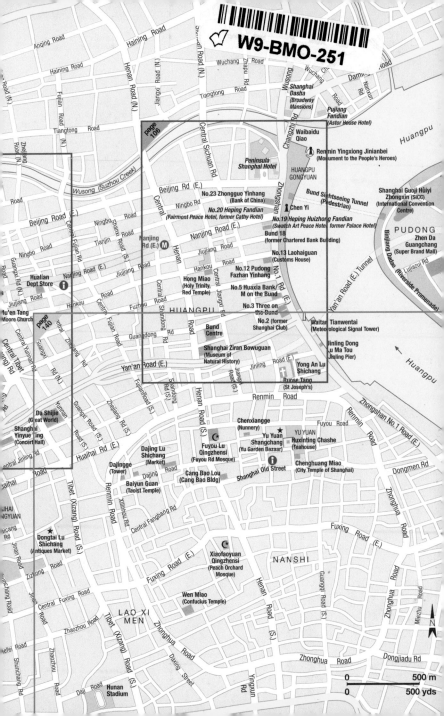

Insight Guides
SHANGHAI

APA PUBLICATIONS **L**

Part of the Langenscheidt Publishing Group

✾ INSIGHT GUIDES

SHANGHAI

Project Editor
Tom Le Bas
Picture Editor
Tom Smyth
Cartography Editor
Zoë Goodwin
Production
Tynan Dean
Series Editor
Rachel Lawrence
Publishing Manager
Rachel Fox

Distribution

UK & Ireland
GeoCenter International Ltd
Meridian House, Churchill Way West,
Basingstoke, Hampshire, RG21 6YR
sales@geocenter.co.uk

United States
Ingram Publisher Services
1 Ingram Blvd, PO Box 3006
La Verne, TN 37086-1986
customer.service@
ingrampublisherservices.com

Australia
Universal Publishers
PO Box 307
St. Leonards, NSW 1590
sales@universalpublishers.com.au

Worldwide
**Apa Publications GmbH & Co.
Verlag KG (Singapore branch)**
7030 Ang Mo Kio Avenue 5
08-65 Northstar @ AMK
Singapore 569880
apasin@singnet.com.sg

Printing

CTPS - China

©2011 Apa Publications GmbH & Co.
Verlag KG (Singapore branch)
All Rights Reserved

First Edition 2003
Third Edition 2011

ABOUT THIS BOOK

What makes an Insight Guide different? Since our first book pioneered the use of creative full-colour photography in travel guides in 1970, we have aimed to provide not only reliable information but also the key to a real understanding of a destination and its people.

Now, when the Internet can supply inexhaustible (but not always reliable) facts, our books marry text and pictures to provide that more elusive quality: knowledge. To achieve this, they rely on the authority of locally based writers and photographers.

Travellers have been drawn to Shanghai since the 1842 Opium War. Today's visitors are more likely to be captivated by the city's fascinating mix of neoclassical historical architecture and cutting-edge modern skyscrapers. This visceral blend of old and new also extends to the Shanghai lifestyle: chic boutique hotels, designer bars and restaurants, and slick shopping. From the classical to the contemporary, *Insight Guide: Shanghai* covers the best the city has to offer.

CONTACTING THE EDITORS

We would appreciate it if readers would alert us to errors or outdated information by writing to:
**Insight Guides, PO Box 7910, London SE1 1WE, England
Fax: (44) 20 7403 0290
email: insight@apaguide.co.uk**

RIGHT: eating *jiaozi* dumplings.

THE CONTRIBUTORS TO THIS BOOK

This new edition was edited by **Tom Le Bas**, senior commissioning editor at Insight's London office, and features a vibrant new design and fresh photography.

The main updater of this edition, **Tina Kanagaratnam**, has lived in Shanghai since 1997, where she runs the communications consulting firm AsiaMedia. Tina, who has been involved in earlier editions of the book, was ably assisted by **Abby Lavin**, **Rebecca Pasquali** and **Ye Beidi**. She scoured the city to update the Places chapters and Travel Tips, and also wrote the Cuisine feature and restaurant listings and fully updated the maps.

Many of the features, written by Shanghai experts for previous editions, have been revised and updated. These include the Shanghainese chapter, written by **Graham Earnshaw**; the Performing Arts and Visual Arts chapters by **Sheila Melvin**; Shopping by **Ceil Bouchet**; and Shanghai Nights by **Lisa Movius**.

Two other writers from the previous edition updated their own work. **Andrew Field**, a lecturer on modern Chinese and East Asian history at the University of New South Wales, wrote the history chapter. **Patrick Cranley**, AsiaMedia's managing director, who has lived in Shanghai for over a decade, was the ideal person to write the chapters on Business and Economy, and Architecture. Patrick was a former chairman of Shanghai's American Chamber of Commerce and is a co-founder of the Shanghai Historic House Association.

Most of the striking new images in this edition were taken by the Shanghai-based photographer **David Shen Kai** and **Ryan Pyle**. The proofreading was undertaken by **Neil Titman**, and the indexing by **Helen Peters**.

THE GUIDE AT A GLANCE

The book is carefully structured to both convey an understanding of the city and its culture and to guide readers through its attractions and activities:

◆ The Best Of section at the front of the book helps you to prioritise. The first spread contains all the Top Sights, while Editor's Choice details unique experiences, the best buys or other recommendations.

◆ To understand Shanghai, you need to know something of its past. The city's history and culture are described in authoritative essays written by specialists in their fields who have lived in and documented the city for many years.

◆ The Places section details all the attractions worth seeing. The main places of interest are coordinated by number with the maps.

◆ A list of recommended restaurants and cafés is included at the end of each chapter.

◆ Photographs throughout the book are chosen not only to illustrate geography and architecture, but also to convey the moods of the city and the pulse of its people.

◆ The Travel Tips section includes all the practical information you will need, divided into five key sections: transport, accommodation, activities (including nightlife, events, tours and sports), shopping, and an A–Z of practical tips. Information may be located quickly by using the index on the back cover flap of the book.

◆ Two detailed street atlases are included at the back of the book, complete with a full index. On the second one, you will find all the restaurants and hotels plotted for your convenience.

PLACES & SIGHTS

Colour-coding at the top of every page makes it easy to find each area in the book. These are coordinated by specific area on the orientation map on pages 100–101.

A locator map pinpoints the specific area covered in each chapter. The page reference at the top indicates where to find a detailed map of the area highlighted in red.

Margin tips provide extra little snippets of information, whether it's a practical tip, a whimsical quote, a historical fact or advice on shopping and eating.

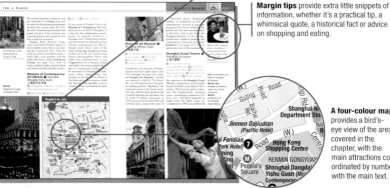

A four-colour map provides a bird's-eye view of the area covered in the chapter, with the main attractions co-ordinated by number with the main text.

PHOTO FEATURES

Photo Features offer an arresting visual coverage of major sights and attractions or special subjects unique to the city. Museum floor plans and detailed close-up pictures bring the subject alive in vivid colour.

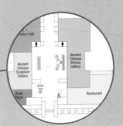

RESTAURANT LISTINGS

Restaurant listings feature the best establishments within each area, giving the address, phone number, opening times and price category followed by a useful review. The grid reference refers to the atlas at the back of the book.

beer in hel, and gindara shioyaki (salt-grilled cod).

Teahouse

The Bund Tea Company
上海茶源有限公司
✉ 100 Dianchi Road,
www.bundtea.com ☎ 6329
0989 ◷ daily Tea Room

TRAVEL TIPS

强艺术中心
g 3, Lane 210, Taikang Road
Tel: 6415 0675
Renowned Shanghai photographer Deke Erh's gallery space is used for exhibitions, concerts and even book readings.

Theatre, Opera & Concerts

Shanghai's stylish new theatres (and a few charming old ones) regularly stage musicals, concerts, dance performances.

Advice-packed Travel Tips provide all the practical knowledge you'll need before and during your trip: how to get there, getting around, where to stay and what to do. The A–Z section is a handy summary of practical information, arranged alphabetically.

Contents

ABOVE: the Jin Mao Tower and other Pudong skyscrapers.

Places

Restaurants & Cafés

Travel Tips

TRANSPORT

ACCOMMODATION

SHOPPING

ACTIVITIES

A–Z of PRACTICAL INFORMATION

LANGUAGE & FURTHER READING

Maps

THE BEST OF SHANGHAI: TOP SIGHTS

Here, at a glance, are the city's must-see sights, from iconic attractions like the Bund and the Oriental Pearl Tower to the charming French Concession and the raucous Yu Garden Bazaar

▷ **Oriental Pearl Tower**
The best time to visit this rocket-like structure is on week-day mornings (when it's infinitely less crowded). You can ride all the way to the top bubble, but the best views are from the second tier. On a clear day, you can see all the way to the Yangzi River. *See pages 227–8*

△ **The Bund**
This architectural cocktail of pre-1949 buildings, once hailed as Asia's Wall Street, is one of the most enduring symbols of Old Shanghai. Take in the spectacular night-time view from one of the restaurant or bar terraces along the Bund itself (like M on the Bund, Bar Rouge or The Peninsula) or gaze across the river from the Park Hyatt or the Pudong Shangri-La. *See pages 105–19*

▽ **Shanghai Museum**
China's best collection of prized Chinese arts and crafts is housed in a build-ing shaped like a giant ancient bronze cooking vessel called a *ding*. *See pages 128–9 and 134–7*

△ **Shanghai Urban Planning Centre** For a sense of where Shanghai is heading as a city and for a good overview of the metropolis, visit this museum on People's Square. Its interesting exhibitions and scale models will give you an idea of Shanghai future. *See page 128*

▽ **Yu Garden and Bazaar**

For a taste of Shanghai's Chinese heart and soul, the Yu Garden area offers temples, a classic Chinese garden, atmospheric teahouses, and busy, narrow lanes full of street life, shopping and food, glorious food. *See pages 143–6*

△ **Xintiandi**

Shopping, dining, drinking and entertainment with character, set in a "village" of refurbished old *shikumen* (stone-gate) houses. *See pages 153–5*

◁ **Former French Concession**

The plane-tree-lined streets of Fuxing Road and Wukang Road in the former French Concession area make for a lovely walk with their chic boutiques, stylish cafés and charming old houses. *See pages 171–9*

◁ **M50**

This artists' enclave near Suzhou Creek is the place to seek out cutting-edge Chinese contemporary art at galleries and artist studios set in old warehouses and factories. *See pages 219–20, 222–3 and 289*

▽ **Lu Xun Park**

Grab a spot at this pleasant green space in the Hongkou area and watch Shanghai's older citizens at play – graceful ball-room dancers, t'ai chi exponents, budding opera singers, and strollers among the lakes. *See pages 218–19*

THE BEST OF SHANGHAI: EDITOR'S CHOICE

Here are our ideas on what to do once you've seen Shanghai's top sights, plus some tips and tricks even Shanghainese won't always know

ONLY IN SHANGHAI

- **Customs House.** Listen to its landmark clock play the Chinese Communist tune *The East is Red* every 15 minutes. *See page 112.*
- **Hairy crabs.** Feast on these delicacies when they are in season (Oct–Nov) at any of Shanghai's fine Chinese restaurants. *See page 71.*
- **Huxinting Teahouse.** Savour a cup of green tea at this century-old teahouse in the middle of a lake. *See page 145.*
- **Site of the First National Congress of** the CCP. This is where Communism first sank its roots in China. *See page 154.*
- **Sunset cocktail.** Catch the sun going down over the Bund, with a glass of champagne in hand, from the M on the Bund terrace. *See page 122.*

SHANGHAI FOR FAMILIES

- **Changfeng Ocean World.** Tanks full of tropical fish, a shark tunnel and even a dolphin show in a park-like setting with a lake for boat rides. *See page 209.*
- **Bund Sightseeing Tunnel.** Board a tram for a ride through a tunnel with flashing images and holograms. *See page 226.*
- **Fuxing Park.** Lush green space for romping around in, a playground with slides, a mini Ferris wheel and even a roller coaster. *See page 156.*
- **Shanghai Museum of Natural History.** A ceiling-scraping dinosaur skeleton, creepy things in jars, and stuffed animals. *See page 121.*
- **Shanghai Acrobatic Troupe.** See amazing feats of contortion at the Shanghai Centre Theatre. *See page 289.*
- **Shanghai Natural Wild Insect Kingdom.** Live bugs in a rainforest setting, and a pond for fishing. *See page 228.*

ABOVE LEFT: the Bund Sightseeing Tunnel.
ABOVE: Customs House clocktower along the Bund.
BELOW: M on the Bund restaurant is one of the city's top tables.

ABOVE: suave Shanghainese and well-heeled expats make up the scene at the red-hot Bar Rouge.

BEST RESTAURANTS

- **Crystal Jade.** Spectacular dim sum and a sophisticated take on Cantonese and Shanghainese dishes – in an elegant (if noisy) Xintiandi setting. Book ahead. *See page 166.*

- **Madison.** Talented chef Austin Hu serves New American cuisine using locally sourced in-season ingredients from China's artisanal and boutique producers. *See page 180.*

- **Mr & Mrs Bund.** Chef Paul Pairet's avant-garde cuisine with global flavours is as stunning as the restaurant's Bund views. Try the foie gras crumble and lemon tart, and book early for a tableside Bund view. *See page 122.*

- **M on the Bund.** Updated Continental classics, dishes from the Mediterranean and Middle East, and one of the best dessert menus and wine lists in town. There are great views of the Bund from the terrace. *See page 122.*

- **Chun.** A two-room Shanghainese eatery serving home-style cuisine – no menu, no English, but delicious, authentic food that pulls in diners in fancy cards and big-time food critics. *See page 166.*

- **Jade on 36.** The sophisticated avant-garde setting in Pudong is matched by adventurous modern cuisine – with outlandish dishes such as foie gras lollipop and citrus shrimp in a jar. *See page 235.*

BEST BARS AND CLUBS

- **Mao Live House.** Features local, national and international acts almost every night of the week. Young locals and expats make up the lively crowd. *See page 292.*

- **Shelter.** The city's best underground dance music venue, located in a 1950s bomb shelter. Local musicians, DJs, alternative dance acts. *See page 292.*

- **Bar Rouge.** Gorgeous bar with red-tinged interiors and terrace with breathtaking views of the Bund and Pudong. Frequented by wealthy Shanghainese and a stylish Euro crowd. *See page 290.*

- **Brown Sugar.** Classy jazz in a Xintiandi setting with delicious cocktails and a slightly older crowd. *See page 291.*

- **The Glamour Bar.** 1930s-style glam reinvented for the 21st century: expect pink and silver interiors, views of the river and the Bund, and long lines at the door. *See page 291.*

- **Jade on 36 Bar.** It's worth crossing the river to Pudong for this slick Adam Tihany-designed bar on the 36th floor. Spectacular views but pricey drinks. *See page 291.*

BEST SHOPPING

- **Cang Bao Building.** Poke around the stalls clustered in the building and you may unearth dusty treasures from Old Shanghai. *See pages 147 and 285.*

- **Madame Mao's Dowry.** Rare, original Cultural Revolution artefacts from furniture to statues, posters, books and more. *See page 286.*

- **Shanghai South Bund Fabric Market.** This Lujiabang Road market has almost every type of fabric under the sun, and tailors on hand to sew whatever you fancy. *See pages 76 and 285.*

- **Suzhou Cobbler.** Hand-embroidered silk Chinese slippers in a historic building behind the Bund. *See pages 110 and 287.*

RIGHT: Shanghai South Bund Fabric Market.

AMAZING SHANGHAI

- **Maglev Train**. The fastest train in the world, the Maglev is one wild and mind-blowing ride. Its top speed? A mere 431km (267 miles) an hour. *See page 270.*
- **Shanghai World Financial Centre**. You might just get neck strain looking up from ground level at the tallest building in China – and the second-tallest in the world. *See page 230.*
- **Neon-lit highways**. Driving on the neon-lit Yan'an Road highway or Nanpu Bridge at night is an almost surreal experience. *See page 226.*

BEST BOUTIQUE HOTELS

- **88 Xintiandi**. Large rooms with separate living areas and kitchenettes, plus a great location. *See page 277.*
- **Jia Shanghai**. Slick and stylish 55-room designer hotel occupying an old apartment building in the heart of Nanjing Road (W). *See page 279.*
- **Hengshan Moller Villa**. Located in a superb 1930s Gothic building, converted into a hotel in 2002; book well in advance. *See page 279.*
- **Mansion Hotel**. A gangster's French Concession mansion, renovated to five-star standards. *See page 277.*
- **Pudi Boutique Hotel Fuxing Park**. Owned by the mass-market French hotel group Accor, but that does not detract from its European-style chic. *See page 278.*

TOP RIGHT: on board the warp-speed Maglev train.
ABOVE: designer interior at Jia Shanghai boutique hotel.
BELOW RIGHT: interior of Hengshan Moller Villa.

UNIQUE ARCHITECTURE

- **Jin Mao Tower**. This pagoda-like structure which fuses Chinese design with Art Deco elements stands out in the Pudong skyline. *See page 230.*
- **Hengshan Moller Villa**. This fairytale Gothic fantasy once owned by a Swedish shipping tycoon is now a small hotel. *See page 184.*
- **Park Hotel**. Concession-era Czech architect Ladislau Hudec's finest Art Deco masterpiece is a landmark along busy Nanjing Road (E). *See page 130.*
- **Shanghai Exhibition Centre**. A wedding cake of a building incorporating a mishmash of architectural styles but

striking nonetheless. *See page 186.*
- **Tomorrow Square**. Its soaring pincer-like roof stands out in the busy People's Square area. *See page 129.*

TRADITIONAL SHANGHAI

- **Jade Buddha Temple**. Primarily known for its two Buddha statues crafted in jade, one in a seated position and the other lying on its side. *See page 220.*
- **Longhua Temple**. Incense-filled courtyards, giant urns of joss sticks, imposing Buddha images and jostling crowds make this one of the city's most popular temples. *See page 196.*
- **Sipailou Road**. All manner of street food sold day and night. *See pages 143 and 151.*
- **Shanghai Arts and Crafts Museum**. See fast-disappearing crafts from yesteryear Shanghai at this grand old mansion. *See page 161.*
- **Shikumen Open House Museum**. Recreates life as it was once lived in a traditional *shikumen* house. *See page 155.*
- **Yu Garden**. A classic Chinese garden in the Old City with pools, pavilions and rockeries. *See page 145.*

BEST WALKS

- **French Concession**. Begin at Fuxing Park, then continue down leafy Sinan Road for a look at Edwardian-style mansions (including the homes of Sun Yat-sen and Zhou En-lai) and the old Russian church. *See pages 156–7.*
- **Behind the Bund**. The streets that criss-cross behind the Bund – Fuzhou Road, Jiujiang Road, Henan Road – are chock-a-block with grand old buildings. *See pages 119–21.*
- **Fuyou Road to Yu Garden**. The narrow lanes around Yu Garden are lined with a mosque, old shophouses selling everything from pickles to wine, and bustling markets. *See pages 141–3.*

ABOVE: Jade Buddha Temple.
RIGHT: Yu Garden, Shanghai's only classical Chinese gardens.

MONEY-SAVING TIPS

Free Views from the lobby levels of high-rise hotels like JW Marriott, Le Royal Meridien, Pudong Shangri-La, Grand Hyatt and Park Hyatt.

Cheap Drinks Many popular bars in Xintiandi, Maoming Road and Hengshan Road have two-for-one deals – usually from 5–7pm – and ladies' nights, where women are exempt from the cover charge. Check websites like www.smartshanghai.com for details.

Set Lunches on the Bund Top tables like Jean Georges, M on the Bund and El Willy offer reasonably priced set lunches *(see pages 122–3, 167)* – a great way to sample their fare and ambience without blowing the budget.

Go Green Entrance to most Shanghai parks is free, and is a great way to get some fresh air and people-watch.

Street Shopping Dongtai Road Antiques Market and the Shanghai South Bund Fabric Market at Lujiabang Road offer more bargains (and fun) than the big and faceless air-conditioned malls.

M50 The artist studios and galleries at at 50 Moganshan Road are open to all – get a free education in Chinese contemporary art.

Buy Bootleg Even the morally upright go weak at the knees when faced with the onslaught of quality knock-offs at Longhua Fashion and Gifts Market.

CHINA'S FUTUREWORLD

Bold and brash Shanghai is where the faded glory of China's treaty port history and its visions for a warp-speed future meld into one

Shanghai's sixth sense – its intangible quality – is the energy that the Shanghainese call *renao* – a superheated buzz that keeps the city on a perpetual simmer. The term was coined for lively Old Shanghai, the Paris of the East, but modern Shanghai's *renao* far surpasses anything that has come before.

Shanghai surprises – no, shocks – on first contact, with images that could only have come from the pages of a sci-fi novel. Walk out of gleaming Pudong Airport and the world's fastest train harnesses electromagnetic levitation technology to whisk you to downtown Pudong in eight minutes flat. The same 30km (19-mile) journey by car would take you an interminable 45 minutes. In the city, neon-glowing elevated highways seem to fly through the air, and the rocket-like Oriental Pearl Tower pierces the sky against the canyon of skyscrapers framing Lujiazui district in Pudong.

At ground level, the city has been re-landscaped and renovated into a sophisticated metropolis. Entire swathes of land have been reinvented – tenements have been turned into parkland, luxury apartments and intelligent office buildings – and roads have been transformed into superhighways. Shanghai leads, and the nation follows: from gourmet coffee to yoga, and contemporary Chinese art to international celebrity chefs, Shanghai does it first and usually best. In this city, fusion is chic, designer is big, mobile phones are small.

The people of this city, they say, are the smartest, savviest, coolest, most progressive citizens in China. When asked how it was that Shanghai people came to be so smart, a former mayor famously replied, "It's not that Shanghai people are smart. It's that smart people come to Shanghai." It is not surprising that Chinese from elsewhere consider the Shanghainese arrogant.

This self-confidence comes, perhaps, from Shanghai's heritage. A treaty port since 1842, Old Shanghai was already Asia's most advanced city in the 1920s, and one of the world's most international cities. It had the tallest buildings and the most fashionable women, and its cosmopolitan citizens traversed the East and West seamlessly.

The city may dazzle with its crisp and newly minted superstructures at first blush, but there are rewards aplenty for those seeking out slivers of its rich history. Glorious Old Shanghai can still be found in the stunning neoclassical buildings along the Bund, in the architecture left behind in the old Concessions, and in the old Chinese *longtang* (lane) neighbourhoods. ❏

PRECEDING PAGES: shopping on Nanjing Road (W); two wheels good – commuting in Nantang. **LEFT:** Pudong district from the top of the World Financial Centre.

THE SHANGHAINESE

The inhabitants of China's richest city are not particularly loved by other Chinese, but that doesn't seem to faze the consumer-oriented Shanghainese

The Shanghainese are very much like their cutting-edge city: smart, hip and – yes – arrogant about it. They are admired, but only grudgingly so, by Chinese from other parts of the country. This doesn't seem to bother the Shanghainese a jot: the self-assured Shanghainese are the New Yorkers of China, convinced that their city is the centre of the world.

A migrant town

Greater Shanghai sprawls over 6,340 sq km (2,448 sq miles) with a population of 19 million, including some 4 million migrant workers from other parts of China. Like New York, it is a port and an immigrant town, with the forefathers of its residents mostly hailing from other cities and districts of East China.

The single-child policy has restricted Shanghai's population growth, but the huge influx of migrants has offset this: in 2009 the population rose above 19 million, up from 16 million in 1990; it is expected to reach 22 million by 2020.

Shanghai was already a thriving city in the 18th century, but it was only after the British blasted open the gates of China with the Opium Wars in the early 1840s, and Shanghai became a treaty port, that the city developed into Asia's

biggest and most progressive metropolis. Shanghai's foreign Concessions became a powerful magnet for economic development as the surrounding areas of East China were torn apart by war and famine over the following decades.

Historically, migrants have had an enormous impact on Shanghai: the southern port city of Ningbo, whose bankers dominated Shanghai's financial industry until the 1940s, was a big influence on the development of Shanghai's language, cuisine and personality. There was also a prominent Cantonese community in 19th-century Shanghai, which had followed the British in as compradors. The foreigners, too, left an indelible imprint on 19th-

LEFT: on the way to work. **RIGHT:** thousands of migrants from the surrounding provinces descend on Shanghai in search of employment.

the surrounding provinces, and even Uighur traders from the northwest of China. The Taiwanese too are becoming a huge force in Shanghai, and it is said there are 300,000 living in the city. Reversing the flow that saw immigrant Shanghainese leave for Hong Kong in the 1940s and 50s, Hong Kong residents – many with Shanghainese roots – have now moved north to seek their fortunes.

Except for a half-century respite after 1949, Shanghai has always had a strong foreign presence. Today, the number of Europeans, Americans, Koreans and Japanese continues to grow dramatically. Exact figures are hard to come by, but there are around 50,000 foreigners, fewer than the number of foreign residents in the 1940s when cosmopolitan Shanghai was hailed as the Paris of the Orient *(see page 34)*. As Shanghai moves to take its place in the pantheon of world-class cities, the authorities are encouraging the influx of foreigners wanting to participate in the new China boom.

Changing lifestyles

China's one-child policy, implemented in 1979 to slow down an explosive population growth rate, has had a huge impact on the life of the Shanghainese. Virtually every young person in Shanghai today is the product of a one-child family. It is natural for parents and grandparents to spoil their only child silly; bratty male offspring are called *xiao huangdi*, or "little emperors". There has been some official concern about this, and children are now encouraged to view cousins as siblings. The policy is also being quietly relaxed – offspring from one-child families who marry a partner who is also an only child are allowed to have two children.

and early 20th-century Shanghai, occupying different enclaves of the city during the Concession years and creating a generation of foreign children who called Shanghai home.

The migration process continues unabated today. Shanghai's economic boom of the past decade has attracted a new wave of immigrants – ambitious Young Turks from the rest of the country, small-time businesspeople from

Until the 1990s, Shanghai was one of the world's most densely populated cities. Then began what is arguably the biggest construction project China has ever attempted – the reconstruction of central Shanghai and the development of vast housing estates around its perimeter. More than 2 million people have been shifted out of the old housing in the central districts since 1995, a process which continues to this day. The *longtang* or lane houses *(see pages 89 and 168–9)* that characterised Shanghainese life for so many decades are fast disappearing. Those that haven't been razed tend to be inhabited by older people. Much is

---

DISPOSABLE MIGRANTS

As in any international city, outsiders who come chasing dreams of prosperity end up doing the dirty work. Most of the jobs Shanghainese deem too lowly – construction, factory jobs, garbage collection and massage – are filled by Chinese from other regions. The majority of migrant labour comes from nearby provinces like Jiangsu, Anhui and Jiangxi. Although migrant labour contributes much to the local economy, and also to the economies of the regions from which the workers come, it is often illegal. Most migrant workers do not have a *hukou* (registration card) licensing them to work in Shanghai. As a result, migrant labour is often underpaid, overworked and exploited.

lost in the process, but then much is gained as well – the old lane houses had no inside toilets or running water, and are often dark and cramped. Younger Shanghainese seem to miss the old alleys much less than sentimental foreigners do, although the older residents do lament the loss of neighbourly *longtang* life. The new standard for Shanghai living today is an apartment in a high-rise block on a housing estate, with a small pet dog yapping to be taken for a run on the small piece of grass outside.

In this new Shanghai, people have something that they have never had before – privacy. In the alleys, everyone knew everything about everyone else; the walls were paper-thin and gossip spread quickly when women washed out the chamber pots in the morning. In the new estates, people tend not to know their neighbours. Life has moved from one extreme to the other.

The young and restless

Young people in Shanghai enjoy an independent urban lifestyle, both native Shanghainese and young migrants who come for university and jobs. They rent – and very quickly buy – their own apartments, live together before marriage, spend more time with their parents and increasingly behave like young people in any major city in the West.

But at the same time there is a growing wealth gap, as urban economic advances create a class of ultra-wealthy conspicuous consumers –

THE SHANGHAINESE DIALECT

Most Shanghainese prefer to speak the lilting local dialect called Shanghaihua instead of Mandarin (or *putonghua*), the official language of China, even though they are conversant with the latter. Although both are written using the same Chinese characters, the Shanghainese dialect is almost completely incomprehensible to Chinese from other parts of the country.

For many years, the Shanghainese dialect was shunned by the local media, but recently, the government relented by allowing a Shanghainese-language radio show to go on air – a reflection of the locals' stubborn use of the dialect to distinguish themselves from the out-of-towners.

ABOVE LEFT: on the streets in Xujiahui.
ABOVE: China's one-child policy means there is a lot of pressure on children to excel.

BMW-driving, Paris-visiting, multimillion-dollar homeowners – and their migrant worker peers, pulling heavy carts full of goods for trade through the city.

There is a technology gap as well, as Shanghainese embrace the world of iPhones and WiFi, obtaining most of their information from the Internet and engaging with the outside world in an unprecedented way, one that leaves their parents and grandparents behind.

Still, because the trajectory is upward and optimistic, there is little adolescent angst or alienation in Shanghai – there is simply too much opportunity.

What makes a Shanghainese?

When they get together, Chinese people love to discuss regional differences in character – and Shanghai people are an obvious target. There is a caricature that all agree upon: Shanghainese are arrogant and aloof, smart but somewhat false, self-conscious and guarded. The men are docile, the women domineering. Everyone seems to have an agenda, everyone seems concerned about impressions, substance often seems secondary. It's partly jealousy, of course, of China's richest and most sophisticated city.

Shanghainese men, according to the cliché, have what it takes to be good at business. They lack the natural openness of northern Chinese. They hesitate before answering because they are mulling over what you may think about what they will say. And they are famous for street arguments that never degenerate into brawls – the Shanghai man, in the famous phrase, "moves his mouth, not his fist". They are supposedly docile at home (ideal husbands for domineering wives, you could say) and don't have a propensity towards alcohol.

Shanghai women are seen as strong-willed and calculating. Certainly they are the country's best-packaged females, a reputation that goes back to the days of the cigarette girl ads in Old Shanghai. A Shanghai man bemoaned the fact that his girlfriend refused to have even the one child permitted by the government. "She says it will ruin her figure and interrupt her career, she won't listen to me." Like most clichés, this one overstates reality, yet contains some truth *(see text box, opposite)*.

ABOVE LEFT: basketball is popular. **TOP:** flashy cars, a sign of the times. **ABOVE:** out and about on Nanjing Road. **RIGHT:** the Shanghainese love to gamble.

Shanghainese men are seldom big drinkers – many foreign beer companies in the 1990s foundered as their business model was based on the mistaken belief that Shanghainese would match their Beijing brethren glass for glass.

Taking the middle road

Someone once said that a Shanghai extremist would be a contradiction in terms, which may well be true. Shanghai people as a whole generally lack the strength of conviction to be extremist. They are too self-involved and calculating, too detached. But that also makes them perfect for administration, politics and management. Shanghainese are also good at business and they understand the art of compromise – qualities that help make this city the commercial capital of China and a magnet for foreign investment.

As in most major world cities, there is some tension between natives of the city and people from the provinces. In Shanghai, the locals are often too ready to make assumptions about others, either seriously or in jest, based on which district they were born in or which school they went to. Some class-conscious Shanghainese are dismissive of those they view as being beneath them – especially people from rural areas. (And it doesn't matter who they are: the Shanghainese famously consider glamorous actress Gong Li a country bumpkin.) Indeed, calling someone a "peasant", a country bumpkin, is one of their most potent putdowns – it means they are not smart enough,

too slow on the uptake, too unsophisticated, too… un-Shanghainese. It feels, just a little, like Manhattan.

Such attitudes, born in Shanghai in the 1920s and 1930s, were stifled first by the Japanese invasion in 1937, then by the Communist takeover in 1949. During the Cultural Revolution years, personal ambitions that would have been condemned as bourgeois by the Communists lay dormant inside their Mao jackets. Then, as the political winds changed direction, middle-class dreams re-emerged.

STRONG WOMEN, WEAK MEN?

History contains some clues that perhaps explain the strength of the Shanghai female and the more delicate nature of the male. Shanghai's character as an immigrant town was formed in the late 19th and early 20th centuries, when the social fabric of old imperial China was falling apart. Shanghai is located close to older cities such as Suzhou, Hangzhou and Ningbo, which were noted for their thriving arts and culture. During imperial times, their Mandarins composed poetry while merchants collected jade, porcelain and

concubines. They were not warriors but a feudal upper middle class. When war and revolution tore China apart from the 1840s until the Japanese invasion in the 1930s, they fled to the safety of Shanghai, their pockets stuffed with jade. The character of Shanghai men, therefore, could have been founded on Old China's intellectual business culture.

The psyche of Shanghainese women can be similarly traced to the time when the city was a refuge for girls escaping the constricting life of Old China – bound feet, concubinage and

slavery. They had to assert themselves to survive, which made them focused and forceful, convinced that the end always justifies the means.

Shanghai people now want to buy their own apartments, drive big cars and send their children to the best schools. And as they move up the social scale, a new generation of immigrants arrives from the farms to handle the menial tasks the locals no longer wish to do.

The Shanghainese are typically more open to ideas from the West – or, as Chinese people from other areas might see it – more slavish in their pursuit of foreignness. It began in the Old Shanghai with something called Yangjingbang Culture, "Yangjingbang" being the name of the creek that separated the French Concession and the Chinese city. The term refers to the amalgam of Chinese and Western ideas and influences into something that was uniquely Shanghainese, in terms of language, clothes, food, lifestyle and attitudes. The trend is visible again today (although other parts of China are catching up).

A few years ago, the Shanghainese would assume that the way the foreigner did it is better. Today, Shanghainese consider both ways of doing things, and sometimes pick one,

TRENDY FASHIONISTAS VS PYJAMA POWER

Shanghainese women are China's fashion trendsetters. They have everything necessary to be so: increasingly sophisticated tastes, high disposable incomes, an insatiable thirst for international trends and, most importantly, attitude. Shanghainese women were China's first to start perming their hair after the Cultural Revolution, and it's no coincidence that fashion magazine *Vogue* started its China edition in Shanghai. Shanghainese women fly to Paris for the summer sales, keep an eye on Japanese fashion, and change their hairstyle with the season.

But it's not all Gucci and Prada. The old Shanghai trend of wearing nightclothes outside on the street is alive and well. Men and women venture out sporting anything from frilly nightie to warm flannel PJs – usually to the market for their morning shopping – which dates from the era when pyjamas were a luxury product and warranted showing off, and is part of the traditional Shanghai *longtang* dweller's sense that the immediate neighbourhood is their living room. Despite stern government campaigns to do away with public PJ-wearing, it appears to be here to stay.

sometimes the other – and sometimes, a uniquely Shanghainese blend of the two.

Conspicuous consumerism

Shanghainese are always looking for bargains – they value quality and follow trends, but are highly price-conscious. As incomes rise, though, the old mode of shopping – to go to a major department store to identify an item, then head for the local knock-off market to buy a copy of the same thing at a tenth of the price – has given way to an insistence on buying the genuine article. Even office girls save up for the real Vuitton, and boutiques in Paris these days employ Chinese-speakers to handle the crowds of Shanghai shoppers who descend on the French capital during the summer sales.

A key feature of the consumerist lifestyle is fads, and Shanghai, which has the highest standards of living in China, follows the latest trends in clothing, mobile phones and nightclubs. Central Huaihai Road, the city's key fashion shopping street, is the epicentre of chic fashion in China. But as quickly as people try to emulate the Shanghai look, it morphs into something else, leaving the "outsiders" (*waidiren*) permanently outside.

Shanghainese girls are now fashion leaders rather than followers – the rest of the country looks here for trends, and Shanghai women seem unconcerned as to what the rest of the world is doing.

Shanghai people are more ambitious, more focused on succeeding than other Chinese. They are less satisfied with comfort, more likely to fight for luxury. But they are not natural politicians or philosophers. While a conversation with a Beijing taxi driver can cover vast territories, it's difficult to get a tight-lipped Shanghai taxi driver even to tell you how business is going.

> People from other parts of China see Shanghainese fashion and lifestyles as something to emulate. Such is the cachet of this premier Chinese city.

Sichuan province in the heart of China is more likely to produce the great Chinese novelists of the 21st century than practical-minded Shanghai – people here tend to be focused on their careers, and leave lofty concerns about the meaning of life to others. Thanks to the Shanghainese, the city will undoubtedly become the powerhouse that drives China through this century, becoming once again the dominant East Asian, if not world, metropolis. ❑

LEFT: a young gymnast in training. **ABOVE:** snapping up shoes at a Shanghai shopping mall.
ABOVE RIGHT: on the catwalk at a fashion show.

THE SHANGHAI STORY

In its transformation from fishing village to bustling trading port and now business centre, Shanghai has survived wars, foreign takeovers, Communism and the Cultural Revolution to emerge as China's leading city

Located near the mouth of the Yangzi River, Shanghai was destined for glory. Its history as a trading port can be traced back to the Song dynasty (960–1279), a period of rapid urbanisation for China, especially in the south. In 1074, the provincial bureaucracy elevated Shanghai from a *hudu* (fishing village) to a *zhen* (commercial town), and in 1159, to that of a *shi* (market town). By 1292, during the early Yuan dynasty (1279–1368), the population of the region around Shanghai had grown so rapidly that officials created a *xian* (county), with Shanghai as its capital. From then on, Shanghai served as a seat of government and eventually became one of the most productive counties in China.

During pirate attacks, guards would sound the alarm and people would flock through one of six gates to enter and seek refuge within the high walls of the city.

In 1404, Ming-dynasty (1368–1644) officials rerouted the Songjiang River into the Huangpu, helping to turn the latter into a navigable waterway. From the 15th century onwards, the Huangpu gradually widened and deepened to become Shanghai's main river. The neglected Songjiang meanwhile withered to its present proportions as Suzhou Creek. With the Huangpu flowing directly into the Yangzi River and out to the sea beyond, Shanghai's fortunes soared.

LEFT: boating down the Yangzi River.
RIGHT: Yu Garden's Huxinting Teahouse.

The walled city

In the 1550s, a wall was built to protect Shanghai from pirates. Most of Shanghai's residents lived outside the city walls, but its wealthy families built their homes inside the walled city, surrounding them with grand gardens. Within the walled city were Buddhist and Taoist temples, as well as government offices, charity halls, guildhalls and private academies where members of the rich families could study for the Confucian examinations.

At the heart of the old walled city were Yu Garden and the Temple of the Town God *(see page 143)*, which became the focal point for public gatherings. In the 15th century, a temple

vided the ideal environment for growing cotton. Cotton cloth became a major cottage industry for villagers throughout the region. By the late Ming period, merchants imported raw cotton to spin and weave into cloth, which was then exported to other parts of China.

By the Qing dynasty (1644–1912), many other industries had grown around the cotton boom. These included the cultivation of indigo for producing *nankeen* (blue cotton cloth), and soybean cake for use as fertiliser in the cotton fields. Soybeans grown in north China were brought to Shanghai, where merchants distributed them to the hinterlands.

In 1684, the Qing emperor lifted restrictions on ocean transport. Although the effect was not immediate, by the mid-1700s merchant ships plying the China coast with beans, grain and other supplies on board were a common sight. Shanghai became a major distribution centre for both maritime and river trade. With thousands of dockworkers towing cargo off the docks to be stored in warehouses, and restau-

was built at this site by the Ming emperor. Called Jinshan Miao, it was reconstructed in 1726 as the Temple of the Town God and dedicated to the spirit of Huo Guang, a famous Ming general. The temple served as a locus of worship for the Shanghai folk, who believed that their Town God possessed the power to ward off pirates, bandits and other marauders. It was also a popular site for festivals, and like today, was a thriving marketplace. The garden that surrounded the temple was originally privately owned by the Pan family. During the Qing dynasty, when the family fell on bad times, it was sold to a group of merchants who turned it into a public space, which it remains today.

Early economy

The key to Shanghai's growth during the Ming dynasty (1368–1644) was the cotton industry. Cotton originated in India but found its way into China in the 13th century. The fertile Jiangnan region surrounding Shanghai pro-

CHRISTIAN INFLUENCE IN EARLY SHANGHAI

Italian Jesuit missionaries converted many educated Chinese, including a Shanghai-born scholar Xu Guangqi (1562–1633) to Christianity. Matteo Ricci (1552–1610; pictured on right), an astronomer for the Ming court, was responsible for exposing the young Xu to Western scientific knowledge.

Over the next few decades, with the aid of the Jesuits, "Paul" Xu promoted Christianity and Western learning in Shanghai. Xu attracted many local scholars into his intellectual circle, with whom he published a number of important Chinese and Western books on agriculture, astronomy, religion and philosophy.

The imprint of Paul Xu and his Jesuit friends on Shanghai may be seen today in the Xujiahui district, where the St Ignatius Cathedral, more popularly known as Xujiahui Cathedral *(see page 194)*, stands tall.

rants and street vendors hawking food to hungry travellers, it must have been quite a sight to walk along the banks of the Huangpu. Adding to the colour, alongside the many merchant and trading ships, sampans and barges, were "flower boats" or floating brothels, carrying girls from Suzhou and other nearby towns.

Rise of the opium trade

In 1760, the Qing emperor restricted all foreign trade to the southern port of Canton (Guangzhou). By 1800, the British were importing into Canton opium that was grown and processed in Bengal. The British exchanged opium with the Chinese for silver, some of which they used to buy Chinese tea. In 1796, the Qing emperor banned the import of opium, but it was too late. By the early 1800s, millions of Chinese had become opium addicts, and silver flowed out of China by the tonne. In 1839, a Chinese official declared a ban on opium and destroyed the British opium supply in Canton, heralding the start of the First Opium War.

Over the next three years, the British Navy decimated Qing defences along the coast, attacking and occupying several port cities, including Shanghai. The British also forced China to open these cities to international trade, heralding the start of a new era in Shanghai's history. Over the next 100 years foreigners took control of the city and turned it – together with help from the Chinese – into a leading centre of international commerce and trade.

> "The expense of a war could be paid in time; but the expense of opium, when once the habit is formed, will only increase with time." – Townsend Harris

Treaty port Shanghai

In 1842, the Qing government signed a treaty with the British to end the First Opium War. Among other things, the Treaty of Nanjing designated five "treaty ports" – including Shanghai – where British nationals could reside in "Concessions" and conduct trade with the Chinese. Other foreign powers soon joined the system with treaties of their own.

The original British settlement was at the confluence of the Huangpu River and Suzhou Creek. The French settled just south of the British along the Huangpu, while the Americans occupied the area north of Suzhou Creek. A series of grand buildings lining the river were erected and the stretch became known as the Bund (see page 107). Then, in 1863, the British and American settlements merged to form an enclave called the International Settlement. Both

LEFT: in the 14th century, cotton growing (and weaving) was a key trade in Shanghai. **ABOVE:** a high wall and moat was built around Shanghai in the 1550s to save it from pirates. **RIGHT:** 19th-centuy opium smokers.

the International Settlement and the French Concession had their own municipal governments, run respectively by British and French nationals. Over the next 50 years, both expanded westward to encompass several square miles of choice real estate south of Suzhou Creek.

At first, the settlements were off limits to Chinese. With the advent of the Taiping Rebellion (1850–64), the rules were relaxed to allow

'NO DOGS OR CHINESE ALLOWED'

During the 1920s, enraged Chinese complained that Shanghai's Huangpu Park *(see page 117)* had a sign at the gates stating "No dogs or Chinese allowed." In actual fact, no such sign existed, although entrance rules at the park did forbid dogs and unaccompanied Chinese from entering, save for Chinese nannies entrusted with European children. The Westerners claimed that the Chinese masses lacked public consciousness; many felt the Chinese would spoil the park with their tendency to spit and litter. Following the Kuomintang revolution of 1926–7, and under pressure from the new government, the International Settlement authorities lifted the ban.

thousands of Chinese refugees to flood into the settlements, where they enjoyed a safe haven.

Lane housing

During and after the Taiping Rebellion, row-house neighbourhoods with *shikumen* (stone gate) or *longtang* (lane) housing sprang up in the settlements, displaying a mixture of Western and Chinese architectural forms. In later years, these spacious lane houses were built smaller and closer in order to accommodate the city's growing population.

> During the 1930s, Shanghai was home to refugees from all over the world. Two of the largest groups from abroad were the White Russians and European Jews.

In a span of 50 years, Shanghai's population grew ten-fold, making it one of the world's fastest-growing cities. The job opportunities in Shanghai attracted both Chinese from neighbouring provinces and foreign nationals from all over the world. By 1930, the total population of Shanghai surged to 3 million, placing it among the top five most populous cities.

A cauldron of revolution

By the early 20th century, Shanghai was a major manufacturing centre. Hundreds of thousands of Chinese men, women and children laboured day and night for pitiful wages in the foreign-owned cotton and silk textile factories. For many Chinese intellectuals, these workers were the most visible sign of the exploitation of China by foreign imperialists.

In 1912, the ailing Qing dynasty gave way to a fledging republic, which soon fell to rapacious warlords. Sun Yat-sen's Nationalist Party (Kuomintang or KMT) headquartered itself in Canton, but Sun spent much of his time in Shanghai. It was in his French Concession mansion that he made a deal with Soviet agents to allow the fledgling Chinese Communist Party (CCP) to join his own party, thus setting the stage for a brutal power struggle between the CCP and KMT over the next 30 years.

Shanghai, with its large worker and student population, was considered the perfect breed-

ing ground for a Communist revolution. In 1921, the CCP held its first meeting in Shanghai's French Concession. During the 1920s, the CCP led workers' strikes and student movements, including the famous May 30th Movement in 1925. Sparked by the murder of a Chinese worker by a Japanese factory foreman, and further inflamed by the shooting of student protestors by Shanghai's Municipal Police, this anti-imperialist movement gathered force throughout the country, paving the way for the erstwhile revolution of 1927, led by Sun's successor, Chiang Kai-shek.

The White Terror

In 1927, Chiang Kai-shek's Northern Expedition made it to Shanghai. The CCP paved the way for the revolution by organising a citywide strike. But Chiang had other plans. After sending delegates to meet with Du Yuesheng (or "Big Ears" Du), one of the leaders of Shanghai's notorious Green Gang, Chiang ordered a purge of the Communists in Shanghai. On 12 April 1927, Green Gang members and Kuomintang soldiers rounded up and executed thousands of Communists operating in Shanghai. Over the next decade, the Green Gang continued to terrorise the city and extorted millions from its wealthy bourgeoisie to fill the coffers of Chiang's government. In return, they were given a virtual monopoly over the city's opium racket.

World War II Shanghai

Yet, the Green Gang was no match for the Japanese military. Japan's defeat of China in

the Sino-Japanese War of 1895 and the resulting Treaty of Shimonoseki, which allowed Japanese to manufacture in China, was the first signal of Japan's extraterritorial ambitions. China, after all, had the a vast depository of resources – mineral and agricultural – that Japan needed to fuel its industrial expansion. In 1931, Japan took Manchuria (which they

THE MOSQUITO PRESS

In 1900, a Shanghai newspaperman discovered that he could sell more papers by including gossip from the city's brothels. Since Shanghai was full of sojourners from all over China, one of the best places to gather or dispense news was at a local courtesan house. News from the brothels gave rise to the institution of the Chinese tabloid or *xiaobao*. Known in English as the "mosquito press", these papers covered the private lives of the city's famous prostitutes.

By the 1920s, *xiaobao* reporters had turned to the lives of Shanghai film stars, reporting about their private lives with abandon. In 1934, a famous actress named Ruan Lingyu committed suicide as a result of scandalous information printed about her in a local paper.

LEFT: a *shikumen* (stone gate) entrance leading to a *longtang* (lane) house. **ABOVE:** Shanghai mob boss, Due Yuesheng. **ABOVE RIGHT:** a young Chiang Kai-shek.

The Rollicking 1930s

Dubbed the "Paris of the Orient", Shanghai was once world-famous for its thriving nightlife scene. By the 1930s, it had over 30 licensed cabarets or "dance saloons" and hundreds of unlicensed ones. They offered dining, drinking and dancing to a live orchestra, as well as pretty female dance partners for the thousands of single men who lived in or visited the city.

High-class dance palaces included the Paramount on Yuyuan Road and Ciro's on Bubbling Well Road. These nightspots, with

their sprung wooden dance floors and African-American orchestras playing the latest jazz tunes, attracted the city's wealthiest – men in tuxedos and women in evening gowns ferried there in their chauffeured cars.

In the middle of the spectrum were dozens of cavernous, albeit lower-class, dance halls such as the Casanova and the Majestic Ballroom. At first such dance halls catered to an elite crowd of Chinese bohemians, but by the 1930s – thanks to the influence of Hollywood films – the Shanghainese came to accept Western practices of dancing, kissing and other forms of intimacy.

Meanwhile, forced by the Depression and

World War II, the more exclusive Shanghai ballrooms began to open their doors to a wider public. These dance halls were filled with pretty Chinese women who danced, drank and flirted with male customers in exchange for tickets, which they then traded with management for cash. The money they earned was used to keep up with the latest fashions in hairstyles, dresses and high heels. Although municipal rules forbade prostitution, to boost their incomes, many of these women engaged in private relations with patrons outside the dance halls.

At the low end of the nightlife scene were the cheap dives that lined the so-called Blood Alley near the Bund, and the Trenches in Hongkou. These rowdy halls catered to thousands of foreign soldiers and sailors stationed temporarily in Shanghai. In joints such as the Venus, Mumm's and the Frisco, the lonely sailor could find a girl of almost any nationality he desired.

From 1937 until 1941, when the foreign settlements operated as neutral zones, Shanghai's residents threw themselves even deeper into the city's hedonistic nightlife. Cabarets, nightclubs and casinos flourished as never before. While patrons cavorted on the dance floor, Chinese staffers and dance hostesses worked behind the scenes to extract information from drunken Axis officers for the sake of the resistance movement. In 1949 the Communist takeover of Shanghai put an end to the city's hedonistic lifestyle, and by 1954, the last of the dance halls were shut down. ❑

LEFT: Shanghainese calendar girl. **ABOVE:** Russian chorus-line girls worked in Shanghai in the 1930s.

renamed "Manchukuo") by force, and in 1932 provoked a war in Shanghai's Zhabei district, killing thousands of Chinese civilians and moving Japanese military personnel into China.

In 1937, Japan finally launched a full-scale invasion of the country from its power base in Manchuria, rapidly occupying the eastern seaboard of China. In December 1937, forces reached the then-capital, Nanjing, where they carried out the horrific Rape of Nanking, brutally torturing, raping and murdering the city's population in a bloodbath that remains an unhealed wound for China. Chiang's government was chased to the interior, Wuhan and Chungking, where they were to spend the ensuing years of war.

The period between 1937 and 1941 was a strange one for Shanghai: the Japanese surrounded the city, operating from their bases in Zhabei and entering the old Chinese city, but they dared not enter the French Concession or the International Settlement, which would have been an act of war against Britain, America and France. Nonetheless, they made their ambitions known, bombing KMT bases in Zhabei and moving in the warship *Udzumi*. Many of the foreigners living in Shanghai took this as a signal to leave, but others – notably Jews fleeing the Nazi threat in Europe – arrived in numbers to replace them.

The Chinese, of course, had no such escape route, but those who were able to fled to the safety of the Concessions. For the rest, it was a horrific time: the Japanese were cruel overlords who looked down upon their subjects.

Private life, too, was not spared during the Mao years. Women traded in their colourful dresses for drab workers' uniforms, and fancy perms gave way to ascetic hairstyles.

Untold numbers of prominent Chinese were called up to "731", the Kempitai (secret police) headquarters where they were tortured, sometimes to death. There were small bright spots, even during this period, like the safe zone in the old Chinese city set up by French priest Father Jacquinot.

When Pearl Harbor was bombed, in December 1941, the Japanese took possession of the International Settlement. (Vichy France, already part of the Nazi collaborationist government, gave up the French Concession to Japanese military control.) Foreigners in the international settlement were enemy nationals, and were made to wear armbands to identify them as such.

It took the Japanese a year to set up the internment camps such as Longhua, made famous in J.G. Ballard's *Empire of the Sun*, and more than a year to set up the Jewish ghetto in

Hongkou. Prior to 1941, Jews – both refugees and long-time Shanghai residents – could live throughout the city, but after the occupation were restricted to the Hongkou "ghetto". They had to apply for permission to enter and depart, even for regular jobs, from a disagreeable Japanese soldier named Goya who is legend among the wartime Shanghai Jewish community. There is an oft-repeated tale among this community that Goebbels wanted the Japanese to set up gas chambers for the Jews in Shanghai in Pudong, but the Japanese demurred.

Food was always scarce, and the invaders were unspeakably cruel to the Chinese, torturing and killing with little mercy. There is a visceral hatred of the Japanese that survives to this day. The 2010 Sino-Japanese dispute over the Diaoyu Islands, which caused holiday trips to Japan and numerous Japanese events in China to be cancelled, was a stark reminder that the Chinese have not forgotten this brutal period.

SHANGHAI FORTUNES

During the 1920s and '30s, Shanghai was famously a place where fortunes could be made, and often lost, with blinding speed.

The richest men in Old Shanghai were the property developers, buying up swathes of real estate in what were often outlying rural areas, and watching the city grow out to them. Men like Silas Hardoon, who arrived penniless from Baghdad and become Shanghai's richest man; Sir Victor Sassoon *(see page 115)*, whose signature buildings still stand (the Peace Hotel, Cathay Cinema, Grosvenor House, the Embankment Building), and Sir Elly Kadoorie, with his portfolio of hotels.

It would not be an exaggeration to say that every major company trading in Old Shanghai had some involvement in the opium trade: opium built the old tongs, the Houses of Jardine, Swire's Sassoons and quite possibly even the New York Astors, whose ships traded in Shanghai in the 19th century.

Compradors, Chinese who acted as go-betweens for foreign traders and local merchants, stuffed their pockets with commissions from both sides, and invested in real estate.

When it came to making fortunes, Shanghai was the place to be: when the KMT's T.V. Soong left Shanghai for New York after the war, he was the richest man in the world.

After the Communists came to power, the entrepreneurial age shuddered to a halt. A large proportion of the business community escaped south to Hong Kong, providing a significant boost to the economy (and long-term prospects) of the British colony. The Shanghainese had to wait until the 1990s before serious money was once again being made in the city.

In 1943, the Allied powers signed an agreement returning Shanghai to Chinese sovereignty. In one fell swoop, 100 years of semi-colonialism came to a sudden, crashing end.

The Communists take over

In 1949, following a four-year civil war between the KMT and Communists, fought mostly in the northeast of China, the People's Liberation Army (PLA) marched southward, taking China's coastal cities. Chiang and his cohorts fled to Taiwan, vowing to return. But they never did; Chiang set up the Republic of China (ROC) with Taipei as its capital.

In May 1949, the PLA "liberated" Shanghai, and, on 1 October, Mao Zedong triumphantly declared the foundation of the People's Republic of China (PRC). Thus began the saga of the the PRC and the ROC, a thorny issue which continues today.

Throughout the 1950s, the CCP made great efforts to clean up the opium, gambling, prostitution and other rackets that had made Shanghai the most notorious city in the world. Shanghai's fame as "Paris of the Orient" *(see page 34)* was dealt a severe blow.

After its "liberation" by the CCP, Shanghai continued to play a leading role in rebuilding the nation. Despite the exodus of many of the city's most talented business managers to Hong Kong and Taiwan, Shanghai still had the greatest concentration of technical know-how, the most diverse and effective educational system, and the most productive workers in China.

For the fledgling CCP, as for the Kuom-

intang and Japanese occupiers who had preceded them, Shanghai provided the industrial and tax support base for building a new and stronger China. Over the next four decades, the central government in Beijing milked Shanghai, siphoning off the city's fiscal revenues to build up other parts of the country.

The Cultural Revolution

In 1966, Mao called upon China's young students and workers to "bombard the headquar-

THE GANG OF FOUR

During the Cultural Revolution years (1966–76), Shanghai became the power base for a group of party leaders, dubbed the Gang of Four after their fall. Its members were Zhang Chunqiao, Jiang Qing (Mao's wife), Yao Wenyuan and Wang Hongwen. They secured their power on the national stage by supporting Mao's radical policies, using Shanghai's newspapers to push their views and to denounce their "revisionist" enemies. Following the death of Mao Zedong in 1976, the Gang of Four was arrested and brought to trial on a long string of charges.

LEFT: starving Shanghainese besiege a food store, 1940.
ABOVE: Mao Zedong visiting a factory. **ABOVE RIGHT:** the PLA marches down the Bund after seizing Shanghai in 1949.

ters" and take the country's political institutions by force. This marked the beginning of the Cultural Revolution. During this period, Shanghai's student and worker population exploded into violent revolutionary activity. Shanghai is China's overachiever, and as if determined to live down her capitalist past, she zealously flew the Cultural Revolution flag. Revolution-drunk Red Guards attacked all vestiges of bourgeois culture, harassing people with Western clothing or hairstyles, and destroying symbols of foreign domination in the city. Although they were raided and plundered, many of the city's churches and other foreign Concession buildings remained intact.

As China's most capitalist and most Western city, though, more Shanghai people were affected by the collective madness of the Cultural Revolution than anywhere else in the country: many left China, but life was miserable for those who did not. Former landlords were "struggled against" and re-housed; English-speakers sent up to the countryside to learn from the peasants; the foreign-educated assigned toilet-scrubbing duties. Although the signature of the Cultural Revolution was to have no rhyme or reason for singling out anyone as a class enemy, Shanghai was so full of bourgeoisie, no one needed to look far for genuine class enemies.

The dragon rises

Following the death of Mao and the rise of Deng Xiaoping, Shanghai emerged from the nightmare of the 1960s and early 70s. The 1980s were marked by gradual improvements in living standards and a heightened sense of optimism, the setbacks of 1989 notwithstanding. In 1992, following the success of economic reforms in Shanghai and other cities in southern China, the CCP began the long process of removing the shackles of a planned economy. With the opening of Shanghai to foreign investment in the early 1990s, the stage was set for an economic and infrastructural boom that was unprecedented in world history.

In 1990, Shanghai's Pudong district *(see page 225)* was set up as a Special Economic Zone (SEZ), and became the showcase for the city's modernisation scheme. Through tax incentives, lowered tariffs and other benefits, the municipal government encouraged foreign enterprises and banks to move into Pudong.

In 1997, the Shanghai Stock Exchange opened in Pudong's Lujiazui financial zone, the new "Shanghai Wall Street". New housing and offices in Pudong were built from the mid-1990s onwards, and have lured many residents and businesses to move across the Huangpu River.

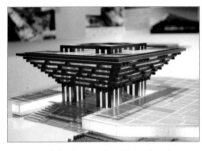

Meanwhile, during the 1990s, the city government constructed an elevated highway system to ease urban traffic, built four suspension bridges spanning the Huangpu River, expanded many of the city's clogged streets, dug a metro line running north–south and another east–west, and constructed the futuristic Pudong International Airport. Two new icons arose in Pudong to dominate the skyline: the Oriental Pearl Tower in 1993, and the Jin Mao Tower in 1998 – the tallest building in China at the time. This title was usurped by the Shanghai World Financial Centre when it opened in 2008. All three buildings tower over the colonial edifices along the Bund across the Huangpu River.

A global metropolis

The 2010 World Expo was declared a huge success, surpassing its goal of 70 million visitors over the six-month period. The Expo gave Shanghai an excuse to clean up and invest in infrastructure – relocating 180,000 households along the way – and the result is a vastly expanded and improved transportation system.

Today, Shanghai continues to transform itself into a cosmopolitan metropolis. The government has built dozens of new public parks throughout the city but at the same time, hundreds of old, decrepit *shikumen* neighbourhoods have been torn down to make way for new high-rises, while others, like the Xintiandi entertainment complex, have been gentrified. Foreigners from Asia, Europe and the Americas have flocked to the city by the thousands to work, bringing with them their cultures, their cuisines and their creative energies.

Yet there is a downside to this growth. Millions of male migrant workers have moved into the city to build its modern infrastructure, while thousands of female migrants fill the city's hostess clubs and massage parlours, providing a range of sexual services. These migrants do not have access to the educational, housing or health services provided to local residents.

In 2006, long-time Party Secretary Chen Liangyu was dismissed after a lengthy investigation and the uncovering of corruption that funnelled hundreds of millions of yuan worth of taxes, property and social security funds into private hands. Government assurances that this is all in the past and things are squeaky clean are taken with a grain of salt by locals, particularly in the corrupt property sector.

With the population rising, the gap between wealth and poverty growing, air pollution levels soaring and an inverted pyramid of ageing residents climbing, Shanghai faces formidable challenges over the next few decades.

Yet despite these problems, the city continues to exude a powerful sense of optimism and a creative energy unrivalled in the world. For those with the means and the moolah, Shanghai is *the* place to be. ❑

LEFT: Lujiazui, the financial and business zone in Pudong.
ABOVE: a model of the China Pavilion for the 2010 Expo.
AROVE RIGHT: gearing up for the good life in Shanghai.

DECISIVE DATES

1074
Shanghai progresses from a humble fishing village *(hudu)* to a commercial town *(zhen)*.

1159
Shanghai's status is further elevated to that of a market town *(shi)*.

1292
A new county is created with Shanghai as its capital seat *(xian)*.

1404
Ming-dynasty engineers build a channel in Huangpu River to keep it from silting, and reroute the Songjiang to exit into the Yangzi River. The Huangpu River becomes the main watercourse for Shanghai.

1554
Following successive attacks by pirates, the citizens of Shanghai petition the government to build a wall around the city.

1684
Kangxi emperor sanctions maritime trade. Shanghai becomes a major distribution centre for both maritime and Yangzi River trade.

1732
Shanghai becomes headquarters of the Jiangsu customs office.

1760
The Pan family auctions off Yu Garden to the public, which is combined with the Temple of the Town God to become Shanghai's largest public space. The Qianlong emperor restricts all foreign trade to Canton.

1826
When the Grand Canal linking the Yellow and Yangzi rivers is blocked, the Qing government turns to Shanghai shipping merchants to transport rice from the Lower Yangzi region by sea to Beijing.

1839
The British launch the First Opium War, and proceed to take China's coastal cities by force.

1842
The British attack and capture the walled city of Shanghai. Qing government is forced to sign the Treaty of Nanjing to end the war. The treaty designates that five ports be open to foreign trade and residence, including Shanghai.

1843
The British establish a settlement in Shanghai near the confluence of Huangpu River and Suzhou Creek.

1849
The French establish their own settlement along Huangpu River, just south of the British settlement.

1853
Small Swords uprising by groups of local rebels put down by settlement forces. The Taipings, another rebel faction and led by Hong Xiuquan, set up their "heavenly capital" in Nanjing.

1854
Land Regulations allow foreigners to lease land "in perpetuity" from Chinese. Americans claim a settlement in Hongkou. Shanghai's Volunteer Corps, made up of various nationalities, is formed to protect the city.

1859
Shanghai's Imperial Maritime Customs is

placed under the charge of the British agent Robert Hart.

1861
Chinese official Li Hongzhang takes control of Shanghai customs and uses revenue gained from it to fund the Huai Army.

1863
The British and American settlements are merged to form the International Settlement.

1864
Decisive Taiping Rebellion is quelled by Qing forces.

1872
Englishman Ernest Major establishes China's first modern newspaper, the *Shenbao*, published in Shanghai's International Settlement. The *Shenbao* continues to run until 1949.

1895
Following China's defeat in the Sino-Japanese War, the Treaty of Shimonoseki allows the Japanese to set up factories in Shanghai as well as in other other treaty port cities. Other foreign powers follow suit.

1912
A weak and battered Qing dynasty gives way to a fledgling republic.

1917
Opium is declared illegal by international agreement. Shanghai becomes a smuggler's paradise.

1919
On 5 June, workers launch several strikes in Shanghai, causing the city's industries to shut down.

1921
Chinese Communist Party (CCP) holds first general meeting in Shanghai, with the goal of establishing trade unions in China's most proletarian city.

1922
Sun Yat-sen, leader of the Nationalist, or Kuomintang (KMT), Party in Canton, meets with Communist International (Comintern) agents in Shanghai and agrees to allow the CCP to join the Kuomintang revolutionary movement.

1924
Du Yuesheng becomes head of the Green Gang, taking power from Huang Jinrong following an incident at an opera house.

1925
May 30th Movement begins in Shanghai when students march to the Shanghai Municipal Police headquarters, only to be shot at by police. Death of 12 students leads to nationwide demonstrations against imperialism.

1927
On 12 April, the KMT, under its new leader Chiang Kai-shek, teams up with the Shanghai Green Gang to enforce violent purge of CCP members in Shanghai. The KMT establishes the Greater Shanghai

FAR LEFT TOP: Shanghai's port in the early days. **LEFT MIDDLE:** Shanghai's ancient city walls. **ABOVE:** Li Hongzhang, the customs chief. **ABOVE RIGHT:** triad boss Due Yuesheng. **RIGHT:** Sun Yat-sen, founder of modern China.

Municipality, and attempts over next 10 years to clean up the city and rid it of Communist influence.

1932
War is fought in Zhabei district between the Japanese military and Cantonese 19th Route Army. Japan wins but is forced to evacuate area under international pressure.

1934
The KMT launches the New Life Movement to clean up Shanghai and other cities, part of a broader initiative to rid cities of decadent Western influences.

1937
Japan invades China. Shanghai is attacked in August, but Concessions are left untouched. The KMT government retreats to the Chinese interior.

1940
In June, the Vichy government of France gives up

the French Concession to Japanese military control.

1941
Following the attack on Pearl Harbor, Japan takes over Shanghai's International Settlement and rounds up Allied nationals.

1943
Agreements between Allied powers and China end extraterritoriality in Shanghai and other treaty ports; Shanghai's Concessions are given up to Chinese sovereignty, ending 100 years of "semi-colonial" rule.

1945
Japan surrenders. US forces occupy Shanghai and other Chinese port cities.

1946
Chiang Kai-shek's KMT returns to Nanjing.

1949
The CCP's People's Liberation Army (PLA) defeats KMT forces, who flee to Taiwan and set up the renegade Republic of China (ROC). Shanghai is "liberated" in May. On 1 October, Mao Zedong announces establishment of People's Republic of China (PRC).

1949–54
CCP shuts down vice industries in Shanghai, including gambling dens, brothels and dance halls.

1950
Start of a campaign to "resist America and assist Korea"; foreigners expelled from Shanghai.

1958
Mao Zedong launches the Great Leap Forward.

1966–76
Cultural Revolution marks the rise of the Gang of Four, who use Shanghai as a propaganda base.

1976
Cultural Revolution ends with death of Mao. The Gang of Four is arrested and brought to trial.

1979
Deng Xiaoping launches the "opening and reforms" era.

1985
Jiang Zemin is named mayor of Shanghai.

1988
Jiang Zemin is succeeded by Zhu Rongji.

1989
Tiananmen crisis rocks Beijing; Jiang and Zhu maintain stability in Shanghai. Jiang becomes the Communist Party Secretary.

1990
Pudong area is designated as a Special Economic Zone. Shanghai becomes "dragon head" of economic development in China.

1992
Deng takes his famous "southern tour", and encourages foreign investment and growth in Shanghai. Municipal revenues are used to build up Shanghai's infrastructure.

1993
The 468-metre (1,535ft) tall iconic Oriental Pearl Tower is opened and becomes the symbol of New Shanghai. Jiang Zemin, the former Shanghai mayor, becomes China's president.

FAR LEFT: Shanghainese refugee, 1937. **LEFT:** statue of Mao Zedong, the founder of Chinese Communism. **ABOVE:** Jiang Zemin, former Shanghai mayor. **RIGHT:** Haibao, mascot for the 2010 Expo.

1998
Jin Mao Tower, then China's tallest building, officially opens. Zhu Rongji, former Shanghai major, is appointed as China's prime minister.

1999
Pudong International Airport opens in time for Fortune 500 Global Economic Forum. Work on the elevated highway system is also completed.

2001
Shanghai hosts the APEC conference.

2002
Despite strong competition, Shanghai wins the bid to host World Expo in 2010.

2003
High-speed Maglev train starts operations, connecting Pudong Airport to the city. Hu Jintao succeeds Jiang Zemin as China's president.

2004
Shanghai hosts the first Formula One Grand Prix race in China.

2005
Construction along the Huangpu River for the 2010 World Expo site begins, relocating some 18,000 to 20,000 households in the process.

2006
Shanghai Party Secretary and former mayor Chen Liangyu is dismissed following allegations of corruption.

2007
Yu Zhengsheng is appointed as Shanghai Party Secretary. Former Shanghai Party Secretary Xi Jinping goes to Beijing as part of the new Politburo Standing Committee, and is identified as possible successor to Hu Jintao.

2008–9
The world goes into recession, but Shanghai, after a brief dip, continues on its growth trajectory, supported in part by infrastructure projects for the World Expo. Completion (August 2008) of China's tallest building, the Shanghai World Financial Centre.

2010
Shanghai hosts a successful World Expo, attracting 76 million visitors over the six-month period and completing a host of infrastructure projects that have considerably improved city living: extended subway lines, additional tunnels to Pudong and widened highways.

BUSINESS AND ECONOMY

Business in Shanghai is not built upon low wages and sweatshop labour. With ready access to an educated workforce and a solid infrastructure, the city is set on steamrolling China's spectacular economic growth

From the incessant clatter of construction that fills the gleaming metropolis of Pudong and the old downtown in Puxi, to the clink of glasses toasting a steady stream of closed deals in conference rooms and restaurants all over the city, Shanghai is hopping

Shanghai beats other major Chinese cities on all counts as a destination for investment. For information on what's hot, check the Shanghai government's business website at www.investment.gov.cn.

with a high-voltage buzz and energy that screams out economic development.

Shanghai has been China's most important commercial city for the past 150 years, and it's hard to overstate the importance of this city to the national economy. With only 1 percent of the country's population, Shanghai generates about 5 percent of the nation's economic output and 25 percent of its total trade.

Since its latest bout of growth began in the early 1990s, Shanghai's economy has expanded by at least 10 percent every year – albeit with a short-lived blip during the global recession in 2008–9. Naturally, the Shanghainese are among the wealthiest in China: it's forecast that they will enjoy a purchasing power equal to or exceeding that of Australians and Italians in the near future. It's little wonder that manufacturing and service companies are beating a path to the city, or that real-estate developers are rushing to build shopping malls, office complexes and apartments that seem to materialise here as quickly as they can be conceived.

Shanghai's thriving retail business forms a sizeable chunk of the service sector, which accounts for more than 40 percent of GDP. The Shanghainese are China's most style-conscious people; the city is filled with packed malls, screaming billboards and sidewalks that sometimes look more like catwalks. Visitors may wish to purchase Chinese silk or porcelain as gifts for family and friends back home, but they can just as easily opt for Ferragamo on Nanjing Road, Versace on Central Huaihai Road or Dolce & Gabbana on the Bund – or any one of the top-flight international designer brands.

Shanghai Renaissance

Shanghai has not always been a great place in which to invest though. In 1949, the very qualities that had made the city a business mecca suddenly turned into an industrialist's nightmare when the city was seized by the Communists. Shanghai's business elite either fled the country or suffered the iniquity of watching their factories nationalised and their personal assets seized. By the late 1950s, Shanghai's business intelligentsia had been driven to the brink of extinction.

During the first 10 years of its rule, the Communist Party tore apart the laissez-faire capitalism of pre-1949 China and instituted in its place a textbook example of a centrally planned economy. All production was set by the state and distributed by the state. In return for labour and loyalty, a citizen's needs were provided from the cradle to the grave by the government. Once assigned to a *danwei* (work unit), it was nearly impossible for someone to transfer to another.

In the early years of the People's Republic,

the central planners soaked up the "economic surplus" from Shanghai and starved the city of resources, in part out of fear that Shanghai's capitalist reflexes could undermine the Communist experiment. This policy was maintained even as Deng Xiaoping's administration began dismantling parts of the state apparatus under the *gaige kaifang* ("reform and opening up") drive in the 1980s.

COMMERCIAL CULTURE

The intangible factor in Shanghai's economic success is the confident, urbane and commercial-minded character of the typical Shanghainese. The parents of most of today's Shanghainese moved to the city decades ago to seek their fortunes – hardworking people with an appetite for risk and the brains to make the best of opportunity. To this day, Shanghai is the lodestone that attracts the most ambitious Chinese from all corners of the country. Shanghainese may refer derisively to the newcomers as *waidiren* (outsiders), but if they are smart, diligent – and a little lucky – they become the new Shanghainese very quickly.

LEFT: prospective buyers surveying a scale model of a condominium – property is much sought after in boom-town Shanghai. **ABOVE:** China is set to conquer the world, with Shanghai as its financial and business weapon.

With the encouragement of both the municipal and central governments, the city has become a production centre for high-tech items like semiconductors and telecommunications equipment. These industries rely on educated workers with good language skills, and this is where Shanghai excels.

Shanghai is the world's second-busiest container port, and is poised to take the top spot in the near future. With China's best highway, rail, air and inland marine infrastructure, Shanghai serves as the logistics centre for much of the country. It is little wonder that the Yangzi River Delta continues to attract high-end manufacturers from all over the world, who know that business in Shanghai is not built upon low wages and sweatshop labour.

Will Shanghai displace Hong Kong?

Shanghai's evolution as the financial centre of China is another driver in the city's economic miracle. China's rapid move towards a market-oriented economy over the past two decades has required the development of modern financial institutions. Pudong's Lujiazui district (see page 225) is home to China's most powerful banks and insurance companies, as well as the Shanghai Stock Exchange.

But despite what some pundits say, Shanghai is not yet able to challenge Hong Kong's position as Asia's financial hub. China's state-owned banks are financially weak; capital markets are in their infancy compared to those in Hong Kong; and it is not likely, despite increased pressure from the West, that the Chinese yuan (RMB) will be made fully convertible until the financial system is more mature.

But the state's economic planners have a good grasp of the reforms necessary to make Shanghai competitive as a financial centre, and are implementing them in a methodical and measured manner. Banks have received government bail-outs, sold stakes to overseas investors and raised additional capital from global markets. The yuan was taken off its longstanding peg to the US dollar in 2005, and its value as determined by a "managed float" has been strengthening gradually since (see box, opposite).

The number and types of financial instruments offered in both the consumer and institutional financial markets are on the rise, and both companies and individuals are able to invest in

After former Shanghai mayors (and Party Secretaries) Jiang Zemin and Zhu Rongji assumed top positions in Beijing, they became lobbyists for Shanghai's economic development. When Deng Xiaoping agreed to loosen Shanghai's reins after 1990, the city reacted like an orchard exposed to warmth after a long winter. Forty years was not long enough to extinguish Shanghai's commercial instincts: the stage was set for the intensive development that began in the 1990s and continues today.

Economic pillars

Shanghai products have maintained their pre-1949 reputation as the best made in the country, and manufacturing continues to be an important pillar of the regional economy. While most economic activity is now driven by market forces, the state has insisted on maintaining a strong hand in the six so-called "pillar industries": information technology, automobiles, chemicals, steel, machinery and biotechnology. Production in these six areas constitutes more than 70 percent of Shanghai's total industrial output.

With wage levels rising, Shanghai manufacturers have moved up the technology curve.

a whole new class of assets, such as gold and foreign equities. With the domestic retail banking industry now open following China's entry to the World Trade Organization, consumers have more financial choices than ever before.

Stereotypical Chinese business meetings focus on gradual relationship-building, but in fast-changing Shanghai, it's likely that your business partners will want to get down to brass tacks as quickly as you do.

Future directions

Shanghai can still be a challenging place to do business. Issues such as non-tariff trade barriers, corruption and intellectual property protection continue to vex some investors, and the legal system will remain a weak link for decades. But doing business in Shanghai gets easier all the time, and the proof is in the seemingly inexhaustible appetite of foreign businesses intent on investing in Shanghai.

China's most cosmopolitan city has been in the public eye during the 2010 World Expo, which saw public investment continue at a high, recession-reversing rate, virtually guaranteeing the city's 10-plus percent annual growth. The city's economy is relatively balanced and driven by so many sectors – manufacturing, services, exports, logistics, domestic and international finance – that growth is expected to continue even after the Expo investment surge is over.

Investors who accept the unique risks presented by China's business environment are betting that its rapidly growing economy will bring them profits on a scale not possible in smaller and more mature markets. Only time will tell if they have read the tea leaves correctly. ❑

LEFT: high-tech industry is the mainstay of Shanghai's thriving economy. **ABOVE:** Shanghai's citizens are among the richest in China. **ABOVE RIGHT:** crunching numbers at the Shanghai Gold Exchange.

FLOATING THE YUAN

Not too many years ago, the thriving black market for US dollars in China proved that the yuan was overvalued at its official exchange rate. Today, an intense debate rages over how overvalued it might be – and whether or not the Chinese government's management of exchange rates is tantamount to currency manipulation, aimed to make Chinese exports cheap abroad.

The yuan has gradually strengthened against international currencies since the switch was made from a US dollar peg to a "managed float" regime in July 2005 – but this hasn't been fast enough for ailing US manufacturers. These companies have made the value of the yuan a political issue that could have far-reaching consequences in the arena of international trade and business.

PERFORMING ARTS

Chinese opera, music, drama, dance and cinema are all staging a comeback in Shanghai, and the city looks set to claim its former glory as a world cultural centre

The Shanghai Grand Theatre *(see page 127)* is a gleaming glass and steel structure, with an aluminium roof that arcs gracefully toward the heavens. The city's first world-class theatre set the standard for performing arts venues across China when it opened in 1999. And if that wasn't enough, a second and equally impressive facility opened in 2005. Located in Pudong, the Shanghai Oriental Arts Centre *(see page 232)*, with its dramatic tinted-glass exterior, resembles a magnolia when viewed from above. Designed by French architects and featuring state-of-the-art technology, both theatres have succeeded in luring the world's top performing arts companies to Shanghai.

It is appropriate that Shanghai should have two of China's best performing arts theatres. It was in this city that many Chinese art forms were incubated, refined and born.

Glory days of the arts

In the 1920s and 30s, Shanghai was the undisputed performing arts capital of China, a magnet for aspiring and established artists from around the country. The greatest Chinese opera stars dazzled audiences with their interpretations of classic operas. Professional storytellers mesmerised crowds in teahouses, relating tales so long they took months to finish. Acrobats, jugglers and contortionists cavorted before crowds in the narrow streets around the Yu Garden. The Shanghai Municipal Orchestra performed the works of classical and contemporary European composers at the Lyceum Theatre, and movies were so popular that it was front-page news when a new cinema opened.

But then came war and revolution, and an entirely new system for governing the arts. After 1949, private opera troupes were disbanded and reorganised under government auspices. Itinerant performers were obliged to stop their wanderings. The foreigners who comprised the bulk of the Shanghai Municipal Orchestra left.

PRECEDING PAGES: Beijing opera actors. **LEFT:** scene from the Kunju opera's staging of *The Peony Pavilion*. **RIGHT:** Shanghai Acrobatics Troupe – not to be missed.

Beijing emerged as the cultural centre of China and Shanghai's performing arts were forced to play second fiddle. Neglect, the passage of time and 10 years of suppression during the Cultural Revolution (1966–76) did great damage to the arts in Shanghai. Yet, somehow, many art forms have withstood the odds and are still being performed today. They divide neatly into those traditional to China and those imported into Shanghai from the West and Japan.

Chinese opera (Beijing-style)

Chief among the traditional performing arts is Chinese opera, a broad term for sung drama that includes more than 360 different varieties. This is a highly demanding art: actors, who begin training as children, must learn to sing and dance, acquire an extensive repertoire of highly stylised gestures and perform acrobatics. It is equally challenging to watch. Few props are used, which means the audience must use their imagination to fill in considerable blanks, characters are role types recognisable only by their make-up and costumes, and interpretative differences are highly nuanced. With so many less challenging modern diversions, Chinese opera today is losing its fans, especially in the cities.

For the past century, Shanghai has been home to four kinds of Chinese opera: Beijing, Kunju, Shaoxing and Huju. Beijing opera is the best known, recognisable by its falsetto singing, vivid make-up, percussion-based music, striking acrobatics and librettos based on the exploits of legendary heroes. In Old Shanghai, Beijing opera was king, with great stars such as Mei Lanfang, renowned male interpreter of women's roles, who was enticed here from Beijing by wealthy patrons.

So seductive was the profusion of performing arts in Shanghai that Beijing opera troupes began to borrow from other art forms and a Shanghai school of Beijing opera developed. Called *haipai*, which is characterised by a willingness to experiment, it was the first to use mechanical scenery and special effects, and to

THE CULTURAL REVOLUTION YEARS: DYING FOR THEIR ART

The Cultural Revolution (1966–76) was a political campaign and power struggle disguised as an effort to create a new socialist culture by ridding China of traditional and Western art forms. It was launched from Shanghai by Jiang Qing (Mao Zedong's wife) and her cronies in the Gang of Four.

For 10 years, virtually all performing arts were banned, except eight "model operas" which Jiang Qing helped create. These included five modern Beijing operas, two ballets and a revolutionary symphony. The Shanghai Beijing Opera Company's *Taking Tiger Mountain by Strategy* and the Shanghai Ballet's *White-Haired Girl* were performed countless times because they had Jiang Qing's offficial sanction.

Although the performing arts suffered immensely during this period, the artistes suffered more. Virtually all significant performers of "feudal" or "Western" arts were subjected to public criticism sessions in which they were humiliated, beaten and locked away in makeshift jails. The tools of their art – instruments, opera costumes, sheet music – were confiscated and burnt. Unable to withstand this cruelty, many artistes gave up and

killed themselves. At the Shanghai Conservatory alone, 17 students and professors committed suicide in the first years of the Cultural Revolution, while the Shanghai Symphony conductor Lu Hongen was executed for criticising Mao Zedong.

adapt scripts from outside the traditional repertoire. This willingness to innovate is criticised by purists, but it has helped Shanghai's Beijing opera company maintain its vitality and remain one of the strongest in the country.

Kunju, Shaoxing and Huju opera

Kunju, named after nearby Kunshan, is sometimes known as the mother of Beijing opera. Its music is gentle and melodic, dominated by the bamboo flute, and its librettos are long and lyrical, read to this day as literary classics. The Shanghai Kunju Company has sparked renewed interest in this dying genre, most recently with *The Peony Pavilion*.

Written by Tang Xianzu in 1598, *The Peony Pavilion* has 55 acts, a cast of 100 and still packs a punch. The erotic, political content of a true-to-the-original production so shocked the authorities that they refused to allow the company to perform at New York's Lincoln Center in 1998 (a more sanitised production was performed a year later).

Shaoxing opera, which originates in Zhejiang province, has a repertoire of mainly tragic love stories like *A Dream of Red Mansions*, with music augmented by violins and cellos. Interestingly, it is performed – and watched – almost exclusively by women. It first became popular in the 1920s – when fans would throw gold and jewellery on stage to their favourite actresses – and has a large cult following of housewives to this day.

Huju is a strictly local opera form sung in the Shanghainese dialect. Rarely performed in theatres, it's sometimes still staged outdoors near the Temple of the Town God, a gathering place for itinerant performers since the Ming dynasty.

Pingtan

Though the wandering performers of Old Shanghai are gone, a few of their arts have survived, notably Pingtan and acrobatics. A respected art form of storytelling with close links to music, Pingtan is usually performed by a man and a woman who use only a fan or a teacup as props but keep audiences spellbound with animated facial expressions and virtuosic musical accompaniment on Chinese string instruments like the *pipa* and *san xian*.

LEFT: a Beijing opera star takes centre stage.
ABOVE: Pingtan storytelling is accompanied by traditional string instruments like the *pipa* and *san xian*.

began writing plays and, in 1933, the China Travelling Dramatic Troupe was founded to take spoken drama from Shanghai to the rest of the nation. Its greatest moment was the 1936 première of Cao Yu's *Thunderstorm*, a tragedy that remains a classic on the Chinese stage.

Drama is still associated with politics and is thus carefully controlled in Shanghai. Though the city still supports several drama companies, it has contributed little to the art form in recent decades. An increasing number of international theatre troupes, whose performances range from Shakespeare to contemporary Asian drama, tour Shanghai more frequently these days, giving audiences a new perspective.

Orchestral music

The Shanghai Symphony Orchestra dates to 1879, when it began as a town band for the International Settlement. Over the years, the band became a symphony, comprising mainly foreigners and, after 1938, Chinese musicians. The presence of so many foreign musicians in Shanghai attracted aspiring Chinese musicians from around the country and led the great music educator Xiao Youmei to establish the country's first music school – now the Shanghai Conservatory – in 1927.

Graduates of the Conservatory were instrumental in persuading the Communist Party that classical music could "serve the people"; many indeed went on to be key forces in the post-1949 development of Western music and opera. Western classical music in turn became a major influence in the reform of Chinese music – traditional instruments were modernised, new instruments were created and Western-style orchestral ensembles were formed. Both the Shanghai Symphony Orchestra and Shanghai Conservatory are strong institutions. The city also supports two other major orchestras, the Shanghai Philharmonic Orchestra and the Shanghai Broadcast Symphony Orchestra.

Contemporary drama

Westerners began introducing their own performing arts and forming acting clubs as early as the 1860s, but their plays had little reach beyond the foreign community. The first spoken drama performed by the Chinese was a 1907 adaptation of Harriet Beecher Stowe's *Uncle Tom's Cabin*, staged by leftist students. In the 1920s, young authors like Tian Han

ACROBATIC ARTS

Acrobatics did not originate in Shanghai but was so popular pre-1949 that the city became a centre for acrobatic troupes from around the country, and the first port of call for circuses and magic shows from overseas. After 1949, acrobatics was promoted heavily by the government as a proletarian art form. It was also one of the few arts permitted during the Cultural Revolution.

Though acrobatics remains popular in rural areas, urban residents tend to view it as peasant entertainment. The audience in Shanghai therefore is comprised primarily of overseas tourists. This is rather unfortunate because the Shanghai Acrobatic Troupe, which performs nightly at the Shanghai Centre Theatre *(see page 289)*, is one of the best of its kind in the world.

Ballroom and ballet dancing

Dance was wildly popular in Shanghai, but more as a participatory activity than as an art form which people watched in a theatre. Dance was closely linked with jazz and – together with movies – was the prime means through which jazz was introduced. In the 1920s and 30s, Shanghai had enough dance halls to support

over 500 jazz bands, mostly comprising Filipino musicians. Ballroom dance remains popular among the Shanghainese today, and the nightclub band circuit is again dominated by Filipinos. Jazz too has made a comeback, and once again many of the musicians are foreign.

Ballet and contemporary dance were brought to Shanghai by the White Russians in the 1920s – Dame Margot Fonteyn in fact began her studies with a Russian ballet teacher in Shanghai *(see page 164)*. After liberation, the Soviet Russians continued to develop the art form, and the Shanghai Ballet School and Shanghai Ballet were founded. Russian classics dominated their repertoire up until the mid-1960s, when Jiang Qing (Mao Zedong's wife and key perpetrator of the Cultural Revolution) encouraged the creation of a proletarian ballet with Chinese characteristics. Classic poses from Beijing opera were integrated into ballet and the choreography was made more "revolutionary", meaning that ballerinas danced with clenched fists and rifles, their eyes ablaze with the fire of class hatred.

The Shanghai Ballet today performs primarily European classics, although they still stage the classic *The White-Haired Girl*, and are moving into experimental East-West collaborations with international ballet companies. There is also the Shanghai Dance Ensemble, which combines elements of contemporary, classical and traditional Chinese dance, and has several rising young stars.

Shanghai has a well-respected modern dance company founded by the renowned dancer

Ballroom dancing is popular in Shanghai, with couples twirling on pavements and parks in the early morning hours.

Jin Xing, a Beijing transplant. Jin Xing – who used to be a colonel in the People's Liberation Army and is as famous for her sex change as for her dancing – is a strong and provocative choreographer whose work is shaking up Shanghai's modern dance scene.

Shanghainese cinema

Cinema also got its start in Shanghai, where the first film ever shown in China was screened in 1896 – as an interlude between magic tricks and a fireworks display in a vaudeville show. The first films made in China were produced by foreigners in Shanghai and the first Chinese-produced films were also made here.

By the 1930s, movies were the biggest form of entertainment, with first-run Hollywood films shown in lavishly decorated auditoriums that could seat nearly 2,000 people. The first Chinese "talkie" was produced in Shanghai in 1931, starring the legendary actress Butterfly

LEFT: Shanghai Symphony Orchestra. **ABOVE:** Jin Xing is a provocative modern dancer. **ABOVE RIGHT:** Shanghai Ballet dancers in a contemporary piece.

Wu, and the industry soon prospered despite the popularity of Hollywood movies.

The Communist Party quickly recognised the usefulness of film as a propaganda tool, and gave the industry much support after 1949. Today, however, Shanghai's film industry is moribund: fewer than 100 feature films are produced annually, and of these only a handful are made in

> Critically acclaimed Chinese movies like Crouching Tiger, Hidden Dragon *are going mainstream, while Chinese movie stars like Gong Li and Chow Yun-fat have made a name for themselves in Hollywood.*

Shanghai, with 80 percent of them losing money. Still, filmmakers like Wang Xiaoshuai, whose *Shanghai Dream*s won the Prix du Jury at Cannes in 2005, are gaining an international reputation.

Shanghai is also marketing itself as a cheaper, more exotic movie-making locale for Hollywood. *Mission Impossible III, The White Countess* and *The Painted Veil* were recently filmed in Shanghai, with many more in the making.

What the future holds

Shanghai's performing arts suffer because the government maintains a contradictory, and ultimately unsustainable, arts policy. On the one hand, the government recognises that performing and other arts are essential to Shanghai's drive to be a major global city, and has built first-rate performance venues and imported popular shows, from the musical *Cats* to pop stars like Elton John. On the other hand, professional arts companies are still treated as government propaganda vehicles. Although their subsidies have been sharply cut, arts groups remain saddled with burdensome quotas for performances at factories and schools. They are required to appear at a political event at a moment's notice, even if it means cancelling a long-scheduled public performance. In addition, all scripts for plays and films must be submitted to cultural censors for approval.

Sadly, the degree of artistic interference in Shanghai negates the many commendable efforts the city is making to become a great cultural centre. Lost – or deliberately overlooked – in the rush forward is the simple fact that Old Shanghai was the nation's performing arts capital because it was open, cosmopolitan and relatively free. Shanghai is fortunate in that so many of its stellar performing arts companies survived a century of war, revolution and chaos. But only when artists are allowed to create and perform with relative freedom will the city have a chance of reclaiming – or exceeding – its past glory. ❏

● *See page 289 of Travel Tips for listings of performing arts venues.*

ABOVE LEFT: movie poster of the award-winning *Shanghai Dreams*. **ABOVE:** shooting a film in Shanghai.

Writing in Shanghai

So important is Shanghai in the history of modern Chinese literature that nearly every great writer of the first half of the 20th century lived here at some point: Lu Xun, Guo Morou, Ba Jin, Mao Dun, Xu Zhimo, Qian Zhongshu, Cao Yu, Tian Han, Ding Ling – the list goes on.

They came for different reasons, but all found themselves in a city primed to support a literary revolution. The Shanghai region had, for centuries, produced great poets, painters and calligraphers – arts that are intertwined in traditional Chinese thinking. When Westerners settled here after the Opium Wars, they spread their own literature and ideas through missionary schools and universities. In time, graduates of these schools began to study overseas and returned with new world views. When the "old culture" of the traditional literati met the "new culture" of the Western-influenced students, great literary ferment was inevitable.

Shanghai became a nucleus of literary experimentation, a role made easier by its commercial base as a printing and publishing centre. The pinnacle of the written word in China had always been poetry, but in Shanghai the novel – written in the vernacular, rather than classical Chinese – became the vogue. Famous examples include Mao Dun's *Midnight*, Ding Ling's *Miss Sophie's Diary*, Ba Jin's *Family* and Qian Zhongshu's *Fortress Besieged*.

Poetry, too, became a form of experiment. New-style bards such as Guo Morou tossed aside the strict technical rules for writing Chinese poetry and immersed themselves in the flowing verse of poets like Whitman and Tagore. Xu Zhimo wrote of love, ideals and freedom, and he lived his life as passionately as he wrote his poetry.

The essay also held an important place in Shanghai's literary world, its greatest practitioner the legendary Lu Xun, who lived and wrote here from 1927 to 1936. He wrote with an acid-tipped pen, criticising the entire fabric of Chinese society. Many of his

> *The Shanghai Literary Festival, held every March and organised by the M on the Bund restaurant, brings together literary luminaries of both the Western and Chinese worlds. See www.m-restaurantgroup.com.*

essays revolved around political or revolutionary topics. He is best known in the West, however, as the author of *The True Story of Ah Q* and *Diary of a Madman*, which lampooned Chinese character and culture.

From 1949 until 1976, political move-

ments forced writers to reflect a vision of socialist "reality" and they produced little of literary merit. When the Cultural Revolution ended, dissident writers left, and some, such as Ma Jian, gained profile in the West. In China, a new generation was finding its voice; in recent years, young writers have published passionate accounts of characters struggling to find love or meaning in the modern city. Wei Hui's sexually charged *Shanghai Baby* has been translated into several languages (but it is banned in China) and the teenage Han Han's novels that condemn China's education system have become nationwide bestsellers. ❑

RIGHT: controversial Chinese writer Wei Hui.

VISUAL ARTS

A heady mix of both traditional and cutting-edge contemporary art forms has made Shanghai an exciting centre of artistic expression

Shanghai's progress in transforming itself into a cultural centre is nowhere more apparent than in the visual arts. Indeed, in less than a decade, the city has become the nation's standard-bearer for museum design and management, and a key centre for contemporary art. Remarkable as this transformation is – especially given that in the 1990s the city was best known in art circles for the speed with which it shut down controversial and experimental avant-garde art exhibitions – it nonetheless feels like destiny.

In recent years, Shanghai has become a centre for Chinese contemporary art. There are big bucks to be made, too – in 2006, Sotheby's and Christie's sold US$190 million worth of Chinese art, a 760 percent increase in two years.

Old Shanghai was an important arena of artistic experimentation, a meeting place for methods and philosophies from China and the West. Its booming economy enabled it to support artists, patrons and collectors, and its cosmopolitan atmosphere made them feel at home. In traditional China, the arts had long been looked upon as a gentleman's pursuit rather than a professional's *métier*, but in brash, business-minded Shanghai it has become acceptable to combine culture with commerce – and still be respected.

LEFT: even the body is a canvas for Shanghai's artists.
RIGHT: Liu Haisu's work is reminiscent of Impressionism.

Chinese painting

Painting is traditionally considered the greatest of the traditional arts in China. It is intimately related to calligraphy, which holds a similarly exalted status, and seal-carving. In Old China, some facility in painting or calligraphy was a virtual requirement for any self-respecting member of the literati, a cultural belief so deeply embedded that to this day Chinese leaders feel obliged to demonstrate their calligraphic skills in public.

As part of the prosperous Jiangsu-Zhejiang region, Shanghai was heir to a tradition of highly accomplished gentlemen painters. Painting was a meditative and philosophical art that was considered as much a reflection of the artist's inner

such Western techniques as perspective and shading, they eschewed them, considering the Chinese way of painting to be infinitely superior.

Western influence

However, as Shanghai became more cosmopolitan in the late 19th and early 20th centuries, a new school of painting called *haishang* developed. *Haishang* is essentially a combination of different styles and techniques, its most distinctive feature being openness to new ideas – it is the visual arts equivalent of Chinese opera's *haipai (see page 52)*. This *haishang* broad-mindedness grew to encompass Western art when the printing industry blossomed at the turn of the 20th century and painters could see reproductions of Western masterpieces. Art students began to paint still lifes and nude models, and to take their easels outdoors and sketch what they saw – methods that were a departure from traditional art.

Shanghai soon became the destination of choice for students interested in Western painting, including renowned painters such as Liu Haisu and Xu Beihong. Liu Haisu studied in Paris and Japan and founded the Shanghai Art School in 1920. A great admirer of such artists as Van Gogh and Cézanne, Liu sparked a scandal when he organised an exhibition of nude paintings, which was quickly shut down by the police. Liu eventually returned to brush-and-ink painting, but his traditional-style works still reveal the influences of his Western education.

Xu Beihong studied in Paris and Berlin and spent much of his career moving between Western- and Chinese-style painting. At its best, his work combines elements of both, as seen in his famous galloping horses, which seem ready to run off the scroll with their flowing brushstrokes and bulging muscles.

moral being as his artistic skill. Brushwork was of paramount importance, its intent to reflect the essence of whatever was portrayed rather than its true appearance. Tradition reigned supreme; a painter who wished to portray a mountain was as likely to study a past master's representations of mountains as to go and look at one himself. Though many Chinese painters were aware of

The vivacity that characterised painting in Shanghai largely ended with the Sino-Japanese War. After 1949, Soviet-style Realism became the main influence, and the subject matter of both traditional and Western-style painting tended to be revolutionary. Traditional paintings often included trains and tractors, and the practice of drawing people dwarfed by landscape ended – workers, peasants and soldiers had to dominate nature, not be overshadowed by it. In the Cultural Revolution, Western-style portrait painting was widely practised but there was only

MUSEUMS APLENTY

When the Shanghai Museum *(see pages 128–9 and 134–7)* built its striking building *(see picture below)* in People's Square in 1996, it was seen as proof that the city was serious about improving its cultural standards. Often cited as the best museum in China, its success fuelled a plan to refurbish and build many more museums in Shanghai, both public and private – the long-term goal is 100. At present, these include the Shanghai Art Museum *(page 127)*, the Shanghai Municipal History Museum *(page 228)*, the Shanghai Urban Planning Centre *(page 128)* and the Shanghai Arts and Crafts Museum *(page 161)*. There is also a costume museum, a maritime museum, a traditional folk arts museum, and many more.

one subject – Mao Zedong. Poster art was also prominent, most of it "red, bright and shiny".

After the Cultural Revolution ended, artists quickly picked up their brushes and began to paint in both traditional and Western styles – many even began to portray Mao in political pop art paintings that have been eagerly snatched up by Western buyers for huge sums of money. Shanghai became a centre for such pop art with painters like Wang Ziwei, who became rich and famous with his trademark style of contrasting Mao with American icons like Mickey Mouse and Donald Duck.

The contemporary art boom

In recent years, Shanghai has become known as a centre for abstract art, often inspired by traditional painting. Chinese contemporary art has, in fact, become one of the hottest commodities in the art world, and Shanghai has cleverly combined culture with commerce to become a major art centre. In 2006, Sotheby's and Christie's sold US$190 million worth of mainly Chinese contemporary art. Chinese avant-garde artists who struggled to scrape a living in the post-Tiananmen era (contemporary art was viewed as subversive then) now sell paintings for hundreds of thousands of dollars – the record is US$2.7 million for a Liu Xiaodong painting, set at a Beijing auction house in 2006.

The works of Shanghai's artists range from Yue Minjun's beaming sculptures to Zhou Tiehai's famous variations on the Joe Camel cigarette ad, and from Ding Yi's vibrant geo-metric abstracts to Zhong Biao's realist oils that often feature Shanghai as a backdrop. The artists come from all over the country, but are drawn to the Shanghai galleries, where, they say, they get both exposure and top dollar for their work.

> Shanghai's reputation as a centre of art is so well known globally that both the Guggenheim and the Pompidou Centre are thinking of opening museums there.

Sculpture, bronze and jade

In Old China, sculpture was primarily seen in temples and at royal tombs. Sculpture grew with Buddhism during the Tang dynasty and many of the greatest examples are Buddhist in character. The Shanghai Museum has an excellent collection of stone Buddha sculptures while the Jade Buddha Temple is home to the exquisite Jade Buddha statues. Interestingly, modern Shanghai is a major producer of Buddha statues; its foundries can cast the huge metal figures that are so favoured these days by monasteries.

The city is also heir to a tradition of Western

LEFT: the Joe Camel cigarette is a recurrent motif in Zhou Tiehai's work. **ABOVE AND ABOVE RIGHT:** Yue Minjun's trademark in both his painting and sculpture are cartoon-like characters with gleeful wide-toothed grins.

sculpture that grew up alongside Western-style architecture in the Concession era. It is perhaps the only Chinese city that has public sculptures of famous figures from arts – the writer Tian Han, the composer Nie Er, and even the Russian poet Alexander Pushkin. The government oversees the creation of sculpture for public areas. These tend towards whimsical crowd-pleasers, such as the many life-size bronze sculptures of typical Shanghainese going about the business of daily life – a young woman talking on a mobile phone, a couple pushing their child in a stroller, a man on a bicycle. Sculpture is also a growing genre for contemporary artists, who create both abstract and realist pieces.

Cast bronzes, carved jades and porcelain were produced by artisans and collected by emperors, literati and wealthy merchants. In addition to beauty and age, bronzes were also prized for their inscriptions and supposed ability to drive away ghosts and evil spirits; jades because they were thought to embody every virtue and to contain much qi, the vital life force; and porcelain for its lustre, feel and melodious ring when

SUZHOU EMBROIDERY: A DYING CRAFT

Embroidery is a craft that has been passed from mother to daughter in rural Suzhou for centuries. At the end of the Qing dynasty, there were 100,000 "embroidery girls" in the area, but the number has since fallen to 10,000, and most of the "girls" are now quite elderly.

Embroidery girls work in their homes on pieces assigned to them by the Suzhou factories. A complex piece – like a dragon robe that might be worn by an emperor – could take one woman stitching alone at least five years to complete. To speed up the process, the girls often work together, stitching towards each other from opposite sides of the frame. They also work together when doing Suzhou's famous two-sided embroidery, in which each side of the cloth is identically embroidered – usually with a cute kitten surrounded by flowers and butterflies.

Although there is great demand for hand-embroidered goods, the craft is slowly dying because peasant families have become prosperous and no longer need the work. The embroidery girls' daughters often have little time for the craft, and the extra cash that grandmothers earn is put to such uses as paying for the college tuition of a granddaughter – who is unlikely to become an embroiderer.

struck. Shanghai was not a major production centre for any of these crafts, but many wealthy collectors lived here and the Shanghai Museum has excellent galleries devoted to each of these.

Embroidery and folk crafts

The Jiangsu-Zhejiang region was the nation's key producer of silk, with imperial silkworks located at Suzhou, Hangzhou and Nanjing until they were closed in 1894. Sericulture is linked with embroidery, and Suzhou became an important centre of this craft. Of the four nationally recognised styles of embroidery – which include Hunan, Sichuan and Guangdong – Suzhou's was considered the most elegant *(see box opposite)*, and was used for the embroidered gowns worn by the emperor and his family. Suzhou was also the main supplier of the embroidered insignia, or rank badges, worn by the nine different lev-

Shadow puppetry has disappeared as a theatrical art, but its magic lives on in exquisite puppets made from donkey or water-buffalo skin. The Shanghai Art Museum has an excellent collection.

els of civil and military officials in imperial China. The market for such robes and insignia ended with the demise of the imperial system in 1912, but the embroidery industry stayed alive because of demand for opera costumes, household items and export goods.

Woodblock printing is an ancient craft that fell into decline after the introduction of mechanical printing in the 19th century, but was revived in Shanghai in the 1920s and 30s by the renowned writer Lu Xun. He hired a Japanese artist-engraver and organised a class for young artists at which he acted as interpreter. Lu encouraged students to depict society as they saw it. The results are often bleak – starving children, downtrodden refugees, industrial landscapes – but nonetheless beautiful; samples from his collection can be seen at the Lu Xun Memorial Hall *(see page 219)*. The craft has remained alive in Shanghai, as have silkscreening and other related methods of artistic printing.

Experimental art

But if attempts to revive folk arts have been less than successful, the government's support of painting, calligraphy, sculpture, photography and even video and performance art is of great significance. This backing is generally indirect, often grudging – untold numbers of experimental art shows have been shut down in the past – and largely a corollary of efforts to ensure that showcase projects like the Shanghai Arts Fair and the Shanghai Biennale become respected international events.

Nonetheless, the result is that Shanghai now has dozens of private galleries that sell the work of local and national artists and a burgeoning community of artists. It has frequent shows of experimental art and the Shanghai Biennale has grown into an important international exhibition. Once again, Shanghai's winning combination of culture and commerce, creativity and connoisseurship has enabled it to emerge as a key centre of the visual arts. ❏

● *See page 288 of Travel Tips for listings of art galleries.*

LEFT: modern sculptures like this are frequently found in parks all over Shanghai. **RIGHT:** contemplating contemporary art at the Shanghai Art Museum.

CUISINE

Shanghainese cuisine is best described as earthy and hearty comfort food – peasant fare, as some call it. But the city is also home to scores of sophisticated eateries that tout celebrity chefs from the major capitals of the world

From crispy fried crullers for an early-morning breakfast to a late-night snack of plump steamed dumplings, it is obvious that Shanghai is a city that loves to eat – 24 hours a day. At first light, cooks begin crowding the astounding produce markets, starting the cycle of shopping, preparing food, eating and endless conversations about food that is central to the Chinese way of life.

The Chinese often greet each other with the words "Ni chi fan le mei yo", which translates as "Have you eaten rice yet?" The emphasis on food in daily life is unmistakable.

For sheer variety alone, Shanghai is one of the best places to eat in China. Dining choices range from itinerant street vendors where take-out is the only option, to swanky celebrity chef eateries like Jean Georges. The geographical diversity is just as breathtaking, with culinary offerings from Africa to Brazil, India to the Mediterranean, the Americas, Europe and Southeast Asia, and styles ranging from the simple to the sublime, fast food and fusion, as well as an impressive array of Chinese regional cuisines.

Comfort food

Shanghai's own cuisine has its roots in hearty peasant cooking, with none of the grand flavour statements and enormous variety or subtle complexities of Cantonese or Sichuan food. With its long-simmered stews and sauces, sweetened for the child in all of us, this is comfort food, not haute cuisine. An insistence on seasonality and freshness lifts it from the ordinary, although Shanghai gourmands say that increased fish farming and hot-housing of fruits and vegetables have irrevocably changed the original flavours of classic Shanghainese dishes.

Shanghai cuisine is a subset of Huaiyang cuisine, which is the lush region located between the Huai and Yangzi rivers. It encompasses both Zhejiang and Jiangsu provinces, a place so rich and fertile that it's known as the land of fish and rice.

LEFT: *xiao long bao* – a Shanghainese speciality.
RIGHT: lunch at Din Tai Fung.

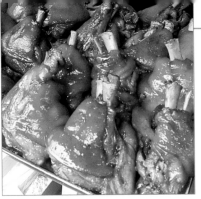

from Yangcheng Lake in Jiangsu province. The crustacean gets its name from the black hair-like filaments found on its legs. To retain their exquisite taste, the crabs are steamed and served with a soy sauce, black vinegar and ginger dip.

The city that grew up on the banks of the Huangpu River is especially fond of its denizens. River fish like yellow croaker *(huang yu)* and carp (crucian carp, variegated carp and black carp) are typically "red-cooked", ie prepared in a sauce of soy and sugar. River eel is cooked in casseroles, clams are stir-fried with ginger and scallions, and mussels are cooked with soy sauce and chilli. The classic Shanghai prawn dish is "crystal prawns", marinated in egg white and brine and stir-fried, while the hilsa herring *(shi yu)*, now rarely prepared, is renowned for its succulent scales. Fish head is considered especially sweet, and, when stewed with *fenpi* (bean starch jelly sheets), soy sauce and red chilli in a clay pot, makes another favourite dish.

Seafood staples

The sea and rivers that feature so prominently in Shanghai's history play an equally important role in shaping its largely seafood-based cuisine. The most famous dish is Shanghai's signature *dazha* or "hairy crab". More popularly known in Asia as "Shanghai hairy crab" *(see page 71)*, the finest versions of this autumn delicacy come

Pork, poultry and veggies

Turning inland, pork plays a more prominent role in the cuisine than poultry: the rustic *tipang*, a great hunk of pork rump on the bone stewed to melting tenderness, is a Shanghai classic, as is *hong shao rou* or "red-cooked" pork, fatty cubes of pork stewed in a soy sauce marinade until they practically melt in the mouth.

Poultry plays only a minor role, featuring in the classic appetiser *zuiji* or "drunken" chicken (chicken marinated in Shaoxing rice wine), *feng ya* or "wind-dried duck", which is dried outdoors and preserved for the winter, and duck and taro soup. There is also Jinhua processed ham, from Zhejiang province, often sliced and steamed with rock sugar and added to fish dishes and soups, or stir-fried with vegetables.

CLASSIC SHANGHAINESE DISHES

Most local food aficionados will agree that the following dishes constitute classical Shanghainese cooking: *dazha* (hairy crab); *tipang* (pork rump); *hong shao rou* ("red-cooked" pork); *shizi tou* ("lion's head" meatballs); *shui jing xia ren* (crystal prawns); fish head with *fenpi*, a jelly made of bean starch; *menbao shansi* (eel casserole); *hong shao huang yu* ("red-cooked" yellow croaker fish); *su ji* or *su ya* (vegetarian chicken or duck); *zuiji* ("drunken" chicken); *shi yu* (hilsa herring); *jiao bai* (wild rice stems); *kao fu* (wheat gluten); *pao fan* (rice dregs made into porridge); *xiao long bao* (pork dumplings); and *shengjie mantou* (pot-stickers; pictured left).

The words "gan bei" or "bottoms up" are uttered when making a toast at hard-drinking and more informal social gatherings. These days, people are more likely to use the more health-conscious phrase "sui yi", which means "drink as much as you want" (or not at all).

Traditionally, the vegetables of Shanghai cuisine – either cooked with meat or as dishes on their own – are fresh from the farm and seasonal, such as fat spring bamboo shoots or their more delicate-tasting winter counterparts, baby lima beans, lily buds, Chinese broccoli, *ji cai* or "shepherd's purse", asparagus lettuce, leafy *mixi*, and the quintessential Shanghai vegetable dish, *jiao bai* (wild rice stems).

Shanghainese cooking styles

With its country roots, the preparation of Shanghai cuisine is far less complex than that of its Cantonese or Beijing cousins, with only three major methods of preparation: *hong shao* or red-cooked (with sugar and soy sauce), stewed or simply stir-fried with ginger and scallions. Garlic is never used in Shanghainese cooking.

Nonetheless, Shanghai's famous style is revealed in its cold dishes, artistically arranged hors d'œuvres of dazzling variety: plates of juli-enned vinegary pickles, tiny raw crabs mari-nated in rice wine called *zuipanxie*, spiced broad beans, "drunken" chicken marinated in wine, and sweet marinated wheat gluten *(kao fu)*, all laid out in picturesque arrays at street stalls.

Bakeries and bortsch

The international influence on Shanghai's design, architecture and fashion also left its culi-nary footprints. Many of the first-generation Communist leaders, notably Deng Xiaoping and Zhou En-lai, spent time in Paris, and it was their passion for croissants, say the Shang-hainese, that perpetuated the Euro-style bak-eries that were first brought to Shanghai by the French. After falling into disfavour during the

Cultural Revolution, Shanghai's neighbourhood bakeries have undergone a renaissance, and today number in the thousands. Their shelves are filled with croissants, brioches, jewel-like teacakes and lighter-than-air sponge cakes.

About the same time that the French were baking croissants, Shanghai's White Russian population, which swelled after the 1917 Russ-ian Revolution, was brewing bortsch. Those Russian restaurants are long gone, but *luo song tang* (literally "Russian soup") is considered by many locals to be a Shanghainese dish.

Shanghai continues seamlessly to incorpo-rate new influences into its cuisine. Not to be outdone by the likes of McDonald's and Burger King which line the streets of Shanghai, the street vendors who fry spring rolls in great bubbling woks of oil now also slice up pota-toes into french fries, accompanied by a watery ketchup, for young schoolchildren.

Seasonal specialities

Shanghai home cooks still define their menus by the season. Each seasonal speciality is eagerly anticipated and then deftly incorpo-rated into dishes – until the next delicacy arrives at the markets.

FAR LEFT: seafood features prominently in Shanghainese cooking. **ABOVE LEFT:** *tipang*, or stewed pork rump, is another Shanghai speciality. **RIGHT:** for the sweet-toothed.

With early springtime come the small, succulent and intensely flavoured strawberries, mulberries, the apricot-like pipa fruit and red cherries, and a brief, glorious season of yellow cherries. The itinerant pedlars in Old Shanghai who would crush the juicy summer *yang mei* berry, a cousin of the bayberry, into a thirst-quenching drink are long gone now, but sugarcane juice vendors still ply the streets of Nanshi, the long mottled stalks of succulent green sugarcane balanced precariously on their bicycles their calling cards.

The Barbie-pink peach blossoms of spring, more substantial and pinker than their famous cherry blossom cousins, yield to summer's Nanhui honey peach, a delicate and juicy thin-skinned white peach with a subtle yet distinctive flavour. The peach has both a round and flat variety, the latter sold as "designer fruit" in the US. Along with the autumn hairy crab, November brings fresh figs from Baoshan, while the winter months see deliciously sweet miniature oranges from the offshore islands.

Street food and snacks

The street food *(see also photo feature on pages 72–3)* in Shanghai primarily comprises snacks, and while it cannot compete with places like Malaysia or Singapore, one can still eat extraordinarily well on street food alone. Expect everything from Muslim-style Xinjiang mutton kebabs to Shanghai dumplings, at all hours of day and night.

Breakfast is almost always eaten on the run, with *you tiao*, the long fried *dough* cruller, a favourite. The classic Shanghai way of eating *you tiao* is to wrap it in a sticky rice cake and eat the two together – experiencing both soft and crunchy sensations in one bite – and wash it down with freshly brewed soybean milk. That same sensation is found in rice cakes *(ci ba)*, deep-fried squares of compressed rice that make a filling breakfast. Another favourite is *pao fan*, the ricepot dregs which are steeped, then made into a *congee*, or porridge. And then there's the more familiar omelette called *jianbing*, cooked on steaming griddles and topped with chilli sauce and rolled up for takeaway.

Bamboo shoots are characteristic of Sichuan and Hunan cuisines, home of lush bamboo forests, but Shanghai's fat spring bamboo shoots, called orchid bamboo shoots because of their lovely fragrance, come from nearby Sheshan in Songjiang county. The bamboo shoot is sliced and often "red-cooked" on its own, as well as used in other dishes. Wintertime brings a more subtly flavoured shoot.

WET MARKETS AND PEDLARS

The wet markets of Shanghai make fabulous theatre as well as a fascinating introduction to Shanghai food: the philosophy of freshness is encapsulated here, where everything is just-picked and fresh-killed, and cooks shop daily, tailoring their menus to the seasons' constantly changing produce. The mind-boggling display of items includes vegetables, fruit, live poultry and seafood, tofu and noodles, and even clothes and household sundries. But it is the itinerant pedlars, wandering Shanghai with shoulder baskets filled with produce from nearby farms, who are the first with the newest offerings, often selling rare delicacies that never make it to the markets.

LEFT: *you tiao*, or fried dough stick, is a classic street snack. **RIGHT:** trays of steaming hot *xiao long bao* at a restaurant in Yu Garden Bazaar in Nanshi.

Snacks and street food are available on virtually every corner of Shanghai, but the best selection of Shanghai snacks is found at Yu Garden Bazaar *(see page 143)*. Such is the fame of Shanghai street food and snacks that hordes of Chinese tourists patiently wait in line at Yu Garden's Nanxiang Mantou Dian, purportedly the best place for *xiao long bao*, the tiny pork-stuffed dumplings with translucent skins for which Shanghai is famous.

The lines are just as long for the so-called pot-stickers, *shengjie mantou*, pan-fried in giant crusty black pans and sprinkled with scallions, and for *anchun jiaozi*, soft, sweet "pigeon-egg" dumplings made with glutinous rice flour and filled with osmanthus flower and mint. *Tang yuan*, glutinous rice dumplings with a sweet filling in a soup of fermented rice, is a traditional New Year delicacy, as is *nian gao*, literally "New Year cake". Other favourite snacks include crisp-crusted *meimao su* or "eyebrow" shortcake, a pastry named for its arched shape and filled with sweet or savoury stuffing, and *chou doufu*, or smelly bean curd, more politely known as

---

FESTIVAL FARE: FROM RICE DUMPLINGS TO ICE-CREAM MOONCAKES

Almost obliterated during the Communist years, Shanghai's festivals and the special food associated with them are now undergoing a renaissance. Chinese New Year, the biggest and most important festival (in Jan or Feb) is a great excuse for the fish-loving Shanghainese to eat fish dishes. *Yu*, or fish, is a homonym for prosperity in Chinese, and is considered an auspicious New Year's dish, along with *tang yuan*, the soft glutinous rice dumpling that always ends the meal. Qingming or the springtime tomb-sweeping day is mostly observed with ceremonies at the gravesites of Communist martyrs, but the *qing* cake, made of glutinous rice paste and stuffed with a sweet filling, has returned. Summer's Dragon Boat Festival is the time to eat *zongzi*, the lotus-leaf-wrapped glutinous rice dumplings. The autumn Moon Festival is the time to gorge on mooncakes filled with sweet lotus-seed paste and a salted egg yolk, but these days creative options like Häagen-Dazs ice-cream mooncakes and gourmet chocolate ones have made serious inroads among the younger Shanghainese.

fermented bean curd and an acquired taste, from Fenxian county on the outskirts of Shanghai.

Unrivalled dining scene

Shanghai's international culinary scene is so spectacular that the city is the only one in China to have its own Zagat Guide. New restaurants open every month, and one local publication lists 35 different types of cuisine in its restaurant directory. Add to that the enormous variety of eateries, from hole-in-the-wall digs to haute cuisine by Michelin-starred chefs, and you have a dining scene that is unrivalled in all of China.

> Among the A-list Michelin-starred celebrity chefs who have opened restaurants in Shanghai are Jean Georges Vongerichten, and brothers Jacques and Laurent Pourcel.

As a city of immigrants, Shanghai's restaurants represent a veritable microcosm of China. Along with the major cuisines – Cantonese, Beijing, Sichuan – are endless variations in between. Sichuan hotpot (*huoguo*) restaurants, at which a pot of chilli-laced bubbling soup, sitting over a flame, is used for dipping and cooking vegetables and meats, are popular, as are dim sum buffets. Sensing opportunity, well-known restaurants have opened branches in Shanghai, including Beijing's famous Quanjude for Peking duck, Hong Kong's legendary Fook Lam Moon and Singapore's Crystal Jade chain of restaurants.

Chinese cuisine trends sweep Shanghai every couple of years or so: first, it was the food of the ethnic Yunnan minority, then came the cuisine of lakeside Hangzhou, followed by spicy Hunan food from Mao Zedong's home province. Now it has gone full circle back to Yunnan, albeit a more sophisticated version.

Local Shanghainese restaurants run the gamut from the tiny four-table Chun, serving homestyle Shanghainese cooking in a studiously unpretentious setting, to Shanghai Uncle's authentic dishes in a glittering banquet hall. The latest Shanghainese restaurant trend sees restaurants like Ye Shanghai and Whampoa Club serving updated versions of old classics in luxurious surroundings (with prices to match).

Shanghai is becoming quite the international dining hotspot, drawing celebrity-chef and Michelin-starred franchises as well as homegrown restaurants manned by talented chefs from around the world. Some are world-class and some are neighbourhood bistros, each adding to the depth of dining out in Shanghai. Perennial local favourite M on the Bund started it all, and its European-Mediterranean menu, well-selected wine list and views of the waterfront are still hard to beat. Across the road, celebrity chef Jean Georges Vongerichten serves *haute* French at Three on the Bund, while down the street at Bund 18, the Michelin-starred Pourcel brothers have opened Sens and Bund. Another Michelin alumnus, Paul Pairet, serves what may be the most avant-garde menu in China at Jade on 36. The exotic Asian eateries Hazara (Indian) and La Na Thai are located in a garden manor while T8 restaurant serves fusion in a refurbished *shikumen* house at Xintiandi. The dining options are as endless as they are exciting. ❑

● *Restaurant recommendations are listed at the end of each chapter in the Places section.*

LEFT: dine on fusion French at Jade on 36 restaurant.

A Feast of Hairy Crabs

The signature dish for "the city above the sea" comes – of course – from its waters. Ancient poets inscribed verses on the joys of savouring "hairy crabs" and sipping wine under a ripe harvest moon, and the tradition endures.

The *dazha* crab, which is indigenous to the lower reaches of the Yangzi River, begins its journey in May, when millions of the migratory crustaceans swim eastwards to the mouth of the river to spawn. The baby crabs swim into connecting rivers and lakes, where they are caught and reared in crab farms. The immense popularity of the hairy

The female crab with her rich, flavourful roe becomes available in October, while the male crab is ready in November. Each female crab bears just a few roe, making it an expensive delicacy. Crab gourmands have strict criteria when it comes to selecting the perfect crab. The crab should be alive and alert. The legs and the hairs should be long, and the crab's apron should be white. Preparation is focused on preserving the prized flesh and the fragrant natural crabmeat flavour: crabs are steamed to a gorgeous shade of vermilion, sometimes with ginger, and are served with a dipping sauce of raw minced ginger, soy sauce and black vinegar.

To eat the crab, the apron and carapace

crab has instigated the development of crab farms throughout the region, but connoisseurs still insist that the crabs from Yangcheng Lake are beyond compare. The unique ecology of this lake – clean and so clear that the sunlight fills its depths – helps to nurture such delectable creatures. (Predictably, there is an industry specialising in fake Yangcheng hairy crabs – so much so that genuine sellers are now developing special crab ID tags.) Genuine Yangcheng Lake crabs all sport distinctive shiny green shells, pearl-white bellies, golden legs covered with long, thick hair – hence their name – and spit foam continuously.

ABOVE: Shanghai hairy crabs and the various implements you need to eat them.

are taken off first, and the roe extracted. Next, the legs are pulled off, and the meat inside mined with a chopstick. A nutcracker is then used for the claws. Finally, the great, succulent chunks of meat inside the main body of the crab are tackled. Everything but the lungs is eaten, and particularly adept crab-eaters can put the entire crab back together after eating it, as if it had never been touched.

Hairy crabs are considered to be "cooling" to the body, so the sherry-like Shaoxing wine is served to rebalance the body's yin and yang. Like those crab gourmands who can put the shell of a whole crab back together again after tearing it apart, the human body, too, needs to return to its pre-crab-eating state. ❑

STREET SNACKS

Shanghai's street food provides more than mere sustenance – it's a chance to experience a fast-disappearing way of life

Shanghai's massive restaurant boom notwithstanding, most locals probably have at least one snack a day. It might be something substantial, like the big and yummy *jian bing* omelettes, or just a piece of fruit on a stick – all sold by the city's itinerant street vendors. The best variety of snacks can be found in the Yu Garden Bazaar, but they can also be found around town, sold by street vendors who are perfectly in tune with the rhythms of Shanghai's hunger pangs: they appear outside schools at the end of the day, around metro stops and outside big office buildings. These vendors, who come from neighbouring provinces, are carrying on an important Shanghai tradition – sharing the foods of their villages with Shanghai, where they will eventually become absorbed into the melting pot that is Shanghainese cuisine.

BELOW: meat and seafood kebabs.

ABOVE: one of the advantages of street food is that, like these spring rolls, it is cooked to order and served piping hot.

ABOVE: candied fruit.

ABOVE: fried dough sticks called *youtiao* (behind) are a breakfast staple throughout China.

LEFT: fried dumplings are one of the most ubiquitous street snacks in the city.

RIGHT: streetside cafés serve simple, delicious dishes such as freshly made noodles in soup for just a few *kuai*.

ABOVE: Shanghai breakfast – *jian bing* and *youtiao* dough sticks.

ABOVE: shrimps from the numerous shrimp farms along the east China coast feature heavily in local cuisine.

ABOVE: vegetable seller – Shanghai is surrounded by farmland so fresh, local produce is easy to find.

BELOW: a speciality of the Muslims who live in China's far west province of Xinjiang are lamb kebabs, grilled over hot coals and served with a sprinkling of chilli powder.

ABOVE: an array of vegetable-based dishes.

SHOPPING

Bold, brash and confident, Shanghai appears
to be on the verge of sidelining glitzy Hong Kong
and reclaiming its former role as China's fashion
and design hotbed

Something for everyone

Today, the Big Four stores have been revamped
and stocked with more stylish goods. Other
department stores have joined them, both in the
traditional shopping areas of Nanjing Road (E)
and Central Huaihai Road and in new areas like
Pudong, Xujiahui and the Bund. International
brand names are well represented in Shanghai,
reflecting the city's increasingly sophisticated
tastes – and strong purchasing power.

> The world's über-luxury brands, from
> Armani to Zegna, are all jockeying for a
> piece of Shanghai, and shiny new malls
> are constantly being built to keep pace.

Local and foreign entrepreneurs – inspired by
Chinese tradition and Shanghai's cosmopolitan
atmosphere as well as the easy access to raw
materials – produce high-quality goods with
unique one-of-a-kind designs. Bespoke clothing,
shoes and even fine china and table linens are an
affordable luxury in Shanghai, but the blatant
knock-offs are still doing a roaring business.
There are also plenty of adventures for intrepid
shoppers if they venture from the main thor-
oughfares and into local markets, backstreets
and private showrooms. Here they can expect a
slice of Shanghai life, with the added bonus of
unique goods and bargains. The warren of shops
around Yu Garden Bazaar *(see page 144)*, for
instance, is where kitsch battery-powered Panda
bears, fake chirping crickets and the like abound.

Shopping in Shanghai, once limited to
cheap knock-offs and kitschy souvenirs,
has evolved to encompass luxury brands,
funky boutiques, couture and just about anything custom-made. China, after all, is the
world's factory, and Shanghai is its showcase.

Between the two World Wars, Shanghai's
shopping culture burgeoned when the "Big Four"
department stores *(see page 131)* were built to
cater to the city's cosmopolitan citizens. When the
austere Communists took over in 1949, the big-
name retailers fled to Hong Kong, leaving their
buildings to be filled with state-produced goods
and surly clerks who seemed to know only two
words: *"mei you"* ("don't have").

Bootleg goods and bargaining

Few people are mourning the demise of the old Xiangyang Market, the legendary knock-off market, because three counterfeit goods markets have sprung up in its place. Most of the vendors have relocated to the Longhua Fashion and Gifts Market *(page 198)*, where hundreds of stalls vie for the shopper's attention with brand-name purses, watches, clothing and accessories, all reflecting the latest trends among Shanghai's fashionistas. (If you don't see a certain luxury brand displayed, chances are that the company's big brass is in town. Just ask, and the shopkeeper will probably pull it out from under the counter.) Also on sale are bootleg DVDs and VCDs, and Game Boy and Nintendo games. But quality can vary. Roughly one out of three copied discs is flawed, and pirated DVDs sometimes don't work on certain high-end DVD players sold in the West.

In-the-know locals rarely buy a knock-off wallet or handbag off the shelf. Instead, they ask to see the shopkeeper's catalogue of "A-Grade" products with brands ranging from Louis Vuitton to Chanel. Do the same, as most merchants speak some English. Once you've chosen the styles you like, the shopkeeper will fetch the goods from his "warehouse". This can take up to 30 minutes. Carefully check the merchandise for scratches and flaws, and then start

LEFT: shoppers outside Metro City shopping mall in Xujiahui. **ABOVE:** selling belts on Shaanxi Road.
ABOVE RIGHT: window dressing along Central Huahai Road, another of the city's shopping drags.

THE FINE ART OF COPYING

Copying has deep cultural roots in China. Since the 6th century, Chinese painters have been judged by the six principles developed by the scholar Xie He, one of which includes copying ancient masters to preserve traditional techniques. The general attitude among the Chinese is that there is nothing wrong with copying. Add to this a burgeoning appetite for cheap counterfeit goods, and it's easy to see why China is such a booming market for knock-offs.

Thanks to consumer education and increased vigilance by companies, the situation is improving – the value of counterfeit goods seized by the US Customs has fallen over the years. And as incomes in Shanghai rise and luxury brands gain a certain cachet among the city's nouveaux riches, trendy Shanghainese are increasingly buying the real McCoy.

has been aged to give it an "antique" look. Shop owners will usually tell you the real provenance of the piece. But, as with all Shanghai shopping, buyer beware. The warehouses will also help ship your purchases home.

In downtown, several boutique furniture shops sell original Shanghai Deco – the uniquely Shanghainese take on Art Deco – pieces from the 1920s and 30s. For smaller curios and more typical Shanghai items from the 1920s and 30s, try the Dongtai Road Antiques Market *(see page 149)*, where opium pipes, cigarette girl retro posters, lanterns, porcelain and other trinkets spill from the street stalls. Flea-market shoppers should also visit the five-storey Cang Bao Building *(page 147)* near Yu Garden, filled with kitsch as well as rare books and maps, Cultural Revolution memorabilia, vintage furniture and clothing. Weekend mornings are the best time to go.

Fabrics and pearls

The sprawling Shanghai South Bund Fabric Market at Lujiabang Road offers a dazzling array of silks, cashmeres and linens. The on-site market tailors are usually not the best with cut and fit, but can usually create decent copies of your own clothing or of one of their own designs (you'll see these on display at the stalls). Generally, the stallholders will speak enough English to facilitate communication. (It also helps that the word "copy" is a word understood by most Shanghai tailors.)

The Silk King stores (there are branches around town) are another option for fabric

haggling. One good rule of thumb is to start at one-third and end at one-half to two-thirds of the original asking price. The final sum will depend on a delicate combination of the seller's disposition and your bargaining skills.

Similarly, fake Rolexes and Longines are only sold surreptitiously. Respond positively to vendors who whisper, "You want watch?" and you will be led to a hidden salesroom in the neighbourhood that is chock-full of glittering watches. With a diligent quality check, and some good-humoured hard bargaining, you should be able to get a nice watch for about RMB 200–300.

Chinese furniture and curios

Most old-style Chinese furniture shops are in the vicinity of Hongqiao Road *(see page 202)* and Wuzhong Road *(see page 204)*. All the shops stock restored and unfinished pieces. Ask to visit the warehouse area, where you can stroll among dusty piles of rickety trunks, kitchen cabinets, calligraphy tables, chairs and wedding chests. Once you have chosen your piece, the store's craftsmen will restore and refinish it to your specifications. Most of the furniture here is newly made of old wood, or

---

ABOVE LEFT: shopping at Dongtai Road Antiques Market.
ABOVE: bolts of Chinese silk in varying colours and patterns. **RIGHT:** Shanghai Tang boutique in Xintiandi.

and clothing. These government-run emporiums offer quality silk as well as a variety of excellent (but pricey) fabrics like cashmere; the tailors on the premises can custom-make clothing for you. As a bonus, they can also create shoes to match your outfit.

The Yangzi River Delta and the network of canals and ponds surrounding Shanghai is home to China's thriving freshwater cultured pearl industry, making cultured pearls one of the best buys in Shanghai. Round, lustrous gem-quality pearls as well as multicoloured Baroque, seed- and coin-shaped pearls are sold at boutiques and at the Hongqiao Pearl Market; jewellery can also be custom-made.

Shanghai chic

The unmistakable Shanghai style is back in the chic boutiques that line the former French Concession streets, where creative minds marry Chinese and Western style *(see photo feature on pages 78–9)* with highly successful results. The trendy shopping and dining Xintiandi area features several of these boutiques, including French-owned Shanghai Trio (gorgeous Chinese-inspired silk, linen and cashmere home and fashion accessories) and Simply Life (lovely home decor with an emphasis on Asian-influenced minimalist items). Next door, Cocoon and Ciococo specialise in exquisite lingerie and sheets. Xinle Road, Maoming Road and Fuxing Road are treasure troves of boutiques, featuring everything from funky local clothing designers to *qipao* tailors.

SoHo meets Shanghai (well, sort of) at the Taikang Road *(see page 158)* art street, which has much more than art – an old factory has been converted into a design incubator for young talent that features art, fashion, design and gift products. Another hotspot for art is M50 *(see page 219 and photo feature on pages 222–23)*. Some of the city's best known cutting-edge galleries are clustered here. ❏
● *See page 284 of Travel Tips for shopping listings.*

THE LURE OF CHINESE SILK

Since ancient times, China has cornered the world's silk market. Legend has it that the concubine Lei Zu discovered the silk-making process when she accidentally dropped a silkworm cocoon into her tea over 3,000 years ago. By 200 BC, the precious "woven wind" fabric was being dispatched to Western markets via the fabled Silk Road. China is still the world's largest exporter of silk, with most of the fabric produced around Shanghai. Peasants raise silkworms less than 100km (60 miles) away in mulberry tree-carpeted Deqing County, near Hangzhou, the heart of China's silk producing region. Naturally, Shanghai is home to all varieties of silk, from stiff brocades to slinky materials.

SHANGHAI CHIC

Many shops sell one-of-a-kind designs, made in Shanghai and fiercely proud of it, that marry the best of East and West

Shanghai's cosmopolitan soul makes for fresh and interesting design work, and that has translated into a treasure trove of unique, proudly made-in-Shanghai items. Invariably, these creations take traditional Shanghai as their inspiration, and then update, update, update – sometimes far into the future. It's retro style, re-imagined, reinvented and re-made for modern Shanghai. Some of these pieces are original, often handmade, and each one a work of art. Their creators, too, are often a fusion mix – Westerners living in (and inspired by) Shanghai, or Shanghainese with a global world view.

Shopping for made-in-Shanghai items is a happy adventure as well: most shops are located in the former French Concession, in spaces and places as fusion as the designs are – charming vintage ateliers and contemporary chic boutiques in style havens such as Xintiandi, Fuxing Road, Taikang Road and Dongping Road.

ABOVE: Chloe Chen incorporates materials from Italy and France with designs from Shanghai and Taiwan.

ABOVE: inspired by a Shanghainese grandmother's silk quilts, Cocoon and Ciococo features luxurious silk fibre bedding as well as nightwear and accessories.

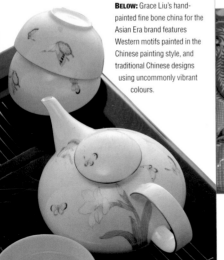

BELOW: Grace Liu's hand-painted fine bone china for the Asian Era brand features Western motifs painted in the Chinese painting style, and traditional Chinese designs using uncommonly vibrant colours.

ABOVE: Denise Huang of Suzhou Cobblers crafts silk slippers in bright colours, then embroiders them with either classical Chinese or whimsical motifs.

ABOVE: Illudeco hand-produces lamps and laterns to order, mixing Chinese and Middle Eastern themes.

ABOVE: the Simply Life chain of stores specialises in Asian-inspired home accessories, like brocade-covered notebooks, photo albums and address books.

ABOVE: founded in Hong Kong, Shanghai Tang's inspiration for its clothing and home furnishings is the inimitable style of Old Shanghai – updated with glowing neon and attitude.

CUSTOM-MADE ANYTHING

One of the great things about Shanghai is that it is possible to get almost anything custom-made. Many a visitor has taken a shine to the city's fabric markets – like the Shanghai South Bund Fabric Market at 399 Lujiabang Road – entering like a gleeful child let loose in a candy store and walking out with a completely brand new wardrobe at bargain prices. Virtually anything in Shanghai can be custom-made: shoes, furniture, bed linen, sweaters – at a fraction of the cost of similar ready-made items.

It sounds too good to be true, and maybe it is. While there are true artisans among those who create Shanghai's custom-made items, they are few and far between. Many more are, instead, unskilled with minimal training, and the results are likely to be less than spectacular.

Fabric market tailors may not give you exactly the couture cut you want (several fittings may be required); the furniture you ordered may not be put together to the highest standards; and the sweater may seem as if it's been knitted for someone else's body. Vendors will fix the problem, if they can, but visitors often don't have the time for repairs. The best course of action is to go only to those who have been personally recommended, or whose work you have seen. And never pay the entire bill until you have collected the goods and are satisfied with them.

ABOVE: getting measured for a new suit. Shanghainese tailors are known for their deft needlework and tailoring skills.

SHANGHAI NIGHTS

Shanghai is once again staking its claim to be considered the "Paris of the Orient". Whether one's taste inclines to sleazy drinking dives, elegant dance clubs, all-night karaoke or just late-night supper, the city can cater for it

The classic 1930s pop song *Ye Shanghai (Night-Time Shanghai)* trilled the tribute, "You really are a city that never sleeps." Shanghai did sleep, for almost half a century, when the Communists outlawed Shanghai's wild nightlife and the licentiousness that made it famous – but today, it's wide awake once more.

The bar and club scene

Like much of modern Shanghai's revival, nightlife owes a large debt to foreign investment. Most of Shanghai's successful bars are opened and run by either Chinese "returnees" who have lived or studied abroad, or by foreigners.

Appearances count for everything in Shanghai, including its bars. Other Chinese cities are dominated by earthy and unpretentious dives, but in Shanghai even the casual is carefully

ultry Chinese girls greeting Western men vith "Hello! Buy me drink!" are a regular xture at bars in Tongren Road. At these laces, a fat wallet (or a foreign passport) an make any man a potential Don Juan.

crafted. Its most famous bars, like Face in the Ruijin Guesthouse and Glamour Bar at the Bund, are posh and pricey, with elaborate decor that rivals the best nightspots in the clubbing capitals of the world – with prices to match.

LEFT: fashionistas at a Xintiandi bar.
RIGHT: Face Bar has Southeast Asian design accents.

Shanghai's bar denizens are as varied as the city itself. Local and foreign students usually congregate at the cheap and cheerful Windows Too in Jing An Plaza, where the drinks start at RMB 10. Another popular haunt is C's Bar, on Ding Xi Road, a basement bar with no cover charge and cheap drinks – and a regular venue for underground rock parties.

At the more expensive nightspots, Western faces are joined by Shanghainese white-collar workers. Shanghai's upwardly mobile and college-educated yuppies, or "Shuppies", who enjoy mid-management positions and salaries their parents never dreamed of, are generally a bored bunch eager for new experiences. Many

Shuppies are also eager to assert their sophistication, which in Shanghai translates to being Westernised, and thus prefer foreign bars.

The moneyed Hong Kong and Taiwanese communities like to spend extravagantly at clubs like Babyface on Central Huaihai Road, Muse on Yuyao Road (part of the New Factories hub of bars, restaurants and creative companies) and old-time favourite Guandii in Fuxing Park.

The new hotspots

Given such conflicting demands, opening a bar in Shanghai is a Darwinian undertaking – most have the shelf life of an open can of club soda. Trend-obsessed barflies follow the "hot new thing", currently Pirates on Xingfu Road, where the artsy crowd sways to underground electro beats. House- and techno-lovers converge in droves at BonBon on Central Huaihai Road for all-night dance sessions. Attica, located on the Bund, with its fabulous views across to the Pudong skyline,

is a jaw-dropping stunner, as is rooftop Bar Rouge at the Bund 18 building.

Xintiandi, now something of a Shanghai institution with its restaurants, bars and shops in refurbished lane houses, draws hordes of tourists as well as local and foreign businesspeople on a daily basis. Current hotspots here include DR Bar, a tiny, super-sleek bar designed by Xintiandi architect Benjamin Wood, TMSK (Tou Ming Si Kao), a beautiful bar sculpted out of brightly coloured glass, and old-time favourite Paulaner Brauhaus, a three-storey French Concession villa with house-brewed beer.

Before Shanghai's nightlife took off in the early 2000s, it was the hard-partying Maoming Road (S) strip that thrived after hours. After 2am curfews were enforced in 2004, bar owners looked for alternative sites. Many moved to Tongren Road, and took with them some of the sexual charge of Maoming Road. The Tongren Road bars are usually frequented by middle-aged Western men on the Chinese girlfriend prowl (the young women prowling back), but there are also places like Blue Frog and the Spot

GAY SHANGHAI

Homosexuality in China was openly condemned during the Cultural Revolution as a "mouldering lifestyle of capitalism". Many homosexuals were persecuted and gay society was forced underground.

Considering that sodomy was only decriminalised in 1997, and homosexuality no longer deemed an illness in 2001, the gay scene in China has come a long way in the past decade, with Shanghai probably the most open about it. Shanghai's gay scene is equal parts Western and Chinese, but it tends to be mainly male-focused. While *lalas* (lesbians) are welcome at some of the *tongzhi* (gay) bars such as Eddy's on Huaihai Road and Pink Home on Gaolan Road, there is only one lesbian bar in the city, Red Bar on Gonghe Xin Road. For the boys, Eddy's Bar and Frangipani Bar & Café (on Dagu Road) provide a relaxed atmosphere. Pink Home and Club Deep are for dancing the night away.

Bar & Restaurant, which have reputations for good pints and friendly service rather than as pick-up joints.

DJ-clubs

Shanghai's booming DJ scene offers mainly hip-hop, R 'n' B, techno, garage and house, mixed by both Chinese and foreign DJs. Recent years have also seen a long list of internationally renowned spinmasters such as Paul Oakenfold and DJ Krush at the decks of Shanghai's top clubs. DJ-driven clubs attract an edgy subsection of Shuppies and younger foreigners. They are also popular with Shanghai's recreational drug-users who, high on Ecstasy, *yaotou* (head-shake) to the trance-like music.

Live rock and jazz

Shanghai has a small but growing live rock music scene *(see page 85)*, led primarily by 4 Live and Yuyintang. Both venues feature mainly Chinese bands, playing anything from electronica to heavy metal and hip-hop. As the music scene has grown, so has the demand for foreign acts to play in Shanghai. Recent foreign bands on the Shanghai stage include the Rolling Stones, Black Eyed Peas and Sonic Youth – to name a few.

Shanghai's jazz and blues scene mainly takes place at the Cotton Club and JZ Club on Fuxing Road, and at the House of Blues on Maoming Road (S). Both local and foreign jazz acts take centre stage here. Many of the five-star hotels also have jazz bars featuring mostly American singers backed by Filipino musicians.

The Peace Hotel's Jazz Bar, a nostalgic favourite despite the somewhat dubious quality of its musicians, reopened in 2010 after renovation.

Local pastimes

While the hipsters live it up at chichi bars, dance clubs and music dives, their elders and their lower-income peers opt for more time-tested activities. The karaoke parlour, or KTV (Karaoke TV), enjoys something of a double life. Outlets draw a steady flow of Shanghainese of all ages and classes, while the point of the less salubrious establishments is the KTV girl, Shanghai's equivalent of the hostess. A customer selects from a line-up of pretty young things to sing with, and pays an hourly rate for her company, with tips for more physical services. The middle-aged Chinese men who frequent such places come in groups, often on expense accounts to entertain clients and government officials.

Moneyed business types also congregate at posh bathhouses like Sea Cloud Garden on Panyu Road. In glaring marble and crystal, these luxurious complexes feature elaborate bathing options: along with sauna, steam room and Jacuzzi are special pools containing pearls or rose petals for purported medicinal benefits.

FAR LEFT: on the dance floor. **ABOVE LEFT:** drinking at Manifesto on Julu Road. **ABOVE:** jazz is king at the Cotton Club in Fuxing Road. **ABOVE RIGHT:** karaoke.

housing, where Shanghainese pass their days and nights socialising with their neighbours, often outdoors in the lanes. Children play football and badminton, teens strum guitars and elderly men compare their pet songbirds. After dinner, the lanes fill with a clacking sound like an invasion of locusts from mah-jong games. Regardless of season, older men prop up tables and carry out stools to play cards. Even as the lanes disappear, the stubborn Shanghainese hold on to their traditions, shifting the setting of their outdoor games to bustling city pavements.

Ordinary Shanghainese with limited means are resourceful at concocting budget forms of entertainment. Ballroom dancing, banned as Western and decadent during the Cultural Revolution, was the rage in the 1980s and remains popular among retirees. Shanghainese toting mini-stereo sets often invade downtown parks like Xujiahui Park and Fuxing Park and also the Bund at dawn and dusk, playing music that sends the dancers twirling merrily.

Shanghai is famous for its insular communities contained in its traditional *longtang* (lane)

After-hours entertainment

Most of Shanghai's bars and clubs ebb around 4am as the revellers stumble homewards, drunk but hungry. Street kitchens start wheeling up their carts, unloading tables and stools, and firing up the coal brickets from 9pm onwards every evening. Shanghai does not have one central area for after-hours street food; instead, stalls are scattered around the downtown area. The traditional staples are wonton soup (*yuntun*), fried noodles (*chao mian* or *chao hefen*) and fried rice (*danchaofan*). Many noodle and dumpling shops downtown close late at weekends, while franchises like the Soy Milk King chain serve breakfast dim sum items like soy milk and *you tiao* (fried dough sticks) around the clock. ❑

● *See page 290 of Travel Tips for nightlife listings.*

ABOVE LEFT: ballroom dancing at Fuxing Park. **ABOVE:** street food for sustenance after the bars close.

SEEDY SHANGHAI

Shanghai's seedier side manifests itself on different levels. "Fishing girls", or *diaomazi*, charge for their company, but not necessarily for sex. The KTV *xiaojie*, or KTV miss, accompanies male karaoke patrons, but for the right tip, is also available for anything from groping and kissing to sex. If a wealthier KTV client takes a shine to a particular *xiaojie*, he may upgrade her to his personal "canary", or *jinse niao*.

Outright prostitution has become more flagrant in recent years. Pimps often approach unaccompanied men while sexily dressed girls preen in a row of so-called "barbershops" along Fumin Road, calling out to men strolling along the pavement. RMB 10 buys a shampoo and scalp massage – while RMB 100 can get you something a great deal more lascivious.

Shanghai Rocks

Gone are the days when the only visible alternative music scene in China was rock. Nowadays, hip-hop, breakcore, breakbeat, dance and electronica, folk as well as rock are part of the scene, with Shanghai being one of the best places in China to experience them all.

Shanghai's rock developed mostly independent of the rest of China, taking its musical influences from abroad rather than from within. Its earliest roots lie in the streetside guitar bands of the early 1980s. With often home-made instruments, groups of neighbourhood youth reinvented tunes by 1970s Taiwanese pop icon Teresa Teng or composed ribald ditties, hoping to outshine rival groups down the block. Shanghai also produced China's first nascent rock star, Zhang Xing, who was so ahead of his time he was arrested in 1985 on charges of hooliganism.

For 15 years, Shanghai rock stewed underground, with only a handful of bands around at any given time, and playing only at obscure dives and underground rock parties. By the late 1990s, however, a few young, ambitious bands such as Crystal Butterfly had secured gigs at more mainstream bars, and their names and songs started to infiltrate public awareness. At the same time, rock parties were being held more often and more publicly, wooing coverage from the reluctant Shanghai media by featuring more established Beijing bands as well as local groups. Now that the city has a number of regular venues, like 4 Live at Jianguo Road and Yuyintang at Yan'an Road (W), Shanghai has the infrastructure needed to nourish its growing rock scene. Bands currently making the most buzz are "noise" group Torturing Nurse, indie rock band Sonnet and garage rock group Banana Monkeys.

Folk music is also slowly creeping into the Shanghai scene, mainly thanks to Bandu Music, a café-cum-bar (as well as record label) in Shanghai's Moganshan art district.

The last few years have also seen the emergence of local and foreign DJs and musicians organising underground music parties at various venues in town, with bars, clubs, art galleries, museums and concept stores hosting these events.

The Antidote, a group of digital musicians and DJs based in Shanghai, regularly play a mix of indie rock, punk, IDM and synthcore at C's Bar. Underground talent such as Ramona Cordova and Kiki (from Chicks on Speed) have also performed in Shanghai. Dragon Dance Studios continue to have their finger in many hip-hop pies around town, and The Lab, set up by DMC China Champion DJ V-Nutz (Gary Wang) and up-and-coming turntablist Fortune (Fu Jun), continues to inspire local as well as foreign musicians and DJs. ❑

ABOVE: getting the crowds worked up at Yuyintang.
RIGHT: spinmaster doing his thing.

ARCHITECTURE

*Mixing Art Deco, Postmodernist,
Song dynasty Chinese, Tudor, über-modern and
just plain kitsch, Shanghai is a stimulating
showcase of architectural treasures*

Even world-weary visitors from the globe's most sophisticated urban centres catch their breath the first time they see Shanghai's skyline. The city is in the middle of the biggest urban building boom the world has ever known, and the sheer size, scale and speed of its reconstruction is astounding. Shanghai's juxtaposition of avant-garde glass and steel structures and its old-world brick and mortar historic buildings is visually arresting – the result is an almost visceral tension between the ultra-modern and the traditional.

Nowhere is this tension as palpable as on the Bund *(page 107)* along the Huangpu River, where the neoclassical Bund buildings face off against the soaring mirrored towers of Pudong. The futuristic Oriental Pearl Tower *(page 227)*, opposite the Bund, is now the most recognised structure in the city. Before it was built, the Bund was the indisputable symbol of the city – a powerful image, to be sure, but also an unwelcome reminder that it was not the Chinese but foreigners who first put Shanghai on the world map.

Look East, or West?

For 40 years after the Communists took over in 1949, construction virtually halted in Shanghai because the Communist leadership feared that the city's capitalist culture could undermine its efforts to create a New China. Thus, when restrictions on Shanghai's development were lifted in the early 1990s, the city was a veritable time capsule of pre-1949 architecture.

Some say the space-age Pearl Oriental Tower, just opposite the Bund, was built to divert attention from the latter – a symbol of the city's "humiliating" colonial past. If so, the tower is a smashing success.

Today, in an effort to catch up with the times, many sections of the city have been razed and replaced with modern high-rises and green open spaces. While it's sad to see so many bricks and beams succumb to chrome and glass, it's vital to remember that Shanghai has always been about

LEFT: the World Financial Centre and Jin Mao Tower.
RIGHT: the Shanghai Art Museum.

being modern. In the 1920s and 30s, that meant Art Deco *(see photo feature on pages 92–3)*, the streamlined, then-futuristic architectural style that is as easily identified with Shanghai as it is with Miami Beach. Well known for its ability to weave outside ideas into the local culture, Shanghai adapted the born-in-the-West Art Deco to China, and it became a symbol of the cosmopolitan, hybrid city. After the recent frenzied building of imported modern designs, the next decade may, similarly, see the emergence of a new architectural style that Shanghai can call its own.

As China becomes less rigid ideologically and more open economically, the Shanghainese are slowly coming to terms with their architectural identity. They still want the latest the world has to offer, but they are also confident enough to celebrate, however subtly, the unique history of their city. So some buildings include design references to lane neighbourhood architecture, and many new office towers are blatant paeans to the Art Deco splendour of old. The rejection of "bourgeois" art, which reached its extreme during the Cultural Revolution of 1966–76, has given way to a rich architectural environment in which themes from all over the world contribute to Shanghai's dramatic skyline.

Shanghai modern

Shanghai's most successful modern buildings include references to Chinese architecture, or push the high-design envelope in some way. The Shanghai Grand Theatre *(page 127)* on People's

---

REACHING FOR THE SKY

In the international quest to build the world's tallest buildings – symbolic or silly as the competition may be – Shanghai is at the forefront. In 2008, the sleek Shanghai World Financial Centre was completed in Pudong. At 492 metres (1,614ft), it ranks third on the list of the world's tallest buildings (after Dubai's Burj Khaifa and Taiwan's Taipei 101). Just next door, the dramatic 1999 Jin Mao Tower has moved down to number six, at 420 metres (1,378ft). For those keeping score, 7 out of 12 of the world's tallest build-

ings are in Chinese cities.

The two tallest buildings west of the Huangpu River are midgets by contrast, though they sit at 42 and 44 on the global list. Both are on Nanjing Road (E): Plaza 66 (288 metres/945ft) and Tomorrow Square (285 metres/ 935ft). These were displaced by the 290-metre (951ft) Wheelock Place in late 2008. The Huaihai Road business district has Hong Kong New World Tower (278 metres/912ft; ranked 58), while Xujiahui sports the Grand Gateway Plaza (262 metres/860ft; ranked 77).

Square does both. Designed by Frenchman Jean-Marie Charpentier, it resembles a hyper-modern transparent temple to the arts – until you realise that the convex curvature of the roof is a clear homage to the heavy roofs and upturned eaves of traditional Chinese palace architecture.

At the time of its completion in 1989, the Shanghai Centre *(page 187)* on Nanjing Road (W) was the only tall building for miles. Its obvious reference to traditional motifs is seen in the simple, strong red columns that support the entrance portico. Less obvious is the monumental reference that architect John Portman designed into the building – it is in the shape of the Chinese character for mountain, *shan* (山).

Next to Shanghai Centre is Plaza 66, a building that is successful despite its non-reference to traditional architecture. Plaza 66 architects Kohn Pederson Fox Associates of New York also designed Wheelock Square on Yan'an Road (W), which has overtaken Plaza 66 as the tallest building west of the Huangpu since its 2008 completion. East of the Huangpu River, the soaring pagoda-like Jin Mao Tower *(page 230)*, is now China's second-tallest building after the Shanghai World Financial Centre *(page 230)*, which opened in August 2008.

Postmodern European architects have been equally popular in Shanghai. The seagull-inspired Pudong International Airport – a 2000 landmark in glass and brushed aluminium – was designed by Paris-based Paul Andreu, who also designed the controversial National Theatre in Beijing. So pleased were Shanghai's leaders with the airport that they hired Andreu to design the ceramic and glass Shanghai Oriental Arts Centre in Pudong *(page 232)*.

> A lane-house doorway – called shikumen – is formed by three pieces of solid stone with rounded upper joints and an inward-opening set of wooden doors leading to a courtyard.

Lane houses

The most typical Shanghainese architectural form is the *lilong or longtang* (lane) neighbourhood, which, until the latest building boom began 20 years ago, was common throughout the city. Lane neighbourhoods *(see photo feature pages 168–9)* typically cover a city block, and have a few entrances from the street that can be locked by iron gates. Within the neighbourhood, lanes are arrayed in a regular matrix pattern, the stone-framed doors *(shikumen)* facing south.

LEFT: Shanghai Grand Theatre. **ABOVE:** Pudong skyline. **ABOVE RIGHT:** a view across the rooftops of Nanshi, the Old City.

First built by foreign entrepreneurs during a period of civil war in the 1850s and 60s when affluent Chinese moved to the foreign enclave for security, the lane houses mutated slowly over 80 years in response to economic forces and changes in architectural taste. Rising land prices impelled developers to shrink each dwelling, while the advent of reinforced concrete enabled

the building of three- and four-storey houses. In the final stages of its evolution, lane dwellings lost their courtyards and came to resemble modern urban apartment buildings.

Since the 1990s, some 75 percent of the city's lane houses have been demolished by a government intent on modernising the city's appearance and decreasing the city-centre population. But adaptive re-use projects such as Xintiandi *(page 154)* have had a strong impact on public perceptions of the value of the old lane houses. More and more Shanghainese now feel that their native architecture is worth preserving.

The magnificent Bund

No visit to Shanghai is complete without a stroll along the Bund *(page 105)*, with its striking panorama of European-style buildings. About half of the 24 structures on the Bund were built during the 1920s, and nine during the first two decades of the century. Most incorporate the neoclassical themes that influenced the design of public buildings during that period. The queen of them all is the regal 1923 Hong Kong & Shanghai Bank building at No. 12 (now the Shanghai Pudong Development Bank), but the most famous is the Art Deco 1929 Cathay Hotel (renamed the Peace Hotel in 1956, and now undergoing major renovations). The 1937 Bank of China, next door, is the only Bund building to incorporate Chinese themes in its design.

Built in 1947, the former Bank of Communications at No. 14 is the youngest building on the Bund, with a stripped-down Art Deco style, while the 1874 neoclassical former British Consulate at Nos 33–53 is the oldest.

French Concession homes

The International Settlement was considered *the* place to do business in Old Shanghai, but from the 1920s onwards, the nouveaux riches of all nationalities preferred the tree-lined streets of the French Concession for their homes. Stroll down Fuxing Road, Wukang Road or Xinhua Road and you'll see the lovely Mediterranean, Tudor and Art Deco homes that set the architectural fashion some 70 to 80 years ago.

Many are private residences, but some are commercial enterprises, such as the magnificent Shanghai Arts and Crafts Museum *(page 161)*. Close by is Taiyuan Villa *(page 161)*, a French Provincial mansion built for the Comte

---

CHINESE ARCHITECTURE

For a Chinese city, there isn't that much Chinese-style architecture in Shanghai. A few examples of Ming dynasty Yangzi River Delta style (Jiangnan) architecture can still be found within the Old Chinese City of Nanshi. These are distinguished by their whitewashed walls, distinctive rooflines, undulating "dragon walls", latticework and keyhole windows. The structures inside Yu Garden are also in the Jiangnan style; be sure to visit the gardens if Suzhou is not part of your itinerary. At nearby Shanghai Old Street (Shanghai Laojie), the newly built buildings mimic the Jiangnan style. Other notable Chinese structures are the Longhua Temple and Jade Buddha Temple, both built in the Southern Song style.

Old Shanghai's cosmopolitan character is reflected in its places of worship, many of which are both architecturally and historically intriguing. Catholic, Protestant, Muslim, Jewish and Russian Orthodox monuments dot the city.

du Pac de Marsoulies, and, later, a favourite haunt of Mao's wife Jiang Qing. An Art Deco masterpiece on Lane 18, Gao'an Road is now the Xuhui District Children's Palace. The former residence of a Swedish businessman on Shaanxi Road (S) is now the Hengshan Moller Villa *(page 184)*, a boutique hotel.

Apartment living was the height of modernity in the 1920s and 30s, and architects were given free rein to use the latest ideas in their designs – like the Normandie apartments *(page 173)*. Art Deco styles, with their emphasis on linearity, verticality and functionality, were perfectly suited to these structures, which dot Frenchtown.

The Shanghai of tomorrow

The pace of change in Shanghai over the past 15 years has been exhausting, and shows few signs of decelerating. The largest urban redevelopment will be the 74 sq km (29 sq miles) of land along the banks of the Huangpu River on the Puxi side. Much of the area will be devoted to green public space, set far from the river's edge and buildings with heights limited to 30 metres (98ft)

to protect precious water views. The area southwest of the Nanpu Bridge was turned into a huge complex for the World Expo in 2010, and the Shiliupu wharf transformed from a no-man's land of dingy warehouses into a waterfront marketplace inspired by Sydney's Rocks area.

Northeast of the Waibaidu Bridge, an international cruise-ship terminal and shopping and entertainment projects are planned to replace the run-down shipyards and warehouses of the Hongkou and Yangpu districts. And on Chongming Island, a rural district within the Shanghai city limits, a huge "carbon-neutral" satellite city will emerge within a few years to accommodate some 500,000 of the immigrants that will continue to flock to Shanghai.

Recent Shanghai urban planning has reflected an almost stereotyped Modernist vision of vertical skyscrapers and landscaped greenbelts criss-crossed by wide avenues and superhighways, as city planners followed the trends set by world-famous architectural gurus. Hopefully, cutting-edge architectural concepts like "designing for density" and "green design" will help Shanghai confront today's daunting urban realities and enable the city to emerge with an architectural style identifiably its own. ❑

LEFT: Peace Hotel (with the green roof) and the Bank of China beside it. **ABOVE:** the Shanghai Arts and Crafts Museum was once a private home.
ABOVE RIGHT: interior of the Moller Villa, now a hotel owned by the Hengshan group.

SHANGHAI DECO

Art Deco was Old Shanghai's signature style – both in its pure form, and fused with Chinese characteristics

Art Deco was Shanghai's signature style: the streamlined, elegant look, born at the Exposition for the Decorative Arts in Paris in 1925, was a metaphor for the new age of skyscrapers, steamships, trains and all things *moderne*. Progressive Shanghai embraced it eagerly, but made it her own by adding Chinese elements to Art Deco, and Art Deco elements to Chinese styles.

Art Deco defined Shanghai's skyline between the late 1920s and late 1940s: the Park Hotel (the tallest building of its day), the Grosvenor House and – most famous of all – the iconic Peace Hotel. Even traditional lane houses were modernised with the addition of Art Deco exterior details.

So completely did Shanghai embrace this style that it permeated virtually all design: furniture, graphic art, even fabric. And so completely did Art Deco become associated with Shanghai that, even today, contemporary architects wanting to add a bit of Shanghai style to their skyscrapers invariably use Art Deco features.

ABOVE: a Shanghai institution and erected in 1929, the Peace Hotel (then the Cathay) was tycoon Victor Sassoon's jewel in the crown – and perhaps the epitome of Shanghai's Art Deco architecture and design. The original entrance, with its dramatic vaulted ceiling, features the vibrant pastels and distinctive ironwork pendant lamps of the period.

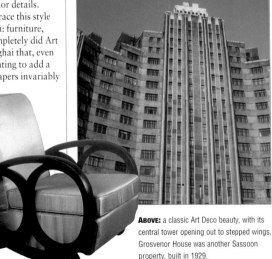

ABOVE: it was characteristic of Concession-era Shanghai to embellish classical Chinese furniture, such as this wooden cabinet, with both Art Deco lines and fruit motifs from traditional Chinese design.

RIGHT: Art Deco used geometric forms liberally, but whereas Western Art Deco used modern materials like steel, Shanghai artisans preferred the traditional dark wood to craft their furniture.

ABOVE: a classic Art Deco beauty, with its central tower opening out to stepped wings, Grosvenor House was another Sassoon property, built in 1929.

RIGHT: Art Deco was everywhere – even in the details. Tycoons like Robert Morriss, owner of the *North China Daily News*, hired artisans to create decorative ironwork with Art Deco motifs – this was to complement the architecture of his sumptuous mansion, now the Ruijin Guesthouse.

ABOVE: Shanghai's nightlife in the 1930s was legendary – hence its moniker as "Paris of the Orient". Partying and dancing demanded a modern, sophisticated building. Enter the Paramount nightclub, built in 1930, with its slim central tower, neon lights and sweeping ballroom.

BELOW: the 1930s and 40s were the golden age of film – and of cinemas. The Cathay Cinema, with its classic Art Deco lines and tapered tower, screened both Hollywood films and those made in Shanghai's booming movie studios.

LEFT: Shanghai's most beloved skyscraper is a 21st-century take on Art Deco. The Jin Mao Tower, designed by American firm Skidmore, Owings & Merrill, is inspired by the proportions of a pagoda and the typical angular stepping and massing of Art Deco design.

ABOVE: this advertisement poster, dating back to the 1930s, is a vignette of the good life in Shanghai: here, the mah-jong-playing ladies are wearing *qipaos* made from fabrics with Art Deco designs, and are seated on Art Deco chairs in a pastel-hued Art Deco house, complete with the classic curve of an Art Deco banister.

ORIENTATION

The Places section details all the attractions worth
seeing, arranged by area. The areas are shown on the
colour-coordinated map on pages 100–1. Main sights
are cross-referenced by number to individual maps

T he limits of this maritime city are defined by its waterways. The Huangpu
River separates Shanghai's newest district, Pudong, literally "east of the
Huangpu", from the rest of Shanghai, or rather Puxi, "west of the
Huangpu". The Suzhou Creek divides the thriving midsection of Puxi from
its quieter northern suburbs. New lines have been drawn, but the shape and
feel of the old foreign Concessions and Nan-
shi, the Old Chinese City, are still discernible.

Shanghai Municipality comprises 18 city
districts and one outlying county (Chongming Island). Streets run north to south and
east to west in grid-like fashion, except for
oval-shaped Nanshi and People's Square, the
latter defined by the old racetracks. The
major streets run the length of the city and
have directional tags: Huaihai (West), Huaihai (Central) or Huaihai (East). Buildings are
usually numbered sequentially, odd numbers on one side of the street and
even numbers on the other; the numbering on the residential lanes (*longtang*)
that run off the main streets has no relationship to the main street numbering.

The 98km (61-mile) outer ring road, A20, takes a lap outside the city limits,
while the inner ring Zhongshan Road loops around the perimeter of Puxi and
Pudong, changing its name in Pudong and east Hongkou before turning back
into Zhongshan Road. The city is bisected from east to west by the Yan'an
Road Elevated Highway and from north to south by the Chongqing Road Elevated Highway. Crossing Huangpu River to Pudong from Puxi can be done
via ferry, metro, the Nanpu, Yangpu or Lupu bridges, or a host of tunnels.

Street signs are in English and Chinese, but most locals will only know a
street by its Chinese name – so a rudimentary understanding of the basic
street translations will hold the traveller in good stead (*see page 271*). Buses
are packed during peak hours, and difficult to use if you don't speak
Chinese. The metro system is an easy way to get around, especially now
that there are 11 lines extending throughout the city; the lines are still being
extended and are linked to an elevated light railway system. Taxis are inexpensive, but hard to get during rush hour and in bad weather.   ❑

PRECEDING PAGES: the Bund facing the Huangpu River; the bright lights of central
Shanghai. **LEFT:** People's Liberation Army soldiers march along the Bund.

SHANGHAI
TOP SIGHTS

Lu Xun Park
pages 218–19

M50
pages 219 and
222–23

*Shanghai Urban
Planning Centre*
page 128

Shanghai Museum
pages 128–29 and
134–37

*Former French
Concession*
pages 171–79

JING A
main map

CHANGNING
main map 206

**HUAIHAI &
HENGSHAN**
main map
172

HONGQIAO
main map 202

**XUJIAHUI &
LONGHUA**
main map 194

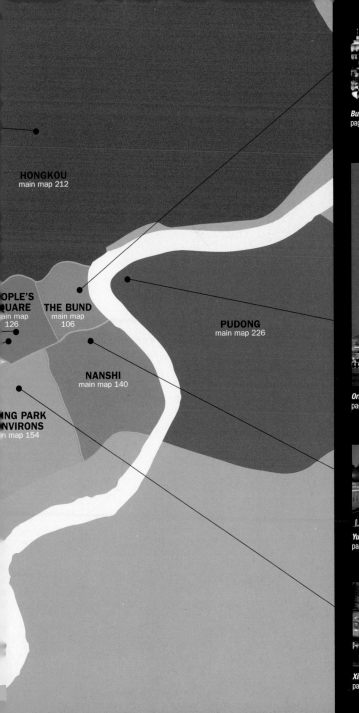

HONGKOU
main map 212

OPLE'S
QUARE
ain map
126

THE BUND
main map
106

PUDONG
main map 226

NANSHI
main map 140

NG PARK
NVIRONS
n map 154

Bund
pages 107–19

Oriental Pearl Tower
pages 227–28

Yu Garden and Bazaar
pages 143–47

Xintiandi
pages 154–55

Central Shanghai

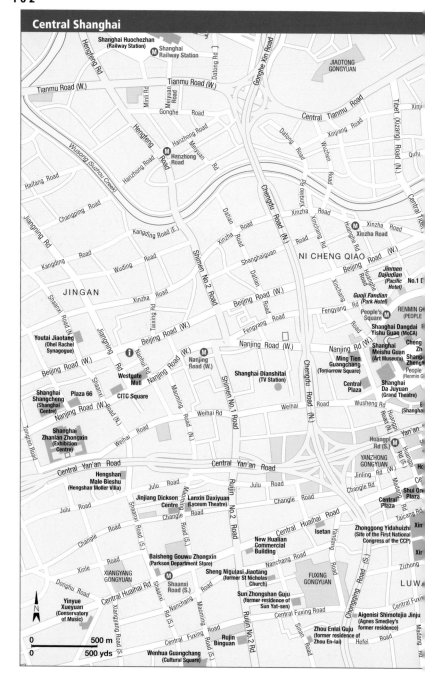

Shanghai Huochezhan
(Railway Station)

M Shanghai Railway Station

JIAOTONG GONGYUAN

Hengfeng Rd

Gonghe Xin Road

Tianmu Road (W.)

Tianmu Road (W.)

Central Tianmu Road

Tibet (Xizang) Road (N.)

Xinji

Minli Rd

Meiyuan Road

Gonghe Road

Xinjiang Road

Central Tianmu Road

Qufu

Wusong (Suzhou Creek)

Hengfeng Road

Hanzhong Road

M Hanzhong Road

Meiyuan Rd

Datong Road

Wuzhen Road

Central Tibe

Haifang Road

Changping Road

Chengdu Road (N.)

Xinchang Rd

Xinza Road

Jiangning Rd

Kangding Road (E.)

Dalian Road

Xinza Road

Huangpie Road

M Xinza Road

Xinza Road

Road

Kangding Road

Wuding Road

Shanghaiguan

NI CHENG QIAO

Beijing Road (W.)

JINGAN

Shaanxi Road (N.)

Xinzha Road

Shimen No.2 Road

Dalian Road

Beijing Road (W.)

Xinchang

Huangpi Road

Jinmen Dajiudian
(Pacific Hotel)

No.1 D

Jiangning Rd

Beijing Road (W.)

Nanhui Rd

Fengyang Rd

Guoji Fandian
(Park Hotel)

RENMIN G
(PEOPLE

Youtai Jiaotang
(Ohel Rachel Synagogue)

Fengyang Road

People's Square M

Shanghai Dangdai Yishu Guan (MoCA)

Beijing Road (W.)

i

Nanjing Road (W.)

Nanjing Rd (W.)

Shanghai Meishu Guan
(Art Museum)

Cheng
Zh

Shang
Zheng

Westgate Mall

M Nanjing Road (W.)

Shanghai Dianshitai
(TV Station)

Ming Tien Guangchang
(Tomorrow Square)

People
(Renmin Gi

Shanghai Shangcheng
(Shanghai Centre)

Plaza 66

Maoming Road (N.)

Central Plaza

Shanghai Da Juyuan
(Grand Theatre)

CITIC Square

Nanjing Road (W.)

Shimen No.1 Road

Chengdu Road (N.)

E
(Shangha

Shanghai Zhanlan Zhongxin
(Exhibition Centre)

Weihai Road

Weihai Rd

Wusheng Rd

Huangpi Road (N.)

Yan'an

Tongren Road

Central Yan'an Road

Central Yan'an Road

Huangpi Rd (S.)

YANZHONG GONGYUAN

Ho

Hengshan Male Bieshu
(Hengshan Moller Villa)

Julu Road

Jinling Rd (W.)

Central Plaza

Madang Rd

Shui On Plaza

Ce

Jinjiang Dickson Centre

Lanxin Daxiyuan
(Lyceum Theatre)

Julu Road

Changle Rd

Taicang Rd

Julu Road

Maoming Road (S.)

Ruijin No.2 Road

Changle Road

Central Huaihai Road

Zhonggong Yidahuizhi
(Site of the First National Congress of the CCP)

Xin

Changle Road

Shaanxi Road (S.)

Isetan

Yandang Road

Xin

New Hualian Commercial Building

Nanchang Road

FUXING GONGYUAN

Xir

Xinle Road

Baisheng Gouwu Zhongxin
(Parkson Department Store)

Sheng Nigulasi Jiaotang
(former St Nicholas Church)

Zizhong

LUW A

XIANGYANG GONGYUAN

M Shaanxi Road (S.)

Nanchang Road

Chongqing Road (S.)

Central Fuxi

Donghu Road

Central Huaihai Rd

Shaanxi Rd (S.)

Nanchang Rd

Sun Zhongshan Guju
(former residence of Sun Yat-sen)

Central Fuxing Road

Aigenisi Shimotejia Jinju
(Agnes Smedley's former residence)

Madang Rd

Yinyue Xueyuan
(Conservatory of Music)

Xiangyang Road (S)

Maoming Road (S.)

Ruijin No.2 Rd

Zhou Enlai Guju
(former residence of Zhou En-lai)

N

Central Fuxing Road

Sinan Road

Hefei Road

0 — 500 m

0 — 500 yds

Rujin Binguan

Wenhua Guangchang
(Cultural Square)

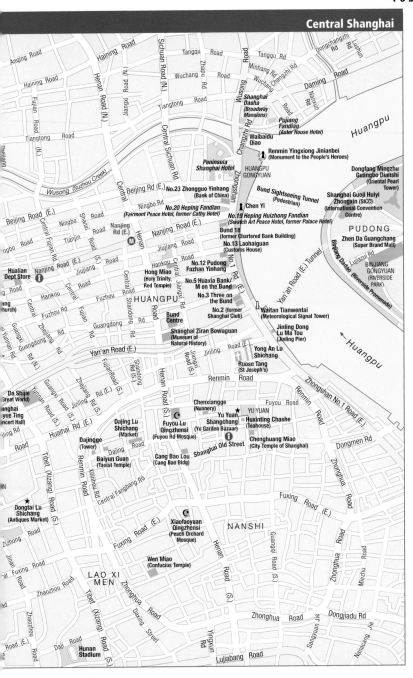

Anqing Road

Haining Road

Haining Road

Henan Road (N.)

Fujian Road (N.)

Tiantong Road

Sichuan Road (N.)

Tangqu Road

Wuchang Road

Zhapu Rd

Zhejiang Rd (N.)

Jiangxi Road (N.)

Central Sichuan Road (N.)

Tiantong Road

Minhang Rd

Tanggu Rd

Changzhi Rd

Wusong Rd

Changzhi Rd

Dongchangzhi Rd

Lishun

Daming Road

Nanxun Rd

Huangpu

Shanghai Dasha (Broadway Mansions)

Pujiang Fandian (Astor House Hotel)

Waibaidu Qiao

Wusong (Suzhou Creek)

Peninsula Shanghai Hotel

HUANGPU GONGYUAN

Renmin Yingxiong Jinianbei (Monument to the People's Heroes)

Beijing Rd (E.)

Central Beijing Road

No.23 Zhongguo Yinhang (Bank of China)

Chen Yi

Bund Sightseeing Tunnel (Pedestrian)

Dongfang Mingzhu Guangbo Dianshi (Oriental Pearl Tower)

Ningbo Rd

No.20 Heping Fandian (Fairmont Peace Hotel, former Cathy Hotel)

Shanghai Guoji Huiyi Zhongxin (SICC) (International Convention Centre)

Ningbo Road

Shanxi Road

Nanjing Rd (E.)

Nanjing Road (E.)

No.19 Heping Huizhong Fandian (Swatch Art Peace Hotel, former Palace Hotel)

ngbo Rd

Tianjin Road

Henan Road

Jiujiang Road

Bund 18 (former Chartered Bank Building)

PUDONG

Nanjing Road (S.)

Jiujiang

Hankou Road

Central Henan Road

No.13 Laohaiguan (Customs House)

Zhen Da Guangchang (Super Brand Mall)

Lujiazui Rd

Hualian Dept Store

Nanjing Road (S.)

Hankou

No.12 Pudong Fazhan Yinhang

BINJIANG GONGYUAN (RIVERSIDE PARK)

Binjiang Dadao (Riverside Promenade)

g Road

Central Shandong Road

Hong Miao (Holy Trinity, Red Temple)

No.5 Huaxia Bank/ M on the Bund

hurch)

Fuzhou Rd

Fuzhou Road

Fujian

No.1 Zhong

HUANGPU

Guangong Rd

Zhejiang Rd

Shandong Rd

No.3 Three on the Bund

Bund Centre

No.2 (former Shanghai Club)

Waitan Tianwentai (Meteorological Signal Tower)

Guandong Rd (N.)

Guangdong Road

Shanghai Ziran Bowuguan (Museum of Natural History)

Jinling Dong Lu Ma Tou (Jinling Pier)

Yuman Rd

Yan'an Road (E.)

Fujian Road (S.)

Shandong Rd (S.)

Jinling Road (E.)

Jiangxi Road (S.)

Yong An Lu Shichang

← Huangpu

ling Rd

Zhejiang Rd (S.)

Henan Road (S.)

Ruose Tang (St Joseph's)

yue Ting

Da Shijie (Great World)

Renmin Road

Renmin Road

Zhongshan No.1 Road (E.)

anghai cert Hall)

Yunnan Road (S.)

Guangxi Road (S.)

Jinling Rd (S.)

Chenxiangge (Nunnery)

Fuyou Road

Renmin

ling Rd

Hualhai Rd (E.)

Fuyou Lu Qingzhensi (Fuyou Rd Mosque)

Yu Yuan Shangchang (Yu Garden Bazaar)

YU YUAN

Huxinting Chashe (Teahouse)

Road

Dajing Lu Shichang (Market)

Shanghai Old Street

Chenghuang Miao (City Temple of Shanghai)

Dongmen Rd

Dajingge (Tower)

Tibet (Xizang) Road (S.)

Renmin Road

Xinbhou Rd

Dajing Road

Cang Bao Lou (Cang Bao Bldg)

Zhonghua Road

Baiyun Guan (Taoist Temple)

Central Fangbang Rd

Zizhong

Dongtai Lu Shichang (Antiques Market)

Road

Fuxing Road (E.)

Xiaofaoyuan Qingzhensi (Peach Orchard Mosque)

Fuxing Road (E.)

NANSHI

Zhonghua Road

Mezhou

Jinan Road

al Fuxing Road

Tibet (Xizang) Road (S.)

Zhonghua Road

Wen Miao (Confucius Temple)

Henan Road (S.)

Guangqi Road (S.)

Zhaozhou Road

LAO XI MEN

Zhonghua Road

Daxing Street

Yingxun Rd

d

Zhaozhou

Zhonghua Road

Dongjiadu Rd

Sangyuan Jie

(E.)

Daji Road

Hunan Stadium

Yingxun Rd

Lujiabang Road

Nanchang Jie

Recommended Restaurantss & Cafés on pages 122–3

THE BUND AND BEYOND

For the visitor, the Bund is the perfect introduction to Shanghai's glorious past – and its even more glittering present. Its stunning examples of European architecture tell stories of pride and subjugation, commerce and culture

"On this small oblong plot of land, about the size of Manhattan Island from the Battery to 58th Street, are jammed all but a handful of the foreign banks and all of the important native ones, all the office buildings, the hotels, the important shops and big department stores, most of the clubs... The industry, the finance, the amusements of the fifth biggest city in the world." So wrote *Fortune* magazine in 1934. Shanghai in the 21st century may be a city defined by a breathtaking warp-speed journey into the future, but the **Bund** (Waitan) remains one of its signature sights. The 2km (1¼-mile) sweep of historic buildings west of the Huangpu River is a Concession-era time capsule, a sepia portrait in a Kodachrome world.

The sight of so many magnificent buildings all at once – each more beautiful, more stately, more glamorous than the last – is nothing short of breathtaking, particularly when the Bund is lit up at night and glows, as if lit from within. Yet Shanghai has a love-hate relationship with the Bund. The stretch of European buildings (despite the Chinese flag flying above each one) has long been a politically incorrect symbol of foreign domination as well as one of the city's most well-known sights. For years the Bund languished as the authorities wrestled over its fate – a conflict that slowed down development plans for the Bund and ironically helped retain its original character.

Today, whatever angst there was over its colonial past has been buried and the Bund is firmly back in the limelight – this time as a premier

Main attractions

SHANGHAI PUDONG DEVELOPMENT BANK
CUSTOMS HOUSE
BUND 18
FAIRMONT PEACE HOTEL
BANK OF CHINA
ROCKBUND ART MUSEUM
ST JOSEPH'S CHURCH

LEFT: exercising in front of the Fairmont Peace Hotel. **RIGHT:** the same hotel, *c.*1932, then called the Cathay.

The Bund and Beyond

Shanghai Dasha
(Broadway Mansions)

Waibaidu Qiao
(former Garden Bridge)

No.'s 33-53
Waitan Yuan
former British
Consulate

No. 31
former Nippon Yusen
Shipping Company

Renmin Yingxiong Jinianbei
(Monument to the People's Heroes)

HUANGPU
GONGYUAN
(HUANGPU PARK)

Peninsula
Shanghai Hotel

No.29 Guangda Yinhang
(Everbright Bank) former Banque de l'Indochine

No.28 Shanghai Renmin Guangbo Diantai
(People's Broadcasting Station)
former Glen Line Steamship Building

Shanghai Waitan Meishuguan
(Rockbund Art Museum)
former Asiatic Society

No. 27 Luosifu (House of Roosevelt)
former Jardine Matheson & Company

No.26 Nongye Yinhang (Agricultural Bank of China)
former Yangtse Insurance Building

No.24 Zhongguo Gongshang Yinhang
(Industrial & Commercial Bank of China)
former Yokohama Specie Bank

No.23 Zhongguo Yinhang
(Bank of China)

Dianchi Road

Waitan Canguang Sui Dao
(Bund Sightseeing Tunnel)

No.20 Heping Fandian
(Fairmont Peace Hotel)
former Cathay Hotel

Chen Yi

No.19 Heping Huizhong Fandian
(Swatch Art Peace Hotel)
former Palace Hotel

No.18 Waitan Shibahao (Bund 18)
former Chartered Bank Building

No.17 Youbang Baoxian Dasha
(American International Assurance AIA)
former North China Daily News

No.16 Zhongguo Zhaoshang Yinhang
(China Merchants Bank) former Bank of Taiwan

No.15 Zhongguo Wai Hui Jiao Yi Zhongxin
(Shanghai Gold Exchange)
former Russo-Asiatic Bank

No.14
former Bank of
Communications

Guangdong Fazhan Yinhang
(Guangdong Development Bank)

Hong Miao
(Holy Trinity, Red Temple)

No.13 Laohaiguan
(Customs House)

No.12 Shanghai Pudong Fazhan Yinhang
(Pudong Development Bank)
former Hongkong and Shanghai Bank

former Shanghai Municipal
Council Building

No.44
former Calbeck &
MacGregor

No.9
former China Merchants
Steam Navigation Company

Metropole

No.17
former Russell
& Company

No.7 Bangkok Bank
former Great Northern
Telegramme Company

former
Hamilton House

former
American Club

No.6 Bund 6
former Commercial Bank of China

No.5 Huaxia Bank, M on the Bund
former Nissin Kisen Kaisha Shipping Building

No.3 Three on the Bund
former Union Assurance Building,
Mercantile Bank of India, London & China

No.2 former Shanghai Club

Waldorf
Astoria

China Minsheng Yinhang
former Bank of
Paris-Golden Cage

No.1 former
McBain Building

Waitan Tianwentai
(Meteorological Signal Tower)

Bund
Centre

former Chung
Wai Bank

Shanghai Ziran Bowuguan
(Museum of Natural History)

Shanghai Danganguan
Waitan Xinguan
(Shanghai Municipal Archives)
former Messageries Maritime

Jinting Dong
Lu Ma Tou
(Jinling Pier)

Yong An Lu Shichang
(Yong An Road Market)

Ruose Tang
(St Joseph's)

Nanjing
Road (E.)

Sichuan Road (N.)

Hubei Road

Suzhou Road (S.)

Wusong Road

Yuanmingyuan Road

Beijing Road (E.)

Central Sichuan Road

Central Jiangxi Road

Ningbo Road

Tianjin Road

Nanjing Road (E.)

Central Henan Road

Zhongshan No.1 Rd (Bund)

Jiujiang Road

Hankou Road

Zhongshan No.1 Rd (E.)

Promenade

Huangpu

Jiujiang Road

Hankou Road

Central Jiangxi Road

Fuzhou Road

Guangdong Rd

Central Sichuan Rd

Fuzhou Road

Central Henen Road

Guangdong Road

Shandong Road

Yan'an Road (E.) (Yan'an Donglu)

Yan'an Road (E.) Tunnel

Zhongshan No.2 Road (E.) Tunnel

former French Bund

Zhongshan No.2 Road (E.)

Jinling Road (E.)

Yong An Road

Sichuan Road (S.)

Jinling Road (E.)

Xinyong'an Road

0   200 m
0   200 yds

N

Recommended Restaurants & Cafés on pages 122–3

dining, entertainment and shopping hub. The renaissance began with the opening of the ritzy M on the Bund restaurant at the Huaxia Bank building, and renovations to the AIG building and the former Hongkong and Shanghai Bank in 1999. In 2004, celebrity chef Jean Georges Vongerichten opened at Three on the Bund. Today there's Dolce & Gabbana at Bund 6, Chinese chic boutique Shiatzy Chen at No. 9, and Cartier at Bund 18, while spiffy refurbishments have brought the glamour back to the Fairmont Peace and Waldorf Astoria hotels.

ALONG THE BUND WàITĀN 外滩

The banks and financial institutions of Old Shanghai's Wall Street were anchored along the **Bund** and also just behind it in the International Settlement area. This is where visitors will find a treasure trove of architectural imprints made by long-forgotten giants.

Like the buildings that line it, the word "bund" is itself a legacy of the colonial era. The British signatories to the 1842 Treaty of Nanjing, which ended the First Opium War and opened Shanghai to foreign trade (separate treaties were signed by the US and France in 1844), brought with them a new vocabulary, some of it borrowed. Bund comes from the Hindi word *band*,

meaning artificial embankment, a word that the British applied to the embanked quay along the shores of the settlements in their Chinese treaty ports and in British colonies from Ceylon to Malacca.

Old Shanghai's maritime soul determined the strategic location of the Bund – on the shore of the Huangpu River where great trading ships sailed in from the Yangzi. Originally a muddy mess with sewage and refuse strewn on its banks, the strip was filled and "bunded" in the late 1880s. Only then did the classic Bund, lined by jetties, with trading houses and financial institutions just behind them, begin to take shape. Waitan, the Chinese name for the area, means "outside beach".

A four-lane highway now runs where once the great mass of coolies hauled crates into the trading houses and rickshaw pullers ran. Remodelled in 2010, the raised promenade has replaced the old jetties, and it's a sign of the times that most of the tourists who pack the promenade want to be photographed against the Pudong skyline *(see page 225)* – not the Bund.

The opulent interior of Tan Wai Lou restaurant – located at the restored Bund 18 building.

LEFT: t'ai chi.
BELOW: the Bund promenade with the Customs House in the background.

TIP

Boats departing on cruises (ranging from 1–3½ hours) of the Huangpu River can be booked at Jinling Pier at the southern end of the Bund, near the Meteorological Signal Tower. Note: there are several booths at Jingling Pier (and some of the signage is in Chinese), so it can be quite confusing. Look out for the Shanghai Huangpu River Cruise Company *(see also page 294)*.

BELOW: night view of the Huangpu River and the Bund.

River cruises

In the pre-aeroplane age, the first sight that greeted vessels approaching Shanghai on the Huangpu River was the Bund. Visitors today can replicate that vision on river cruises from the **Jinling Pier** (Jinling Dong Lu Ma Tou) *(see margin note)*. The cruise boats slide past an eye-popping array of freighters, ships and barges – a sign of the vibrant activity in China's largest port – and give you panoramic riverside views of the Bund and Pudong.

Shanghai Municipal Archives ❶ Shànghǎi Dàngànguǎn Wàitān Xīnguǎn 上海档案馆外滩新馆

✉ 9 Zhongshan No. 2 Road (E); www.archives.sh.cn ☎ 6333 6633
🕓 daily 9.30–11.30am, 1–5pm
💰 free 🚇 Nanjing Road East + taxi

Across the street from Jinling Pier is the **Shanghai Municipal Archives**. This was the **former French Messageries Maritime Building**, an Art Deco high-rise and one of the few original buildings left south of Yan'an Road, on the former Quai de France, (the part of the Bund within the French Concession). Inside are a coffee bar and photo exhibits chronicling Shanghai's history.

Meteorological Signal Tower ❷ Wàitān Tiānwéntái 外滩天文台

✉ 1 Zhongshan No. 2 Road (E)
☎ 6321 6542 🕓 Bund Museum, first floor: daily 9am–5pm 💰 free
🚇 Nanjing Road East + taxi

The boats that ply the river once received periodic typhoon warnings from the 31-metre (102ft) tall redbrick signal tower, north of Jinling Pier. Jesuit priests at Xujiahui Observatory would telephone in weather information to what was then known as the Gutzlaff Signal Tower. One of Shanghai's few Art Nouveau structures, the tower was built in 1908. It now houses a ground-floor photographic exhibition of the Bund buildings, a bar and an outdoor terrace café with excellent perspectives of the length of the Bund.

pans at the prime Bund-facing end of the L-shaped bar, with the social scale falling as one moved further away – has been recreated and the colonnaded Grand Hall and the caged lifts remain. The heritage building is now all suites while a new tower rises behind, all glitz and gloss to match the new Shanghai.

Three on the Bund ❹
Wàitān Sānhào 外滩三号

Next, at **No. 3**, the 1916 **former Union Assurance Building** now goes by the swanky name of **Three on the Bund** – housing the eponymous **Jean Georges** restaurant *(see page 123)*, owned by the French celebrity chef, along with designer shopping and restaurants serving contemporary fusion (**Laris**) and Shanghainese fare (**Whampoa Club**). Three on the Bund opened in 2004, after a seven-year and US$50-million interior makeover supervised by American architect Michael Graves. This was one of the first Bund buildings to undergo such an extensive refurbishment.

The interior was completely gutted and retrofitted with a more

Designer shop at Three on the Bund.

THE MAIN BUND BUILDINGS

Continue north and cross Yan'an Road (E), the old border between the Quai de France and the International Settlement, to the beginning of the Bund proper at **Zhongshan No. 1 Road (E)**. Only highlights along this stretch – which faces the Bund promenade along the Huangpu River – are described in the following pages *(for a list of all the Bund buildings, see page 118)*.

For orientation purposes, the first building you will see is at **No. 1**, the **former McBain Building**, dating back to 1915, and now used as offices.

Waldorf Astoria Shanghai on the Bund ❸ Shànghǎi Waitan Hua Er Dao Fu Jiudian
上海外滩华尔道夫酒店

The old boys' club that controlled Shanghai ran it from the leather-and-whisky-soaked confines of the **former Shanghai Club** at **No. 2**, now the **Waldorf Astoria**. Built in 1911, membership to this club was restricted to white men of a certain class. The famous Long Bar, whose seating was then subject to a strict hierarchy – bank managers and tai-

LEFT: Meteorological Signal Tower.
BELOW: the atrium of the restored Three on the Bund Building.

DRINK

The cognoscenti sip classic Martinis at M on the Bund's Glamour Bar *(see right)*, from where there are amazing views of both the Bund and Pudong. For a slightly diffferent waterfront view, have a drink at the rooftop Bar Rouge at Bund 18 *(see page 290)*.

contemporary look featuring cool marble and monotones. Detractors sniff and dismiss it as looking too much like a faceless hotel with little indication of its historic past, save for its tiny lobby area and facade. Its fans retort that the restoration reflects the cutting-edge style of modern Shanghai.

Huaxia Bank ❺ Huáxià Yínháng 华夏银行

At **No. 5**, the **former Nissin Kisen Kaisha Shipping Building**, dating to 1925, is today occupied by **Huaxia Bank**, but its most famous contemporary tenant is the **M on the Bund** *(see page 122)* restaurant (entrance at 20 Guangdong Road), the favourite restaurant of many Shanghai residents, and the hip **Glamour Bar**, one floor below. Restaurateur Michelle Garnaut has revived Shanghai glamour in 21st-century fashion, enhanced by the city's best view of the Bund.

Bund 6 ❻ Wàitān Liuhào 外滩六号

Shanghai's constant rebuilding missed out the rare Victorian Gothic

RIGHT: No. 44 Fuzhou Road, the former offices of Calbeck & MacGregor.
BELOW: rooftop dining at Three on the Bund.

edifice of the **former Commercial Bank of China** at No. 6 for many years. Refurbished in 2006 into a slick, if nondescript, shopping and dining emporium now known as **Bund 6**, it is the home of **Dolce & Gabbana's** flagship store and Japanese restaurant **Sun with Aqua** *(see page 123)*. A US$30-million refurbishment has erased all signs of the original structure (save for the facade), so you'll have to use your imagination to remember it as it once was: the original Municipal Council Hall, housing the governing body of the International Settlement. This was also where the Shanghai Volunteer Corps billeted its mercenary Russian troops until 1937.

Fuzhou Road ❼ Fúzhōu Lù 福州路

Duck into **Fuzhou Road**. Just behind **No. 9** of the Bund is the oldest Bund building, the squat 1850s stone Gothic **former Russell & Company warehouse** at 17 Fuzhou Road, today an apartment building with a unique trio of shops in the street-facing part of the building: **Blue Shanghai White**, where owner Haichen designs beautiful ceramics inspired by classic blue and white pottery; **Suzhou Cobbler**, with its exquisite hand-embroidered silk Chinese slippers; and, between the two, **Studio Rouge**, a stylish contemporary Chinese art gallery. Also part of the same building is an Italian restaurant called **Tartufo Ristorante**.

The quaint Tudor-style building across the street, at **No. 44**, used to house the offices of wine importers **Calbeck & MacGregor**; it is now occupied by Chinese companies. Down the road at No. 60 is **House of Blues and Jazz**, one of the city's best live jazz venues.

Shanghai Pudong Development Bank ❶

Shànghǎi Pǔdōng Fāzhǎn Yínháng 上海浦东发展银行

Head back up the Bund to see the **former Hongkong and Shanghai Bank** at No. 12. "Dominate the Bund" was the instruction given by the bank owners to architects Palmer & Turner. Today, the domed neoclassical building, once hailed as "the grandest building east of the Suez", is still the beauty of the Bund. Now occupied (and renamed), the bank remains guarded by a pair of bronze lions *(see box page 112)*. Opened in 1923 and restored in 1999, the bank's magnificent 2,000-sq-metre (21,500-sq-ft) banking hall and adjacent office building are open to the public during working hours;

at weekends only the entrance lobby is open.

No expense was spared on the building of this edifice, with almost every piece crafted overseas. The four marble columns that support the banking hall, each weighing more than 7 tonnes and hewn from a single piece of marble, are among only six solid marble pillars of this size in the world – the other two are found in the Louvre Museum in Paris.

Above the octagonal entrance lobby is the spectacular domed mosaic ceiling: eight panels depicting the eight cities in which the bank had its branches in 1923, along with the eight words of the bank's motto, "*Within the Four Seas all men are brothers*". The 12 signs of the zodiac ring the dome, and panels on the walls illustrate, in Latin, 16 lofty qualities, including temperance, truth and prudence. When the Communists seized Shanghai in 1949, the bank, worried that the mosaic would fall victim to the proletarian cause, had it hidden under layers of thick white paint, where it remained during the half-century that the

Close-up of an ornate entrance leading to one of the Bund's most magnificent buildings, the Shanghai Pudong Development Bank.

BELOW: one of the Bund's must-see sights, the grand Shanghai Pudong Development Bank.

Shanghai now has its own younger, stronger version of Wall Street's "Charging Bull" on the Bund, looking towards Pudong. Created by the same artist, Arturo Di Modica, the bull was unveiled for the Expo and symbolised Shanghai's ambitions as a global financial centre.

RIGHT: the stunning domed ceiling of the Shanghai Pudong Development Bank.
BELOW: one of a pair of lions guarding the entrance of the Shanghai Pudong Development Bank.
BELOW RIGHT: the Customs House.

building served as the seat of the Shanghai Municipal Government. Only when the Shanghai Pudong Development Bank began restoration work was it revealed.

In the left-hand corner, where foreign exchange transactions are now handled, stood a separate bank for Chinese customers; it was once decorated in the bright reds and shiny golds favoured by its clientele. All that remains today are the Chinese designs in the ceiling mouldings, cornices and ventilation covers, and in the Chinese characters for fortune in the trim and on the walls. The bank manager's offices, now VIP meeting rooms, still have their original parquet floors and Bund views.

The fourth floor, under the domed rooftop, once housed the Royal Air Force Club of Shanghai. Restoration work found no signs of the seal of the RAF and the images of World War I aircraft that the Fly Boys were said to have laid in mosaic on the floor.

Customs House ❾
Lǎohǎiguān 老海关

The old **Customs House** at No. 13 was first located in a Chinese temple that was destroyed in an 1853 Taiping uprising. It is still used as a branch of the Customs House today, and visitors can enter only during office hours; access is restricted to the lobby.

A castle-like Gothic brick building took its place before this neoclassical Palmer & Turner building and its distinctive clock tower was

Banking on Bronze Lions

Mythical dragon-lion creatures flanking Chinese doorways are traditional, but the Western-looking lions that guard the main entrance of the Shanghai Pudong Development Bank are an unusual sight. The four bronzes were cast by sculptor Henry Poole: two for the branch in Hong Kong and two for the Shanghai branch, and the mould was then broken. Contemporary accounts tell of locals who rubbed the lions for good luck until the beasts acquired a golden sheen on their teeth and faces. A rumour began to spread among the local Chinese that the lions were, in fact, made of gold.

The lions disappeared during the Japanese Occupation; it was assumed they had been melted down but in fact they had been stored in the basement of a musty old museum. Today, one of them can be seen at the Shanghai Municipal History Museum *(see page 228)*. The replica lions guarding the bank meanwhile continue to be rubbed and patted till this day for good luck.

built in 1925. Fondly referred to as the "Big Ching", the clock tower sounded every 15 minutes until the Cultural Revolution, when its chimes were replaced with loud-speakers that broadcasted revolutionary slogans. The clock chimes were restored in 1986 and both clock and chimes were overhauled in 2007, in part to ensure that its chimes can be heard above the street's din. The Communist People's Peace Preservation Corps once holed up in the Customs House to fight for the liberation of Shanghai, and a carving in the entrance lobby commemorates its contribution. Inside, strips of jarring neon outline the low ceiling, while an interior dome mimics the grander one in the Pudong Development Bank next door. The mosaic here depicts the different types of Yangzi junks.

China Merchants Bank ❿
Zhōngguó Zhāoshāng Yínháng
中国招商银行

There is more colonial history at **No. 16**, the **China Merchants Bank** – Japanese colonial history. Like the other banks along the bund, it can be visited during working hours. Built as the Bank of Taiwan in 1924 during the Japanese occupation of Taiwan, the bank's main gallery features blossoms on the tops of the columns, original alabaster lamps and a second-floor gallery from which bank managers still carry out their supervisory duties.

AIA Building ⓫ Yǒubāng
Bǎoxiǎn Dàshà 友邦保险大厦

The **American International Assurance** or **AIA Building** (**No. 17**) was the Bund's tallest when it was completed in 1923 as the North China Daily News Building – the "Old Lady of the Bund". The oldest and most important newspaper in the city at the time, the *North China Daily News* operated here from

1864 to 1951. At some point during the 1930s, the building also rented space to the American Asiatic Underwriters, founded in Shanghai in 1919. The firm went on to become the insurance giant AIA, and leased its old premises back after extensive renovations. The lobby is open during office hours so be sure to have a look at its interior. Look up as you climb the staircase before the entrance to see the original cast iron lamps hanging beneath the gold mosaicked ceiling.

Bund 18 ⓬ Wàitān Shíbāhào
外滩十八号

The 2006 Unesco Asia Pacific Heritage Award of Distinction was given to **Bund 18**, at what else but No. 18, easily the best example of historic preservation on the Bund. The **former Chartered Bank of India, Australia and China** is home to the **Mr & Mrs Bund** *(see page 122)* eatery, as well as current hot nightspot **Bar Rouge** and the **Cartier** boutique.

Venice-based Kokai Studio's chief architect Filippo Gabbiani and his team took pains to do a proper

Step into the lobby of the Customs House to see the mosaic depiction of Chinese junks on the ceiling.

BELOW: the China Merchants Bank (left) and the AIA Building.

A trio of Venetian glass chandeliers greet visitors at the entrance lobby of the Bund 18 building.

RIGHT: cleaning the entrance to Bund 18. **BELOW:** looking towards the Peace Hotel along the newly developed walkway on the west side of the Bund.

restoration rather than gutting and rebuilding the 1923-built structure – it took them two years and US$15 million (compared to the less successful Three on the Bund which cost a whopping US$50 million). Based on a thorough and detailed analysis, the original structure was impeccably restored: the 70-year-old marble was cleaned, the wood was treated and many of the original details (such as the staircase banisters and windows) were retained.

Swatch Art Peace Hotel ⓭
Hépíng Huìzhōng Fàndiàn 和平汇中饭店

At **No. 19** is the **Swatch Art Peace Hotel** (an annexe of the Peace Hotel). The hotel is a joint venture between China's Jin Jiang hotel group and the Swatch company of Switzerland. This stately Edwardian red-brick structure, with an ornate wood-panelled and gilt Edwardian lobby, was originally built in 1906 as the **Palace Hotel** and now houses luxury watch boutiques and a swanky hotel. Just outside the original Art Nouveau revolving doors, a panel commemorates the 1909 meeting of the International Opium Commission. Ironically, it was in this city – whose foundations rested on the right to trade in opium – that the world's first steps towards narcotics controls were taken.

Fairmont Peace Hotel ⓮
Hépíng Fàndiàn 和平饭店

The star of the Bund is the fabulous Art Deco **Fairmont Peace Hotel** at **No. 20**, reopened in 2010 after a much needed renovation. Built in 1929 as the luxurious **Cathay Hotel**, and originally located on the fourth to seventh floors of Sassoon House, the

Recommended Restaurants & Cafés on pages 122–3

hotel was considered Shanghai's finest – and tycoon Victor Sassoon's *(see box below)* showpiece. Scion of the great opium-trading firm E.D. Sassoon, Victor Sassoon's domination of the city's property market defined the skyline at the time. In addition to his taste for the high life and fast women, Sassoon was apparently also enamoured of greyhound racing – then a popular Shanghai pastime. Two greyhounds dominate the carvings below the hotel's roof and on the exterior.

The first of three buildings designed by the British architectural firm Palmer & Turner on this stretch of the Bund, the Cathay Hotel was a legend in a city of legends. Pure spring water from the so-called Bubbling Well *(see page 183)* flowed from silver taps into its imported marble tubs, and every luminary who came to town stayed here: Charlie Chaplin, George Bernard Shaw and Noel Coward; the last wrote *Private Lives* in his Cathay suite. It was renamed the Peace Hotel in 1956.

The renovation has retained many of the interior details of the public areas: the stunning Chinese Art Deco ceilings of the Dragon-Phoenix restaurant, the classic Art Deco detailing of the Grill Room (now a private room), and the magnificent ballroom, where Sassoon held his fabled fancy-dress parties. The tycoon's penthouse suite is now a dining room. The roof garden offers gorgeous views of the Bund, where Shanghai famously danced as the Communists knocked, and of the modern Pudong skyline. The ground-floor jazz bar still features the Old Jazz Band – a group of elderly (average age: 77) jazz musicians playing vintage tunes.

Bank of China ⑮ Zhōngguó Yínháng 中国银行

Next door to the Peace Hotel at **No. 23** is another Palmer & Turner building. Its harmonious blend of Chinese, classical and Art Deco themes conspire to make the **Bank of China** a fusion jewel (open during working hours). Reminiscent of an ancient drum tower and built in 1935, the building was commissioned by H.H. Kung two years before the Japanese occupied Shanghai. Kung was the

Across the road from the Peace Hotel stands the statue of Marshal Chen Yi, on the spot where a statue of British diplomat Sir Harry Parkes had stood before it was melted down by the Japanese. One of China's legendary "10 marshals", Chen Yi "liberated" Shanghai on 25 May 1949. He later became the city's first mayor and served as foreign minister.

BELOW LEFT: entrance to the Swatch Art Peace Hotel.
BELOW: David Sassoon.

The Savvy Sassoons

The Sassoon fortune began when David Sassoon (1792–1864), a Sephardic Jew originally from Iraq, expanded his business empire by setting up a branch in Shanghai in 1845. His goal, and that of nearly every businessman in the city at the time, was to cash in on the opium trade. And cash in he did: it was not long before one-fifth of the opium trade brought into China was transported on the Sassoon fleet. In 1918, Sir Victor Sassoon, a fourth-generation Sassoon, inherited the family business from his uncle, Jacob Sassoon. Victor arrived in Shanghai in 1923, and immediately set about changing the city landscape. Known as much for his flamboyant costume parties and horse and greyhound racing as for his business acumen, Victor started more than 30 companies in Shanghai. His legacy, however, was the real estate he left behind: the Peace Hotel, Grosvenor House, Cathay Hotel, Cathay Cinema, Hamilton Building, Metropole Hotel and Embankment Building.

The wide stretch between the Bund buildings and the Huangpu River is a legacy of its use as a towpath in the old days when trackers would pull in the boats. The 1845 Chinese Land Regulations stipulated a space of at least 9 metres (30ft) between the buildings and the river shore.

RIGHT: the elongated domed glass ceiling at the Industrial and Commercial Bank of China.
BELOW: the Bank of China's banking hall.

Kuomintang finance chief, Bank of China director and the husband of Ai Ling, one of the famous Soong sisters. Acquired by the Kuomintang government after World War II, the building is best remembered as the institution responsible for the ruinous hyperinflation of post-war China.

The building features traditional Chinese elements like a blue-tiled Chinese roof, ancient dragon designs on the bronze entrance gates, cloud motifs on the columns and lattice-work panels on the facade. The steps leading into the main banking hall are in three groups of nine – like Beijing's Temple of Heaven. The Chinese theme continues in the beamed ceilings of the marbled lobby and the square pillars. The Bank of China asked Palmer & Turner to make its building taller than Sassoon House next door, and so it was – until an indignant Victor Sassoon countered by adding a green cupola on his roof.

Industrial and Commercial Bank of China ⑯ Zhōngguó Gōngshāng Yínháng 中国工商银行

The final building in the Palmer & Turner trilogy along this stretch, at **No. 24**, is the classical Greek-themed **Industrial and Commercial Bank of China**, or the **former Yokohama Specie Bank**, built in 1924. Enter during office hours to see its capacious banking hall with its elongated domed glass ceiling, marble columns topped by gold fretwork and giant alabaster pendant lamps.

House of Roosevelt ⑰
Luosifu 罗斯福

The next highlight is at No. 27, now the House of Roosevelt, located in what was one of the main hives of commerce in Old Shanghai, the **former Jardine Matheson & Co. Building**. Completed in 1922, it was known as Joyful and Harmonious Trading House, or "*yihe yanghang*" in Chinese. One of the great old *hong* or trading houses of Concession-era Shanghai, the granite-clad seven-storey building, with its once resplendent marble and terrazzo floors and high-ceilinged offices, was located across from Jardine's own jetty. House of Roosevelt is a collection of bars, restaurants and shops with

Recommended Restaurants & Cafés on pages 122–3

Shanghai's largest wine cellars, and fabulous rooftop views.

Former British Consulate ⑱

The oldest buildings on the Bund proper are the very last ones: the **former British Consulate**. The British Consulate oversaw the development of Shanghai from its perch at the end of the Bund, and the buildings included the consul's residence at **No. 34**, now being renovated as a state guesthouse. Built in 1873 on a site acquired by Shanghai's first British Consul, Sir Rutherford Alcock, the buildings have a simple dignity and a commanding location that befitted the British Empire.

Next to the consulate is the landmark **Peninsula Shanghai Hotel** *(see page 275)*. Owned by another well-known Jewish family, the Kadoories, it is their first foray back to the city where they made their fortune after they fled their spectacular Marble Hall *(see page 189)* in 1949. The new hotel has quickly become Shanghai's "it" place to stay and features the excellent restaurant **Sir Elly's** *(see page 122)*.

Huangpu Park ⑲ Huángpǔ Gōngyuán 黄浦公园

✉ 500 Zhongshan No. 1 Road (E)
☎ 5308 2636 ⓒ daily 6am–6pm
ⓖ free 🚇 Nanjing Road East + taxi

Across the street is **Huangpu Park**, the former Public Gardens. Laid out in 1868 by a Scottish gardener brought to Shanghai specifically for the job, the park was the purported site of the famous "No dogs or Chinese allowed" sign *(see text box page 32)*. Although no such physical sign existed, unwritten park rules that denied the entry of dogs and unaccompanied Chinese to the compound were humiliating, especially since the park was financed by municipal taxes that were paid by both Chinese and foreigners. Today, a Socialist-Realist statue stands at the site of the old British bandstand, and in the mornings, many Chinese gather in front of it to practise t'ai chi.

Along the waterfront facing the park is the **Monument to the People's Heroes** ⑳ (Renmin Yingxiong Jinianbei), its three towering pillars commemorating those who

The three pillars of the Monument to the People's Heroes are a tribute to Shanghai's war heroes.

BELOW: mural at the base of the Monument to the People's Heroes.

An A–Z of the Bund

Everyone knows of the Peace Hotel, but what about the other Bund treasures? This is a complete listing of all the buildings along the Bund

This walking tour covers every single building along the Bund. It begins with the first building on the southern end, at Zhongshan No. 1 Road (E), and ends with the former British Consulate at Nos 33–53. (There is the occasional gap where a building was demolished, or, in the case of No. 4, an unlucky number in China, simply glossed over.)

No. 1 Former McBain Building. Dates back to 1915, now used as offices.

No. 2 Waldorf Astoria Shanghai. Dates from 1911.

No. 3 Former Union Assurance Building (later Mercantile Bank of India, London and China), now a restaurant and shopping complex called Three on the Bund. Built by Palmer & Turner in 1916.

No. 5 Former Nissin Kisen Kaisha Shipping Building, now the Huaxia Bank, with M on the Bund restaurant as co-tenant.

No. 6 Former Commercial Bank of China, and headquarters of the original Municipal Council, which ran Shanghai. Now Bund 6, housing designer shops and restaurants.

No. 7 Former Great Northern Telegramme Company, now Bangkok Bank Building.

No. 9 Former China Merchants Steam Navigation Company, now home to Taiwanese designer boutique Shiatzy Chen.

No. 12 Shanghai Pudong Development Bank, formerly Hongkong and Shanghai Bank. Built in 1923 by Palmer & Turner.

No. 13 Customs House. A neoclassical Palmer & Turner building with a clock tower, built in 1925. Now a branch of the main Customs House.

No. 14 Former Bank of Communications, now used by Shanghai Trade Union Bank of Shanghai.

No. 15 Former Russo-Asiatic Bank, now Shanghai Foreign Exchange.

No. 16 Former Bank of Taiwan, now China Merchants Bank.

No. 17 Former North China Daily News Building, now the American International Assurance Building. The tallest on the Bund when it was completed in 1923.

No. 18 Formerly the Chartered Bank of India, Australia and China. This 1923 building was restored and is now known as Bund 18, housing ritzy restaurants and designer boutiques.

No. 19 Former Palace Hotel; now Swatch Art Peace Hotel.

No. 20 Former Cathay Hotel; now Fairmont Peace Hotel.

No. 23 Bank of China. The only Chinese-style building on the Bund. Still retains its original function.

No. 24 Former Yokohama Specie Bank, now Industrial and Commercial Bank of China.

No. 26 Former Yangtse Insurance Building, now the Agricultural Bank of China. The building once housed the Italian Chamber of Commerce and the Danish Consulate.

No. 27 Former Jardine Matheson & Co. Building, now House of Roosevelt.

No. 29 Former Banque de l'Indochine, now Everbright Bank.

No. 31 Former Nippon Yusen Shipping Company, demolished in 2005.

Nos 33–53 Former British Consulate, now being renovated as a state guesthouse. ❑

died fighting the Opium Wars, the May 4th Movement and Liberation.

WEST OF THE BUND

The area west of the Bund, part of the old International Settlement, is dotted with a treasure trove of old buildings. The grid of narrow streets, occasionally interrupted by landmark new high-rises such as the 50-storey **Bund Centre** on Guangdong Road and the 66-storey **Le Royal Meridien** on Nanjing Road (E), still manages to create a retro aura. The work of the International Settlement surveyors is still evident in the logical grid behind the Bund; streets running north to south bear the names of Chinese provinces while those going east to west are named after China's cities.

Just behind the British Consulate is an area, now planned for redevelopment as a cultural and entertainment hub, that was once home to Old Shanghai's social institutions, such as the YWCA, the Royal Asiatic Society and the Rotary Club. Known as **Waitan Yuan**, this 7-hectare (16-acre) site is being redeveloped in three phases.

Rockbund Art Museum ㉑
Shànghǎi Wàitān Měishù Guǎn 上海外滩美术馆

✉ 20 Huqiu Road (near Yuanmingyan Road and East Beijing Road) ☎ 3310 9985 ⌚ Tue–Sun 10am–6pm
🎟 RMB 15 🚇 Nanjing Road East

The first completed phase is the Rockbund Museum, set in the former Royal Asiatic Society Building, which was completed in 1932 and designed by British architect George L. Wilson with an Art Deco exterior combining elements of Western and Chinese architecture. British architect David Chipperfield's 2007 renovation has created a pleasant juxtaposition between the historical architecture and the current exhibits of modern art, spread across the four floors.

Guangdong Development Bank ㉒ Guǎngdōng Fāzhǎn Yínháng 广东发展银行

One block west along **Hankou Road**, the old street of publishers, at the corner of Sichuan Road, stands the **former Joint Savings Society Building**, today the **Guangdong Development**

The soaring 66-storey Le Royal Meridien at Nanjing Road (E) is a striking landmark just west of the Bund area.

BELOW:
night-time panorama of the magnificent Bund buildings.

Bank. It was designed by Ladislau Hudec (1893–1958), the Czech architect who fled to Shanghai (and stayed there) after he escaped while en route to a POW camp in Siberia. Hudec's other architectural jewels include the Moore Church *(page 131)* and the Park Hotel *(page 130)*.

Holy Trinity Church ㉓
Hóng Miào 红庙

Running parallel to Hankou Road is **Jiujiang Road**, the old banker's street, lined with stately banks in styles ranging from Victorian to Art Deco. At the junction with Jiangxi Road stands the 1866 **Holy Trinity Church**, a classic 19th-century Gothic church in eye-catching red brick – hence its Chinese name Hong Miao, or Red Temple. The church – tucked behind trees and other adjoining buildings and hardly visible from the road – is being renovated and there are plans to reconsecrate it as a church in the future.

More old buildings

Two blocks west of the Bund at the intersection with **Fuzhou Road** and **Central Jiangxi Road** ㉔ are a quartet of buildings – three Art Deco skyscrapers and a low-rise building. On the northeast corner is the **Metropole Hotel** and on the southeast corner its almost identical twin, the **former Hamilton House** (now apartments), which also houses the eponymous French restaurant. Both were built by Victor Sassoon in the 1930s and designed by Palmer & Turner. On the northwest corner is the squat **former Shanghai Municipal Council Building,** now government offices; a manhole cover nearby reads "SMC PWD" (Shanghai Municipal Council Public Works Department). A short walk east of Fuzhou Road at **No. 209** is the lovely red-brick Georgian-

RIGHT: vegetable vendor at Yong An Road Market. **BELOW:** a mammoth skeleton of the Sichuan dinosaur at the Shanghai Museum of Natural History.

Recommended Restaurants & Cafés on pages 122–3

style **former American Club**, built in 1924 and now standing empty.

Shanghai Museum of Natural History ㉕
Shànghǎi Zìrán Bówùguǎn
上海自然博物馆

✉ 260 Yan'an Road (E) ☎ 6321 3548 🕐 Tue–Sun 9am–4.30pm 💰 RMB 5 🚇 Nanjing Road East

Located three blocks west of the Bund, this museum houses some of the Royal Asiatic Society's collection in a stately 1923 neoclassical building – formerly the Cotton Goods Exchange. The exhibits trace everything from amoebas and a ceiling-scraping Sichuan dinosaur skeleton on the first floor to mammals on the third. This is a rare old-style museum in modern Shanghai, with plenty of atmosphere together with poorly stuffed and formaldehyde-soaked specimens.

Across the street is the red-brick Art Deco tower of the **former Chung Wai Bank**, owned by Shanghai's chief mobster Du Yuesheng, now an office building. Next door is the **Bund Centre**, designed by John Portman Associates, the complex includes the **Westin** hotel, apartments and offices.

AROUND YAN'AN ROAD

The area of the Quai de France, or French Bund, south of Yan'an Road, gets much less attention than its British counterpart, in part because most of its waterfront buildings have been razed. The streets behind the waterfront, though, are untouched for now, a warren of markets, small shops and lane residences.

Yong An Road Market ㉖
Yǒngān Lù Shìchǎng
永安路市场

One block west of the Bund at the intersection of Jinling Road and Yong An Road is the **Yong An Road Market** (daily 5.30am–8.30am), a lively street market that blankets two blocks of Yong An Road in the early mornings. Vendors sell an array of vegetables, fruits, chickens, fish, turtles and frogs, along with tofu, noodles, dumplings and clothes. The street also specialises in sewing supplies, and each shop, a different product: ribbons in one, buttons in another, thread in a third.

St Joseph's Church ㉗
Ruòsè Táng 若瑟堂

✉ 36 Sichuan Road (S) ☎ 6328 0293 🕐 open to visitors Sat–Sun 1–4pm 💰 free 🚇 Nanjing Road East

A few minutes' walk west are the lovely Gothic spires of the Catholic **St Joseph's Church**, rising like a fairytale castle next to the school it adjoins. Dating back to 1861, a large stained-glass rose window of Christ dominates the French-built church. Also of interest are the four niches holding statues on the building facade. The church underwent a facelift in 2007 and was given a fresh lick of paint. On Sunday mornings a church service is held in Chinese at 9.30am. ❏

The stained-glass rose window of Christ at St Joseph's Church.

Every neighbourhood in Shanghai still has a glassed-in box displaying the day's paper, a way of making sure that the party's message reaches the people.

BELOW: St Joseph's Church.

BEST RESTAURANTS AND CAFÉS

Chinese

Lost Heaven Yunnan Folk Cuisine
花马天堂云南餐厅
⊠ 17 East Yan'an Road, near Sichuan Road (S), www. lostheaven.com.cn 🕻 6330 0967 🕒 daily L & D. **$$** [p322, C2]
Enjoy exotic food from Yunnan (and its near neighbours, Tibet, Thailand, and Burma) in a subdued, temple-like atmosphere. You can find dishes with a variety of spices, from simmered vegetables in tamarind juice to Miao Tribe hot and sour prawns. This four-floor establishment also includes a bar and handicrafts store.

Tan Wai Lou
滩外楼
⊠ 5/F, Bund 18, Zhongshan No. 1 Road (E); www.vol group.com.cn 🕻 6339 1188 🕒 daily L & D. **$$$$** [p322, C2]

Filippo Gabbiani, who designed the award-winning Bund 18 building, also designed Tan Wai Lou, fitting it with his striking crimson chandeliers and spicy red glass walls. The Taiwanese-Cantonese-Western fusion menu sometimes works (and sometimes doesn't). Dishes include fusion Cantonese dim sum and sashimi with foie gras, but the presentation, which takes its cue from the Japanese, is always perfect.

Whampoa Club
黄浦会
⊠ 5/F, Three on the Bund, entrance on 17 Guangdong Road; www.threeonthebund. com 🕻 6321 3737 🕒 daily L & D. **$$$$** [p323, C2]
Hong Kong designer Alan Chan has created a dazzling, over-the-top setting for avant-garde Shanghainese cuisine. Whampoa serves a menu of Shanghainese-inspired dishes that is a mix of fusion and classic. Highlights include foie gras on sweet red dates, "popcorn" fried shrimp, tea eggs with caviar and a version of red-cooked pork.

Continental/Fusion

M on the Bund
米氏西餐厅
⊠ 7/F, 5 Zhongshan No. 1 Road (E); www.m-restaurant group.com 🕻 6350 9988 🕒 daily L & D. **$$$$** [p323, C2]
Shanghai's first independent fine-dining restaurant is still tops for its sophisticated takes on classic Continental and Mediterranean dishes, great views of the Bund and contemporary design inspired by the 1930s. Classic dishes here include the slow-baked salt-encased lamb and a de luxe version of that famous Aussie meringue dessert, Pavlova.

Mr & Mrs Bund
⊠ 6/F, Bund 18, 18 Zhongshan No. 1 Road (E); www. mmbund.com 🕻 6323 9898 🕒 daily D, Mon–Fri L **$$$$** [p322, C2]
This modern eatery by Paul Pairet has a relaxed yet chic atmosphere and serves global French fare with family-style service. They are especially known for their foie gras crumble and to-die-for lemon tart, but have over 250 classic dishes to choose from, along with a great view of the Bund.

New Heights
新视角餐厅酒廊
⊠ 7/F, Three on the Bund, entrance on 17 Guangdong Road; www.threeonthebund. com 🕻 6321 0909 🕒 daily L & D. **$$$** [p323, C2]
Occupies prime position on top of the refurbished old Union Assurance Building, with a terrace that overlooks the river and Bund. The menu is best described as eclectic, with well-executed Western dishes like steak, pasta and savoury pies as well as Asian standards like Hainanese chicken rice and laksa.

Sir Elly's
艾利爵士餐厅
⊠ 13/F, 32 Zhongshan No.1 Road (E); www.peninsula. com 🕻 2327 6756 🕒 daily L & D. **$$$$** [p322, C1]
The Peninsula's top table is old-school fine dining: high ceilings, chandeliers and discreet service in plush rooms overlooking the Bund and the Pudong

LEFT: Posh M on the Bund restaurant.
RIGHT: delectable dishes at Tan Wai Lou restaurant.

skyline. The menu features the finest ingredients from around the world, including lobster, diver scallops and wagyu beef. The second-floor patio overlooks the Bund.

Stiller's Restaurant

德国餐厅

✉ The Cool Docks, 6-7/F, Bldg 13, 505 Zhongshan Road (S); www.stillers-restaurant.cn ☎ 6152 6501 ⏰ daily D. $$$$ [p323, E4]
Chef Stefan Stiller has a well-deserved reputation in Shanghai for excellent cuisine. His contemporary Continental menu features classic dishes with a modern twist, in a sophisticated interior with fabulous views of the river and Pudong from the patio.

Table No. 1

外滩第一台

✉ 1–3 Maojiayuan Road ☎ 6080 2918 ⏰ daily, L & D. $$$$ [p323, E4]
Chef Jason Atherton, a former Michelin-starred chef (at Gordon Ramsay's Maze in London), has been getting rave reviews for Table No. 1 (even though he's not based here – the man in the kitchen is Scott Melvin, former Maze sous chef). No matter, the food is delicious – try the clams a la plancha and the squid ink risotto – and the setting, in the industrial-chic confines of the boutique Waterhouse Hotel, is one of Shanghai's most remarkable.

French

Allure

艾露法国餐厅

✉ 8/F, Le Royal Meridien, 789 Nanjing Road (E) ☎ 3318 9999 ⏰ daily L & D. $$$$ [p322, A2]
Allure's chef Michael Wendling was a student of three-star Michelin chef George Blanc, and it shows: Wendling's menu comprises superbly executed dishes with a strong southern French and Mediterranean flavour. Allure's glass and black marble interiors contrast with the traditional flavours, but complement the futuristic architecture of Le Royal Meridien, one of Puxi's tallest buildings.

Hamilton House

汉弥尔敦餐厅

✉ 137 Fuzhou Road, near Middle Jiangxi Road, www.hamiltonhouse.com.cn ☎ 6321 0586 ⏰ daily L & D. $$$ [p322, C2]
Two blocks off the Bund, this classic French restaurant takes its name from its location in the historical building designed by architects Palmer & Turner in 1934. The restaurant's stylish Art Deco interior adds a touch of modern class to the historic corner. Oyster naige and Duck done Two Ways are some of the chef's accomplished creations.

Jean Georges

✉ 4/F, Three on the Bund, entrance on 17 Guangdong

Road; www.threeonthebund.com ☎ 6321 7733 ⏰ daily D, Mon–Fri L. $$$$ [p323, C2]
Celebrity chef Jean Georges Vongerichten's Shanghai outpost has been beautifully executed. The clubby, almost masculine, interior, with views of the river, was designed by Michael Graves. In the kitchen, chef Eric Johnson produces Jean Georges's trademark Asian-inspired French cuisine: menu highlights include foie gras brûlée with sour cherries, salmon with pickled green mango, and "themed" dessert plates featuring a quartet of delectable desserts using the same ingredient.

Japanese

Sun with Aqua

东京和食

✉ 2/F, Bund 6, Zhongshan No. 1 Road (E) ☎ 6339 2779 ⏰ daily 11am–11pm. [p322, C2]
The Bund's first Japanese restaurant is a dazzling spot: a shark aquarium (at the bar) entertains diners, as does the open kitchen where Japanese chefs do a contemporary take on Japanese cuisine – like an excellent *yakiniku kamameshi* –(barbecued beef in rice) and *gindara shioyaki* (salt-grilled cod).

Teahouse

The Bund Tea Company

上海茶源有限公司

✉ 100 Dianchi Road, www.bundtea.com ☎ 6329 0989 ⏰ daily Tea Room 4–10pm, Tea Shop 9am–10pm. $ [p322, C1]
Sip a cup of tea while soaking up some history at this historic British tea trade company building, built in 1908. You can find an assortment of teas here to taste or purchase, including green, black and flower teas.

Prices for a three-course meal for two people, excluding drinks:

$ = under RMB 250
$$ = RMB 250–500
$$$ = RMB 500–800
$$$$ = over RMB 800

Recommended Restaurants & Cafés on page 133

PEOPLE'S SQUARE

The main city square area contains the best of modern Shanghai, including a world-class museum of Chinese artefacts, another devoted to art, and a magnificent theatre. But there's also the crush of Nanjing Road, with its remarkable concentration of shops

The People's Square area is Shanghai's centre, its exact geographical midpoint in fact, according to the city's mapping and surveying department. Shanghai's main metro lines all converge at this town square, transporting people from all over the city to its cultural and political hub.

WITHIN PEOPLE'S SQUARE

The core of People's Square today is Showcase Shanghai: world-class museums, a theatre, five-star hotels, and the imposing Shanghai City Hall in the middle of it all. The buildings, all raised during the late 1990s and each one a significant architectural statement, seem to have been lifted from a futuristic urban planner's utopia. They also symbolise Shanghai's arrival as a city that can compete on its own merit on the world stage. With these buildings, no longer does the city government have to take pride in the historic Bund buildings, long a symbol of foreign oppression.

People's Square ❶ Rénmín Guǎngchǎng 人民广场

Ⓒ daily 24 hours Ⓖ free
🚇 People's Square

Although there is little to remind you of the past in **People's Square** itself, the place was once so brazenly bourgeois during the Concession years that it had to be razed and paved over before it was fit for proletarian Shanghai. The perimeter of People's Square, bounded by Nanjing Road (W), Huangpi Road (N), Central Xizang Road and Wusheng Road, once defined pre-Liberation Shanghai's racecourse, where millionaires would ride their steeds, and their wives would wager fans and sun-bonnets because

Main attractions
SHANGHAI ART MUSEUM
SHANGHAI GRAND THEATRE
SHANGHAI URBAN
   PLANNING CENTRE
SHANGHAI MUSEUM
MOORE CHURCH

LEFT: relief from the sweltering summer heat in People's Square. **RIGHT:** communal exercises at People's Park.

Catching up on the latest gossip at People's Park.

betting money was too, too vulgar. The wartime Japanese command used the racetrack as a holding camp and the post-war Kuomintang government turned it into a sports arena. By 1952, the new Communist government had paved over part of the racetrack into a parade ground and turned the rest into a park for recreation.

People's Park (Renmin Gongyuan), just behind People's Square, is much smaller today than it was during the Concession days. Still, the park has pretty tree-lined paths, a small lake, rock gardens and the night-time haunt called **Barbarossa Lounge** *(see page 133)*, with its exotic *Arabian Nights*-inspired decor and sweet-smelling sheesha smoke.

Museum of Contemporary Art (MoCA) ❷ Shànghǎi Dāngdài Yìshù Guǎn 上海当代艺术馆

✉ 231 Nanjing Road (W), in People's Park; www.mocashanghai.org

☎ 6327 9900 ⏰ daily 10am–9.30pm
ⓔ RMB 20 🚇 People's Square

In one corner of People's Park is the **Museum of Contemporary Art**, popularly known as MoCA Shanghai. It is the city's first independent contemporary art museum, funded by a Shanghai-born Hong Kong millionaire and focused on international and Chinese contemporary art. MoCA, though small, shows some of the more cutting-edge, thought-provoking modern art in the city: controversial French photographers Pierre and Gilles have exhibited here, as has Guggenheim's Art in America, which was hailed "the most in-depth exhibition of contemporary modern art to be presented in Shanghai". Exhibitions, which change every two months, are on the first two floors of this three-storey glass structure, while the **Art Lab Cafe and Bar**, with an outdoor terrace overlooking the park, is on the third.

BELOW: Barbarossa Lounge at People's Park.

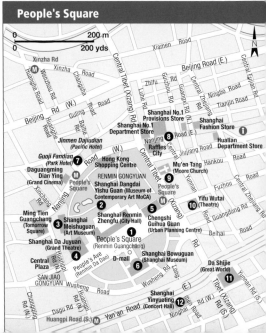

People's Square

0 — 200 m
0 — 200 yds

Xinzha Rd
Xinzha Road
Wenzhou Road
Huanghe Road
Beijing Rd (W.)
Guling Road
Baihe Road
Huaihe Road
Chengdu Road (N.)
Xiamen Road
Zhifu Rd
Guhzou Rd
Guangxi Rd
Central Zhejiang Rd
Central Tibet (Xizang) Road
Ningha Road
Beijing Road (E.)
Central Fujian Rd
Tianjin Rd
Ningbo Road

Shanghai No.1 Provisions Store
Shanghai No.1 Department Store
Shanghai Fashion Store
Jinmen Dajiudian (Pacific Hotel)
Nanjing Road (E.)
Raffles City
Jiujiang Road
Hualian Department Store
Guoji Fandian (Park Hotel) ❼
Hong Kong Shopping Centre
Mu'en Tang (Moore Church)
Hankou Road
Daguangming Dian Ying (Grand Cinema)
RENMIN GONGYUAN
People's Square
People's Square ❾
Fuzhou Road
Central Zhejiang Rd
Shanghai Dangdai Yishu Guan (Museum of Contemporary Art MoCA)
Yunnan Road
Yifu Wutai (Theatre) ❿
Ming Tien Guangchang (Tomorrow Square)
Shanghai Meishuguan (Art Museum) ❸
Shanghai Renmin Zhengfu (City Hall)
Chengshi Guihua Guan (Urban Planning Centre)
Guangdong Rd (E.)
Beihai Road
Shanghai Da Juyuan (Grand Theatre) ❹
Central Plaza
People's Ave (Renmin Da Dao)
People's Square (Renmin Guangchang) ❶
D-mall
Shanghai Bowuguan (Shanghai Museum) ❻
Da Shijie (Great World) ⓫
SAN JIAO GONGYUAN
Wusheng Road
Yan'an Road (E.)
Wusheng Rd
Tibet (Xizang) Rd (S.)
Yunnan Rd (S.)
Chongqing Rd (N.)
Dagu Rd (N.)
Shanghai Yinyueting (Concert Hall) ⓬
Ninghai Rd
Huangpi Road (S.) 🚇 Yan'an Road (S.)

Shanghai Art Museum ❸
Shànghǎi Měishù Guǎn
上海美术馆

✉ 325 Nanjing Road (W); www.sh-art
museum.org.cn ☎ 6327 2829
🕐 daily 9am–5pm ⓔ RMB 20
🚇 People's Square

Virtually the only remnant of People's Square racetrack's glory days is the 1933 Shanghai Racing Club, today the **Shanghai Art Museum** – located just adjacent to MoCA. The letters SRC are still engraved over the granite building entrance, "Big Bertie", the nickname given to the clock tower, still ticks, and the horse heads on the ironwork banisters are still intact, but the RMB 70 million renovation in 1999 removed the Turkish baths and bowling lanes, along with some of

its old-world charm. Temporary exhibits of traditional as well as contemporary artwork occupy the museum's three floors (although the quality can vary from one exhibition to the next), and it also hosts the Shanghai Biennale. On the rooftop, palettes have yielded to palates at the contemporary American restaurant **Kathleen's 5** *(see page 133)*, with its spectacular views of the surroundings.

Shanghai Grand Theatre ❹
Shànghǎi Dà Jùyuàn
上海大剧院

✉ 300 People's Avenue;
www.shgtheatre.com ☎ 6372 8702
(tickets), 6372 3833 🕐 tours on Mondays only 9–11am ⓔ Ticket price (for tours): RMB 40 🚇 People's Square

Just opposite is the **Shanghai Grand Theatre**, designed by much-lauded French architect Jean-Marie Charpentier. The futuristic glass confection has flamboyantly upturned eaves – mimicking a traditional Chinese roof – that glow magically at night when the lights come on. Completed in 1998 and dubbed the

Waiter with a dessert plate at Kathleen's 5 restaurant, perched on the rooftop of the Shanghai Art Museum.

LEFT: contemporary art exhibit at Shanghai Art Museum.
BELOW LEFT: Shanghai Art Museum used to be a horse-racing club.
BELOW: performance at the Shanghai Grand Theatre.

Martial arts display at the forecourt of the Shanghai Urban Planning Centre.

"Crystal Palace" by locals, the 1,800-seat, 10-storey theatre has a packed season of ballet, classical music and opera, as well as imported Broadway musicals and revolutionary operas. Tours, which take place only on Mondays, give you access to the high-tech stage; otherwise catch a performance here to appreciate its excellent acoustics.

Shanghai Urban Planning Centre ❺ Shànghǎi Chéngshì Guīhuà Guǎn 上海城市规划馆

✉ 100 People's Avenue; www.supec. org ☎ 6372 2077 ◷ Tue–Thur 9am–5pm, Fri–Sun 9am–6pm ◉ RMB 30 (audio guide); RMB 20 ▣ People's Square

To the east, just past the **Shanghai City Hall** (closed to the public), is the **Shanghai Urban Planning Centre**. Designed by Xing Tonghe of the Shanghai Architectural Institute, the centre helps to make some sense of the Shanghai building frenzy. Nearly a twin of the Grand Theatre in terms of design, the square building has the same clean lines of the

former, though its startling flat roof is an almost kitschy departure.

The mezzanine floor tells the story of Shanghai's development from fishing village to Concession, the second floor houses temporary exhibitions, while the third floor focuses on the government's efforts at providing modern housing, with visitors offered a virtual tour of Shanghai in the "360 Degree Virtual Hall". The 500-sq-metre (5,380-sq-ft) scale model of downtown Shanghai depicts every building over six storeys high, including ones as yet unbuilt. The fourth floor displays the city's plans for the 21st century; visitors can also design their own city, while the top floor offers a cáfe with one of the best views in town. A re-creation of the Sino-Western architecture and *longtang* (lane) houses that dominated the pre-Liberation era is found in the basement.

Shanghai Museum ❻ Shànghǎi Bówùguǎn 上海博物馆

✉ 201 People's Avenue; www.shanghai museum.net ☎ 6372 3500 ◷ daily 9am–5pm ◉ free; Acoustiguide rental RMB 40 (plus RMB 400 or passport for deposit) ▣ People's Square

A landscaped plaza fronts Shanghai Museum across the street. The neatly manicured gardens and flowerbeds are dominated by a soaring musical fountain, whose jets cool Shanghai children during the steamy summer months. Allow a full morning, at least, to tour the museum. Designed by Chinese architect Xing Tonghe (who also designed the Shanghai Urban Planning Centre), the massive five-storey granite structure was officially opened in 1996.

Shaped like a *ding*, an ancient round bronze tripod cooking vessel, the museum focuses on the arts and crafts of China in its 11 permanent galleries, arranged thematically across

extensive collection of Chinese paintings in the **Chinese Painting Gallery**, the **Ancient Chinese Jade Gallery** and the colourful **Chinese Minorities Nationalities Gallery**. *See also photo feature on pages 134–7.*

AROUND PEOPLE'S SQUARE

People's Square's attraction as the city centre appealed to Concession-era Shanghai too, and one of its great attractions was that all around the sparkling core – like an antique frame – is a historic ring of the legends that defined the Shanghai of yore: the tallest hotel, the best theatre and the wildest entertainment. These wonders of Old Shanghai now stand in the shadows of several modern high-rise structures, creating a rich and contrasting texture. Today, it's the plush **JW Marriot** hotel (contained within the skyscraping and pincer-edged **Tomorrow Square** building) that looms over the old-world **Park Hotel** and glitzy malls overshadow Shanghai's original "Big Four Department Stores" along busy Nanjing Road (E), the city's main shopping thoroughfare.

EAT

The Acoustiguide is a great resource for more in-depth overviews and insights of Shanghai Museum's galleries. The guides at the entrance of each gallery can also provide more detailed information if required.

four floors. Beautifully laid out and lit, with informative introductory panels in each gallery, the museum houses one of the largest collections of Chinese art in the world – rivalling Taipei's National Palace Museum – and is easily the best in the country.

Museum highlights include the **Ancient Chinese Bronze Gallery**, which features one of the world's finest and most comprehensive collections of bronzes; and the **Ancient Chinese Ceramic Gallery**, which traces this born-in-China craft from the Neolithic Yellow River cultures to the Qing dynasty. Other must-sees include the nation's largest and most

LEFT: a *ding*, an ancient Chinese bronze cooking vessel.
BELOW: the Shanghai Museum is shaped like a *ding* vessel.

For those who can't be bothered to walk, hop on one of the trams than ply up and down the length of pedestrianised Nanjing Road (E), for only RMB 2. Bear in mind, however, that the trams are incredibly slow, so it might actually be quicker on foot.

RIGHT: the Art Deco Park Hotel dates back to 1934. **BELOW:** Nanjing Road East.

Park Hotel ❼ Guójì Fàndiàn
国际饭店

✉ 170 Nanjing Road (W); www.jinjianghotels.com ☎ 6327 5225 🚇 People's Square

Continue northeast along **Nanjing Road (W)** for a look at the gracious old buildings that once defined progressive Shanghai. In his memoirs, Shanghai-born architect I.M. Pei recalls coming out of the nearby **Grand Cinema** (Daguangming Dian Ying) – built by Czech architect Ladislau Hudec – when he saw the just-completed 24-storey **Park Hotel**, another Hudec masterpiece. Immediately Pei took out his pencil and began drawing the Park Hotel's Art Deco outline, citing this moment as the inspiration for his career. The hotel's interior has been renovated and its status as Asia's tallest building long since surpassed, but the Park's brown-tiled tower still dominates this section of Nanjing Road (W).

Built in 1934 for the Joint Savings Society, the Park Hotel also served as the first hotel school for Chinese students. During the Cultural Revolution years, the hotel was draped with revolutionary banners ("Do not forget the class struggle" and "Politics is in command") because it symbolised decadence. Step into the lobby to see the marker for the geographical centre of Shanghai.

Next door is the **Shanghai Sports Association**, formerly the Foreign YMCA Building, with its beautiful beige brick exterior and third-storey rooftop garden.

Continue east along Nanjing Road (W). When the eight-storey **Pacific Hotel** (Jinmen Dajiudian) was built in 1924 at 108 Nanjing Road (W) as the Union Insurance Building, it was the tallest building in the city and its bell tower was used by ships for navigation.

Nanjing Road (E) shops ❽

Head east along Nanjing Road (W), following the curve of the old racetrack for about five minutes, for a glimpse of where young Shanghai shops and eats – **Raffles City** (268 Central Xizang Road). The shopping mall is filled with brand names like French Connection and Starbucks,

Recommended Restaurants & Cafés on page 133

and also houses an IMAX Theatre.

From here, it's a short five-minute walk east to the **pedestrian section** of **Nanjing Road (E)**, once the city's pre-eminent shopping street. The street, with its bright, flashy neon lights and carnival-like atmosphere, is now over-shadowed by swankier malls else-where in the city, but it's still packed with Chinese tourists, particularly the pedestrian strip from **Tibet Road** (Xizang Lu) eastwards to as far as **Central Henan Road**. A giant screen broadcasts propaganda, couples snug-gle at street corners and a tourist tram plies the walking street. Most of the older shops have now acquired a glossy look, including Shanghai's famous "Big Four" department stores, staples of Old Shanghai which have all been refurbished and updated for a new generation: **No. 1 Department Store** (formerly Sun) at 800 Nanjing Road (E); **Shanghai No. 1 Provisions Store** (formerly Sun Sun) at 700 Nan-jing Road (E); **Hualian Department Store** (formerly Wing On) at 635 Nanjing Road (E), with a roof garden; and **Shanghai Fashion Store** (formerly Sincere) at 660 Nanjing Road (E).

Moore Church ❾
Mù'ēn Táng 沐恩堂

✉ 316 Xizang Road (M) ☏ 6322 5069 ⏱ Services: Sun 7.30am, 9am, 2pm and 7pm ⓔ free
🚇 People's Square

South of Nanjing Road (E) is the red-brick **Moore Church**. Originally named the Arthur J. Moore Memor-ial Church after the Texan who donated funds for its construction in the late 1920s, the Methodist church was rebuilt by the Czech architect Ladislau Hudec in 1931. The struc-ture features Hudec's characteristi-cally innovative design elements, like the concave-and-convex brickwork that is used to encase the structure. Used as a middle school during the Cultural Revolution, it was the first church in Shanghai to reopen post-Cultural Revolution (in 1979) and the first to consecrate bishops (in 1988).

Subterranean shopping

From Moore Church, descend into the **Hong Kong Shopping Centre** (Xiang Gang Zhongxin; accessible through People's Square metro

The Shanghai Sports Association (Shanghai Tiyu Hui), next to the Park Hotel, was where enemies of the state were held for questioning during the Cultural Revolution. It was here that the daughter of author Nien Chieng (Life and Death in Shanghai) perished.

BELOW: Moore Church.

The area east of Fuzhou Road covering Yunnan Road, Guangdong Road and Central Zhejiang Road is also known as Little Xinjiang. It's a great place to explore; vendors sell the delicious piping-hot, Xingjiang pitta-style bread and barbecued sticks of meat, and you'll come across sharp-featured Xinjiang people.

RIGHT: Beijing opera performer at the Yifu Theatre.
BELOW: Shanghai Philharmonic Orchestra rehearsing at the Shanghai Concert Hall.

station exit 1), at the corner of Tibet Road and Fuzhou Road, for a little underground shopping. The subterranean mall leads to **D-mall** (Dimei Gouwu Zhongxin; entrance also north of the People's Square fountain), an underground rabbit warren of hip fashion boutiques. Fearful that the 1960 Sino-Soviet split would precipitate a nuclear war, Mao exhorted the people to "dig deep, store grain and resist hegemony". The result was underground bomb shelters like this that snake under most of Shanghai.

Yifu Theatre ⑩
Yifū Wǔtái 逸夫舞台

About a block south, at 701 Fuzhou Road is the **Yifu Theatre**, which hosts regular performances of colourful Beijing opera (1.30pm and 7.15pm; tel: 6322 5294) as well as other forms of traditional Chinese opera.

Great World ⑪
Dà Shìjiè 大世界

Three blocks south is an ornate wedding-cake structure, on the corner of Yan'an and Tibet Road. This is the infamous **Great World** whose colourful history is part of Shanghai lore. Controlled in the 1930s by the head of the French Concession's Chinese detective squad, Huang Jinrong, or "Pockmarked" Huang, this was a world of smoky gambling dens, where scions of Shanghai's first families lost their fortunes, of dance hostesses, and of the staircase that led to nowhere – where desperate souls who had lost it all could take the quick way out.

The ongoing renovations have retained the famous exterior, while the interior will be completely refurbished by Xing Tonge of Shanghai Museum fame. Completed renovations include the first floor, now filled with small souvenir and food shops.

Shanghai Concert Hall ⑫
Shànghǎi Yīnyuètīng
上海音乐厅

One block west along Yan'an Road is the 1930 neoclassical **Shanghai Concert Hall**, esconced in a lovely park setting. The concert hall, originally the Nanjing Theatre, received an interior refurbishment recently, and is now home to the **Shanghai Philharmonic Orchestra**, the city's second major orchestra (Tickets available from www.culture.sh.cn/english).

BEST RESTAURANTS AND CAFÉS

Chinese

Mao Zhu Shi Jia Xiang Cai
毛主席家乡菜

✉ 168 Yun Middle Road (S) ☎ 6360 6226 ☻ daily 8am–10.30pm. $ [p322, A2]

Chairman Mao's Family Restaurant, as the name translates, pays tribute to Mao Zedong's hometown cuisine – hot, spicy Hunan food. The house special is Mao's favourite, *hong shao rou*, tender pieces of fatty pork belly, served with red chillies and whole cloves of garlic. The place is always crowded, but the service is efficient so seats free up quickly. An English menu is available, although the staff's English is limited. Photos of the most popular dishes are pasted on the walls.

Yang's Fry Dumplings
小杨生煎

✉ 1/F, Shanghai No.1 Food Store, 720 Nanjing Road (E) ☎ 6322 2777 ☻ daily 9.30am–10pm. $ [p322, B2]

Two busy chefs here fry up *shengjianbao* – pan-fried pork dumplings oozing with lovely juices – in giant woks. Yang's is found at the far end of the first floor of Shanghai No. 1 Food Store. Note: only takeaway is available.

Continental

Barbarossa Lounge
芭芭露莎

✉ People's Park, 231 Nanjing Road (W); www.barbarossa.com.cn ☎ 6318 0220 ☻ daily 11–2am. $$ [p322, A2]

Located amidst the greenery of People's Park, this Middle Eastern-inspired place is better known for its bar than its restaurant, and perhaps for good reason. The menu offers a range of pastas, Moroccan tagines, and fish and meat dishes – all good, but somehow lacking those authentic Middle Eastern flavours.

iiiit!

✉ 1/F, World Trade Tower, 500 Guangdong Road ☎ 6362 0567 ☻ Mon–Sat 8am–9pm. $ [p322, B3]

Focuses on good-quality ingredients and tasty sandwiches, salads, paninis, pizzas, cakes and fresh juices. Especially good is the eggplant and provolone panini and the zesty lemon square. Free WiFi available.

Kathleen's 5
赛马餐饮

✉ 5/F, Shanghai Art Museum, 325 Nanjing Road (W); www.kathleens5.com.cn ☎ 6327 2221 ☻ daily 11.30am–11pm. $$$

[p322, A3]

This rooftop restaurant serving Continental cuisine at the Shanghai Art Museum has stunning views over People's Square. At lunch the place attracts the business crowd, and in the evening, couples on dates. Although some of the dishes need a little fine-tuning, Kathleen's should not to be missed if you're in the area, especially to see the sunset with a drink in hand.

Italian

Art Lab
摩卡咖啡

✉ People's Park, 231 Nanjing Road (W) ☎ 6327 0856 ☻ daily 10am–midnight. $$ [p322, A3]

Located on the top floor of the Museum of Contemporary Art, this eatery serves Mediterranean-style dishes which are perfectly complemented by

the style of the dining room – which also serves as an exhibition space. Enjoy the great city and park views from the outdoor terrace.

Café

Wagas
沃歌斯

✉ 227 Huangpi Road (N), at Central Plaza ☎ 5375 2758 ☻ daily 7am–10pm. $ [p322, A3]

A great place for a coffee or a quick meal, this chain serving Western cuisine can be found all around town. Enjoy healthy gourmet panini, salads, pasta and an assortment of homemade cakes and smoothies. Free WiFi available.

Prices for a three-course meal for two people, excluding drinks:

$ = under RMB 250
$$ = RMB 250–500
$$$ = RMB 500–800
$$$$ = over RMB 800

RIGHT: chef with his creation at Kathleen's 5.

SHANGHAI MUSEUM

China's finest collection of ancient arts and crafts are housed in this modern museum shaped like a *ding* food vessel

THE FIRST FLOOR:
ANCIENT CHINESE BRONZE GALLERY

This is one of the world's finest and most comprehensive collections of Chinese bronzes, including very rare pieces going back to China's first dynasty, the Xia (21st to 16th century BC). Highlights include a Shang dynasty square *lei*, or wine vessel, with finely-crafted dragons; a Western Zhou dynasty bell embellished with tigers; and an enormous *jian* wine vessel, with four mythical creatures grasping the rim and peeking into it – taken from the tomb of King Fu Chai of the Wu Kingdom.

ANCIENT CHINESE SCULPTURE GALLERY

This gallery features beautifully rendered sculptures from the Warring States period through the Ming dynasty, most of it religious in theme. The Buddha sculptures reflect the artistic styles of the period, from the delicate, ethereal figures of the Northern Qi and Sui periods to the realistic depictions of the Tang dynasty and the classical figures of the Song dynasty.

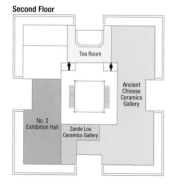

LEFT: the finely wrought Buddhist statues in the Ancient Chinese Sculpture Gallery illustrate how the early images of Buddha, depicted with distinctly Indian features, gradually take on a more Chinese appearance as Buddhism becomes more and more entrenched in China.

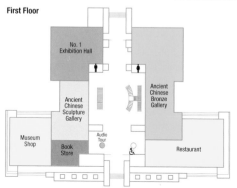

First Floor

No. 1 Exhibition Hall

Ancient Chinese Sculpture Gallery

Ancient Chinese Bronze Gallery

Museum Shop

Book Store

Audio Tour

Restaurant

Second Floor

Tea Room

Ancient Chinese Ceramics Gallery

No. 2 Exhibition Hall

Zande Lou Ceramics Gallery

LEFT & BELOW: the bronze items on display in the Ancient Chinese Bronze Gallery are laid out chronologically, and include exquisitely wrought food vessels called *ding* (left), and wine vessels (below), some in the shape of mythical creatures.

THE SECOND FLOOR:
ANCIENT CHINESE CERAMIC GALLERY

This gallery traces this born-in-China craft from the Neolithic Yellow River cultures to the Qing dynasty, including the development of celadon. Especially beautiful are the delicate Tang dynasty Sancai ceramics with their three-colour glazes, and blue and white Ming and Qing pieces. The Zande Tower Ceramic Gallery, adjacent to the main ceramics exhibit, displays 130 masterpieces from the Jin to the end of the Qing dynasty, many of which are Qing imperial ware. As you exit, there is also a fascinating potter's workshop, model kilns and, sometimes, pottery-making demonstrations.

ABOVE: there are over 500 pieces in the Ancient Chinese Ceramic Gallery. This pomegranate-shaped vase with a turquoise glaze dates back to the reign of Emperor Qianlong (1736–95).

Third Floor

- Chinese Painting Gallery
- Chinese Calligraphy Gallery
- Chinese Painting Gallery
- Chinese Seal Gallery
- Liangtuxuan

Fourth Floor

- Chinese Minority Nationalities Art Gallery
- Chinese Coin Gallery
- Ancient Chinese Jade Gallery
- Chinese Ming and Qing Furniture Gallery
- No. 3 Exhibition Hall

LEFT: the Chinese Painting Gallery's 120 masterpieces, dating from the Tang dynasty, are displayed behind glass panels arranged along corridors. Automatic sensors cast light onto the paintings only when the viewer is in front of them.

THE THIRD FLOOR:
CHINESE PAINTING GALLERY

This is where you'll find a rotating exhibit of the country's largest and most extensive collection of Chinese paintings, including Tang and Song dynasty album leaves and hand scrolls, and masterpieces such as the *Eight Noble Monks* by Liang Kai, *Misty River and Mountains* by Wang Shen, as well as works by masters of the Yuan, Ming and Qing dynasties.

RIGHT: seals, or *chops*, feature elaborately designed knobs that vary according to the rank of the owner. Royalty and important officials had separate seals for private and official use.

CHINESE CALLIGRAPHY GALLERY

This is perhaps the most challenging gallery for foreigners who can't read Chinese. It traces the development of this ancient form of brushstroke writing, from early inscriptions on tiny oracle bones to flowing Qing dynasty scripts. The chronological display shows the development of the art, featuring major styles and the works of the masters.

CHINESE SEAL GALLERY

The world's first gallery devoted to the Chinese seal displays 500 intricately carved seals from the museum's stored collection of 10,000. The seals, which cover the period from the Western Zhou to the Qing dynasty, served as signatures in ancient letters and contracts. On display are seals made of ivory, jade, amber and crystal.

ABOVE: the rare pieces of ancient calligraphy in the Chinese Calligraphy Gallery include examples of different writing styles, as well as early paper rubbings from stone and bronzes. There are four basic writing styles: *zhenshu* (regular script), *caoshu* (cursive script), *lishu* (official script) and *zhuan shu* (seal character script).

THE FOURTH FLOOR:
CHINESE MING AND QING FURNITURE GALLERY

The furniture gallery showcases the spare, clean lines of Ming dynasty furniture, as well as the more Baroque influence of the Qing era. It offers a look at originals of much-copied pieces, and an insight into the unique Chinese method of joining two pieces of wood, which uses no nails.

ABOVE: in the Furniture Gallery, rooms are laid out with antique pieces as they would have been in a traditional Chinese house.

ANCIENT CHINESE JADE GALLERY

The museum's impressive collection of jade features a display that runs from the Neolithic period to the Qing dynasty, with a range of jade objects used for ritual, burial and as ornamentation.

ABOVE: jade was supposed to bestow immortality on the wearer, and the collection at the Chinese Jade Gallery includes objects that were used by royalty and nobles, such as these intricately carved wine vessels and ritual ornaments.

CHINESE MINORITY NATIONALITIES' ART GALLERY

This gallery – always a hit with the children because of its visual appeal – showcases over 600 handicrafts from China's 56 ethnic minorities: costumes, textiles, embroidery, metalware, sculpture, pottery, lacquer ware, food and water vessels, and a stunning collection of wooden masks.

ABOVE & RIGHT: exhibits at the Chinese Minority Nationalities' Art Gallery include carved wooden masks used in rituals and dances, and handcrafted fishing boats made without the use of nails.

CHINESE CURRENCY GALLERY

This gallery displays currencies through the ages – from the shell money of the Neolithic period to the gold Persian coins from the Silk Road. There is also currency from the Concession-era banks.

RIGHT: the Chinese Currency Gallery displays ancient copper coins with a square hole in the middle, which allowed a string to be threaded through. Less common are coins in the shape of ingots, spades and knives.

NANSHI

Visit the famous Yu Garden and its adjoining bazaar
by all means, but to see the real China, wander around
the Old City's narrow lanes and crowded markets for
the sights and sounds of a vanishing way of life

A 1934 guidebook to the city, published by Shanghai's University Press, warned that "Shanghai is not China". For a peek at the real China, the book suggested a visit to its Chinese City – advice that still applies today. While parts of Shanghai's original city, **Nanshi** ("Southern City") may be self-consciously Chinese, like a theme-park vision of Ming China, the spirit of the Old City remains very much alive in the tightly packed lanes and crowded old markets along the backstreets, full of the constant din of *renao*, the electric buzz that defines Shanghai.

There is still plenty of life in the lanes, but every day great swaths of Nanshi fall to the wrecking ball. Its 19th-century wood and brick Chinese architecture is being replaced by new tourist-friendly malls and green space. A walk along an old lane may be rewarded by scenes of children playing in the streets, chamber pots being washed out, and women shelling peas outside century-old doors.

A refuge for the lawless

By law, Shanghai's Chinese population was supposed to live in the Old City during the Concession era, but that stricture quickly broke down. Developers found that building housing for Chinese who were seeking the safety of the policed Concessions during the Taiping Rebellion was too lucrative to miss out on.

The Chinese soon lived throughout the Concessions – they paid taxes, but had no voice in the municipal government – leaving the Old City a squalid ghetto that remained purely, utterly Chinese, with its mysterious maze of lanes, exotic sights and strange smells. It was a lawless

Main attractions

BAIYUN TAOIST TEMPLE
CHENXIANGGE NUNNERY
YU GARDEN BAZAAR
HUXINTING TEAHOUSE
YU GARDEN
SHANGHAI OLD STREET
CONFUCIUS TEMPLE
DONGTAI ROAD ANTIQUES MARKET
DONGJIADU CATHEDRAL
MUSEUM OF FOLK ART

LEFT: Yu Bazaar ablaze with lights and lanterns during the annual Lantern Festival.
RIGHT: performance at Yu Bazaar.

It's not uncommmon to see people dressed in their pyjamas on the streets of Shanghai, and especially so in the back lanes of the Old City. The practice dates from the time when only the better off could afford to wear pyjamas; night-clothes thus became a status symbol.

place that foreigners did not dare visit – save the missionaries who came to convert the heathen. For some – like the rebels plotting to overthrow the government, gangsters and criminals – it was a place in which to hide.

Some 2,000 years before foreigners arrived, a small fishing town called Hu already existed on the site of today's Nanshi. Renamed Shanghai in 1280, the original settlement here grew and became rich, although it never gained any historical importance. In the 1550s, Japanese pirate incursions instigated the building of a 4.8km (3-mile) long and 8-metre

(27ft) high wall and a moat enclosing the city. The structure had two watchtowers and six gates that were firmly locked at midnight. The Kuomintang demolished the wall, but its contours still define the 4-sq-km (1½-sq-mile) area of Nanshi. The "walls" today are the high-speed highways of Renmin Road and Zhonghua Road.

ALONG RENMIN ROAD

Just along **Renmin Road**, which today defines the western and northern limits of the Old City, as well as just off it, are several historic sights and temples worth seeing.

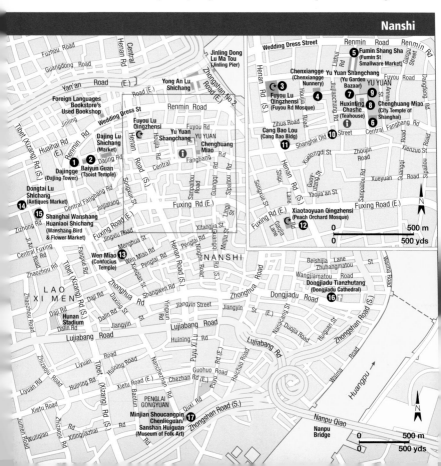

Nanshi

Recommended Restaurants & Cafés on page 151

Dajing Tower ❶
Dàjìnggé 大境阁

✉ 269 Dajing Road (at Renmin Road)
🕐 daily 9am–4pm 💲 RMB 5
🚇 Dashijie

The only remaining section of the city wall makes an ideal entry point to the Old City. **Dajing Tower** is a 1995 recreation of the wall, attached to a refurbished Ming temple – the former War Gods Temple, which was built in 1553. The "Exhibition of the History of Old Shanghai Town", inside the building, is entirely in Chinese, but offers an interesting collection of photographs of life in the old days – its festivals, markets and history, along with a miniature model of the Old City's original layout.

Baiyun Taoist Temple ❷
Báiyún Guàn 白云观

✉ 239 Dajing Road (at Renmin Road)
🕐 daily 8am–4.30pm 💲 RMB 5
🚇 Dashijie

Turn left as you exit Dajing Tower for a look at the **Small North Gate**, the only original city gate still standing.

Just adjacent, the quietness of **Baiyun Taoist Temple**, which dates back to 1873, belies its historical importance for Shanghai's Taoists. In 1882, Taoist monk Xi Zhicheng extended the temple on this site, called Leizu (Ancestor of Thunder). In 1888, when Xi brought over 8,000 scriptures from Beijing's Baiyun Temple, Leizu was renamed Baiyun Temple.

The temple's three halls were built in 1892, but sustained major damage during the Cultural Revolution, including the destruction of its magnificent collection of paintings and scriptures. The restored Baiyun now proudly displays its seven bronze Taoist gods that survived the Cultural Revolution and is once again a functioning temple. Baiyun also serves as the headquarters for Shanghai's Taoist Association, as well as a research centre for Taoist culture.

FUYOU ROAD TO YU GARDEN
Continue south along **Henan Road (S)** and turn right into **Fuyou Road** where a mosque, a nunnery and some bargain shopping are clustered.

Statue of a Chinese deity at the Baiyun Taoist Temple.

BELOW: part of the Old City wall at Dajing Tower.

TIP

Chinese markets are not for the faint-hearted. Not very different from a small zoo, there are live chickens, pigeons, snakes, frogs, turtles, prawns and fish, any of which are killed and cleaned in front of the customer to guarantee freshness.

Fuyou Road Mosque ❸
Fúyòu Lù Qīngzhēnsì
福佑路清真寺

✉ Fuyou Road at Henan Road (S)
ⓒ daily 6am–7pm ⓖ free 🅿 Yuyuan

Right at the junction is **Fuyou Road Mosque**, whch comprises three connecting halls. This is a run-down but still intact Qing-era Chinese courtyard building that was the city's first mosque, built in 1853 by Muslim traders and still used today.

Chenxiangge Nunnery ❹
Chénxiānggé 沉香阁

✉ 29 Chenxiangge Road ⓒ daily 7am–4pm Ⓡ RMB 5 🅿 Yuyuan

Further down Fuyou Road on the right, the vibrant mustard walls of **Chenxiangge Nunnery** indicate Shanghai's largest Buddhist nunnery (entrance around the corner, along Chenxiang Road). Pan Yunduan, who created the Yu Garden, established this temple in honour of his mother in 1600. After a brief interlude as a factory during the Cultural

Revolution, the temple was restored in 1994. Its centrepiece is a gilded Buddha, and there is a collection of 18 gilded *arhats* (Buddhist saints).

Charming back lanes

Heading east on **Fuyou Road** leads to one of the area's prime attractions for shoppers: the **Fuyou Road Merchandise Mart** (Fuyou Lu Shichang) and the **Fumin Street Smallware Market ❺** (Fumin Shang Sha; both daily 8am–5pm). These two warehouse-sized clusters of stores are stocked with what seems like everything under

RIGHT: Taoist statues at Baiyun Temple.
BELOW: Chenxiangge Nunnery dates back to the 1600s.

the sun. China is the world's factory, and these markets seem to sell it all – and at heavily discounted prices too. The range of goods is truly mind-boggling, and combing the market, plus the shops outside the buildings, will take a dedicated shopper hours.

From Fuyou Road, turn right into **Anren Street**, a historic lane where life goes on as it has for centuries, to **Central Fangbang Road**.

Turn left here and follow the street until it becomes a lane lined with 19th-century buildings filled with old apothecaries, pickle stores with gigantic jars, and Shaoxing wine merchants, transporting you into a medieval time warp.

Foodies should take a detour off the street to **Sipailou Road**, lined with some of the city's most delicious street food: from fried noodles, dumplings, kebabs and breads to cotton candy pumped from vintage machines and sugared fruit speared onto sticks.

YU GARDEN AREA

This is the Shanghai of classical gardens and temples, teahouses, bazaars and traditional delicacies. But this is Shanghai, after all, so expect an Old China that is perpetually being reinvented, the bazaars tarted up, the traditional delicacies given creative twists, and the antiques remade.

City Temple of Shanghai ⑥
Chénghuáng Miào 城隍庙

✉ 249 Central Fangbang Road
🕐 daily 8.30am–4.30pm 💰 RMB 10
🚇 Yuyuan

Return along Central Fangbang Road to the **City Temple of Shanghai** (formerly known as the Temple of the Town God), dedicated to the gods that protect Shanghai. Each city in Old China had a town god temple that served as its hub, a place where traders gathered and festivals were celebrated; this tradition continues at the adjoining bazaar. Built in 1726, the Temple of the Town God succeeded the 15th-century Jinshan Miao (Golden Hills Temple) and, like the latter, is dedicated to the legendary general Huo Guang. After it was used as a factory during the Cultural Revolution, images of the general and his Taoist deities have been restored – look out for the ones sporting British bowler hats.

Temple bells are rung on special festival days.

Yu Garden Bazaar ⑦
Yù Yuán Shāngchéng 豫园商城

✉ 218 Anren Street 🕐 daily 7am–late night 🚇 Yuyuan

LEFT: vendor at the Fumin Street Smallware Market.
BELOW: gilded deities at the City Temple of Shanghai (formerly the Temple of the Town God).

The Huixinting Teahouse is supposed to be the subject of the "Blue Willow" pattern plates, first created in 1790 by Josiah Spode during the heyday of the china trade. He based it on an original pattern called the Mandarin.

Exit the temple and turn right to enter **Yu Garden Bazaar** – a bold and brash, vehicle-free, reinvented Ming-era Chinese experience centred around speciality shops and delicious local snacks (but there's Starbucks and Häagen-Dazs too).

Among the bazaar's newly minted Ming-style buildings housing restaurants, food stalls and hundreds of small speciality shops is a labyrinth of lanes, made all the more confusing by the pressing crowds. The central plaza is an endless source of entertainment: toy vendors demonstrate their products, street performers awe the crowds, and tourists bounce along in sedan chair rides – just like in the days of the Old City.

There are larger department stores selling overpriced jewellery and antiques, but the individual speciality shops make for more interesting browsing. A sight to behold are the shops specialising in goods like chopsticks, canes, buttons, fans, kites and scissors. The bustling commerce spills out onto the streets that ring the bazaar, and these are lined with more shops selling everything from Chinese decorations to kitchen equipment.

RIGHT: noodles at Yu Garden Bazaar.
BELOW: delicate Yixing teapots.
BELOW RIGHT: shoppers in Yu Garden Bazaar.

Famous Shanghai snacks

Yu Garden Bazaar is known for its snacks. Follow the signs to **Nanxiang Mantou Dian** *(see page 151),* which is encircled by the most popular food stalls in the bazaar. Domestic tourists line up here for a taste of Shanghai's famous delicacies: the bite-sized, translucent *xiao long bao* (pork dumplings) from Nanxiang, *anchun jiaozi* (sweet glutinous rice pigeon-egg dumplings) and *meimao su*, or eyebrow-shaped shortcakes. The queues for the

Yixing's Tiny Teapots

At the Huixinting Teahouse, waitresses pour tea from the tiny maroon-brown spout of a Yixing teapot, the vessel that tea connoisseurs say brews the finest tea. Made from the purple clay found only in Jiangsu province's Yixing county, the teapots are unglazed, both inside and out, and this porous quality allows it to become seasoned over time from both the colour and flavour of the tea. Usually, only one type of tea is used in a pot to maintain its purity.

The Yixing teapot was first created during the 10th century, and flourished during the Ming dynasty. The tiny teapots were originally created for personal use. During the Ming dynasty, their owners carried around the pocket-sized teapots, and tea would be drunk directly from the spout.

Tea experts say that a quality teapot should be rough, both on the outside and on the inside, make a clear sound when struck, and the tea should pour out from the spout in a smooth arc.

Recommended Restaurants & Cafés on page 151

snacks are almost always worthwhile, but for those who can't be bothered and don't mind paying more, there are Nanshi's famous restaurants. Places such as **Shanghai Classic Restaurant** *(see page 151)*, which has been in business since 1875, and **Green Wave Pavilion** *(see page 151)* all serve the famous snacks along with a menu of Shanghainese dishes – but unless you're there for breakfast, the atmosphere is too much that of a tour-bus stop.

Huxinting Teahouse ❽
Húxīntíng Cháshè 湖心亭茶社

✉ Yuyuan Bazaar, opposite Yu Garden
☏ 6373 6950 🕒 daily 8am–9pm
🚇 Yuyuan

Cross the zigzag **Bridge of Nine Turnings** (Huxinting Qiao) – which seems to have acquired a few more turns over the years. The theory is that evil spirits cannot turn corners, thus protecting **Huxinting Teahouse**, found at the end of the bridge and set in the centre of a man-made lake.

Perhaps because the five-sided teahouse, with its classical pointed roof, has hosted the likes of Queen Elizabeth and Bill Clinton, a cup of tea here costs RMB 50. Still, sipping delicate Chinese tea from a Yixing teacup on the second floor, to views of willows and the tops of the trees in Yu Garden, is a rare experience. If you prefer a caffeine-free version, opt for one of the flower teas (like the fairy jasmine). Most tourists get a thrill when they see the flowers unfurling after hot water is poured into the glass teapot.

Yu Garden ❾ Yù Yuán 豫园

✉ Yuyuan Bazaar, opposite Huxinting Teahouse; entrance also at 218 Anren Street 🕒 daily 8.30am–5.30pm 🎫 RMB 40 🚇 Yuyuan

At the centre of the bazaar is Shanghai's most famous garden, the 16th-century **Yu Garden**. Referred to in local maps and literature as Yuyuan Garden, it occupies the northern part of the Old City. The garden was built in 1577 by Ming dynasty official Pan Yunduan to please his elderly father – "Yu" means peace and comfort. After years of neglect,

The Bridge of Nine Turnings that leads to Huxinting Teahouse.

BELOW: rock gardens and pavilions at the Yu Garden.

TIP

Unfortunately, Yu Garden is often invaded by huge tourist groups with loudspeaker-blasting guides, crowding what is meant to be a space for quiet contemplation. To avoid this, visit at 8.30am, when the gardens open.

RIGHT: porcelain statues on sale at Yu Garden Bazaar.
BELOW: Shanghai Old Street (Shanghai Laojie).
BELOW RIGHT: cheap shoes for sale on Shanghai Old Street.

the garden was restored in the mid-18th century.

Yu Garden, its walls encircled by an undulating dragon, is a petite 2-hectare (5-acre) classical Suzhou-style garden that has all the ingredients that create a microcosm of the universe – the defining hallmark of the classical Chinese garden. It has 30 pavilions connected by bridges and walkways, and interspersed with fishpools, rockeries and ingenious views.

The **Grand Rockery** (Dajiashan), a 2,000-tonne gigantic sculpture of pale yellow rocks from Zhejiang province, stands 14 metres (46ft) tall as the centrepiece of the garden, with the best views from the aptly named **Hall for Viewing Grand Rockery** (Dajiashan Tang) that stands just opposite the rocks.

On the garden's east side is the enormous **Exquisite Jade Rock** (Yu Ling Long), acquired by the Pan family when the boat carrying the rock to the emperor in Beijing sank off the coast of Shanghai. Also on this side is the **Hall of Heralding Spring** (Dianchun Tang), which in the early

1850s served as the headquarters of the Small Swords Society, the local branch of the Taiping rebels. A small museum in the hall recounts the Taiping Rebellion, now embraced by the Communist government as China's first large-scale peasant uprising.

Shanghai Old Street ❿
Shànghǎi Lǎojiē 上海老街

✉ Central Fangbang Road at Henan Road (S) 🕐 shops open daily 8am–6pm 🚇 Yuyuan

Exit the bazaar the same way you came, and continue down Central Fangbang Road to **Shanghai Old Street**, which runs for a section along Central Fangbang Road, east of Henan Road, and ends roughly at

Recommended Restaurants & Cafés on page 151

Anren Street. The street is lined with two-storey buildings that progress architecturally from the Ming to the Qing and to the Kuomintang eras. The shops sell traditional Chinese-themed souvenirs: the famous "purple clay" Yixing teapots, Chinese lanterns and crafts, tea blends, temple paraphernalia and antiques.

Also on this street is the retro **Old Shanghai Teahouse** (Lao Shanghai Chaguan) at 385 Fangbang Road *(see page 151)*, where you can capture the soul of Old Shanghai over a leisurely cup of tea, sipped amidst surroundings filled with historical maps, pictures and collectables.

Cang Bao Building ⑪
Cáng Bǎo Lóu 藏宝楼

✉ 459 Fangbang Road ⓒ daily 5am–5pm 🚇 Yuyuan

Close to the junction of Central Fangbang Road and Henan Road is **Cang Bao Building**. The five-storey building with the Chinese roof, the tallest structure in the area, is fairly quiet on weekdays, but turns into a lively antiques market at weekends.

Then, as early as 5am, traders begin laying out their wares on the top floor, and shop owners from all over the city begin jamming the aisles.

The Cang Bao Building is a successor to the former Fuyou Road Sunday "ghost" market and still has that street market feel to it; most of the "antiques" are obviously scrounged from homes and have more sentimental than antique value. Even if you don't buy anything, just browsing gives an insight into Old Shanghai. This is especially true on the fourth floor, where vendors sell relics from the Concession era, such as monogrammed cutlery from the old clubs, factory cards, photographs from the old studios, rare books – some from old Shanghai libraries – and Cultural Revolution memorabilia.

The third-floor furniture corner has a good supply of Shanghai Art Deco pieces from the 1920s and 1930s, including fixtures such as doorknobs, while the first and second floors have smaller collectables, including vintage clocks, watches and genuine Shanghai advertising posters from the 1930s.

Settle down with a cup of tea at Old Shanghai Teahouse (see left) and enjoy its collection of memorabilia.

BELOW: ethnic pottery at Cang Bao Lou.

Statue of Confucius at the temple named after him.

BELOW: Peach Orchard Mosque caters to Shanghai's minority Muslim population.

Peach Orchard Mosque ⑫
Xiǎotáoyuán Qīngzhēnsì
小桃园清真寺

✉ 52 Xiaotaoyuan Road ⏱ daily 8am–7pm ⓒ free 🚇 Yuyuan

Turn right as you exit Cang Bao Building, head west across busy Henan Road and then south across Fuxing Road (E) to **Peach Orchard Mosque**, where Shanghai's Chinese Muslim community, the Hui people, worship. The mosque, with its distinctive green spheres on the roof, was built in 1917 and renovated in 1925, but is surprisingly modernist with its restrained fusion of Arabic, Western and Chinese architecture. Look out for the round Art Deco windows more frequently seen in the French Concession area.

Confucius Temple ⑬
Wén Miào 文庙

✉ 215 Wen Miao Road ⏱ daily 9am–4.30pm ⓒ RMB 10 🚇 Laoximan

Students – and their anxious parents – still pray at the **Confucius Temple**, just south of the Peach Orchard Mosque, especially during "black June", the time of the gruelling three-day college entrance exams. As Confucius is the patron of scholars, the literary theme is strong here.

Of note are the **God of Literature Pavilion** (Kui Xing), with its Chinese arched roof, and the **Respecting Classics Tower** (Zunjing), a library for Chinese classics that also served as the state library during the Kuomintang period, and a lecture hall. The last served a less than literary purpose during the Taiping Rebellion as the headquarters of the rebels' Shanghai branch, the Small Swords Society.

The origins of the temple date back to the 13th century, but what you mostly see is an 1855 reconstruction. Its relatively new sheen comes from more recent renovations after its destruction by the Red Guards during the Cultural Revolution years. The literary theme continues in an informal Sunday book market, adjacent to the temple in a courtyard surrounded by recreated temple buildings.

Recommended Restaurants & Cafés on page 151

BEYOND NANSHI

South of Nanshi is an area undergoing change from 1970s housing blocks to modern high-rises. Scattered here and there are unexpected gems well worth seeking out, like a 19th-century Spanish church and a delightful museum devoted to Chinese folk art.

Dongtai Road Antiques Market ⑭ Dōngtái Lù Shìchǎng 东台路市场

✉ Dongtai Road at Liuhekou Road
🕒 daily 10am–5pm 🚇 Renmin Square + taxi

Take a brief detour out of the Old City – yet stay within its spirit – at the **Dongtai Road Antiques Market**. Located west of Nanshi, this is Shanghai's biggest antiques market, with 100 booths as well as two-storey shophouses, all selling a mix of genuine antiques and pure kitsch, including fresh-from-the-factory repros of china figurines depicting Cultural Revolution-era heroes.

A delightful stop is **Store No. 107**, which specialises in vintage lighting fixtures, many from grand houses and restaurants that have since been torn down. Garrulous owner Zhi Zhong Pan and his wife, who only speak Chinese, have one of the city's best collections of lights and Concession-era memorabilia (the Shanghai Museum has its eye on several pieces).

Shanghai Wanshang Bird & Flower Market ⑮ Shànghǎi Wànshāng Huāniǎo Shìchǎng 上海万商花鸟市场

✉ Dongtai Road 🕒 daily 8am–5pm
🚇 Renmin Square + taxi

Shanghai's increasing wealth has meant a proportionate increase in luxury items – such as pets. An entire menagerie of animals are sold on the eastern side of Dongtai Road at the **Shanghai Wanshang Bird & Flower Market**. The covered pet section is stocked with puppies, kittens, rabbits, hamsters and pot-bellied pigs, and a good selection of birds and impressive handmade cages.

During the summer cricket season, an entire segment is devoted to the chirping insects – valued either for their singing prowess or fighting skills.

Songbirds, Wanshang Market.

BELOW LEFT: Dongtai Road Antiques Market.
BELOW: crickets for sale at Shanghai Wanshang Market.

Confession booth at Dongjiadu Cathedral.

Keeping crickets as pets is a tradition that goes back to the Tang dynasty. These critters are kept in special containers made from ceramic or bamboo. It's not uncommon to see grown men hunched over these creatures, coaxing them to either shrill merrily or to do battle with other crickets.

Dongjiadu Cathedral ⓰
Dǒngjiādù Tiānzhǔtáng
董家渡天主堂

✉ 185 Dongjiadu Road   ☎ 6378 7214   🕐 Services: Mon–Sat 7am, Sun 6am, 8am   🚇 Laoximen

The southeast quadrant of the Old City is a wasteland of ugly government-built apartments and razed construction scdites. Thus, coming upon the beautiful **Dongjiadu Cathedral** is all the more surprising. The Moorish Baroque church, built by the Spanish Jesuits in 1853 and originally called St Xavier Cathedral, was Shanghai's first Catholic church. Restored in 2007, it is still an active church, holding daily mass in Chinese at 7am, with two services on Sunday at 6 and 8am.

RIGHT: Museum of Folk Art.
BELOW: altar and sacristy at Dongjiadu Cathedral.

Museum of Folk Art ⓱
Mínjiān Shōucángpǐn
Chénlièguǎn/Sānshān Huìguǎn
民间收藏品陈列馆/三山会馆

✉ 1551 Zhongshan Road (S)
☎ 6313 5582   🕐 daily 9am–4pm
💲 free   🚇 Xizang Nan Lu

Shanghai has an estimated 100,000 collectors, and many of these exhibit their often arcane collections at the **Museum of Folk Art**. Past exhibitions here have included butterflies, tiny shoes for bound feet, cigarette labels from the 1930s, school badges and ship models. The Chinese-style museum building with its carved beams and upturned roofs is worth a visit on its own. Built in 1909 as the Sanshan Guild Hall (Sanshan Huiguan) with funds raised by a Shanghai-based Fujian fruit dealer, the hall is the only remaining one of several Chinese-style structures that used to line this area. ❏

BEST RESTAURANTS AND CAFÉS

Chinese

Green Wave Pavilion
绿波廊
✉ 115 Yuyuan Road (in Yu Garden); www.lubolang.com
☎ 6328 0602 ⏰ daily 7am–12.30am. $$ [p323, C3]
Dim sum, particularly the signature crabmeat dumplings, are the speciality at this Yu Garden fixture. Located next to the historic Huxinting Teahouse and the lake. The state-run restaurant has hosted heads of state and the crowned heads of Europe, from Queen Elizabeth II to the Clintons and Fidel Castro.

Nanxiang Mantou Dian
南翔馒头店
✉ 85 Yuyuan Road (in Yu Garden) ☎ 6355 4206 ⏰ daily 7am–8pm. $ [p323, C3]
Long lines attest to the reputation of Nanxiang's dumplings, a favourite of the late *New York Times* reviewer Johnny Apple. Situated opposite Huxinting Teahouse, the restaurant's signature *xiao long bao* (bite-sized dumplings filled with pork or crabmeat), and a scalding hot soup, are among the best anywhere – with tender skins and succulent fillings. If you want to skip the queue, head for the air-conditioned third floor, where reservations

can be made with a minimum spend of RMB 60 per person.

Shanghai Classic Restaurant
上海老饭店
✉ 242 Fuyou Road; www.laofandian.com ☎ 6355 2275 ⏰ daily L & D. $$ [p322, C3]
It has been operating since 1875, and this has given it plenty of time to perfect the classic Shanghai dishes it does so well. Now located on the second floor of a hotel just outside the Yu Garden complex, its famous dishes include red-cooked Hui fish, eight-treasure duck (stuffed with a mix of glutinous rice and eight ingredients including dates, mushrooms and chicken) and braised river shrimp.

Food Street

Sipailou Road
四牌楼路
⏰ daily 7am–6pm. [p323, C4]
Small restaurants and makeshift stalls line Sipailou Road, selling everything from peanut candy, pounded in front of you, to fresh hand-pulled noodles, Xinjiang lamb sandwiches and bread, *xiao long bao* dumplings and fresh sugarcane

juice. The best approach: wander from stall to stall, like the locals, snacking and tasting.

Teahouses

Huxinting Teahouse
湖心亭
✉ 257 Yuyuan Road (in Yu Garden) ☎ 6373 6950 ⏰ daily 7am–7pm. $ [p323, C3]
A classic Old China teahouse offering a variety of teas as well as snacks, all of which is rather expensive given what it is. The tables upstairs offer beautiful views of the willows and treetops of Yu Garden, just opposite.

Old Shanghai Teahouse
老上海茶馆老菜馆
✉ 385 Central Fangbang Road ☎ 5382 1202 ⏰ daily 9am–6pm. $ [p323, C4]
This second-floor teahouse, overlooking Shanghai Old Street, is a nostalgic slice of Old Shanghai. The owner's museum-quality collection

of Shanghai memorabilia is on display – his *qipao* (cheongsam) collection is especially notable – and the menu includes a wide range of Chinese teas as well as coffees.

Xianmingju
仙名茗居
✉ 249 Central Fangbang Road (inside the City Temple of Shanghai) ☎ 6320 1008 ⏰ daily 8.30am–5.30pm. $ [p323, C3]
Xianmingju has a unique location inside the City Temple of Shanghai, and a pretty Old China setting, furnished with Qing-era wooden furniture. The tea prices are too high for locals, so the teahouse is usually empty, making it a nice spot for a quiet break from this buzzing area.

Prices for a three-course meal for two people, excluding drinks:

$ = under RMB 250
$$ = RMB 250–500
$$$ = RMB 500–800
$$$$ = over RMB 800

RIGHT: dumplings at Nanxiang Mantou Dian.

FUXING PARK AND ENVIRONS

The streets of the French Concession, where ideological idols like Sun Yat-sen and Zhou En-lai once lived, still hold treasures of its elegant past in the form of old churches and mansions. Many have been turned into restaurants and nightspots

I n Old Shanghai, it was said, the British in the International Settlement would teach you how to do business, but in the French Concession, you would be taught how to live. That remains true in the well-preserved area surrounding Fuxing Park, the old heart of the **French Concession** that is today the soul of the city's good life. Lucien Bodard's description in *Les Français de Shanghai* still rings true: "A charming residential area dotted with imposing villas and large avenues with their venerated names... sidewalk cafés, boutiques with the latest styles, nightclubs... French savoir faire, elegance and gentility reigned supreme in the Concession."

The reality today is not much different. One of the most expensive districts in the city, the Fuxing Park neighbourhood continues to attract high-living sybarites of all nationalities, clustered into an area that boasts the city's largest concentrations of luxury shopping and stylish dining within an urban landscape of refurbished historic buildings, sleek high-rises and *longtang* (lane) housing. There's a bit of an edge here, as well, contributed by its legacy of revolution that came from a time when the

French Concession was a lawless place that allowed rebellion to brew.

AROUND XINTIANDI

Around 12 minutes on foot south from People's Square and just off Central Huaihai Road is **Xintiandi**, the city's first adaptive re-use project – in architecture speak – of an old *longtang* (lane) neighbourhood. Since its opening in 2001, Xintiandi has quicky become the city's premier shopping and entertainment hub and the model copied around the country.

Main attractions
XINTIANDI
SHIKUMEN OPEN HOUSE MUSEUM
FUXING PARK
FORMER RESIDENCE OF
  SUN YAT-SEN
TIANZI FANG
RUIJIN GUESTHOUSE
SHANGHAI ARTS AND CRAFTS
  MUSEUM
OKURA GARDEN HOTEL
JINJIANG HOTEL

LEFT: alleyway off Taikang Road.
RIGHT: Xintiandi at night.

Xintiandi ❶ 新天地

✉ 2 blocks bounded by Taicang, Zizhong, Madang and Huangpi (S) roads; www.xintiandi.com 🚇 South Huangpi Road

All taxi drivers in Shanghai will know **Xintiandi** (meaning New Heaven and Earth), a two-block area of refurbished *shikumen* houses that is one of the city's most popular restaurant-bar-entertainment complexes. *See also page 89 and photo feature on pages 168–9.*

Xintiandi's buildings offer a clutch of gourmet restaurants, haute couture boutiques and a modern cinema. Brand names fill the old houses, like sophisticated fusion restaurant T8, Shanghai Tang's brightly coloured modern interpretations of traditional Chinese designs and even a Vidal Sassoon salon. Don't expect much authencity though; some of the structures are new and in all the houses, the insides have been gutted and only the grey brick facades have been retained. But without a doubt, Xintiandi has almost single-handedly made lane houses cool again.

Site of the First National Congress of the Communist Party of China ❷ Zhōnggòng Yīdàhuìzhǐ 中共一大会址

✉ 76 Xingye Road (between the 2 blocks of Xintiandi) ☎ 5383 2171 🕐 daily 9am–4pm 🎟 free; limit of 2,000 visitors per day 🚇 South Huangpi Road

TIP

Taxis are plentiful around Shanghai except when it's raining. The best solution in wet weather is to get in line at a hotel or shopping centre taxi rank. Taxi lines may be long, but at least you're assured of a taxi at the end. For those who can't be bothered to wait, the metro is the next best option.

RIGHT: wax figure tableau at the site of the First National Congress of the CCP.

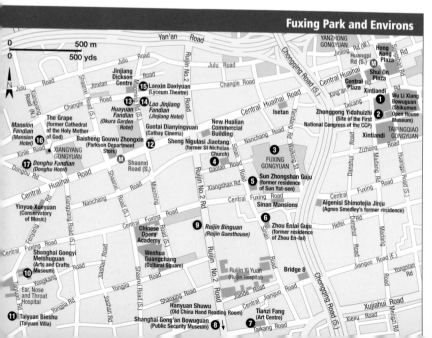

Xintiandi exists because the developers could not build higher than the Communist Revolution's most famous legacy: a 19th-century brick lane house that was the home of delegate Li Hanjun. It was here, in 1921, that the Communist Party of China was formed. The table around which the 13 delegates, including a young Mao Zedong, held their first secret Congress, is set with 13 stools and 13 teacups, as if waiting for the return of the delegates. Although that first Congress wasn't completed here – the delegates fled on the eighth day when news of the illegal gathering reached the ears of the French Concession's gendarmes – this remains one of Chinese Communism's most sacred sites.

An adjacent exhibition hall recounts the history of the Chinese Communist Party, with grainy pictures of the original delegates, film clips showing the horrors of the capitalist treatment of workers, some of the finest Concession-era artefacts in the city, and a dramatic wax-figure tableau of the first Congress. The gift shop has a selection of postcards, photographs, books, Mao buttons and pins with the iconic image of the First Party Congress building.

Shikumen Open House Museum Wū Lǐ Xiāng Bówùguǎn 屋里厢博物馆

✉ Lane 181 Taicang Lu, House 25
☎ 3307 0337 ⏰ Sun–Thur 10.30am–10.30pm, Fri–Sat 11pm–11pm
⊙ RMB 20 🚇 South Huangpi Road

Also located in Xintiandi, this small museum recreates the interior of an authentic lane house, also known as *shikumen* (the name refers specifically to its stone-framed entrance). Containing photographs and models, it's a fitting memorial to the hundreds of old houses surrounding Xintiandi that were felled to create the adjacent lake and this sprawling development.

AROUND FUXING PARK

To the west of Xintiandi past Chongqing Road is **Yandang Road**, a pleasant walking street lined with modern Chinese restaurants as well as Italian ice cream parlour **La Perla**, at No. 21. This is the best way to access the sights around Fuxing Park.

Xintiandi is a favourite photo stop for couples on their wedding day.

BELOW: a recreated study room at the Shikumen Open House Museum.

Marx and Engels immortalised in granite at Fuxing Park.

Fuxing Park ❸ Fùxīng Gōngyuán 复兴公园

✉ 2A Gaolan Road; entrances also on Yandang Road and Central Fuxing Road ⏰ daily 6am–6pm ⓔ free 🚇 South Shanxi Road + taxi

Laid out by the French in 1909 and originally known as the French Park, **Fuxing Park** – which served briefly as a Japanese parade ground – honours its heritage with European landscaping, albeit interspersed with Communist symbols. Statues of Karl Marx and Friedrich Engels smile benevolently upon the carnival of Chinese martial arts, aerobics, sword play, ballroom dance and t'ai chi exercises that awaken the park at dawn each day. In front of the children's playground is **Park 97** (entrance at 2 Gaolan Road), a collection of hip restaurants and nightspots.

Former St Nicholas Church ❹ Shèng Nígǔlāsī Jiàotáng 圣尼古拉斯教堂

Exit the park on Gaolan Road and cross Sinan Road to the former Rus-

sian Orthodox **St Nicholas Church**. Today it is a business address, but back in its heyday, this elaborate jewel of a church was frequently used for weddings, and served the White Russians who flooded Shanghai after the 1917 Russian Revolution.

The figure of Christ, surrounded by 12 apostles, no longer graces its onion-shaped domes, nor are the four patron saints of Moscow on its four walls. Even the portrait of Chairman Mao on the entrance facade, painted during the Cultural Revolution to protect the church

RIGHT: Former St Nicholas Church.
BELOW: singing practice in session at Fuxing Park.

from desecration, disappeared during the 2004 renovation.

Former Residence of Sun Yat-sen ❺ Sūn Zhōngshān Gùjū 孙中山故居

✉ 7 Xiangshan Road; www.sh-sunyat-sen.com/e1.htm 📞 6437 2954
🕒 daily 9am–4.30pm; guided tours Mon–Fri 10.30am, 2pm, 3pm
🎫 RMB 8 🚇 South Shanxi Road

South along Sinan Road, just one block away, is the **Former Residence of Sun Yat-sen**. The Kuomintang Party that Sun established in 1905 sought to replace the ailing Qing dynasty with democratic leadership, and finally succeeded in 1911. Considered the father of modern China, Sun – who has the distinction of being the only political figure revered by Chinese both in Taiwan and the mainland – lived here with his wife Soong Ching Ling from 1918–24.

The taped introduction of the tour reveals a China on the brink of modernity. Among the plush Chinese carpets, artwork and gleaming blackwood furniture – all supposedly originals despite the house having been looted by the Japanese – is a 1924 picture of Sun and Soong in front of the first aeroplane in China.

Sinan Mansions
Sī nán gōng guǎn 思南路 近复
This new lifestyle hub in the Xintiandi mould features a series of restaurants (California Pizza Kitchen, Boxing Cat Brewery) and shops linked by outdoor piazzas, the Hotel Massent, condominiums and office space, and vintage-style villas (some historic, some exact replicas).

Former Residence of Zhou En-lai ❻ Zhōu Enlái Gùjū 周恩来故居

✉ 73 Sinan Road 📞 6473 0420
🕒 daily 9.30am–4pm 🎫 RMB 2
🚇 South Shanxi Road

Tree-shaded Sinan Road, lined with houses that are inspired by a dozen different architectural styles, is also the site of the **former Residence of Zhou En-lai**. This is where Zhou, the first prime minister of the People's Republic of China, lived in 1946 when he was head of the Shanghai branch of the Communist Party.

The house, a Spanish-style villa, is simply furnished, with most of it devoted to the underground revolution. Communist newspapers were produced on the second floor, and the third floor housed a dormitory for comrades who needed a safe house. From the porch, the Kuomintang surveillance house across the road that kept a constant watch on Zhou is visible.

In a separate building, an exhibition hall documents Zhou's life; a statue of the young Zhou with fresh flower offerings at his feet is a testament to his status as one of China's best-loved leaders.

SOUTH & WEST OF FUXING PARK

South of Fuxing Park are a number of sights that are fairly dispersed.

Sun Yat-sen statue at his former Shanghai residence. Sun is regarded as the father of modern China.

BELOW:
Sun Yat-sen lived here from 1918 to 1924.

TIP

If you like what you see at the Tianzi Fang, be sure to visit the very happening M50 arts enclave at 50 Moganshan Road *(see pages 219 and 222–3),* just north of Suzhou Creek.

ABOVE: potter at work at his Taikang Road studio.
BELOW: traditional Chinese garments in the Feel Shanghai store on Taikang Road.

There is contemporary cutting-edge art at Taikang Road but also old-world charm at the Ruijin Guesthouse and Taiyuan Villa.

Tianzi Fang ❼ 田子坊

Sinan Road continues south until it intersects with **Taikang Road**. This is where a number of shabby-chic old warehouses and factories have been turned into an arts space hosting a collection of funky galleries, boutiques, restaurants and shops. The area is anchored by a 3,200-sq-metre (34,445-sq-ft) former candy factory that now serves as the studios of several creative shops like **L'Atelier Mandarine** and **Jooi Design** (both at

No. 3, Lane 210). Well-known photographer Deke Erh also has a gallery here, the **Shanghai Deke Erh Centre** (Erh Dongqiang Zhongxin) at No. 2 Lane 210.

The nearby artsy quarter known as **Bridge 8**, located in an old auto repair centre on Jianguo Road, at No. 8, pulls in a more bohemian crowd with its design stores, creative companies and stylish cafés.

Shaoxing Road Shàoxīng Lù 绍兴路

Past **Ruijin Hospital** (Ruijin Yi Yuan) at 197 Ruijin No. 2 Road, one of the city's major hospitals, which is set in the tranquil grounds of the former French Aurora University, is charming **Shaoxing Road**. A short walk along the road leads to the antique-filled atmospheric salon of the photographer Deke Erh, the **Old China Hand Reading Room** (Hanyuan Shuwu) at 27 Shaoxing Road (tel: 6473 2626). This is a good place to browse through architecture books; particularly apt is *Last Look*, which is part of a series on Old Shanghai architecture photographed by Erh and written by the noted Shanghai architectural historian Tess Johnston. Directly opposite, at No. 90, is a leather studio called Shu, where bags and shoes in every imaginable colour are skilfully handmade by local artisans.

At No. 25 is the cosy **Vienna Café** *(see page 167),* which serves delicious Austrian delights and holds film

viewings on Thursday evenings. Walk down the road a little further to find the **OV Gallery**, at No. 19. Artists who have exhibited here include Harbin native Zhang Dali, whose depictions of migrant workers can be found in the Saatchi Gallery in London. A few doors down, at No. 9, the **Shanghai Kunju Opera Troupe** can often be heard rehearsing. To sneak a peek, ask to go to the second floor.

Shanghai Public Security Museum ⑧ Shànghǎi Gōng'ān Bówùguǎn 上海公安博物馆

✉ 518 Ruijin No. 2 Road ☎ 6472 0256 ⊙ Mon–Sat 9am–4.30pm ⊙ RMB 8

At the southern end of Ruijin No. 2 Road is the **Shanghai Public Security Museum**, which crime connoisseurs will revel in. See the wax figure of a red-turbaned Sikh guard and a pistol with a gold folding handle that crime boss "Pockmark" Huang once carried, as well as a selection of photographs and artefacts that offer glimpses of Shanghai's evil under-

belly – including pornographic porcelain vases and hand-painted courtesan's cards. The exhibits at this three-floor museum can be gruesome but are always fascinating.

Ruijin Guesthouse ⑨ Ruìjīn Bīnguǎn 瑞金宾馆

✉ 118 Ruijin No. 2 Road ☎ 6472 5222 ⊙ South Shanxi Road

Further north the busy traffic choking Ruijin No. 2 Road yields to the sprawling lawns and grand manor houses of the **Ruijin Guesthouse**, the former Morriss estate. H.E. Morriss Jr, son of the founder-owner of the *North China Daily News*, built the

Office buildings near Xintandi

LEFT: Shanghai Public Security Museum.
BELOW: the old lanes off Taikang Road.

Red Shanghai

Few people associate Communism with brash and business-minded Shanghai, but this is where the Red Revolution started

Shanghai's capitalist veneer may belie her Communist soul, but make no mistake, the city's Communist legacy is something her citizens are extremely proud of. After all, this is where Chinese Communism was born, and where the beginnings of the revolution were shaped. This was where many of Shanghai's Communist luminaries lived and worked. To ensure that Prada doesn't eclipse the Party, the government has started a "red tourism" campaign, focused on sites that were key to the birth of New China, identifying some 20 sites of interest across the city.

Visiting these places offers an interesting insight into contemporary Chinese history, and to the importance of Shanghai in the growth and shaping of the Chinese Communist Party. It also serves as a reminder that despite outward appearances, Communism remains a force in modern Shanghai.

No one seems to see anything contradictory about this unholy marriage between the brashly capitalist and communist. Perhaps this is because Chinese Communism was born in a consumerist paradise; indeed, Shanghai has always produced some of the best of both breeds – from real estate tycoons to the radical Gang of Four.

Red tourism in Shanghai begins with the Site of the First National Congress of the Communist Party of China *(page 154)*, a must-stop on domestic tours. But there are plenty more – like the Longhua Martyrs Cemetery *(page 197)*, where hundreds of young Communists were rounded up and executed by the Kuomintang troops. Of interest too are the homes of the men and women who led China's revolutionary struggle: names familiar outside of China, such as Sun Yat-sen *(page 157)*, Zhou En-lai *(page 157)*, Soong Ching Ling *(page 174)* and even a young Chairman Mao, who lived in Shanghai with his wife and two sons before embarking on the Long March. There are also names that are famous only within China, such as Chen Yun and Cai Yuanpei *(page 189)*.

There are charming little finds, such as the offices of the *Bolshevik* newspaper, and the League of Left Wing Writers Museum *(page 217)*, which celebrates the writers who articulated and agitated the ideas of revolution. There is the memorial hall to Lu Xun *(page 219)*, whose writing inspired a generation of revolutionaries. There are statues scattered around town: Chen Yi *(page 115)*, the marshal who liberated Shanghai and later became the city's first mayor after the Communist victory, on the Bund; and Nie E'r, the composer of the national anthem, on Central Huaihai Road. There are sites of famous events, such as Aomen Road, where the May 30th Movement began, as well as more obscure ones. It's a very different side to Shanghai – but one well worth exploring. ❏

LEFT AND ABOVE: symbols of Chinese Communism.

Recommended Restaurants & Cafés on pages 166–7

estate with its four villas in 1928. An avid horse and greyhound breeder and racer, Morriss would walk his greyhounds through a back door in the estate and out directly to the greyhound race track, the Canidrome (which was demolished in 2006).

Building 3 of Ruijin Guesthouse, which houses the **Art Deco Garden Bar & Café** (tel: 6472 5222), has a magnificent piece of stained glass depicting a tiger in a jungle. It is Shanghai's only surviving piece of stained glass from the Siccawei (Xujiahui) Orphanage glass workshop – the rest were smashed to bits during the Cultural Revolution. The Morrisses lived well until the very end; the date on the stained glass is 1949 and the last Morriss lived out his years in the estate's gatehouse.

Maoming Road (S)
Màomíng Nán Lù 茂名南路

Leaving the Ruijin Guesthouse by the Maoming Road gate takes one to a charming street full of restaurants and cafés. This was one the heart of Shanghai nightlife. Today, even old-time favourite **Blue Frog** at No. 207–6 *(see page 167)* is a tamer haunt.

North of Central Huaihai Road, however, Maoming Road (S) takes on a completely different and more genteel character *(see page 162)*.

Shanghai Arts and Crafts Museum ⑩ **Shànghǎi Gōngyì Měishùguǎn 上海工艺美术馆**

✉ 79 Fenyang Road ☎ 6437 0509
🕙 daily 8.30am–4.30pm 💲 RMB 8
🚇 Changshu Road

Set in lush grounds, the **Shanghai Arts and Crafts Museum** is housed in a grand whitewashed mansion, its curved façade reminiscent of the American White House. It was originally designed by Czech architect Ladislau Hudec in 1905 for the director of the French Compagnie des Tramways. At one point, it was

also the home of Shanghai's first mayor, Chen Yi. Today, it has been converted into a fine museum.

Downstairs is the museum's collection of dying traditional crafts – bamboo, jade, ivory, embroidery, costumes, snuff bottles and paper lanterns – while upstairs, visitors can see the artisans at work.

Taiyuan Villa ⑪ **Tàiyuán Biéshù 太原别墅**

✉ 160 Taiyuan Road ☎ 6471 6688
🚇 Hengshan Road + taxi

A five-minute walk south from the museum, past the Shanghai Ear, Nose and Throat Hospital, is **Taiyuan Villa**. This mansard-roofed mansion looks as if it should be set in the rolling countryside of France.

Built for the Comte du Pac de Marsoulies in the 1920s, it was General George C. Marshall's residence – when it became known as Marshall House – while he was trying to broker a last-minute deal between the Communists and the Kuomintang. During the Cultural Revolution years, the house was taken over by

Strolling along Maoming Road.

BELOW: a crafts demonstration at the Shanghai Arts and Crafts Museum.

Taiyuan Villa has been home to the likes of General George C. Marshall as well as Mao Zedong's wife. Today, it has been turned into a guesthouse.

BELOW: a mall poster along Central Huaihai Road – one of Shanghai's most popular shopping strips.

Mao Zedong's infamous wife, Jiang Qing. It was later turned into a guest-house and a new wing was added together with a swimming pool. But the interior of the old house was kept intact, including the spiralling wrought-iron staircase, dark wood panelling and the Comte's coat of arms in the fireplace. The villa now houses **Roosevelt Steak House**.

CENTRAL HUAIHAI ROAD AND NORTH

Head back north on Shaanxi Road (S) to **Central Huaihai Road**. One of Shanghai's major streets, Huaihai Road cuts an east–west swathe through the city and is one of Shanghai's most popular shopping strips, with stores such as Tiffany, Apple, Uniqlo and the Sony Gallery as well as big department stores like **Parkson**, Japanese giant **Isetan** and IT mall **Hong Kong Plaza**.

Also on this strip (roughly between Isetan and Ruijin No. 2 Road) are a number of wedding boutiques (see box opposite), displaying flamboyant bridal and ball gowns in a range of colours and styles to suit the fickle bride-to-be's every desire.

Cathay Cinema ⑫ Guótài Diànyǐngyuàn 国泰电影院

✉ 870 Central Huaihai Road at Maoming Road (S) ☎ 5403 2980
🚇 Shanxi Road (S)

North of Central Huaihai Road, **Maoming Road (S)** takes on a more rarefied and genteel air, as typified by a clutch of old-world buildings. The first building of note is the Art Deco **Cathay Cinema**, at the corner of Central Huaihai Road and Maoming (S) Road. This lovely Art Deco classic opened in 1932. Part of the real-estate moghul Victor Sassoon's empire (which included the nearby Cathay Mansions and Grosvenor House, along with the Peace Hotel on the Bund), the cinema showed Hollywood movies in its heyday; today it screens both Hollywood and Chinese fare.

Okura Garden Hotel ⑬ Huāyuán Fàndiàn 花园饭店

✉ 58 Maoming Road (S); www.garden
hotelshanghai.com ☎ 6415 1111

Recommended Restaurants & Cafés on pages 166–7

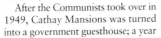 Shanxi Road (S)

Further up Maoming Road (S), on the left, is the **Okura Garden Hotel**. With its spreading lawns and cool fountains, it is a welcome oasis after the buzz of Huaihai. The original entrance lobby (on the Maoming Road side) of this **former Cercle Sportif Français**, or French Club, still features the glittering gold mosaic, polished marble columns and a dramatic stairway, all designed in 1926 by the French Concession's master architect, Paul Veysseyre.

The Cercle Sportif Français – which once had 20 lawn tennis courts, an indoor pool, a rooftop terrace for dancing and a ballroom with a stained-glass ceiling that is still intact – became Mao Zedong's private retreat on his Shanghai trips, before its conversion into a hotel in 1982. This could be the reason why the Grecian nudes holding up the ballroom lobby's columns were not destroyed during the Cultural Revolution but were merely covered up.

There is no doubt that Mao was definitely the reason for the eight-room reinforced concrete bunker, built in case of a nuclear attack. The bunker – the entrance of which is found in the inconspicuous garden shed by the fountain and is usually locked – connects to the old Jinjiang Hotel (Lao Jinjiang Fandian) across the street.

Jinjiang Hotel ⑭ Lǎo
Jǐnjiāng Fàndiàn 老锦江饭店

✉ 59 Maoming Road (S); www.jinjiang hotels.com ☎ 6258 2582 🚇 Shanxi Road (S)

There are several buildings at this site, chief of which is the historical **Jinjiang Hotel** (not to be confused with the new Jinjiang Towers). The brainchild of Jewish tycoon Victor Sassoon, the Jinjiang – formerly called **Cathay Mansions** – was a risky investment when he commissioned the British firm Arnhold & Company to build it in 1928. It was the first high-rise to be built on swampy ground, and there was no guarantee that downtown sophisticates would want to live in what was then the countryside. As it turned out, Cathay Mansions was so successful that Sassoon built two more housing complexes on the premises, the **Grosvenor House** (now luxury apartments and an all-suite hotel) and the low-rise **Grosvenor Gardens**, now converted into offices.

After the Communists took over in 1949, Cathay Mansions was turned into a government guesthouse; a year

The famous Grecian nudes on the ballroom columns at the Okura Garden Hotel.

LEFT: part of Okura Garden Hotel was the French Club during the Concession days.
BELOW: a bridal shoot.

Shanghai's Blushing Brides

As the sepia wedding photos in the antiques markets show, Shanghai's brides have been dressing up in clouds of tulle for over 100 years. After a brief post-Cultural Revolution respite (when gowns yielded to Mao suits), the wedding-belle dream has burst into full flower. More specifically, the wedding-gown photo. The gowns displayed in the ritzy Central Huaihai Road boutiques are not for walking down aisles – they are worn exclusively for the all-important bridal portrait, the most important day in a Shanghai bride's life. Bridal photo packages include dresses, make-up and hairstyles. Brides get to choose from gowns of virginal white, Scarlett O'Hara red, bright blue festooned with flowers, or off-the-shoulder taxicab yellow, and they are photographed against fake backdrops of Paris or along futuristic Pudong. It's not cheap – wedding-photo packages can run to RMB 100,000 – but as Shanghai brides will tell you, a wedding day lasts 24 hours, but pictures are for ever.

North on Maoming Road, on the corner with Changle Road, is the newly renovated **Lyceum Theatre**, built in 1930 as the home of the British Shanghai Amateur Dramatic Club – and where the great ballerina Margot Fonteyn performed as a girl (she was known as Margaret Hookham then). Fonteyn's family lived in Shanghai between 1927 and 1933 when her father worked as an executive in the British Tobacco Company. Much later, China's opera legend Mei Lanfang also took command of the Lyceum's stage. Today, the beautifully restored Art Deco theatre hosts acrobatics and Chinese opera – but Fonteyn is still remembered in a portrait in the lobby.

ABOVE: the Art Deco Jinjiang Hotel was formerly known as the Cathay Mansions.
BELOW: the Lyceum Theatre, where Margot Fonteyn once danced.

later the hotel's name was changed to the Jinjiang Hotel. The Jinjiang secured its place in contemporary Shanghai history as the venue where US President Richard Nixon and Chinese Foreign Minister Zhou En-lai signed the Shanghai Communiqué in 1972, the first step towards normalising US–China relations.

Thankfully, the 2003 restoration has kept intact the theatre's European-style architecture and arched ceilings while introducing unobtrusive modern lighting and sound systems.

Lyceum Theatre ⓯ Lánxīn Dàxìyuàn 兰心大戏院

✉ 57 Maoming Road (S) at Changle Road 📞 6256 5544 (box office) 🚇 Shanxi Road (S)

Surrounding streets

Cross Maoming Road (S) to **Changle Road** where at No. 400 is the stylish **Jinjiang Dickson Centre**,

Recommended Restaurants & Cafés on pages 166–7

offering upmarket boutiques like Zegna and Gucci.

Across from JJ Dickson is "*qipao* row", a string of boutiques specialising in the traditional high-necked and form-fitting Chinese silk dresses as well as several small Japanese *yakitori* restaurants. Particularly good is the tiny **Yakitori Fukuchan** *(see page 167)*, serving delicious barbecued morsels of meat and seafood.

Parallel to the north is **Jinxian Road**, a very traditional Shanghai street where you will find **Chun** *(see page 166)*, a tiny four-table eatery serving home-style Shanghai cuisine that has won rave reviews from the likes of the *New York Times*.

Heading two blocks west at **Xinle Road** are the sapphire-hued onion domes of the former **Cathedral of the Holy Mother of God**. Stripped of its former glory, part of this 1931 Russian Orthodox church is now home to a Shanghainese restaurant called **The Grape** *(see page 166)*. Inspired by the Cathedral of the Saviour in Moscow, the church used to hold over 2,500 worshippers in its heyday. Locals say its paintings of six cute cherubim and seraphim, now long gone, resembled the faces of the local artist's lovers.

Opposite at No. 82 Xinle Road is the boutique **Mansion Hotel ⑯** *(see page 277)*, which occupies a meticulously restored old manor house, said to have been the headquarters of Du Yuesheng, a 1930s Shanghai mafioso. **Magnolia Restaurant & Lounge** on the fifth floor offers exquisite views of the city from both the dining room and terrace, but the food is just so-so – stick with a drink.

Continue down Xinle Road and take a detour left along **Donghu Road** towards the old wing of the **Donghu Hotel ⑰** (Donghu Fandian). This was a generous gift to Shanghai mafia chief Du Yuesheng in 1937 from a grateful disciple, though he never actually lived here. The adjacent restaurant, **The 7** *(see page 166)*, serves Shanghai cuisine in a grand brick villa overlooking a lawn. Opposite, at No. 20, in a 19th-century villa, is hot Spanish restaurant **El Willy** , along with Japanese sensation **Sushi Oyama** on the floor above *(see page 167)*. ❑

The Cathedral of the Holy Mother of God is today, rather ignominiously, used as a restaurant.

BELOW LEFT: taking it easy on Changle Road.
BELOW: shoppers on Xinle Road.

BEST RESTAURANTS AND CAFÉS

American

CPK

诗碧阁 Shibige

✉ Sinan Mansions,Fuxing Road; www.cpk.com.cn
☎ 5465 4800 ◷ daily L & D. **$$** [p325, E2]
Gourmet pizzas with a variety of creative toppings (don't miss Shanghai-inspired dishes like the roasted duck pizza) are this California-based restaurant's speciality. Located in the upscale lifestyle hub Sinan Mansions, overlooking Fuxing Park.

Chinese

1931 Bar & Restaurant

名古

✉ 112 Maoming Road (S)
☎ 6472 5264 ◷ daily 11–2am. **$** [p325, D2]
Intimate dining in nostalgic Shanghai 1930s surroundings with music from the era playing on an original phonograph. The decor is a mix of chintzy flowery wallpaper, dark wooden furniture and 1930s

posters of *qipao*-clad women, with the menu offering home-style Shanghainese dishes.

The 7

大公馆

✉ 7 Donghu Road ☎ 6415 6666/6415 7777 ◷ daily L & D. **$** [p325, C1]
Situated in an old villa overlooking a manicured lawn, this eatery serves classic Shanghainese dishes – red-cooked pork, *xiao long bao* dumplings, hairy crabs in season – in an atmosphere that hints of slightly decaying colonial elegance.

Chun

春

✉ 124 Jinxian Road
☎ 6256 0301 ◷ Mon–Sat L & D. **$** [p325, D1]
Tiny hole-in-the-wall eatery serving home-style Shanghainese cooking by owner Lan-Lan, which has earned rave reviews from legendary *New York Times* reviewer Johnny Apple. No English is spoken and there is no written menu

– owner Lan Lan will discuss the menu with you (bring a Mandarin-speaker along), based on available ingredients. Still, there are staples, like red-cooked pork and glutinous rice cake with crab, and stuffed snails.

Crystal Jade

翡翠酒家

✉ 2/F, Nos 6–7 South Block Xintiandi, Lane 123, Xingye Road ☎ 6385 8752
◷ daily L & D. **$** [p326, A1]
Pan-China cuisine, with a focus on Shanghainese and Cantonese fare, plus top-notch dim sum. Favourite dishes include the *dan dan mian* – spicy Sichuan noodles with a chilli and peanut sauce, *cha shao bao* – fluffy barbecued pork buns, and *hong shao rou*, a classically Shanghainese pork dish. With sleek, contemporary decor, this place is *always* packed – reservations essential.

Din Tai Fung

鼎泰丰

✉ 2/F, No. 6, South Block Xintiandi, Lane 123, Xingye Road ☎ 6385 8378
◷ Mon–Thur 11am–midnight; Sat–Sun 11–1am. **$** [p326, A1]
The house special here is the Shanghai signature dish, *xiao long bao* –

steamed dumplings filled with pork, ginger and garlic, and a scalding hot broth. The *New York Times* called the original Din Tai Fung (in Taiwan) one of the world's 10 best restaurants, and its Shanghai counterpart upholds that reputation.

The Grape

葡萄园

✉ 55 Xinle Road; www.sh grape.xinwen365.com
☎ 5404 0486 ◷ daily 11am–midnight. **$** [p325, D1]
The Grape serves simple but tasty Shanghainese food. What's unusual is that it occupies part of an old Russian Orthodox church. Inside, the decor is a bit uninspiring, but the food is authentic and the service attentive. English menus make this a popular spot with foreigners.

Guyi Hunan Restaurant

古意

✉ 89 Fumin Road ☎ 6249 5628 ◷ daily 11.30–4am. **$** [p324, C1]
Always bustling, its spicy Hunan cuisine is the star – dishes arrive smothered in mounds of chilli. Hotpot is also its speciality. Also worth trying: spicy ribs, string beans in chilli and garlic, and the fried bananas for dessert.

LEFT: the plush Crystal Jade restaurant at Xintiandi.
RIGHT: T8 at Xintiandi.

Continental

Blue Frog
蓝蛙

✉ 207–6 Maoming Road (S); www.bluefrog.com.cn
📞 6445 6634 ⏱ Mon–Thur & Sun 11–2am, Fri & Sat 11–3am. **$$** [p325, D2]
An American menu of burgers, steaks, big salads and gooey desserts makes this a popular spot for brunch, lunch and dinner. The well-stocked bar, with ample drink specials, ensures that it practically heaves into the wee hours.

Citizen Café
天台咖啡

✉ 222 Jinxian Road; www.citizenshanghai.com
📞 6258 1620 ⏱ Mon–Fri 11am–12.30am, Sat and Sun 10am–12.30am. **$** [p325, D1]
Located in an atmospheric French Concession lane, this café serves simple, but delicious Continental dishes and desserts. Tasteful interior with original wooden floors, and smart sofas and chairs. Its weekend brunch dishes – pancakes, eggs and baked items – are very popular.

El Willy
迪雅居

✉ 20 Donghu Lu 📞 5404 5757 ⏱ Mon–Sat L & D. **$$$** [p325, D2]
Authentic tapas and rich paellas – along with an excellent wine list – in a chic, cosy French Concession garden villa. Part of the whole experi-

ence is chatting with Spanish chef Willy Trullas Moreno, a local celebrity.

Osteria
✉ 226 Jinxian Road
📞 6256 8998; www.osteria spirit. com ⏱ daily L & D. **$$** [p325, D1]
A petite two-storey Italian eatery on one of the city's funkiest streets, Osteria has a comfortable understated chic, with exposed brick walls, concrete and hardwood floors and muted tones. A young, hip crowd comes here for their signature super-fresh oysters and antipasti, and stays on for the Italian classics – and a well-crafted wine list.

Vienna Café
维也纳咖啡馆

✉ House 2, No. 25 Shaoxing Road; www.shanghai vienna.com 📞 6445 2131
⏱ Mon, Thur, Fri & Sat 8am–10pm, Tue & Sun 8am–8pm. **$** [p325, E2]
Authentic Austrian food – dark bread, sausage and the legendary chocolate Sacher Torte – is the draw at this relaxed yet sophisticated café. Dark wooden chairs and round, marble-topped tables add to the old European feel.

Fusion

T8
✉ House 8, North Block Xintiandi, Lane 181 Taicang Road; www.t8shanghai.com
📞 6355 8999 ⏱ Mon D only, Tue–Sun L & D. **$$$** [p326, A1]

The much-lauded T8 serves a fusion Mediterranean/Asian menu with subtle flavours and elegant presentation. Housed in a refurbished *shikumen* house in Xintiandi, the decor is modern with Asian influences, and the overall feel is sleek and refined.

Indian

The Tandoor
锦江孟买餐厅

✉ Jinjiang Hotel, South Building, 59 Maoming Road (S) 📞 6472 5494 ⏱ daily L & D. **$$** [p325, D1]
Shanghai's very first Indian restaurant when it opened in 1994, Tandoor is still considered the best. Authentic North Indian fare, with dishes cooked in the clay tandoor a speciality, is served in an upscale environment.

Japanese

Sushi Oyama
大山寿司 Dashan Shousi

✉ 2/F, 2 Donghu Road
📞 5404 7705 ⏱ Mon–Sat D. **$$$$** [p325, C1]

Chef Takeo Oyama serves up what is widely considered the best sushi in a city that has plenty of top-quality Japanese cuisine. The restaurant is tiny, comprising one wooden bar-top counter, a tatami dining room on the second floor of the French Concession villa, and a second private tatami dining room. There is no menu – chef Oyama serves the best of what is available on the day.

Yakitori Fukuchan
福烤锦花

✉ 223 Changle Road
📞 5403 6270 ⏱ daily D. **$** [p325, D1]
A tiny gem, always packed with Japanese regulars, *yakitori* (grilled meats and seafood) is the speciality here. No English menu, but some staff speak English.

Prices for a three-course meal for two people, excluding drinks:
$ = under RMB 250
$$ = RMB 250–500
$$$ = RMB 500–800
$$$$ = over RMB 800

LIFE IN THE LANES

Lane houses and community life are becoming a thing of the past as Shanghai morphs into a modern city of glass and steel

Over 70 percent of Shanghai residents were born and raised in *longtang* (or lane) neighbourhoods, but these communities are now endangered by progress. The *longtang*, Shanghai's vernacular domestic architecture, is more than just a building style: it's a way of life. These attached dwellings – each with its *shikumen* (stone-gate) entrance – separated by lanes and surrounded by an exterior wall, are thriving hubs of community life.

Because the lane houses are cramped, the internal lanes are treated as extensions of residential living spaces: here, laundry is done and hung up to dry, hair is washed in wooden basins, and peas are shelled. The communities are tightly knit, quarrelling like families and sticking together in times of trouble.

As more and more Shanghainese move out to modern apartments and lane houses fall to the wrecking ball, Shanghai stands to lose far more than a piece of its architecture – it's losing part of its culture.

ABOVE: a typical back street in Old Shanghai. Cramped living quarters mean that chores are often performed in the

ABOVE: hanging up the laundry, a common sight in Shanghai's lanes.

LEFT: an elderly resident of one of old Shanghai's lane houses.

ABOVE: every available space in the lanes is used up for hanging laundry. There are no secrets here, as any Shanghainese who grew up in a lane neighbourhood will tell you.

快餐店

XINTIANDI AND THE SHIKUMEN MUSEUM

In 2001, an old lane neighbourhood was gutted and reborn as a modern shopping and entertainment venue called Xintiandi. It's not historic preservation really – some entirely new structures were built and only the grey brick facades were preserved – but defenders of Shanghai's old architecture generally approve of the project for its success in raising awareness of the value of the city's historic buildings.

Xintiandi's Shikumen Open House Museum pays tribute to the lane house, albeit one belonging to a wealthy family – conditions in a typical abode would be much less attractive. The museum recreates the interior of a 1920s seven-room house, furnished with period furniture and memorabilia, from kitchen stove tops to the jade hair clasp on the dressing table and the scratchy jazz played on the gramophone. There are bedrooms, a kitchen, sitting room, study and the *tingzijian*, the garret above the kitchen, often rented to struggling writers (and from which the term for a genre of literature was coined).

ABOVE AND RIGHT: the recreated bedroom and courtyard area at the Shikumen Open House Museum in Xintiandi.

ABOVE: more and more old neighbourhoods fall to the wrecker's ball as lane houses are eschewed in favour of modern high-rises.
BELOW: Xintiandi is Shanghai's 21st-century lane neighbourhood, its converted buildings now a swanky shopping and nightlife hub. Gentrification is one way of saving lane houses from demolition.

Recommended Restaurants & Cafés on pages 180–81

HUAIHAI AND HENGSHAN

The boundaries of the French Concession extend to this part of the city. View stately mansions – once the home of tai-pans, consuls and concubines – during the day, and hole up in the city's best jazz bars at night

This section of the upscale Huaihai and Hengshan neighbourhood – part of the elegant French Concession – has a split personality, drawing sedate, highbrow residents as well as a trendy crowd. Diplomats, high-ranking party officials and Shanghai's new rich are attracted to the area's wide tree-lined boulevards, spacious historic villas with expansive gardens, new luxury apartments, and the rare quality of *anjing* – tranquillity – in a downtown location.

Even the *laobaixing* (Chinese parlance for the average man) in this part of Shanghai aren't so common. Former missionary school graduates frequent the parks and markets in this area, some still living in the shabby grandeur of apartments and villas built by their families more than half a century ago. Most are just waiting for someone to come along and pay the multimillion-dollar price tags that these properties command today.

CENTRAL HUAIHAI ROAD

Central Huaihai Road is a major artery that cuts across from the east to the west of the city. The eastern section of Central Huaihai Road is a brash consumer paradise *(see page 162)* but here, where it parallels **Hengshan Road** to the south, it is toned down, reflecting the character of its residents.

Yet it's not all well-behaved matrons in this part of the city. A trendy crop of boutiques and restaurants attracts the hipster crowd, while nightfall sees Shanghai's party animals heading for the area's neon-lit strip of bars, clubs and restaurants – and the best jazz in town.

Main attractions
NORMANDIE APARTMENTS
SOONG CHING LING'S FORMER RESIDENCE
FUXING ROAD

LEFT: the former home of TV Soong, brother of Soong Ching Ling, now Sasha's restaurant. **RIGHT:** strolling down Fuxing Road.

TIP

Behind the Normandie building *(see page 173)* on Wukang Road are manhole covers that read "CMF 1935" – Conseil Municipal Français (French Concession), 1935. There is also a good supply of vintage French fire hydrants in the area.

BELOW: the French Consul-General's Residence.

French Consul's Residence ❶
Fǎguó Lǐngshìguǎn 法国领事馆

The country manors of the French Concession were located here along Central Huaihai when this was the Avenue Joffre. The size and grandeur of these villas have made them a prime diplomatic enclave today. The corner of Central Huaihai Road and Urumqi Road has a number of consulates, the flags of four nations flying over vintage mansions. Prime among these is the Mediterranean-style **French Consul-General's Residence** (not open to the public) at 1431 Central Huaihai Road. It was built in 1921 for the French Basset family, and later home to colourful characters such as high-living American tai-pan Frank Raven, who scandalised Shanghai when he was jailed for fraud.

The residence changed hands several more times over the years, becoming the French Consul's residence in the 1980s. The house, with its original tiled floors, circular sun-room and lush garden, is not open to the public, but curious visitors can see the roof and cheerful sunflower tiles that line the top of the house over high walls.

US Consulate-General ❷
Měiguó Lǐngshìguǎn
美国领事馆

Across the street at 1469 Central Huaihai Road, straight-backed guards protect the rambling mansion that has served as the **US Consulate-General** (not open to the public) since 1980. The neoclassical Western-style house was built in the early part of the 20th century for a prominent Chinese entrepreneur and Qing government minister, Shang Shu.

After stints as the residence of the Jardine Matheson tai-pan and the Swiss Consulate, it was bought by Rong Hongyuan of the Rong family, one of Shanghai's wealthiest industrial dynasties. The gorgeous ground-floor rooms are intact because it was

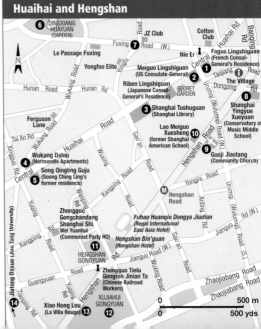

placed under lock and key during the Cultural Revolution.

"Secret Garden"

✉ Lane 1487 🕐 Mon–Fri 8am–11.30am, 1–4.30pm 🎫 free 🚇 Shanghai Library

This tiny overgrown garden, tucked at the end of a lane neighbourhood, and next to the Japanese Consulate, is a lovely, little-known oasis. The pond features an old, haunting statue of a little girl holding a ball. Neighbours say she drowned while chasing the ball and her distraught father memorialized her with this statue.

Shanghai Library ❸
Shànghǎi Túshūguǎn
上海图书馆

✉ 1555 Central Huaihai Road; www.library.sh.cn/english 📞 6445 5555 🕐 daily 8.30am–8.30pm 🎫 free 🚇 Shanghai Library

The white-tiled **Shanghai Library**, next to the Japanese Consul's residence, enhances the stately air of the this area. This spacious, light-filled

facility, which opened in 1996, claims to be Asia's largest library. It has collections of old and rare Chinese books, the Chinese Cultural Celebrities Manuscript Library, and a genealogy section for Chinese throughout the diaspora. Of particular note is a rare 8,000-volume Ming-dynasty edition of the *Taoist Scriptures*. Check out the automated 24-hour return system, a marvel of technology, located just past the entrance of the library, above the driveway.

Normandie apartments ❹
Wǔkāng Dàlóu 武康大楼

Further west along Central Huaihai Road, at the corner with Wukang Road, is the unmistakable red-brick **Normandie** apartment block, a local landmark that dominates the north side of the street. Strongly reminiscent of Manhattan's Flatiron building, the Art Deco structure is known locally as the Titanic because of its remarkable resemblance to the great cruise liner.

Built in 1924, the Normandie – then known as the Intersavin Society (ISS) apartments – was constructed with 76 apartments on six floors and

The Art Deco Normandie apartments are now a much-sought-after residence. Many are being gutted and modernised inside.

BELOW: Shanghai Library.

The Chinese say of the three Soong sisters: "May Ling loved power, Ai Ling loved money, but Ching Ling loved China." Pictured here is a statue of Soong Ching Ling at her former residence.

RIGHT: upmarket shopping in Ferguson Lane.
BELOW: gardens at Soong Ching Ling's Former Residence.

30 servants' quarters. Today, more than 700 people fit into that space and the building is starting to look a bit grimy. But thanks to the Shanghai real-estate boom, several apartments in the building have been bought over and renovated – the beginning of gentrification.

Soong Ching Ling's Former Residence ❺ Sòng Qìnglíng Gùjū 宋庆龄故居

✉ 1843 Central Huaihai Road
📞 6437 6268 🅒 daily 9am–4.30pm
🅰 RMB 20 🄟 Shanghai Library

The **Soong Ching Ling Residence**, across from the Normandie, is where Dr Sun Yat-sen's young widow lived from 1948, having donated their Xiangshan Road house (*see page 157*) as a museum, until she moved to Beijing in 1963.

Today, Soong's house stands as a monument to her, and as a triumph for the Communist Party, to which she remained loyal despite her family's leadership roles in the opposing Kuomintang government. A recent renovation opened up the second

floor, allowing visitors to visit Soong's bedroom suite, with furniture given by her parents at the time of her wedding in 1915, and that of her faithful maid, Li Yan E.

Downstairs, the living and dining rooms are lined with photographs of Soong with a host of legends from Mao to Nehru. A modern building in the compound documents the extraordinary Soong clan in letters and artefacts, and in the garage sit two ebony limousines: a 1952 Jim presented by Stalin and Soong's own Chinese Red Flag. The lane behind the house makes for a nice, tree-shaded walk.

Ding Xiang Garden ❻ Dīngxiāng Huāyuán 丁香花园

Head back across the street to the Normandie apartments. Turning right down Wukang Road for about five minutes will lead to **Ferguson Lane** complex, a "lifestyle hub" with a collection of stylish eateries, boutiques selling one-of-a-kind products, and a spa.

From here, it's a 10-minute walk northwest to the lovely oasis at 849 Huashan Road called **Ding Xiang Garden**. The stucco-and-wood English-style house, with its porches

Recommended Restaurants & Cafés on pages 180–81

and gingerbread trim, was built in 1900 by an American architect. The Qing dynasty reformer Li Hongzhang acquired the house for his favourite concubine Clove (Ding Xiang), and stored his vast collection of books here. The building and garden is the exclusive preserve of retired party cadres, but the **Xian Yue Hien** restaurant *(see page 180)* in the compound allows both access and delicious views of the garden and its pavilion, all surrounded by walls topped with writhing dragons.

FUXING ROAD ❼

Exit Xian Yue Hien restaurant and turn left onto **Fuxing Road**, which, with its vintage villas and canopy of lovely plane trees, is a classic French Concession street. Today, a clutch of trendy restaurants, shops and jazz bars have taken root here.

At No. 299 is another lifestyle hub – **Le Passage Fuxing**. Within refurbished lane houses are **Rouge Baiser**, a boutique specialising in hand-embroidered linen, and **Ginger Café** *(see page 181)*, serving a mixed Asian and Western menu.

Take a short detour right onto **Yongfu Road**, where you'll find **Le Platane** boutique at No. 127. The brainchild of a former *Vogue Australia* editor and a French lawyer, this is a treasure box of clothing, jewellery and housewares.

Continue further down Yongfu Road to **The Yongfoo Elite** (tel: 5466 2727) at No. 200. This early 20th-century antique-filled mansion, once the home of a prominent Shanghai family who fled to Hong Kong in the wake of the Communist takeover, is now a restaurant. The food, unfortunately, is abysmal, but the lovely setting – which includes a lovely garden, shaded by century-old trees – and authentic Old Shanghai feel make it worth stopping by for a drink.

Jazz haunts

Jazz was Old Shanghai's signature tune – 1,200 jazz bands, it is said, performed here in the 1930s – and New Shanghai seems to have embraced it as well. Two of the city's best clubs are located on Fuxing Road. At No. 46 is **JZ Club** *(see page 292)*, a three-storey space that is the

Ginger Café at Fuxing Road makes for a lovely lunch stop when sightseeing in this area.

BELOW LEFT: jazz performer at JZ. **BELOW:** relaxing over coffee at Ginger Café.

Silk purses at the Simply Life boutique at Dongping Road.

heart of the Shanghai jazz scene. The city's best local and out-of-town players perform here, jamming late into the night. Across the street, at the intersection with Central Huaihai Road, is the dark and smoky **Cotton Club** *(see page 292)*, a local legend in Shanghai jazz and blues circles. Its house band plays jazz standards with such verve that even Wynton Marsalis stopped by to jam some years ago when he was in town.

HENGSHAN ROAD

From the Cotton Club, head south down leafy **Hengshan Road**. This enclave plays host to a collection of lively bars and restaurants, beginning with the old expat favourite **O'Malley's** *(see page 181)*, a popular Irish pub in a vintage garden villa, at No. 42 Taojiang Road, which is just off Hengshan Road.

The eating and drinking (and shopping) options continue on **Dongping Road** (also off Hengshan Road) in the next block. There is cosy and colourful tapas bar and restaurant **Azul** at No. 18 *(see page 181)*; locavore chef Austin Hu's

RIGHT: O'Malley's Irish pub on Hengshan Road.
BELOW: the bar at Sasha's restaurant; the building once belonged to the powerful Soong family.

Madison, upstairs, and **Sasha's** *(see page 181)* at No. 11, where French cuisine is served on the second floor in an old-world setting.

The Village at No. 6 is yet another "lifestyle" hub – complete with spa. Also on this street is the original **Simply Life** boutique at No. 9 with its Asian-inspired home accessories, **Simply Thai** at No. 5C *(see page 181)*, serving piquant Thai cuisine amid elegant minimalist decor, and **The Blarney Stone**, at 5A (tel: 6415 7496), one of the city's more authentic Irish pubs – complete with Irish lads and lassies and stick-to-your-ribs pub grub.

Shanghai Conservatory of Music Middle School ❽
Shànghǎi Yīnyuè Xuéyuàn
上海音乐学院

✉ 5 Dongping Road ⓒ Grounds open for events only ▣ Hengshan Road

The gates in the middle of Dongping Road lead to the grounds of the Shanghai home of the powerful Soong family, who once lived here like dynastic royalty. Some of these Western-style brick villas today house the **Shanghai Conservatory of Music Middle School**, while others play host to chic restaurants.

The building housing **Sasha's** restaurant *(see above)* was the home of T.V. Soong, the most prominent of the three Soong sons, who served as the Kuomintang finance minister and was once said to be the richest man in the world. The villa next to Sasha's was the home of Kuomintang leader

Chiang Kai-shek and Soong May Ling, the sister of Ching Ling and a power-broker in her own right. Adjacent to Chiang's residence was the home of H.H. Kung, financial wizard, Bank of China head, briefly Kuomintang finance minister, and husband of Soong Ai Ling, the oldest sister. Only Ching Ling lived apart from the rest of the Soong clan, and only Ching Ling remained in China.

Community Church ❾
Guójì Jiàotáng 国际教堂

✉ 53 Hengshan Road 📞 6437 6576 🕒 English services on Sun at 2 and 4pm; Chinese services at 4.30am, 10am and 7pm 🚇 Hengshan Road

Back on Hengshan Road, a five-minute walk south leads to the ivy-covered **Community Church**, founded by a group of Americans around 1925. The beautiful red-brick Protestant church, with its rosewood pews and high ceilings, is worth a visit at any time of the day – if the guards let you in – but particularly during services. Chinese-language services are especially

popular, with the congregation often spilling onto the lawns. To curb proselytising, Chinese nationals must worship separately from foreigners. The latter may attend the Chinese services, as celebrities from Jimmy Carter to Bishop Tutu have in the past, listening to the translated service through headphones.

Former Shanghai American School ❿

The stately red-brick building across the street from the Community Church is the **former Shanghai American School**, the first signpost of the American community that once flourished here. The school was set up in 1912 to educate the children of American missionaries and moved to this location in 1923. By 1934, a booming Shanghai saw enrolment at the school pass the 600 mark. Designed by American architect Henry Murphy to resemble the Independence Hall in Philadelphia, the building today houses a naval research facility. The school is closed to the public – but can be admired from the street.

TIP

Newly woven reed-wattle fences are an old sight making a comeback in this neighbourhood. Look for the fences around Soong Ching Ling's house, the Shanghai Communist Party Headquarters and the red-brick mansion on the corner of Kangping and Wukang roads.

BELOW: wedding ceremony at the Community Church.

Hengshan Road bar strip

Just before Hengshan Road's well-known bar strip begins, next to the old Shanghai American School, is the Gibson Guitar Store, a gorgeous two-storey palace for guitar-lovers at the throbbing disco-beat **Boiling** (10 Hengshan Road). The bars along Hengshan Road can be a little seedy and they offer none of the glitz and glamour of the Bund. Still, there are plenty of options for late-night party animals, from the Latin-inspired beats at **Zapata's** (9 Dongping Road, House 11) to the raucous **SBS** (Shanghai Band Sanctuary; 191 Hengshan Road) and the downright seedy **Hello** (237 Hengshan Road).

Hengshan Park ⑪
Héngshān Gōngyuán 衡山公园

✉ corner of Hengshan Road and Wanping Road ⓒ daily 6am–6pm
ⓖ free ⎇ Xujiahui

A leisurely 10-minute walk from the Hengshan Road bar strip past the modern **Regal International East Asia Hotel** at 516 Hengshan Road, and the refurbished 1934 **Hengshan Hotel** (Hengshan Bin'guan) at 534 Hengshan Road, takes you to the pocket-handkerchief sized **Hengshan Park**.

Formerly called Pétain Park, it was originally laid out by the French in 1935, and although it has been re-landscaped since, the 75 years' worth of lush greenery has given the park an almost tropical feel. It is a popular place; beginning at dawn, the park buzzes with t'ai chi practitioners in one corner, fan dancers in another, and elderly ballroom dancers waltzing to the tunes of yesteryear in the space in between.

ABOVE AND BELOW:
Xujiahui Park.

Recommended Restaurants & Cafés on pages 180–81

Xujiahui Park ⑫ Xújiāhuì Gōngyuán 徐家汇公园

✉ corner of Hengshan Road and Wanping Road ◔ daily 6am–6pm
◉ free 🚇 Xujiahui

The pristine, manicured grounds of **Xujiahui Park**, which is part of the city's ongoing greening project, is a short walk south. The park was landscaped as a microcosm of Shanghai – the bridge is the Yanan Lu highway; La Villa Rouge, the Concessions; and the old China Rubber Factory smokestack, the industrial zone.

La Villa Rouge ⑬
Xiǎo Hóng Lóu 小红楼

✉ Xujiahui Park, 811 Hengshan Road
☎ 6431 6639 🚇 Xujiahui

The **La Villa Rouge** is now Restaurant Martin (serving Spanish Fusion cuisine), housed in a historic redbrick villa within Xujiahui Park.

In its former life as the EMI Studios, this was where some of Shanghai's most famous voices were recorded, including Zhou Xuan, the legendary "golden throat" of the 1930s, and Nie Er, the composer of the Chinese national anthem. The building remained as a recording studio throughout Shanghai's turbulent history, first under the Japan-

ese, then the Kuomintang, and finally as the Shanghai branch of China Records.

Jiao Tong University ⑭
Jiāotōng Dàxué 交通大学

✉ 1954 Huashan Road;
www.sjtu.edu.cn/english 🚇 Xujiahui

From the park's western edge, head northwest – a 15-minute walk along Huashan Road – to Shanghai's prestigious **Jiao Tong University**. This is China's second-oldest university, which counts China's leadership among its graduates. The extensive campus is dotted with stately early 20th-century buildings, now home to the university's renowned science and engineering faculties. The **C.Y. Tung Maritime Museum** (daily 1–5.30pm; free), dedicated to the late Shanghai-born shipping tycoon and housed in a refurbished 19th-century dormitory, has exhibits on the history of Chinese shipping and the legacy of the Tung family's shipping business. (C.Y.'s son, Tung Chee Hwa, was the first post-colonial chief executive of Hong Kong.) ❏

TIP

At nearby Kangping Road is the ominous grey building that houses the unmarked Headquarters of the Shanghai Communist Party (Zhongguo Gongchandang Shanghai Shi Wei Yuanhui). It is closely guarded by sharp-looking soldiers with equally sharp eyes – watch for a moment too long the shiny black cars with darkened windows driving past the gate and you'll be sent on your way.

BELOW: La Villa Rouge, another beautiful French Concession villa now turned restaurant.

BEST RESTAURANTS AND CAFÉS

American

Boxing Cat Brewery

拳击猫啤酒屋 Quanjii
Mao Pijiu Wu

✉ 82 Fuxing Road (W)
☎ 6431 2091 ex 801;
www.boxing catbrewery.
com ⏰ Mon–Fri 5pm–2am,
Sat–Sun 10am–2pm. **$$$$**
[p324, B2]

Southern American fare
is served at this hip
restaurant and micro-
brewery, set in a three-
storey Bauhaus building.
Barbecue pulled pork
sandwiches, Southern
gumbo, fried chicken with
biscuits and gravy and
red velvet cake are all on
the menu,along with four
different types of home-
brewed beer – and a pool
table and table football.

Madison

✉ 3/F, 18 Dongping Road
☎ 6437 0136 ⏰ daily D,
Sat–Sun brunch. **$$$$**

[p324, C3]

One of Shanghai's hot
new restaurants, led by a
talented chef, Madison
serves New American cui-
sine with distinctly Shanghai flavours, usually
locally sourced in-season
ingredients from artisan
and boutique producers.

Chinese

Di Shui Dong

滴水洞

✉ 1 Dongping Road
☎ 6474 7052 ⏰ daily L &
D. **$$** [p325, C3]

Spicy Hunan cuisine is the
speciality in this small,
casual restaurant. Di Shui
Dong's spicy chicken, with
piles of red chillies, and
spicy *mapou* tofu are all
delicious, but the crowds
come for its famous hot-
pot – big pots of chilli-
laced bubbling stock, in
which diners cook meat,
tofu and veggies.

South Beauty

俏江南

✉ 28-1, Taojiang Road
☎ 6445 2581 ⏰ daily L &
D. **$$$** [p324, C3]

Features Cantonese and
Sichuan dishes in a
Zen-like contemporary
Chinese interior, albeit
one that is buzzing. Spe-
cials include an array of
appetisers served in a
lacquered box, "rock and
roll" salad, hot and spicy
crab, house-made tofu
and whimsical desserts.

Xian Yue Hien

申粤轩

✉ 849 Huashan Road
☎ 6251 1166 ⏰ daily L &
D. **$$** [p324, B2]

This gourmet Cantonese
restaurant (with a touch of
Shanghainese) is set in
the gorgeous historic Ding
Xiang (Clove) Garden, the
love nest of reformer Li
Hongzhang and his fav-
ourite concubine, Clove.
Refined, high-quality Can-
tonese cuisine and lunch-
time dim sum is served
overlooking the garden.
Specialities include
shark's fin soup, drunken
prawns and goose.

Yang's Kitchen

杨家厨房

✉ Lane No. 9, 3 Hengshan
Road ☎ 6431 3028
⏰ daily L & D. **$** [p324, C3]

Set in a renovated vin-
tage French Concession
villa with a courtyard for
alfresco dining in warm
weather. Yang's Kitchen
serves a refined version
of home-style Shanghai
cooking. Its classics
include shrimp with
garlic, drunken chicken,
Mandarin fish and egg-
plant casserole.

Continental

Boonna 2

布那咖啡

✉ No. 57 Fuxing Road (W)
☎ 6433 7142 ⏰ daily
7–1am. **$** [p324, B2]

The second, more spa-
cious branch of this
popular Australian café.
Nice paintings and pho-
tography on the walls
and a menu of salads,
sandwiches and juices.
WiFi access helps make
it the remote office of
many a Shanghai entre-
preneur.

Coffee Tree

咖啡树

✉ 376 Wukang Road
☎ 6466 0361 ⏰ daily
9am–10pm. **$** [p324, B3]

Located in the Ferguson
Lane lifestyle hub,
Coffee Tree is a popular
casual alternative to the
more serious-dining
Franck's, in the same
hub. Rustic wooden
floors, specials on the

LEFT: interior murals at Sasha's restaurant.
RIGHT: the garden terrace at Simply Thai restaurant.

chalkboard and home-style dishes like lasagne, quiche and apple crumble give it a country café feel. In nice weather, most people sit in the courtyard.

Ginger Café
金格咖啡

✉ 299 Fuxing Road (W) (at Huashan Road), No. 1; www.gingercafe.cn
📞 6433 9437 ⏰ daily 9am–11pm. $ [p324, B2]
Located in a refurbished lane house, Ginger is a chic, intimate space patronised by the trendy folks who shop at Le Passage Shanghai, the lifestyle hub in which it is located. Ginger serves a café menu of Asian and Western favourites, from laksa to quiche, and some of the best desserts in town. In mild weather, ask for a table at the outdoor terrace.

Keven Café
凯文西餐厅

✉ 525 Hengshan Road
📞 6433 5564 ⏰ daily 7.30–2am. $ [p324, B4]
Shanghai's version of a diner, with a menu devised by a former Hilton chef. Keven serves good, wholesome food that ranges all over the map (from a mean version of Indonesian fried rice to home-style tuna sandwiches and great breakfasts).

O'Malley's Irish Pub
欧玛莉餐厅

✉ 42 Taojiang Road (at Urumqi Road); www.omalleys

irishpub.com 📞 6474 4533
⏰ daily 11–2am. $$$ [p324, C3]
An authentic Irish pub in a charming French Concession villa, O'Malleys serves up Guinness on tap and authentic Irish pub grub (corned beef and cabbage, black pudding) in a wood-panelled interior. A pool table and dartboard provide entertainment in colder weather, but when it's warm, being outside on the green lawn is the place to be.

Sasha's
萨莎

✉ 9 Dongping Road (at Hengshan Road), House No. 11; www.sashas-shanghai.com 📞 6474 6166 ⏰ daily L & D. $$$ [p324, C3]
Continental cuisine, served in the former home of T.V. Soong, the brother of Soong Ching Ling. The elegant second floor, with wooden floors, high ceilings and fireplace, is the setting for Sasha's adventurous, often experimental dishes.

French

Franck
恒威 Hengwei

✉ Ferguson Lane, 376 Wukang Road 📞 6437 6465 ⏰ daily L & D. $$$ [p324, B3]
French brasserie cuisine, beautifully executed and served in a casual-chic space. Its terrace space is perfect when the

weather is good. Beef tartare, confit de canard, tomato and mozzarella salad, cherry clafoutis and very smooth service – but a bit overpriced.

Italian

Pasta Fresca di Salvatore
沙华多利

✉ No. 4 Hengshan Road; www.pastafresca.com
📞 6473 0789 ⏰ daily L & D. $$ [p324, C3]
Simple, straightforward Italian cuisine that has been a Shanghai favourite for over a decade. Pasta Fresca serves a range of pastas, pizzas and entrees in a rustic, if a little kitschy, Italian setting. Great for families.

Latin

Azul

✉ 18 Dongping Road (at Urumqi Road) 📞 6433 1172
⏰ daily L & D. $$$ [p324, C3]
Cosy tapas restaurant Azul offers a fusion blend of Peruvian-Mexican tapas (with the

occasional Chinese touch) and pitchers of sangria. The low tables and floor seating are popular with groups, while upstairs has windows overlooking leafy Dongping Road.

Thai

Simply Thai
天泰餐厅

✉ 5C Dongping Road; www.simplythai-sh.com
📞 6445 9551 ⏰ daily L & D. $ [p324, C3]
Minimalist elegance at Shanghai's oldest Thai restaurant is the setting for cuisine so authentic that the restaurant caters for Thai royalty when they're in town. Dining outside on the deck overlooking the gardens of the Music Conservatory is one of the city's great pleasures.

Prices for a three-course meal for two people, excluding drinks:
$ = under RMB 250
$$ = RMB 250–500
$$$ = RMB 500–800
$$$$ = over RMB 800

上海静安寺山门重建落成庆典

Recommended Restaurants & Cafés on page 191

JING AN

Expect a mixed bunch of sights in this area, from posh hotels and swanky shopping malls to the Gothic fantasy Moller Villa, the architecturally confused Shanghai Exhibition Centre and the garish Jing An Temple

P remium office buildings, showy shopping malls and a constellation of five-star hotels define the prestigious business and commercial area of **Jing An**, home to some of the city's most expensive real estate. Outside the foreign Concessions until the boundaries expanded in 1899, Jing An's wide open spaces attracted the Hardoons and the Kadoories, two of the richest Jewish families in Old Shanghai. Each built concrete symbols of their wealth – magnificent mansions just minutes away from each other. Here, too, were the Bubbling Well Cemetery and the Bubbling Well Temple, whose Chinese name – Jing An, or "Tranquil Repose" – gives the area its name, as well as the legendary Paramount nightclub.

The cemetery has yielded to a park, the actual "Bubbling Well" has long been smothered by a busy highway, and the lavish Hardoon mansion has become the site of a Sino-Soviet symbol of friendship. But not everything is radically different. Prayers are offered still at Jing An Temple (while it is undergoing renovations), they're dancing again at the Paramount, and Shanghai's moneyed class is flocking to the area's malls and shops.

JING AN'S EASTERN FLANK

Although Jing An's eastern flank is only steps away from its glittering heart, its mix of run-down buildings, small shops and the occasional high-rise give it the feeling of being much more remote – the downmarket part of an upscale neighbourhood. A walk through the streets of these neighbourhoods yields both a look into the lives of downtown residents – lively, crowded lanes, snack vendors on every corner – and some interesting historic artefacts from Shanghai's past.

Main attractions

HENGSHAN MOLLER VILLA
SHANGHAI EXHIBITION CENTRE
JING AN TEMPLE
PARAMOUNT
MUNICIPAL CHILDREN'S PALACE
CHINESE PRINTED BLUE NANKEEN
EXHIBITION HALL

LEFT: worshippers gathered around the giant incense burner at Jing An Temple.
RIGHT: posing at Shanghai Exhibition Centre.

Hengshan Moller Villa ❶
Héngshān Mǎlè Biéshù
Fàndiàn 衡山马勒别墅饭店

✉ 30 Shaanxi Road (S); www.moller
villa.com 📞 6247 8881 🚇 Shimen
No. 1 Road + taxi

RIGHT: Eric Moller, the
original owner of Moller
Villa, had a fascination
for horses.
BELOW: the fairytale
Moller Villa is now a
boutique hotel owned
by the Hengshan group.

The fairytale steeples and spires of
the **Hengshan Moller Villa** rise like
a Gothic fantasy. The sheer grandeur
of the place – the rich wood panelling throughout, the elaborate
carving, the chandeliers dripping
crystal – bring alive the glamour of
old Shanghai. After spending the
post-Liberation years as the Communist Youth League, the house that
Swedish shipping magnate Eric
Moller built in 1936 has been
restored to its Old splendour as a
boutique hotel owned by the Hengshan group. Moller was a passionate
racer of horses, and a statue of his
favourite steed stands in the garden;
its body is reportedly buried in the
grounds. Take in the sight with a cup
of tea at the Vie en Rose café in the
grounds.

Ohel Rachel Synagogue ❷
Yóutài Jiàotáng 犹太教堂

✉ 500 North Shaanxi Road
🕐 Closed to the public; open to
worshippers on Saturdays 🚇 Shimen
No. 1 Road + taxi

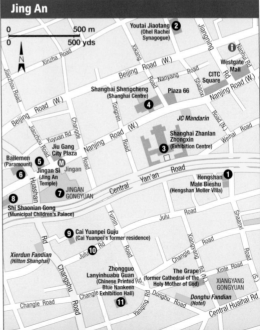

The ivy-covered Greek Revival **Ohel Rachel Synagogue**, to the northwest, was built in 1920 by Jacob Sassoon in memory of his wife Rachel. The synagogue, facing Jerusalem, served as the spiritual home for the city's wealthy Sephardic Jewish community until 1952. It was used as a stable by the Japanese during World War II and later as a warehouse and lecture hall, complete with a portrait of Mao over the ark, during the post-Liberation years.

In 1998 the synagogue was renovated and sanctified for the visit of former US First Lady Hillary Clinton and Secretary of State Madeleine Albright. Shanghai's Jewish community is allowed use of the building four times a year for worship.

Next door is the former **Shanghai Jewish School**, established by Horace Kadoorie in 1932. Both the synagogue and school are part of the Shanghai Education Bureau compound, and are visible from the street, but not open to the public.

NANJING ROAD (W) AT JING AN

Nanjing Road's westernmost flank,

Nanjing Road (W), dominates the Jing An area. Much has changed on Nanjing Road since the time it was called Bubbling Well Road and a 1930s guidebook claimed it was "one of the seven most interesting streets in the world".

The fashion vibe begins at the **Fenshine Fashion & Gift Market** on the corner of Naning and Chengdu roads, a sprawling three-storey building filled with fashion knock-offs. Heading west on Nanjing Road (W), grimy 1930s apartment buildings yield to Starbucks cafés, one in every other block. Things get more upscale on the north side of Nanjing Road (W), which is wall-to-wall with designer malls: CITC **Square**, **Westgate Mall** and **Plaza 66**, where Shanghai's yuppies flock to sip lattes, slurp on Häagen-Dazs sundaes and shop at Burberry and the landmark Louis Vuitton store, in the shape of a giant suitcase. In stark contrast, sunburnt fruit pedlars from the countryside stand outside the gleaming malls, balancing shoulder poles carrying baskets full of the season's offerings.

Celebrating the Jewish festival of Hanukkah at Ohel Rachel Synagogue.

BELOW: celebration at the Ohel Rachel Synagogue – the nine candles are lit to celebrate the Jewish festival of Hanukkah.

RIGHT: a book exhibition at the Shanghai Exhibition Centre in Jing An.
BELOW: the ornate Sino-Soviet-built Shanghai Exhibition Centre. The Plaza 66 building is on its right.

Directly across the street from Westgate Mall is **Meilongzhen** (No. 22 Lane, 1081 Nanjing Road (W); tel: 6253 5353), one of the city's most famous Chinese restaurants. Located in a pink-brick French-style mansion once used as the Communist Party headquarters, it serves Shanghainese delicacies in a vintage dining room.

Just behind Nanjing on Wujian Road is a bustling pedestrian street packed with fast-food outlets and the occasional local stall like **Yang's Fry Dumplings** (see page 191).

Shanghai Exhibition Centre ❸ Shànghǎi Zhǎnlǎn Zhōngxīn 上海展览中心

✉ 1000 Central Yan'an Road ◷ daily 9am–5pm 🚇 Shimen No. 1 Road or Jing An Temple + taxi

The **JC Mandarin** at 1225 Nanjing Road (W), along with the **Shanghai Exhibition Centre** next door, sits on the sprawling grounds of *Aili*, one of the Concession-era's most sumptuous estates. *Aili* (or "Beloved Li") belonged to Silas Hardoon, a

Sephardic Jew who arrived penniless in Shanghai and worked his way up from watchman to Shanghai's richest man. His estate, named after his half-French, half-Chinese wife, Luo Jialing *(see margin note left)*, was once dotted with pretty pavilions, arched bridges, lakes and bamboo groves.

The Shanghai Exhibition Centre was one of the many buildings constructed in major Chinese cities during the 1950s as an expression of the common cause of the Soviet Union and the People's Republic of China. Designed by a Russian architect, the 9.3-hectare (23-acre) centre was created on a scale for a giant and in a cacophony of styles, incorporating kitschy Communist stars, Christmas wreaths, a Roman central dome and a Socialist-Realist Atlas sculpture – all topped by a 106-metre (348ft) tall gold-plated steeple, inspired by Russian Orthodox church architecture.

Famous names like Mao Zedong, Deng Xiaoping and Georges Pompidou have all passed through these portals, but it's no longer *the* place in China to host exhibitions. A 2002 renovation gave it a new lease of life, and it still remains popular for exhibitions, openings and events.

Shanghai Centre ❹
Shànghǎi Shāngchéng
上海商城

✉ 1376 Nanjing Road (W); www.shanghaicentre.com ☎ 6279 8600 ⊙ stores open 9am–7pm
🚇 Jing An Temple + taxi

Across the street, the John Portman-designed **Shanghai Centre** is at 1376 Nanjing Road (W). The city's first international residential, business and hotel complex is ground zero for the expatriate population, who need never leave its comforts. There is an upscale grocery shop, clinic, tennis courts, a pool, the **Portman Ritz-Carlton Hotel** (Boteman Lisi Kaerun Jiuan) and its clutch of restaurants. The **Shanghai Centre Theatre** (Shanghai Shangcheng

Juyuan) within the complex is the home of the **Shanghai Acrobatic Troupe** *(see pages 54 and 289)* which carries on a 2,000-year-old tradition that would dazzle even the most jaded soul.

Jing An Temple ❺
Jìngān Sì 静安寺

✉ 1686 Nanjing Road (W)
☎ 6256 6366 ⊙ daily 7.30am–5pm
💲 RMB 10 🚇 Jing An Temple

Two blocks west is the landmark **Jing An Temple**, which has stood at this location since 1216, when the lapping waves of the Suzhou Creek eroded the foundations of the original temple, built on its banks in 247. Originally called Hudu Chongyuan Temple, it was renamed Jing An in 1008, but became more popularly known as pre-1949 Shanghai as the Bubbling Well Temple – named after the natural springs that stood at the intersection of Nanjing Road (W) and Wanhangdu Road, and considered supernatural by locals.

Dedicated to Sakyamuni Buddha, the temple lost many of its statues

Praying for good luck and blessings at Jing An Temple.

BELOW: monk standing before a giant urn at Jing An Temple.

Jing An Temple, Shanghai's richest temple, was once famous for its equally wealthy and flamboyant abbot, the towering Khi Vedhu, who kept seven concubines and had an entourage of White Russian bodyguards.

and scriptures during the Cultural Revolution, when it served as a factory. It also lost most of its old architecture with an ill-conceived renovation project that began in 2002. The temple is still being renovated, but the street-facing main halls done up in Burmese teak have been completed, and the front courtyard is filled with incense again. The pavilion housing the copper Hongwu Bell, which dates from the Ming era, has also been recreated in teak. A temporary building, often filled with the chants of the faithful, houses images of 18 *arhat* (Buddhist saints). Funds are being raised for a gold Sakyamuni Buddha which will be placed in the new Grand Hall, currently under construction.

The temple is noted for its rare Mi shrines from a sect that is all the more unusual because its modern development dates to the Communist era. The Mi sect is a branch of Buddhism with its own gods and practices, which originated in India and flourished briefly in China during the Tang dynasty, before spreading to Japan. Mi then disappeared in China, before the monk Zhisong revived it in 1953, when Jing An's Mi shrines were first built. Yet the vicissitudes of the Cultural Revolution and Zhison's own death put paid to the revival. Jing An's Mi shrines are reputedly undergoing renovation, yet remain out of view. To the rear of the temple, however, a massive, gilded Thai-style tower is being built.

Paramount ❻
Báilèmén 白乐门

✉ 218 Yuyuan Road ☎ 6249 8866
🕐 daily from 7.15pm onwards
🚇 Jing An Temple

Just west of Jing An Temple is the **Paramount**. One of Old Shanghai's great nightclubs, a 2001 renovation removed all trace of the original and created a bar and nightclub for the New Shanghai. The Paramount is undergoing a second renovation, but remains open with just one bar operating (and no nightclub).

Jing An Park ❼ Jìngān
Gōngyuán 静安公园

✉ 1649 Nanjing Road (W), entrance also on Huashan Road 🕐 park is free but entrance to the "Eight Scenes of Jing An Temple" within the park costs RMB 3 🚇 Jing An Temple

RIGHT: Jing An Park.
BELOW: the bright lights beckon at the Paramount nightclub.

Recommended Restaurants & Cafés on page 191

Directly across the street from Jing An Temple is where elderly men sit on benches shaded by the plane trees that once lined the entrance to Bubbling Well Cemetery (Yong Quan), **Jing An Park**'s previous incarnation. The well has long since been paved over, but the park has built a reproduction of the eight famous scenes of ancient Jing An Temple at one corner. The idyllic **Bali Laguna** restaurant *(see page 191)* in the park serving Indonesian cuisine has an outdoor terrace that overlooks a lily pond.

SOUTH OF YAN'AN ROAD

The area south of Yan'an Road, the old dividing line between the International Settlement and the French Concession, is much more residential. Plane trees line the streets, and the shopping and dining options are on a much more boutique scale.

Municipal Children's Palace ❽ Shì Shàonián Gōng 市少年宫

✉ 64 Central Yan'an Road ☎ 6248 1850 ◉ free (but call to arrange visit) 🚇 Jingan Temple

West of Jing An Park, across Huashan Road, is the **Municipal Children's Palace**, where gifted children are trained in art, music, drama, dance and, more recently, computers. There are several Children's Palaces in the city, but this is the largest and most visited. Originally built as the **Marble Hall** – marble was used throughout the house, particularly in the gorgeous fireplaces and hallways – for the wealthy Jewish Kadoorie family, the mansion was completed in 1924 after six years of construction. Run by a coterie of 43 servants, this was the first house in the city to have air conditioning. Visitors can come here and watch apple-cheeked children perform under the 5½-metre (18ft) tall chandeliers in the magnificent ballroom.

Cai Yuanpei's Former Residence ❾ Cài Yuánpéi Gùjū 蔡元培故居

✉ No. 16, Lane 303 Huashan Road ☎ 6248 4996 ◉ Tue–Sun 9–11.30am, 1–4.30pm ◉ free 🚇 Changshu Road

Monument to Cai Yuanpei (1863–1940) – the famous Chinese educator, scholar and politician.

BELOW: the Municipal Children's Palace was known as Marble Hall in the Concession days. This was where the wealthy Jewish Kadoorie family lived.

TIP

For great city views, take a night ride in the glass elevator to the 39th floor of the Hilton Hotel (Xierdun Fandian) at 250 Huashan Road.

Close-up of Chinese blue nankeen cloth.

RIGHT: exhibits at the Chinese Printed Blue Nankeen Exhibition Hall.
BELOW: dining at Mesa.

It's a 10-minute walk south, past the **Hilton Shanghai** (Xierdun Fandian), to **Cai Yuanpei's Former Residence**, a German-style villa where the great education reformer Cai Yuanpei lived in 1937. An exhibition tells the life of the man who was the first Kuomintang minister of education and past president of Jiao Tong University.

Julu Road nightlife

The restaurants and bars of **Julu Road** 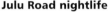 are just across the street. Once one of Shanghai's raunchiest bar strips, Julu Road (Julu Lu) has gone upscale and with its cross street, **Fumin Road** (Fumin Lu), is home to a host of chic restaurants – including trendy fusion restaurant **Mesa** *(see opposite)* and stylishly hip Japanese eatery **Shintori** *(see opposite)* – galleries and cafés.

A right turn on **Fumin Road** leads to galleries like **Madame Mao's Dowry** (at No. 207), which specialises in early modern Chinese design, and **Baoluo** restaurant *(see opposite)*, where customers wait in line for its delicious Shanghainese food.

Chinese Printed Blue Nankeen Exhibition Hall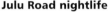
Zhōngguó Lànyìnhuābù Guǎn
中国蓝印花布馆

No. 24 Lane 637, Changle Road
5403 7947 | daily 9am–4.30pm
free | Changshu Road

A right turn from Fumin Road into Changle Road reveals a vista of "Tudor-bethan" houses, leading to the **Chinese Printed Blue Nankeen Exhibition Hall**. Here, in a lovely Concession-era villa, are displays of Shanghai's famous indigo blue cloth.

Local lore credits the famous Jiangsu province weaver called Huang Dapo with bringing this wax-resistant dying technique (much like batik) to the Jiangnan area, where it was applied to *nankeen* cloth, a brownish-yellow fabric woven from the indigenous *gossypium religiosum* cotton. The fabric is named after Nanking, now Nanjing, the capital of Jiangnan.

The small museum here documents the process of making *nankeen* cloth, in which wax is first poured onto hand-cut stencils which feature designs linked to folk tales or traditional symbols. The cloth is dunked into a steaming dye bath of indigo leaves – indigo that first came to China from India via the Silk Road – after which the wax is scraped off to reveal the designs. The museum also features a small collection of antique *nankeen*, while the adjoining shop sells clothes, fabrics and accessories, all made of *nankeen* fabric. ❏

BEST RESTAURANTS AND CAFÉS

Chinese

Baoluo

保罗酒楼

✉ 271 Fumin Road 📞 5403 7239 🕐 daily 24 hours. **$** [p325, C1]

Locals patiently stand in line at this neighbourhood restaurant for the classic home-style Shanghainese food (a favourite of *New York Times* food critic Johnny Apple) – drunken crab, "strange-flavoured" eggplant and *cao fu* (wheat gluten) are among the specialities. The decor is simple, but the service is efficient.

Lynn

琳怡中餐厅

✉ 99-1 Xikang Road 📞 6247 0101 🕐 daily L & D. **$$** [p321, C3]

A chic Shanghainese restaurant, with an upscale environment but restrained prices. Dishes include the classics of Shanghai fare: redcooked pork, *xiaolong bao* dumplings, steamed yellow croaker, and other local favourites.

Yang's Fry Dumplings

小杨生煎

✉ 54 & 60 Wujiang Road 🕐 daily 10.30am–11pm. **$** [p321, D3]

A tiny restaurant and takeaway that is a Shanghai institution. The "fry dumplings" in question are *sengjianbao*, fried and topped with sesame and chives, and stuffed with a mixture of ground pork and ginger. They contain a scalding broth within, so be careful when you bite.

Continental

Baker & Spice

保罗贝香

✉ 1/F, Shanghai Centre, 1376 Nanjing West Road 📞 5404 2733 🕐 daily 7am–9pm. **$** [p321, C3]

Baker & Spice carries a tempting array of hard-to-find (in Shanghai), reasonably priced, freshly baked goods. This is the place to come for a variety of breads, muffins, cakes, pastries, sandwiches and even jams and pâtés in a pleasant boutique bakery. There is another branch on Anfu Road.

Element Fresh

新元素

✉ Shanghai Centre, 1376 Nanjing Road (W); www.elementfresh.com 📞 6385 8752 🕐 daily 7am–11pm. **$$** [p321, C3]

A light-filled Californiastyle eatery (branches all over Shanghai) with big breakfasts, as well as wraps, pastas, sandwiches, salads and smoothies (plus more substantial dinners).

Fusion

Mesa

魅莎

✉ 748 Julu Road 📞 6289 9108; www.mesa-manifesto.com 🕐 daily L & D. **$$$** [p325, C1]

A lovely urban oasis housed in a renovated electronics factory, Mesa serves creative modern Australian cuisine. Seafood is the heart of the menu, and owner-chef Steve Baker incorporates fusion elements to create unique dishes. Upstairs, Manifesto bar draws a fashionable, late-night crowd.

Indonesian

Bali Laguna

巴厘岛

✉ 189 Huashan Road; www.balilaguna.com 📞 6248 6970 🕐 daily L & D. **$$** [p320, C4]

A pretty lakeside setting in Jing An Park, with a

wooden interior and sarong-clad staff, make this the closest thing to Bali in Shanghai. The food is reliably good and includes dishes like *rendang* (spicy beef) and satay, but the flavours aren't terribly authentic.

Japanese

Shintori

新都里无二

✉ 803 Julu Road 📞 5404 5252 🕐 Mon–Fri D only, Sat–Sun L & D. **$$$** [p325, C1]

Very hip, nouvelle Japanese bistro frequented by a sophisticated, cosmopolitan clientele. The sushi and sashimi are amazing, as are the updated takes on classic Japanese dishes.

Prices for a three-course meal for two people, excluding drinks:

$ = under RMB 250
$$ = RMB 250–500
$$$ = RMB 500–800
$$$$ = over RMB 800

ABOVE RIGHT: sea bass on a bed of risotto at Mesa.

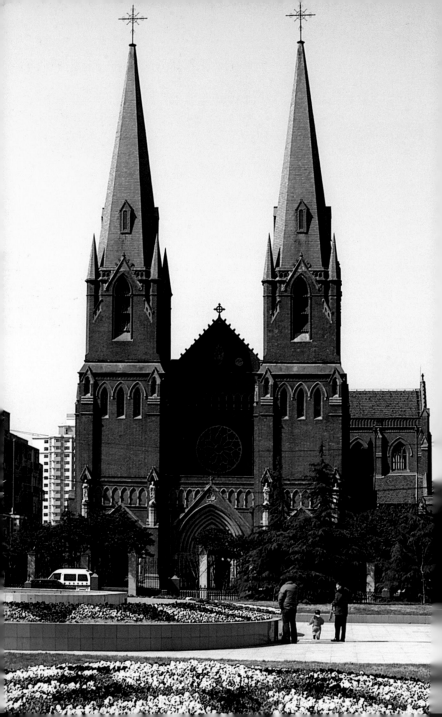

Recommended Restaurants & Cafés on page 199

XUJIAHUI AND LONGHUA

South of downtown Shanghai are shopping malls galore.
But scattered in this area are gems such as the French
Gothic St Ignatius Cathedral, the city's most authentic
Chinese temple at Longhua, and the lush Botanical
Gardens – perfect for an escape from the city

An improbable combination of mass-market shopping and two of the city's most revered holy sites, the Xujiahui and Longhua areas bristle with a chaotic cacophony of mega-malls and skyscrapers, all heightened by the confused flow of traffic at the confluence of eight roads. Crossing over from tranquil Xujiahui Park and the elite Huaihai/Hengshan neighbourhood *(see page 171)*, it is almost as if an invisible line has been crossed – and in a way, it has.

AROUND XUJIAHUI

Xujiahui lies on the western border of the former French Concession. The area still offers the real-estate bargains that attracted the churches, temples, airports and prisons of yesteryear. Today, it houses cathedrals of commerce, and condominiums for yuppies who can't afford the prices downtown.

Meaning "Xu family village", Xujiahui is named after China's first Catholic family. Ming court official Xu Guangqi or Paul Xu *(see text box page 30)* was born here in 1562 and was Jesuit missionary Matteo Ricci's first convert as well as his personal assistant. Xu's legacy lived on for centuries afterwards, sometimes in unexpected ways: illustrious Xu descendants include another Shanghai first family, the Soongs (on their mother's side).

Shanghai Library Bibliotheca Zi-ka-wei ❶
Shànghǎi Túshūguǎn Xújiāhuì Cángshū Lóu
上海图书馆徐家汇藏书楼

✉ 80 Caoxi Road ☎ 6487 4095 ext 208 ⏰ Mon–Sat 9am–5pm; library tours on Sat 2–4pm but call ahead to reserve ⓔ free 🚇 Xujiahui

LEFT: St Ignatius (or Xujiahui) Cathedral.
RIGHT: Bibliotheca Zi-ka-wei.

The lovely **Shanghai Library Bibliotheca Zi-ka-wei** is part of that Xu legacy. Built in 1847 on land that had been donated by Xu for the founding of a Jesuit community, this was the first public library in Shanghai. The three-storey building originally served as the priests' residence, while the adjacent two-storey building, then as now, holds the Jesuit library.

The ground floor of the two-storey building is designed in the style of a classic Qing library, while the beautiful upper storey is a fine copy of the Vatican Library. The Bibliotheca holds 80,000 volumes in several languages, and includes collections inherited after their original owners fled Shanghai in the wake of the Communist takeover, including the collection of the Royal Asiatic Society. Look out for the fine wooden carving of St Ignatius of Loyola on his deathbed, and another of St Francis in the public reading room on the second floor. The ground floor is taken up by an art gallery.

Wedding photos outside St Ignatius.

RIGHT: the upper level of the Bibliotheca is a copy of the Vatican Library.
BELOW: the Gothic interior of St Ignatius.

St Ignatius Cathedral ❷
Xújiāhuì Tiānzhǔtáng
徐家汇天主堂

✉ 158 Puxi Road ☎ 6438 4632
🕐 Sat–Sun 1–4pm, Mass (in Chinese) on weekdays at 7am, Sat at 7am and 6pm, and Sun at 6am, 7.30am, 10am and 6pm 🚇 Xujiahui

The soaring twin towers and flying buttresses of the French Gothic **St Ignatius Cathedral** (also known as **Xujiahui Cathedral**) is another legacy of Xu's Jesuit community. The very first St Ignatius Cathedral was built here in 1846. Named after the founder of the Society of Jesus order, the cathedral has remained essentially unchanged since a 1910 expansion – with the notable exception of the

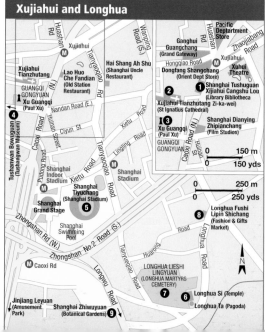

Recommended Restaurants & Cafés on page 1!

dramatic amputation of the 50-metre (165ft) twin tower and destruction of the stained-glass windows during the Cultural Revolution, when the church was forcibly closed.

The towers are now back in place, and new stained-glass windows, designed and created by a glass studio operated by nuns, are installed in the upper windows. The fascinating stained-glass panels take into account their Chinese context, with Chinese symbols and images rendered like traditional papercuts. A large rose window features a phoenix, surrounded by the Chinese zodiac. The church grounds feature a lovely grotto with a statue of the Virgin Mary with floral offerings at her feet. Services in Chinese are held daily and masses at Christmas and Easter are especially popular.

Guangqi Park ❸ Guāngqǐ Gōngyuán 光启公园

✉ 17 Nandan Road 🄲 6am–6pm ⓖ free 🚇 Xujiahui

The meteorological observatory that Xu established on the grounds of Xujiahui Cathedral is gone now, but its legacy lives on at the **Shanghai Meteorological Bureau**, a five-minute walk south of the cathedral.

Just next to the Bureau on a grassy plot of land is a **Statue of Paul Xu**, the scholar who made all this possible. Turn right just past the statue onto Nandan Road to pay your respects to Xu at his tomb at leafy **Guangqi Park**. Xu was buried here in 1641, and the tomb was last renovated in 1903. The ornamental columns and stone sculptures of goats and horses that lead to the tomb – the traditional "Spirit Way" – were added then.

Tushanguan Museum ❹ 土山湾博物馆 Tushanwan Bowuguan

✉ 55 Puihuitang Road 🄲 5424 9688 🄲 Tue–Sun 9am–6pm ⓖ free 🚇 Xujiahui

Located in the old Jesuit orphanage that taught Western arts and crafts to its charges – and is considered the cradle of Western art in China – this high-quality museum showcases the exquisite work made at

TIP

The spitting habit that you frequently witness comes from the Chinese belief that excess phlegm must be cleared, at the risk of ill health. The more refined may spit into handkerchiefs or trash cans, but if you hear a throat being cleared noisily – move!

BELOW: workers put the finishing touches to the ceremonial gate (*pailou*) on display at the Tushanguan Museum.

TIP

If you choose to have dinner at the Old Station Restaurant (see right and page 199), be sure to ask for a table, not in the restaurant proper, but in one of the two antique train carriages out in the gardens. Take note of the building too – this was a former Catholic convent.

the orphanage. There are paintings, photographs, prints and woodcarvings, but the highlight is a *pailou*, or ceremonial gate, made for the San Francisco World Fair in 1915 and returned to Shanghai in 2010, the year of the Expo.

Shopping and eating

Continue north along **Caoxi Road** to one of the few Jesuit buildings to survive the redevelopment of Xujiahui. After a tasteful restoration, the old Catholic convent, south of the cathedral, is now occupied by the **Old Station Restaurant** (Lao Huo Che Fandian). It serves Shanghainese cuisine in an interior embellished with beautiful floor tiles, carved wood and coloured glass (see page 199).

Continue along Caoxi Road to the intersection, where there is a different kind of shrine – this one to shopping. Here, the skyscrapers, traffic, giant ads and TV screens make it look like Times Square on speed. Sunlight floods the glass dome of the **Grand Gateway** (Ganghui Guangchang) mall, the city's largest, and on the escalators that glide up six floors

BELOW: snooker at Shanghai Grand Stage.

– four levels of shopping and two of restaurants and entertainment centres, plus a street-level food alley. The mall, which opened in 2000, has eclipsed its predecessors, the mid-market **Orient Department Store** (Dongfang Shangchang) at 8 Caoxi Road (N) and the **Pacific Department Store**. Computers and electronics are also a speciality of the area, found in places such as **Best Buy** in Fei Diao Tower (1065 Zhaojiabang Road).

Shanghai Stadium ❺
Shànghǎi Tǐyùchǎng
上海体育场

✉ 666 Tianyaoqiao Road
🚇 Shanghai Stadium

Continuing south on Tianyaoqiao Road leads to the east gate of the 80,000-capacity **Shanghai Stadium**, built in 1997 to host the China National Games. One of the projects "built to enhance people's lives", the stadium underwent a major spruce-up in 2007 for the Special Olympics Summer Games. More recently, this was the site of preliminary football matches for the 2008 Olympics.

Next door (and part of the same complex), the **Shanghai Grand Stage** hosts a wide variety of concerts, from the Rolling Stones to Hong Kong pop stars like Sandy Lam. If you'd like to do more than just watch, the stadium has tennis and badminton courts open to the public.

LONGHUA AREA

Heading southeast to **Longhua Road** leads to downtown Shanghai's only pagoda and temple, worth making the trek to as it's one of the city's most authentic Chinese places of worship.

Longhua Pagoda and Temple ❻ Lónghuá Tǎ Hé Sì
龙华塔和寺

✉ 2853 Longhua Road 📞 6456 6085
🕐 daily 7am–4.30pm; no entry to tower
💰 RMB 10 🚇 Long Cao Station

Recommended Restaurants & Cafés on page 199

The maroon wood and brick octagonal **Longhua Pagoda** looks as if it popped straight out of ancient China. The 44-metre (140ft) tower, whose tinkling bells on upturned eaves could once be heard all the way to the Huangpu River, was first built in AD 242 by a nobleman from the Wu Kingdom, although its current shape dates from an AD 922 reconstruction.

Rebuilt several times over the centuries, the pagoda served as a flak tower equipped with anti-aircraft guns during World War II, and was papered over with propaganda during the Cultural Revolution. Today, a modern shopping plaza, featuring Chinese-style buildings around the pagoda, has unfortunately robbed it of some of its languid charm.

Across the street stands the rambling **Longhua Temple** complex. With its incense-filled courtyards, giant joss burners and imposing Buddha images, this atmospheric temple is Shanghai's largest and most active. If there's one temple that you should see in Shanghai, this is it. Originally founded in AD 345, the Chan (Zen) Buddhist temple has been rebuilt several times over the years, and is considered a particularly fine example of Southern Song architecture. The current structure dates back to the 10th century.

Longhua contains some significant Buddha images: Sakyamuni Buddha's Bodhisattva form, in the **Hall of** **Heavenly Kings**, and in the **Maitreya Hall**, the Maitreya (or Future) Buddha incarnation, known as the "cloth bag monk". The temple's **Grand Hall** features a gilded meditating Sakyamuni Buddha, under a spiralling dome, with a statue of Guanyin (the Goddess of Mercy) in the rear, while the **Three Saints Hall** showcases the three incarnations of the Buddha.

Striking Longhua's **bronze bell**, cast in 1894 and weighing 6,500kg (14,330lbs), exactly 108 times (to erase the 108 worries of Buddhist thought) has become a Shanghai New Year's Eve tradition, as has the reinstituted Chinese New Year temple fair, China's largest, full of folk traditions and dances. The fair's popularity has led to another being held in the spring.

Longhua Pagoda is a key landmark in south Shanghai.

Shanghai Longhua Martyrs Cemetery ❼ Lónghuá Lièshí Língyuán 龙华烈士陵园

✉ 180 Longhua Road ☎ 6468 5995
🕐 daily 9am–3.30pm 💲 free
🚇 Long Cao Station

Exit the temple and enter this cemetery, which commemorates a tragic moment in Shanghai's history.

LEFT: multi-armed Guan Yin image at Longhua Temple.
BELOW: burning incense at Longhua Temple.

Memorial statue at the Longhua Cemetery of Revolutionary Martyrs.

Hundreds of idealistic young Communists were killed during what has become known as the White Terror, the ruling Kuomintang's reign of terror against the Communists, carried out in Shanghai by the notorious Green Gang. On 12 April 1927, these revolutionaries were pulled from their homes, rounded up and taken to the execution grounds at what was then the Longhua Garrison. Each April, Longhua's orchard of peach trees blossoms in remembrance, looking remarkably like the tissue-paper flowers made for funerals.

The cemetery today is all landscaped gardens and high-tech fountains, with a blue-glass Louvre-esque pyramid and a Memorial Hall dedicated to the Communist martyrs. Outside, an eternal flame burns in front of a Herculean sculpture being swallowed up by the earth, and the marble graves of the martyrs lie in a semicircle.

A corner of the park features the tiny prison cells of the KMT **Songhu Garrison Headquarters**, later the infamous Longhua prison camp – the setting for much of J.G. Ballard's

BELOW: Shanghai Botanical Gardens.

1984 autobiographical account of the Japanese Occupation of Shanghai, *Empire of the Sun*. But the focus here is the ill-treatment of Communist revolutionaries by Chiang Kaishek's army, with exhibition rooms featuring re-creations of the prison and photographs of those martyred.

Longhua Fashion and Gifts Market ❽ Lónghuá Fúshì Lǐpǐn Shìchǎng 龙华服饰礼品市场

✉ 2465 Longhua Road Ⓒ daily 9am–7.30pm 🚇 Long Cao Station

Many of the vendors from Shanghai's infamous Xiangyang Market at downtown Central Huaihai Road – known for its fake goods and illegally acquired genuine products – relocated to the **Longhua Fashion and Gifts Market** after Xiangyang was shut down in 2006. The volume of stalls at the market, just south of the cemetery, is overwhelming – 600 stalls on three floors, packed cheek to jowl with clothing, shoes, hats, suitcases and much more. But despite the presence of a handful of touts, the market – perhaps because of the out-of-the-way location – lacks the crowds, the buzz and the energy of its predecessor.

SOUTH SHANGHAI

This area is close enough to commute, but far enough away to provide space for greenery and relaxation. The attractions range from the lush greenery of the Botanical Gardens to two artificial playgrounds for the family.

Shanghai Botanical Gardens ❾ Shànghǎi Zhíwùyuán 上海植物园

✉ 1100 Longwu Road 📞 5436 3369 Ⓒ summer daily 7am–6pm, winter daily 8am–5pm Ⓐ RMB 15 garden only, RMB 40 includes Bonsai Garden

The **Shanghai Botanical Gardens**, located about 2km (1¼ miles) south of

Longhua Pagoda, is a rambling green vista of lakes, pine trees and over 9,000 plants. It is known for its bonsai collection in the Penjing Garden, the Orchid Garden, medicinal plants and a pair of 18th-century pomegranate trees, as well as its spring and autumn flower festivals. Fans of Shanghai's blue and white *nankeen* fabric should pay their respects at the Huang Dapo Memorial Temple in the grounds: Huang is the legendary figure who brought the technique of *nankeen*-dyeing to the Jiangsu region.

ing pirate ship and the haunted house attractions.

Jinjiang Amusement Park
Jǐnjiāng Lèyuán 锦江乐园

✉ 201 Hongmei Road 📞 5420 4956
🕐 daily 8.30am–5pm 💰 RMB 70

West of the Botanical Gardens, in Minhang district, is **Jinjiang Amusement Park** – usually sparsely attended despite its claim to fame as home of the world's second-largest Ferris wheel. The Ferris wheel is new, but the rest of the amusement park has seen better days – nonetheless, kids universally seem to enjoy the swing-

Dino Beach Rèdài Fēngbào
Shuǐshàng Léyuán
热带风暴水上乐园

✉ 78 Xinzhen Road 📞 6478 3333
🕐 daily 9am–9pm, until later from mid-July to mid-August 💰 RMB 150

Also in Minhang is **Dino Beach**, which has the world's biggest wave pool, along with whitewater rafting, slides, tubes and a huge man-made beach. It's a good way to cool down in summer, but weekends see huge crowds. ❏ **ABOVE:** Dino Beach.

RESTAURANTS AND CAFÉS

Chinese

Fwuh Luh Pavilion
福禄居

✉ 603B, 6/F, Grand Gateway, 1 Hongqiao Lu 📞 6407 9898 🕐 daily L & D. **$$$$**
[p324, B4, off map]
Fwuh Luh's location in a mall belies its luxury – both of the food and the setting. Fwu Luh is as glamorous as its Hong Kong film-star owner, with deep red walls and delicate ebony chopsticks. It serves a sophisticated version of

Yangzhou cuisine, known for the subtlety of its flavours; the spectacularly tender duck is a highlight.

Old Station Restaurant
上海老站

✉ 201 Caoxi Road (N)
📞 6427 2233 🕐 daily L & D. **$$** [p324, B4, off map]
Fine Shanghainese cuisine served up with a slice of nostalgia in this beautiful former convent, its antique tiles and polished wood still intact.

Diners can choose to be seated in the old-world dining room or in one of the two gorgeously restored antique trains parked in the garden: an 1899 German-built carriage once used by the empress dowager, or the 1919 Russian beauty that Soong Ching Ling rode in.

Continental

Bistrow by Wagas

✉ 151–153A Grand Gateway, 1 Hongqiao Lu; www.wagas.com.cn
📞 6448 2852 🕐 daily 7.30–1am. **$**
[p324, B4, off map]

Wagas, a chain of delis, goes upscale with Bistrow. Dishes include house-made pâté, the famous Bistrow Burger, grilled salmon, and home-style desserts such as carrot cake and lemon meringue pie. Different menus are offered to suit whatever time of the day or night you visit.

Prices for a three-course meal for two people, excluding drinks:
$ = under RMB 250
$$ = RMB 250–500
$$$ = RMB 500–800
$$$$ = over RMB 800

Recommended Restaurants & Cafés on page 209

HONGQIAO AND CHANGNING

The suburb of Hongqiao, where expatriates live in high-walled compounds, contains a few scattered sights like the Soong Ching Ling Mausoleum and a zoo. Middle-class Changning, which is fast catching up, is home to leafy Zhongshan Park and some architectural gems

There's a much more suburban feel in the western districts of Hongqiao and Changning, with their big houses, schools, megamarts and shopping. Lying outside the central downtown core, land is cheaper, something that parks, warehouse shops, office buildings and hotels are taking advantage of.

The same was true when the area lay outside the Concession borders, when tycoons built their country estates here, to allow them to live in the manner of the landed gentry. Remnants of their old lives still linger here – mansions, gardens and churches dot the area, adding to the character.

HONGQIAO

The expatriates on corporate packages and wealthy Chinese who live in Hongqiao's high-walled compounds, each bigger and fancier than the last, are merely the latest to seek the lifestyle of the gentry in Hongqiao. A century ago, this was all rolling land, perfect for large country estates, horseback riding – and the unique Shanghai Paper Hunt. Brought to Shanghai in the late 19th century by military officers who had "hunted" in other parts of the world, paper hunting involved a 16km (10-mile)

cross-country ride on horseback, following a twisting, turning trail of paper to the finish line.

Soong Ching Ling Mausoleum ❶ Sòng Qìnglíng Língyuán 宋庆龄陵园

✉ 21 Songyuan Road ☏ 6275 4034, ext 541 ⏰ daily 8.30am–5pm
🎫 RMB 5

There is perhaps no more concrete evidence of foreign presence in Shanghai than the **"Foreigners Tomb Area"**

Main attractions
SOONG CHING LING MAUSOLEUM
ANTIQUES SHOPS AND WARE-
HOUSES AT HONGQIAO ROAD
AND WUZHONG ROAD
CHANGNING DISTRICT CHILDREN
PALACE
ZHONGSHAN PARK
CHANGFENG OCEAN WORLD

LEFT: leafy Zhongshan Park in autumn.
RIGHT: Soong Ching Ling Mausoleum.

in the **Soong Ching Ling Mausoleum**. Built in 1909 as the International Cemetery, the tombstones here bear identical stone markers and strange spellings ("Feliks, Nanooer, Eoolc, Marly Jone"), indicating that the original graves were moved and new markers recreated. Some of Shanghai's famous names lie here: Sir Elly Kadoorie, whose magnificent Marble Hall still stands as the Municipal Children's Palace *(see page 189)*, and Lady Laura Kadoorie, who died trying to rescue her children's nanny when an earlier home went up in flames. Joseph Sassoon Gubbay and Aaron Sassoon Gubbay, a branch of the family who built the Peace Hotel, also rest here, having died within three days of each other in August 1946.

There are more luminaries in the adjacent "celebrity cemetery", where the tombstones are carved in the likeness of the dead. Here rest patriots, war heroes and martyrs. The centrepiece of course is Soong

Ching Ling's gravesite, with a white marble statue in her likeness set above the grave. The grave itself is marked by a simple stone slab and surrounded by pine trees.

One of the three Soong sisters and wife of Sun Yat-sen, Ching Ling is the only one of the influential Soongs who remained in China. Children come here to pay homage to the childless Soong, who was instrumental in setting up the Shanghai Children's Palaces – an after-school programme offering children training in art, music, dance and drama.

The **Soong Ching Ling Exhibition Hall**, located near the main entrance, recounts Soong's life as an exemplary Communist and is filled with all sorts of interesting memorabilia and artefacts documenting her life.

Antiques Row

Head west along Hongqiao Road to the so-called **Antiques Row** ❷. Cavernous shops here such as Alex's

Soong Ching Ling's tombstone lies in the only cemetery left in Shanghai today. Modern Shanghai cremates the dead.

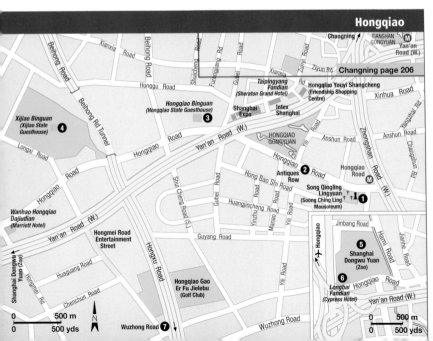

Recommended Restaurants & Cafés on page 209

Xijiao State Guesthouse ❹
Xījiāo Bīnguǎn 西郊宾馆

The well-guarded **Xijiao State Guest-house** at 1921 Hongqiao Road *(see page 280)*, about a 10-minute walk west, is where notables like the Queen of England and the Emperor of Japan have stayed in the past. The complex includes a stunning Frank Lloyd Wright-inspired house, now Building No. 4, built for a Chinese entrepreneur in 1949. Set on a sloping hill, its sliding roof, use of glass walls and an indoor garden with a Japanese bridge create a link between the interior and exterior. A stream runs through the peaceful compound, whose vast lawns include a lake and pavilions.

Antique altar table at one of the Hongqiao Road antiques shops.

Shanghai Zoo ❺ Shànghǎi Dòngwù Yuán 上海动物园

✉ 2831 Hongqiao Road ☎ 6268 7775 ext 8000 ⏰ daily 7.30am–5pm 💰 RMB 30 (children up to 1.4 metres free)

Continuing west on Hongqiao Road leads to the rolling grounds of the former Hungjao Golf Club, which became the **Shanghai Zoo** in 1954.

LEFT: Hongqiao Road antiques shop.
BELOW: the sprawling grounds of Xijiao State Guesthouse.

Antiques (No. 1970; tel: 6242 8734) are an antiques-lover's dream, offering a window into a China when bridal dowries arrived in wedding baskets, ginger was preserved in porcelain jars, and washbasins and chamber pots were commonplace. Some of the cabinets, chairs, altar tables and beds have already been refinished; watching the craftsmen at work is a real treat. Be aware that with Qing-era antiques dwindling, reproductions are common these days.

Hongqiao State Guesthouse
❸ Hóngqiáo Bīnguǎn 虹桥宾馆

Continuing west along Hongqiao Road, there is some exceptional accommodation, starting with the **Hongqiao State Guesthouse** at 1591 Hongqiao Road *(see page 280)*. Set within some 40 hectares (100 acres) of lush gardens is a collection of vintage villas in architectural styles ranging from Art Deco to Spanish Colonial. The sprawling lawns and shady trees assure the privacy of its long-term residents and VIP guests.

The grounds are dotted with pavilions, and the streams are stocked with swans, pelicans and Mandarin ducks, but the zoo, like most zoos in China, is hardly idyllic. The lethargic Giant pandas, a symbol of China, are on most tourist agendas, but far nicer are the chimp habitats, funded by the local branch of Jane Goodall's environmental organisation, Roots & Shoots. Kids will enjoy feeding the ducks and stroking the goats at the petting zoo.

Cypress Hotel ❻ Lóngbǎi Fàndiàn 龙柏饭店

Further west is another unique lodging, the **Cypress Hotel**, at 2419 Hongqiao Road *(see page 280)*. It is set in the verdant country estate of Jewish millionaire Victor Sassoon, who built the Peace Hotel *(see page 114)*. His half-timber faux-Tudor mansion, formerly called **Sassoon Villa**, and scene of many a wild party given by the avid horse-racer and man about town in the 1930s, still stands next door. The mansion is being renovated at the time of writing.

RIGHT: Giant panda at the Shanghai Zoo.
BELOW: Sassoon Villa on the grounds of the Cypress Hotel – where many a wild party was thrown in its heyday.

South of Hongqiao Road

Head south, across Yan'an Road, to the **Hongmei Entertainment Street**, a lively food street which is popular with expatriates who live nearby. Packed with branches of favourite downtown restaurants and bars (like Simply Thai, Blue Frog, Big Bamboo) as well as local restaurants, it's a nice place for a lesiurely dinner or a night out at the pub.

The 18-hole **Hongqiao Golf Club** (Hongqiao Gao Er Fu Jielebu) – another reason why expats favour this area – is a little further south, with the entrance at 567 Hongxu Road.

Continue south along **Hongxu Road** to **Wuzhong Road ❼**; a clutch of good antiques shops and warehouses are found along both roads. On Hongxu Road is the well-respected **Shanxi Antique Furniture** (No. 731; tel: 6401 0056). Wuzhong Road is equally good for antiques and furniture. One of the best (and most honest) stores, **Hu & Hu** used to be here until it moved further south to No. 8 Caobao Road (tel: 3431 1212; www.hu-hu.com). The friendly owner, Marybelle Hu, is a veteran of Sotheby's, and her shop offers both antiques and reproductions as well as custom-made pieces.

CHANGNING

Up-and-coming **Changning** district, which borders Hongqiao to the north, is in the process of revamping itself. New luxury apartments, offices and hotels are fast coming up in an area that was formerly in the "B" list

Recommended Restaurants & Cafés on page 209

realm. Still, its pre-Revolution ambience, from the days when the area attracted a heady brew of revolutionaries, missionaries and spies who sought land and a life removed from the law, still exists. Between the tall office towers, the lanes are still filled with working-class people, many of whom live packed five families to a floor in vintage apartments or squeeze several families into houses originally built for just one family.

Xingguo Guesthouse ❽
Xīngguó Bīnguǎn 兴国宾馆

At the edge of this one-time renegade neighbourhood, in the old French Concession area, is a touch of old-world gentility at the **Xingguo Guesthouse** (78 Xingguo Road). Commissioned in 1934 by the Butterfield and Swire company, British architect Clough Williams-Ellis created an English country estate complete with playing fields on the serpentine curve of Avenue Haig, now Huashan Road. Today, the vast lawns and spreading camphor trees meander around an architectural mélange of French, Italian and neoclassical white-

washed mansions, which still evoke a gracious weekend-in-the-country air. Butterfield and Swire quit China in 1950, but the mansion remained in favour with another powerful figure. Whenever he was in Shanghai, Chairman Mao Zedong enjoyed staying at **Building Number One**, with its dramatic, sweeping staircase, stately Ionic columns and wide outdoor terrace.

Today, the guesthouse is a preferred government official accommodation. Now under the management of the **Radisson Plaza Xingguo Hotel** *(see page 280)*, Number One is renovated and still a guesthouse (but only open to long-term guests when it is not occupied by state visitors). The other old houses on the estate serve as

Changning is full of lovely old houses like this one, but unfortunately many are run-down, with several families squeezed in cheek by jowl.

LEFT: wrought-iron staircase at Building Number One in the Xingguo Guesthouse. **BELOW:** Chinese furniture on sale at a Wuzhong Road shop.

offices and restaurants. More recent 1990s prefab houses occupied by expatriates sit on the old playing fields, while the Radisson Plaza Xingguo's modern high-rise hotel lies on the cusp of the estate.

No. 3 Middle School for Girls ❾ Dìsān Nǚzhōng or Shìsān Nǚzhōng 第三女中 or 市三女中

Jiangsu Road, north of the hotel, is a bustling thoroughfare lined with shabby office buildings, shops and the occasional ostentatious former residence of a Kuomintang official. On the corner with Wuding Road, a vestige of the street's old incarnation as Edinburgh Road surfaces. The Gothic turrets and stained-glass windows of the **No. 3 Middle School for Girls** (ask for permission to enter) indicate the building's origins as the McTyeire School for Girls, founded in 1890 by the Southern Methodist Mission and named after Bishop

No. 3 Middle School for Girls was formerly known as the McTyeire School. This was where the famous Soong sisters were educated.

RIGHT:
students at the No. 3 Middle School for Girls.

Holland McTyeire, the Mission's head in China and then chancellor of Tennessee's Vanderbilt University.

McTyeire was once the city's most exclusive school for the daughters of Shanghai's elite. When the precocious Soong Ai Ling entered its gates at the age of five, her enchanted older classmates made her the school mascot, dubbing her "Soong tai-tai" (Madam Soong). Three decades later, the world would come to know the Soong sisters – Ai Ling, Ching Ling and May Ling, McTyeire girls all – as the wives of wealthy banker H.H. Kung, Kuomintang leader Sun Yat-sen and General Chiang Kai-shek, respectively.

After a brief respite as a co-educational school during the Cul-

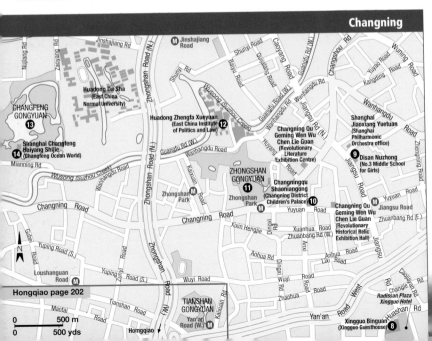

tural Revolution, the city's privileged daughters are back at the renamed top-ranked girls' school. Dressed in egalitarian uniforms, they line up in the shadow of the dove-grey Gothic buildings for classes. Every spring, the girls still play baseball, a McTyeire American tradition that has somehow survived Communist China.

Shanghai Philharmonic Orchestra office Shànghǎi Jiāoxiǎng Yuètuán
上海交响乐团

Two blocks north and around the corner on Wuding Road (W) at No. 1498 is the **office building** of the **Shanghai Philharmonic Orchestra** (ask for permission to enter), its black ironwork gates embellished with treble clefs and the orchestra logo. The orchestra inherited the mansion from the Shanghai Opera School, which had claimed it after the Communist victory – Western opera apparently not being bourgeois enough to be outlawed. A stone fountain, its edges carved with grimacing masks, is found in the garden, while inside, sensitive restoration has returned the mansion to something of its former glory.

Changning District Children's Palace ⑩
Chángníngqū Shàoniángōng
长宁区少年宫

✉ No. 31, Lane 1136, Yuyuan Road
☎ 6252 4154 to arrange for a visit
🚇 Jiangsu Road

Just a few houses west, the florid Teutonic castle-like exterior of the **Changning District Children's Palace** hints at its colourful history. The dream house of the Kuomintang minister of transportation, Wang Boqun, created a stir when it was built in 1930 as a gift for his second wife – the house was overly ostentatious and Wang's new wife, Bao Zhining, was almost 30 years his junior. The sprawling 5,000-sq-metre

(53,820-sq-ft) garden once had small bridges with flowing water and pavilions nestled among the flowers and trees. The main building's marble columns, Gothic arches, 32 rooms and fireplaces are still intact.

During the Japanese Occupation (1937–45), it became the home of the head of the Japanese-endorsed Kuomintang puppet government, the traitor Wang Jing-wei. After the war, Kuomintang spies took over the house and it became a prison and execution ground for Communist revolutionaries. Pressed into use as government offices after 1949, the building has served peaceably as the local Children's Palace since 1960, its after-school activities programme offering gifted children training in art, music, dance and drama.

Girls at the Changning District Children's Palace practising the pipa.

Zhongshan Park ⑪
Zhōngshān Gōngyuán
中山公园

✉ 780 Changning Road ⏰ daily 6am–6pm 💲 free 🚇 Zhongshan Park

A futuristic-looking glass pyramid two blocks west encases the metro

BELOW: Changning District Children's Palace was built in 1930 as the home of a Kuomintang minister.

Flying a kite at Zhongshan Park.

BELOW: t'ai chi session at Zhongshan Park – a familiar sight at most parks in Shanghai.

stop at **Zhongshan Park** and serves as a design accessory to the slick, landscaped plaza that fronts it.

Inside the park, the contours of the Concession-era Jessfield Park remain. Jessfield was said to be named after a little girl called Jessie, who was rescued from the circus in Hongkou by a wealthy Portuguese gentleman. He sent her to university in America with a missionary chaperone, and later married her – naming his country estate after her. Anchored by a lotus-filled lake, the grounds are a favourite weekend destination for children who love the carnival atmosphere with its games, rides and proximity to McDonald's, just outside the park gate.

Mornings and evenings see t'ai chi practitioners and ballroom dancers doing their thing at this leafy park.

East China Institute of Politics and Law ⑫
Huádōng Zhèngfǎ Xuéyuàn
华东政法学院

The back entrance of the park on Wanhangdu Road leads to the leafy green campus and syncretic Sino-Anglo buildings of the **East China Institute of Politics and Law** (1575 Wanhangdu Road). It was founded in 1878 by the American Episcopal Mission as St John's University, the Harvard of China, which accounts for the campus's distinctly Ivy-League-on-the-Huangpu feel. St John's alumni once occupied the highest echelons of Shanghai and overseas Chinese society. Originally part of the Jessfield estate, the campus, with its century-old trees, makes for a nice stroll. The headmaster's house fuses 19th-century gingerbread design with classical Chinese eaves and roof.

Changfeng Park ⑬
Chángfēng Gōngyuán
长风公园

☒ 25 Daduhe Road ⊙ daily 6am–6pm ⊚ free ▣ Jinshajiang Road

Northwest and across Suzhou Creek, sprawling **Changfeng Park** is a breath of fresh air in a gritty neighbourhood, particularly during the spring flower festival when vibrant tulips, daffodils

and peonies bloom, and sculptures are fashioned from flowers.

Changfeng Ocean World ⓮
Shànghǎi Chángfēng Hǎiyáng Shìjiè 上海长风海洋世界

✉ Gate 4, Changfeng Park, 451 Daduhe Road ☎ 6223 5501 Ⓒ daily 8.30am–5pm Ⓖ RMB 110 adults, RMB 80 children 1–1.4 metres
🚇 Jinshajiang Road

Within Changfeng Park is **Changfeng Ocean World**, Shanghai's first modern aquarium. Designed with a South American jungle theme, the lush greenery enhances the aquatic exhibits, which include re-creations of rivers, rainforests and oceans. At its popular shark tunnel, oversized toothy sharks and giant rays swim overhead as you walk beneath; certi-

fied divers can arrange for a swim with the sharks. Children especially love the "touch pool", which allows a hands-on experience with sealife such as starfish, shrimps and crabs. There is also an adjoining 2,000-seat stadium for shows with dolphins and whales. ❑

ABOVE: marine life at Changfeng Ocean World, in Changfeng Park.

RESTAURANTS AND CAFÉS

American

Johnny Moo
音特美式奶牛餐厅
Yinte Meishi Nainiu Canting
✉ Block D, 3219 Hongmei Road ☎ 5175 9189
Ⓒ daily 9am–10pm. **$**
[p324, A2, off map]
A retro American diner with a spotted-cow decor dishing up retro American food: think classic cheeseburgers, milkshakes, fries and sundaes. A big favourite with

families and international schoolkids.

Continental

Da Marco
大马可意大利餐厅
✉ 103 Dongzhu'anbang Road, Golden Bridge Garden ☎ 6210 4495 Ⓒ daily L & D. **$$** [p324, A1]
Delicious, authentic Italian cuisine in a simple setting has made Da Marco's a long-time favourite with Italian expats. Pastas, soups, a variety of pizzas, seafood and meats, plus a decent wine list.

Le Bouchon
勃逊
✉ 1455 West Wuding Road; www.lebouchon-shanghai.

com ☎ 6225 7088
Ⓒ Mon–Sat, D only. **$$**
[p320, A4]
A delightful bistro that serves country-style southern French cuisine in a cosy, slightly quirky space (there's a tree growing in the middle of the dining room). Pâté, crêpes, salads, quiches, house-made desserts and a great wine list.

Chinese

1221
✉ 1221 West Yan'an Road ☎ 6213 2441 Ⓒ daily L & D. **$$** [p324, A2]
Accessible Chinese cuisine – thanks to an English menu and English-speaking staff – in a contemporary setting, Serves a wide à la carte menu and also dim sum. Favourites include the

braised eggplant, crispy duck, lemon chicken and the "eight treasure tea", poured dramatically from teapots with long spouts.

Thai

Simply Thai
天泰
✉ 28 Hongmei Entertainment Street, Lane 3338; www.simplythai-sh.com ☎ 6465 8955 Ⓒ daily L & D. **$$** [p324, A2, off map]
The city's western outpost of this popular, very authentic Thai restaurant has a slicker, more contemporary and pareddown look, but the rich, spicy cuisine is the same. Serves both the Thai classics for which it has become famous – curries, papaya salad, mango with sticky rice – plus innovative creations.

Prices for a three-course meal for two people, excluding drinks:

$ = under RMB 250
$$ = RMB 250–500
$$$ = RMB 500–800
$$$$ = over RMB 800

Recommended Restaurants & Cafés on page 221

HONGKOU

This unassuming area north of Suzhou Creek took major roles on the historical stage: it was the base for Japanese occupying forces, the home of the acerbic Chinese writer Lu Xun and the largest Far East refuge for Jews fleeing Nazism in Europe

Drab blocks of government housing and grimy warehouses are still what primarily define the character of the **Hongkou** district, the area north of the Suzhou Creek. Apart from the memorial hall to Chinese writer Lu Xun as its major tourist attraction, this is a very local area, without the mass-market appeal of Shanghai's big-name draws. Still, Hongkou has a rich history of its own that, until recently, was virtually untouched. But a renaissance is beginning: the old warehouses on Moganshan Road have been transformed into the city's best-known art district; a Cultural Street commemorates the great literary uprisings of the early 20th century; and the new Shanghai Port International cruise-ship terminal will add five-star hotels and restaurants.

Hongkou was little more than vegetable farms and swamps when Bishop William Boone – the first Anglican bishop in China – established the American Episcopal Church Mission here in 1848. It wasn't until six years later, in 1854, that the American Consul raised the US flag in Hongkou to com-memorate the official establishment of the American Settlement – which subsequently merged with the British Settlement to form the International Settlement in 1863. By 1900, the Japanese had established their presence here too. It made perfect sense, therefore, for the International Settlement to locate its support systems, like post offices, prisons, warehouses and waterworks, in Hongkou, given its combination of space and easy proximity to the financial district.

Main attractions
SHANGHAI POST MUSEUM
OHEL MOISHE SYNAGOGUE
GONGQING FOREST PARK
DUOLUN ROAD AREA
M50 ART GALLERIES
JADE BUDDHA TEMPLE

LEFT: historic Duolun Road in Hongkou.
RIGHT: Waibadu Bridge, which was built in 1907, spans Suzhou Creek.

ABOVE: Broadway Mansions and Waibadu Bridge.

Kuomintang leader Chiang Kai-shek had big plans for Hongkou, but the Japanese Occupation of Hong-kou and Zhabei in World War II materialised before his plans could. Hongkou also played a major war role as the home of both the Japan-ese occupying forces and stateless Jewish refugees (see page 214) flee-ing Hitler's Germany to one of the few places that would accept them.

NORTH OF SUZHOU CREEK

Cross into Hongkou the old-fash-ioned way, across **Waibaidu Bridge** (Waibaidu Qiao) which spans the Suzhou Creek – and much of the his-tory of Hongkou. Until 1856, the only way to cross Suzhou Creek into Hongkou was by ferry, but when the International Settlement found that inconvenient, a British entrepreneur decided to build a wooden bridge, naming it Wills Bridge after himself. His system of making the Chinese pay one copper coin for crossing the bridge while allowing foreigners to cross on credit didn't go down well, and the bridge was eventually dis-mantled and replaced by a floating bridge. In 1907, it was replaced by the steel Waibaidu Bridge (known in English then as Garden Bridge).

During the Japanese Occupation, the bridge served as the demarcation line between occupied Hongkou and Zhabei, and the International Settle-ment; it was guarded by turbaned

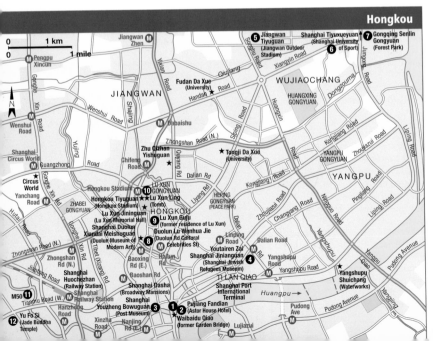

Recommended Restaurants & Cafés on page 221

Sikh policemen from the British forces on the Bund side and Japanese soldiers on the occupied side. Today, the bridge is an excellent vantage point for views of Pudong to the east and the Suzhou Creek to the west.

Broadway Mansions ❶
Shànghǎi Dàshà 上海大厦

✉ 20 Suzhou Road (N); www.broadwaymansions.com ☎ 6324 6260 🚇 Nanjing Road East + taxi

Across Waibadu Bridge, on the western side, is the 22-storey Art Deco facade of the **Broadway Mansions**, one of Asia's first high-rises, and built in 1934 as a hotel. The building is best remembered as the wartime Foreign Correspondents Club, which occupied the top six floors. From this perspective, some members recorded Shanghai's most memorable events: the 1937 Japanese bombing, and, in 1949, watching Marshal Chen Yi march in to "liberate" Shanghai.

A 2006 renovation has retained the high ceilings and spacious rooms, but not all the original details. The 18th-floor terrace offers stunning views of Suzhou Creek, the Bund and Pudong.

Astor House Hotel ❷
Pǔjiāng Fàndiàn 浦江饭店

✉ 15 Huangpu Road; www.pujianghotel.com ☎ 6324 6388 🚇 Nanjing Road East + taxi

The Victorian building on the eastern side of Waibadu Bridge is the **Astor House Hotel** – once one of Shanghai's most elegant hotels. Today, it has been downgraded to a modest three-star hotel. Built in 1910, the Astor attracted luminaries such as Charlie Chaplin and Albert Einstein in its heyday. The hotel was also famous for a number of Shanghai firsts: the first electric light, telephone, talkies, dance ball – even the taxi. Local lore has it that an

Astor House bellboy, handsomely rewarded for recovering a Russian guest's wallet with its contents, spend a third of it on a car. That car became Shanghai's first taxi and spawned the Johnson fleet, now known as Qian Sheng taxi. The interior architecture remains, its sweeping staircases and grand galleries recalling its past splendour.

Shanghai Post Museum ❸
Shànghǎi Yóuzhèng Bówùguǎn 上海邮政博物馆

✉ 250 Suzhou (N) Road ☎ 6362 9898 🕐 Wed, Thur, Sat, Sun 9am–5pm 🎫 free 🚇 Nanjing Road East + taxi

The **Shanghai Post Office**, a short walk west, still dominates the area, much as it did when it was built in 1924 to serve both foreigners and Chinese. Today, it is still the city's main post office. The **Shanghai Post Museum** is tucked at the back of the second floor and offers a good perspective on the history of the Chinese postal service – plus astounding views of Shanghai from its roof-terrace.

The Astor House Hotel.

BELOW: a re-creation of bygone postal days at the Shanghai Post Museum.

Jewish Sanctuary

Shanghai was a safe haven for many Jewish fleeing Nazi Europe. Hongkou, where they mostly lived, became a Jewish ghetto of sorts

Shanghai has always had a Jewish presence, beginning with the Sephardic Jewish families such as the Sassoons, Hardoons and Kadoories who built their vast fortunes in the city. They were followed by the Russian Jews, who fled the anti-Jewish pogroms and upheavals of early 19th-century Russia. During the 1930s, the new wave of Jews arriving in Shanghai were those fleeing the Holocaust in Europe.

For many European Jews, the smashing of the synagogues by rampaging anti-Jewish mobs in 1938 was the final push they needed to be convinced to leave their homeland, but the doors throughout the world were closed: Shanghai was the only place that did not require a visa or family connections. As a result, between 1938 and 1940, some 20,000 European Jews arrived in Shanghai.

In Austria, Jewish persecution reached a frenzy after it was annexed by Nazi Germany in March 1938. Although Shanghai did not require visas for entry, Jews who wanted to flee Austria were not allowed to leave unless they had visas to prove to the Nazis that another country had accepted them.

In order to help them, the Chinese Consul-General to Austria, a dapper young man named Ho Fengshan, quietly granted several thousand visas to Austrian Jews – with Shanghai as the end destination. Ho knew the visas were only a means of escape for Austrian Jews; in reality many of the visa recipients went on to other parts of the world. Under his watch, the Chinese Consulate in Vienna issued an average of 500 visas a month over the two-year period of his term from 1938–40. Ho is regarded today as China's Schindler and has been honoured by Israel.

The Japanese, who occupied Shanghai then, herded the Jewish refugees into a "designated area for stateless persons" in a section of Hongkou. The impetus for this was a visit by the butcher of Warsaw, Joseph Meisinger, who arrived with canisters of poisonous gas in Shanghai and suggested that concentration camps be set up on Chongming Island for the Jewish community.

The Japanese declined, instead insisting that all "stateless persons" move into the Hongkou ghetto. Times were difficult and food was scarce, but the refugees made the best of what they had, creating a "Little Europe" with cafés, delis and even a theatre – with financial help from longer-established Jewish families. Leaving the ghetto, for those who went to school or work outside, required a pass. They also had to bow low to the Japanese sentries when crossing Waibadu Bridge; failure to do so invited abuse.

As hard as life was under the Japanese in Shanghai, many refugees look back fondly on their time in the city. It was a time when people pulled together. And it was a time that saved many from almost certain death. ❏

ABOVE: Jewish refugees in Hongkou.
LEFT: Ho Fengshan, the Chinese Schindler.

Recommended Restaurants & Cafés on page 221

Just west of the post office, along Suzhou Creek, is the startlingly modern **Embankment House**. Built by the Sassoons *(see page 115)* in 1932, this was Shanghai's largest apartment house at the time, with 194 rooms; today it is rapidly becoming gentrified as Shanghai's new rich purchase and renovate the spacious apartments.

EAST HONGKOU

Heading east, along the Huangpu River, is the historic **dock area**, the cradle of Shanghai industry and once lined with the factories that fuelled Shanghai's growth. Now transformed into the **Shanghai Port International Terminal** with a host of high-rises surrounding it, the area will retain some of its historic warehouses – notably the castle-like **Yangshupu Waterworks** (Yangshupu Shuichang). Located by the waterfront at Yangshupu Road, it was built by the British in 1881. The waterworks has buildings for each step of the water filtration process and Victorian equipment that is still used today. From the Yangshupu Waterworks building, there are beautiful views of the majestic Yangpu Bridge.

Shanghai Jewish Refugees Museum ④ Yóutàirén Zài Shànghǎi Jìniànguǎn 犹太人在上海纪念馆

✉ 62 Changyang Road ☏ 6512 6669 ◷ daily 9am–5pm ⊙ RMB 50 🚇 Dalian Road + taxi

The Hongkou redevelopment zone, bordered by Zhoujiazui Road in the north, Wusong Road in the west and Dalian Road in the east, has destroyed what was left of "Little Vienna", Hongkou's old Jewish neighbourhood that provided a safe haven for some 20,000 refugees during World War II.

A few old buildings are left, at the heart of them the **Ohel Moishe Synagogue**, founded by the Russian Ashkenazi Jews in 1927. Today, the synagogue is the **Shanghai Jewish Refugees Museum**. It commemorates the exodus of Jewish people who fled from Europe to Shanghai during World War II, and who settled mostly in this area. The museum features exhibitions of historic pictures.

North of Yangshupu Waterworks, a plaque in **Huoshan Park** (Huoshan Gongyuan; daily 6am–6pm; free), on Huoshan Road, commemorates the area as the "designated area for stateless refugees" between 1937 and 1941. Back in the day, Huoshan Road and Zhoushan Road were homes to the Broadway Theatre and the original Vienna Café. Former US Treasury

The castle-like turrets at Yangshupu Waterworks – built by the British in 1881.

LEFT: furniture used by yesteryear Jewish at Ohel Moishe Synagogue. **BELOW:** view of Yangpu Bridge from Hongkou.

Shanghai University of Sport; its architecture fuses Western Art Deco with Ming-dynasty design.

BELOW: lush Gongqing Forest Park is the perfect antidote to the frenzy of Shanghai city.

Secretary Michael Blumenthal and pop artist Peter Max were some of the more famous Jewish migrants who lived in Hongkou as World War II refugees. Today, this area has reverted to being almost entirely Chinese.

YANGPU DISTRICT

Head northeast from Hongkou along Siping Road to one of the city's best-kept secrets. Chiang Kai-shek built his "new city" centre here in Yangpu district. If Chiang had had his way, this planned city would have showcased his new government. The Communists put paid to his plans, but the buildings still remain, classic examples of the fusion of Art Deco and Ming Chinese styles that defined the so-called Nanjing Decade architecture.

The first "new city" building on the wide boulevard is **Jiangwan Outdoor Stadium ❺** (Jiangwan Tiyuguan; daily 5.30am–1pm) at 346 Guohe Road, with its plain white, almost Grecian exterior decorated with Chinese designs in ornamental plaster. The jewel in the crown, though, is the **Shanghai University of Sport ❻** (Shanghai Tiyuxueyuan), housed in the former City Hall at 650 Qiu Yuan Huan Road. A stunning two-storey building with more than a touch of Forbidden City architecture, the interior is now being used as office space for university staff. From the steps of the old City Hall, two other Chinese-style buildings are visible, both of which are now being used as classrooms.

Gongqing Forest Park ❼
Gòngqīng Sēnlín Gōngyuán
共青森林公园

✉ 2000 Junjong Road; www.shgqsl.com Ⓒ daily 6am–5pm Ⓡ RMB 7 Ⓗ Hailun Road + taxi

A 15-minute drive from here leads to the very picturesque **Gongqing Forest Park**, where visitors can ride on horseback, boat on the lake, fish in the pond, have a barbecue, or simply enjoy lying on the grass – a luxury in Shanghai, where this most harmless and enjoyable activity is forbidden in most parks. This vast expanse of forested parkland offers a nice getaway from the buzz of the city.

Recommended Restaurants & Cafés on page 221

No. 2, Lane 201, Duolun Road
6540 8126 daily 9.30am–4pm
RMB 5 Dong Baoxing Lu

Lu Xun, together with other progressive writers, was instrumental in founding the League of Left Wing Writers. One of the writer's houses has been turned into the **League of Left Wing Writers Museum**. The former Chinese Arts University, where the league was founded in 1930 to "struggle for proletarian liberation" through writing, has preserved its interior. Collections of the league's works are showcased, along with an exhibition on the lives of the five martyred writers who were executed by a Kuomintang firing squad at the Longhua garrison during the Communist witch hunts in 1927 *(see page 198)*.

DUOLUN ROAD AREA

Considered the father of modern Chinese literature, Lu Xun was part of a circle of literati who lived around **Duolun Road**. His literary railing against social injustice earned him a place in the pantheon of modern China's most celebrated personalities. Hongkou takes great pride in the fact that Lu Xun chose to live in this area from 1927 until his death in 1936, and commemorates his presence at every opportunity.

Duolun Road Cultural Celebrities Street ⑧ Duōlún Lù Wénhuà Jiē 多伦路文化街

Duolun Road & Sichuan Road (N)
Baoxing Road East

Lu Xun territory, in the heart of Hongkou, begins at this pedestrian street where there are teahouses, art galleries, antiques shops and cafés to linger at. In addition, several of the old houses, in styles ranging from Shanghainese *shikumen* (stone gate) houses to Swiss villas, have been restored as museums. The 550-metre (1,804ft) L-shaped stretch of Duolun Road is also dotted with life-size bronze figures of the celebrities who lived here, posing here and there along the street.

League of Left Wing Writers Museum Zhōngguó Zuǒlián Jìniànguǎn 中国左联纪念馆

Shanghai Duolun Museum of Modern Art Shànghǎi Duōlún Xiàndài Měishùguǎn 上海多伦现代美术馆

27 Duolun Road; www.duolunart.com 6587 2530 Tue–Sun 10am–6pm RMB 10
Dong Baoxing Lu

TIP
Shanghai's summer plum rain season is a constant downpour that lasts for two to three weeks in mid-June. The rains are named after the plum fruit that are harvested during this period.

LEFT: Duolun Road.
BELOW: tribute to Lu Xun (left) in bronze at Duolun Road Cultural Celebrities Street.

Take the metro to Baoshan Road in Zhabei, and nearby, on Baoyuan Road, you'll find traditional Chinese crafts such as custom-made cotton comforters, shoes and hand-hammered woks for sale. These crafts are kept alive by enterprising locals.

Located at the southeast end of Duolun Road, this box-like, almost windowless seven-storey facility is China's first modern museum of contemporary art, featuring experimental works by both international and Chinese artists as well as art-related workshops and events. Although the publicly funded museum tries to adhere to the principle of originality and internationalism, the government connection means that it avoids exhibits that are too controversial. For this reason it pales in comparison to the more funky (and independent) M50 galleries *(see opposite)*.

Duolun Road's other sights

From the museum's upper floor, the distinctive Chinese tiled roof of neighbouring **Hongde Church** (Hongde Tang), built in 1928, can easily be seen among other low-rise red roofs.

Stop by for coffee at the **Old Film Café** (No. 123) with its film memorabilia and screenings of old Chinese movies. Further down the road are several mini-museums featuring Mao buttons, chopsticks and clocks. The lavish Moorish-style house at the end of Duolun Road was the home of financier H.H. Kung, husband of Ai Ling, one of the Soong sisters.

RIGHT: body art exhibition at the Shanghai Duolun Museum of Modern Art.
BELOW: entrance to the Shanghai Duolun Museum of Modern Art.

Lu Xun's Former Residence ❾
Lǔ Xùn Gùjú 鲁迅故居

✉ No. 9, Lane 132, Shanying Road
🕐 daily 9am–4pm 💲 RMB 8
🚇 Hongkou Football Stadium

A short walk northeast leads to this plain red-brick Japanese Concession house where Lu Xun lived from 1933 until he succumbed to death from tuberculosis in 1936. Smaller than the homes in the European Concessions, the simply furnished house, in keeping with Lu Xun's character, is left just as it was when he lived here. Among the items on display is a clock showing the exact time Lu Xun died – 19 Oct 1936 at 5.25am.

Lu Xun Park ❿ Lǔ Xùn Gōngyuán 鲁迅公园

✉ 146 Jiangwan Road (E)
🕐 daily 6am–6pm 💲 RMB 2
🚇 Hongkou Football Stadium

The centrepiece of Lu Xun territory, this lovely park contains both the writer's tomb and a memorial hall. The park's peanut-shaped pond area, which attracts early morning ballroom dancers and t'ai chi practitioners, is a refreshing spot of greenery after Hongkou's gritty streets, and is very popular with the locals.

A bronze seated figure of Lu Xun welcomes visitors to the **Tomb of Lu Xun** (Lu Xun Ling) within the park. The inscription on the tomb is by Mao, and the trees on either side of the grave were planted by Zhou En-lai and Lu Xun's widow.

The **Lu Xun Memorial Hall** (Lu Xun Jininguan; daily 9am–4pm; tel: 6540 2288; free), at the eastern end of the park, has recreations of his study, newspaper articles and photos from the period, as well as translations of works by and about him.

Zhu Qizhan Art Museum
Zhū Qǐzhān Yìshùguǎn
朱屺瞻艺术馆

580 Ouyang Road; www.zmuseum. org 5671 0741 Tue–Sun 10am–4.30pm free Hongkou Football Stadium

This contemporary art museum (a 10-minute walk northeast of Lu Xun Park) opened in 1995 in honour of the famous Chinese painter and calligrapher Zhu Qizhan, whose works are prominently displayed. Although the museum later introduced contemporary art by other artists, the focus of its displays is narrow, usually only exhibiting paintings and photography.

SOUTH OF SUZHOU CREEK

The area west of Duolun Road, towards the converted art warehouses of M50, is all new high-rises and new roads, dotted with occasional old houses. To the southwest is the Jade Buddha Temple tucked behind big, mustard-coloured walls.

M50 ⑪

50 Moganshan Road most galleries open daily 10am–6pm Shanghai Railway Station + taxi

For a look at the heart of Shanghai's exciting contemporary art scene, head southwest to the Suzhou Creek area and the art galleries at **M50** on **Moganshan Road** *(see photo feature on pages 222–3)*. The warehouses in this once-seedy neighbourhood that formed the backbone of Shanghai's industry are now experiencing an artistic renaissance.

Well-known galleries, which represent some of the hottest young talent

Visitors at the Lu Xun Memorial Hall.

BELOW LEFT:
calligraphy demonstration at Lu Xun Park.
BELOW:
statue of Lu Xun.

The Legacy of Lu Xun

Modern China's most revered literary figure was a product of the May 4th Movement in 1919. The movement affected the politics, economics, language and literature of the time, and is regarded as a cultural watershed. For young Chinese idealists like Lu Xun (1881–1936), it was about social justice for the downtrodden.

Lu Xun's legacy was a radical new style of writing called *bai hua*, or plain language, that turned its back on the flowery classical style understood only by scholars. The very first *bai hua* short story, *Diary of a Madman*, was a brutal satire of the Confucian society he wanted to eradicate. His most famous work, however, is *The True Story of Ah Q*, another jab at Confucianism. Lu Xun railed against the social ills of his time and his politically correct ideology appealed to the Communists, who, ironically, tried to make him their poster boy. Yet he never joined the Communist Party as he was too radical for Mao's China.

Aficionados of modern art should not miss the cutting-edge art galleries at M50.

BELOW: worship inside the Jade Buddha Temple.

in China, include **ShanghART Gallery** (Bldg 16; daily 10am–7pm; tel: 6359 3923; www.shangartgallery.com) and **Art Scene Warehouse** (Bldg 4; Tue–Sun 10.30am–6.30pm; tel: 6277 4940; www.artscenechina.com). There are also interesting, smaller galleries and artists' workshops.

Jade Buddha Temple ⑫
Yù Fó Sì 玉佛寺

✉ 170 Anyuan Road; www.yufotemple.com ☎ 6266 3668
🕐 daily 8am–4.30pm 💲 RMB 20
🚇 Shimen No. 1 Road + taxi

South of Suzhou Creek is one of Shanghai's major religious attractions, the **Jade Buddha Temple** – almost hidden among the surrounding area's sprawl of factories and government housing. The temple's Song-style architecture belies the fact that it is relatively new, dating only from 1918. This is one of Shanghai's most popular temples, mainly thanks to the presence of a pair of exquisite jade Buddhas from Burma.

In 1882, the monk Hui Gen of nearby Putuoshan Island returned from his pilgrimage to Burma with five Sakyamuni Buddha images, each one carved from a single piece of jade. Transporting all the heavy statues back to the island by ferry – particularly the largest, which weighed 1,000kg (2,200lbs) – proved impossible, so two were left behind in Shanghai, and a temple was built that same year to house them. The original temple burnt down in 1918 and was replaced with the Jade Buddha Temple on the same site. Hui Gen took the other three jade statues back with him to his monastery on Putuoshan, but these have since disappeared.

The walled temple is entered through the *san men* ("three gate") entrance, referring to the "three extrications" that every Buddhist must make in this material world in order to enter into a spiritual state of emptiness. The temple's five halls include the **Hall of Heavenly Kings**, which has an enormous gilded image of the laughing Maitreya Buddha, and the **Grand Hall**, with the image of the Sakya-

ABOVE: Hall of the Reclining Buddha, Jade Buddha Temple.

muni Buddha meditating on a lotus, flanked by the 20 warrior-like heavenly kings.

The temple's main draw are the two legendary jade Buddhas, housed in separate halls. On the second floor of the **Jade Buddha Hall** is the seated Sakyamuni Buddha, all of 1.92 metres (6⅓ft) tall and resting in a glass case. The creamy white, almost luminous statue of the beatifically smiling jade Buddha, draped with a gem-encrusted robe and seated in the lotus position, shows Buddha at the moment of enlightenment.

On the ground floor of the **Hall of the Reclining Buddha** is the other smaller but much more exquisite reclining jade Buddha at 96cm (37in), depicting a tranquil Sakyamuni, with the same beatific smile, at the moment of death. Don't confuse this with a larger polished stone version of the reclining Buddha, just opposite in the same hall.   ❏

RESTAURANTS AND CAFÉS

American

Blue Frog
蓝蛙

✉ Room 102A, Building 6, Daning LifeHub, 1918 Gonghexin Road; www.blue frog.com.cn ☎ 6631 3920 ⏰ Mon–Thur & Sun 9am–midnight, Fri & Sat 9–2am. **$$** [p322, C1, off map]

A Shanghai standby with branches around town, Blue Frog serves classic

> Prices for a three-course meal for two people, excluding drinks:
> **$** = under RMB 250
> **$$** = RMB 250–500
> **$$$** = RMB 500–800
> **$$$$** = over RMB 800

American home-style dishes – from burgers and macaroni and cheese to Caesar salad in a simple, stylish setting. Heineken and Tiger beers are on tap, with Happy Hour 2-for-1 deals on most beverages from 4–8pm daily.

Papa John's
棒约翰

✉ Room 101–102, Building 8, Daning LifeHub, 1918 Gonghexin Road; www.papa john shanghai.com ☎ 5603 7272 ⏰ daily 10am–10pm. **$$** [p322, C1, off map]

Tasty American-style thick-crust pizzas served in a casual envi-ronment, with service to match. Salads, soups and a range of desserts are also available, including a lip-smacking apple pie.

Chinese

Xindalu Chinese Kitchen
新大陆中国厨房

✉ 1/F, Hyatt on the Bund, 199 Huangpu Road ☎ 6393 1234 ext 6318 ⏰ daily L & D. **$$$$** [p323, C1]

The best Peking duck in Shanghai, in an elegant, contemporary space. Xinadalu roasts them the old-fashioned way, in a Beijing oven with apple wood and red dates. The menu also includes Shanghai and Hanghou dishes.

Café

Bandu Music Café
半度雨篷咖啡

✉ 1/F, Building 11, 50 Moganshan Road; www.bandumusic.com ☎ 6276 8267 ⏰ Mon–Fri & Sun 10am–6.30pm, Sat 10am–10pm. **$** [p323, C1]

This artsy little café serves mainly basic Chinese snack food such as dumplings and noodles, although pizzas are also available. It's located next to the Bandu Music Shop, which is dedicated to Chinese folk music, the café hosts free live folk music performances every Saturday evening.

CUTTING-EDGE ART AT M50

Forget about stuffy museums – the best of Chinese contemporary art is found at M50, a collection of funky warehouse art galleries

ABOVE: M50's art galleries are housed in the old British warehouses and factories that fuelled Shanghai's industrialisation during the Concession days. The large spaces and high ceilings allow artists to display large canvases – like these by the artist Wei Ye.

The hub of the Chinese contemporary art boom in Shanghai is M50, a funky catch-all name given to this collection of galleries in old warehouses at 50 Moganshan Road, near Suzhou Creek. Just a few years ago, these Concession-era warehouses were dilapidated spaces inhabited by galleries looking for low-cost storage. Today, the space has been reinvented and many of the galleries – and the artists – have taken on a sophisticated veneer that can only come from selling expensive – very expensive – art.

A stroll through the galleries, which carry everything from well-known artists to newbies, photography to installation, is a free tour of Chinese contemporary art that is better curated, and more current, than at any museum. And no wonder, as every important contemporary Chinese art gallery in Shanghai is represented at M50, along with artist studios *(see page 288)*.

ABOVE: for many visitors, one of the highlights of visiting M50 is to meet the artists and discuss their work with them. Pictured is the artist Yi Zhou.
RIGHT: in addition to paintings, M50's spacious galleries and outdoor spaces display contemporary Chinese sculpture, like this one by Xu Huiqiang.

ABOVE: the range of artwork on view at M50 ranges from naïve to realist to avant-garde, sometimes all in one studio. Here, artist Xu Huiqiang ponders his work.

BELOW: in addition to galleries, M50 is also home to artist studios such as this one, where well-known contemporary painter Pu Jie works on his canvases.

BELOW: Island 6, an old flour mill, once owned by the Shanghai industrialist Rong Yiren, is located just behind M50. It is a non-profit, artist-run arts centre, the first of its kind in Shanghai.

ABOVE: ShanghArt at Building 16 (www.shangartgallery.com) was the first gallery to promote Chinese contemporary art and artists, and one of the first to use a Moganshan Road warehouse as gallery space.

LEFT: painter Ding Yi became famous for both his canvases covered with tiny squares of colour, and his funky Moganshan Road studio – Ding Yi was one of the pioneer artists to begin working here.

Recommended Restaurants & Cafés on page 235

PUDONG

Once empty marshland, Pudong's futuristic facade has taken on several global superlatives – the world's longest cable bridge, the fastest train, the highest hotel and China's tallest building are all here

Pudong is Future Shanghai. Anchored by the rocket-like Oriental Pearl Tower, this zone east of the Huangpu River with its forest of glittering skyscrapers (not one was built before 1990) looks like the set of a space-age film. Much of Shanghai's fast-forward progress since 1990, when plans to develop Pudong as a special economic area were first announced, has been telescoped into this 350-sq-km (135-sq-mile) area. Large tracts have been carved out as development zones – like the Waigaoqiao container port, the Jinqiao export processing zone and the Zhangjiang High-Tech Park.

As the face of 21st-century Shanghai, Pudong is the showcase for the best, the brightest and the most advanced. This is the site of China's tallest building, Asia's largest stock exchange, the world's longest cable bridge, a US$2 billion showcase airport, technologically sophisticated exhibition centres and state-of-the-art museums and theatres. Pudong is an urban planner's utopia: high-rises interspersed with large sweeps of greenery and straight boulevards – man and nature coexisting with industry and commerce.

Most of modern Pudong is quite a contrast to its pre-1990 self – when it was a country village on the wrong side of the tracks, a place of grinding poverty where ruined gamblers came to "*tiao Huangpu*" – jump into the river – and where the bodies of sailors who perished in the trading ships were buried.

LUJIAZUI DISTRICT

Economic incentives have lured both the world's financial giants as well as the Shanghai Stock Exchange, the

Main attractions

BUND SIGHTSEEING TUNNEL
CHINA SEX CULTURE MUSEUM
ORIENTAL PEARL TOWER
SHANGHAI MUNICIPAL HISTORY
   MUSEUM
RIVERSIDE PROMENADE
JIN MAO TOWER
SHANGHAI WORLD FINANCIAL
   CENTRE
SHANGHAI SCIENCE AND
   TECHNOLOGY MUSEUM
SHANGHAI ORIENTAL ARTS CENTRE
SHANGHAI EXPO CHINA PAVILION
XINCHANG ANCIENT TOWN

LEFT: Jin Mao Tower flanked by acrobats.
RIGHT: looking out from Jin Mao Tower.

ABOVE: getting to Pudong the surreal way through the Bund Sightseeing Tunnel.

Shanghai that the namesake river was not spanned until the 1990s. Until then, the only way to get across to Pudong was a 5-minute ride on a ferry from **Jinling Pier** at the southern end of the Bund. The ferry (daily 6am–10pm) still makes for an atmospheric ride, with boats and barges sliding past. On landing at Dongcheng Road, it is but a short walk to the main Lujiazui sights.

In contrast, the **Bund Sightseeing Tunnel** (Waitan Canguang Sui Dao) on Zhongshan No. 1 Road (near the Chen Yi statue and opposite the Fairmont Peace Hotel; RMB 50 round trip, RMB 40 one way) is the almost surreal 21st-century way to travel: train cars – accompanied by flashing lights, waving "people" on the tracks and scenes projected onto the tunnel walls – whisk visitors to Pudong.

It takes a little longer to cross by road, via either the **Yangpu Bridge** (Yangpu Qiao) or **Nanpu Bridge** (Nanpu Qiao), the world's longest

Futures Exchange and the Diamond Exchange to the **Lujiazui financial zone** (Shanghai's own Wall Street). This is the city's ultra-modern business and museum district, with the tallest buildings in China, and, indeed, the world: the Shanghai World Financial Centre, at 492 metres (1,614ft), is the third-tallest in the world, and the Jin Mao Tower, the sixth.

Getting to Pudong

Pudong, meaning "east of the Huangpu", was so insignificant to

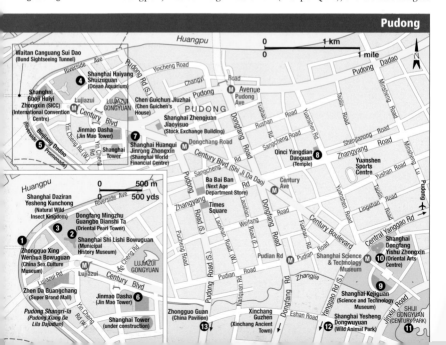

Recommended Restaurants & Cafés on page 235

and fourth-longest cable bridges, respectively, but the dramatic spider-webbed bridges and the travel on elevated highways make the experience worthwhile. The most popular – and least interesting – crossing is via the **Yan'an Road (E) Tunnel**, which suffers from horrible jams. The government has announced plans for six additional tunnels and bridges by 2020; until then, the fastest way to cross to Lujiazui is by metro.

China Sex Culture Museum
① Zhōngguó Xìng Wénhuà Bówùguǎn 中国性文化博物馆

✉ 2879 Riverside Avenue 📞 5888 6000 ⓒ daily 8am–9pm Ⓜ RMB 20; RMB 65 with return Bund Sightseeing Tunnel ticket 🚇 Lujiazui

Located one level below the Bund Sighseeing Tunnel exit, the **China Sex Culture Museum**, a small branch of the main museum in Tongli *(see page 255)*, features sex-themed artefacts from ancient China. It's both an interesting and educational museum, but not one for the kiddies: exhibits include porcelain figures of copulating couples in a variety of positions, phalluses and depictions of bestiality and homosexuality. Some of the more memorable exhibits include a woodcarving of a man with a startlingly large phallus and a donkey saddle mounted with a wooden penis, used as punishment for wayward women in ancient times.

Exhibit at the China Sex Culture Museum.

Oriental Pearl Tower **②**
Dōngfāng Míngzhū Guǎngbō Diànshì Tǎ 东方明珠广播电视塔

✉ 2 Lujiazui Road 📞 5879 1888 ⓒ daily 8am–9.30pm Ⓜ RMB 85–135, depending on type of ticket 🚇 Lujiazui

However you choose to arrive in Lujiazui, begin your visit at the iconic **Oriental Pearl Tower**. This symbol of modern Shanghai, which looks like a Jetsons-era rocket ready for take-off, elicits great passion in locals and mock horror in overseas tourists. The 468-metre (1,535ft) tall television tower, the world's third-tallest, has a series of silver and cranberry-coloured "pearls" along its length, three of which are opened to visitors.

BELOW: Pudong's glittering skyline.

TIP

Many visitors make the mistake of taking the lift to the third and highest "pearl" (called the Space Capsule) at the Oriental Pearl Tower. But at 350 metres (1,092ft), this is almost too high. Much better views are to be had from the second pearl at 263 metres (862ft).

BELOW: Old Shanghai is realistically created at the Shanghai Municipal History Museum.

Tickets are priced according to which parts of the tower you visit, but what's recommended is buying the RMB 85 ticket (which also gives you access to the Shanghai Municipal History Museum; see below). This ticket will zip you vertically in the high-speed lift – travelling at an ear-popping 7 metres (23ft) per second – to the observation deck on the second accessible bauble, perched at 263 metres (862ft). Here, compass points and landmarks are displayed prominently on the windows. The 360-degree view of the city is one of the best ways to orientate yourself, provided it's a clear day. A (mediocre) revolving Chinese restaurant is located at 267 metres (876ft), and above that, the third sphere (called the Space Capsule) at 350 metres (1,092ft) – almost too high for the views to be much good.

Shanghai Municipal History Museum
Shànghǎi Shì Lìshǐ Bówùguǎn
上海市历史博物馆

✉ Basement of the Oriental Pearl Tower 📞 5879 3003 🕐 daily 9am–9pm 💲 RMB 35 (museum only; combination tickets with Oriental Pearl Tower also available) 🚇 Lujiazui

Not to be missed is the **Shanghai Municipal History Museum** in the basement of the Pearl Tower. The two-storey museum takes you through Shanghai's history, with a Chinese spin on the imperialist invaders. The museum's excellent audiovisual exhibits and dioramas include re-creations of an early stock exchange, traders and artisans at work, 19th-century cobblestone streets and an arrogant tai-pan's office (complete with voice recording). There is also the original bronze lion from the Hongkong and Shanghai Bank *(see page 112)* and a gun from the Opium War's Wusong battles, in addition to models of Old Shanghai architecture. This is one museum both adults and kids will enjoy.

Shanghai Natural Wild Insect Kingdom ❸ Shànghǎi Dàzìrán Yěshēng Kūnchóng Guǎn 上海大自然野生昆虫馆

✉ 1 Fenghe Road 📞 5840 6950 🕐 daily 9am–5pm 💲 RMB 35 adults, RMB 20 under-18s 🚇 Lujiazui

A short walk west of the Oriental Pearl Tower is the **Shanghai Natural Wild Insect Kingdom** – a sure hit with the kids. There are exhibits of scorpions, spiders and all manner of creepy crawlies in several galleries, all given a tropical, somewhat tacky, jungle setting. In addition, there are interactive insect shows (weekends only) that allow the audience to touch and feel the creatures, as well as an indoor lake; kids can catch (and keep) the fish with nets supplied.

Shanghai Ocean Aquarium ❹ Shànghǎi Hǎiyáng Shuǐzúguǎn 上海海洋水族馆

✉ 158 Yin Cheng Road (N); www.sh-soa.com 📞 5877 9988

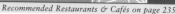
🕐 daily 9am–6pm 🎫 RMB 110 adults, RMB 70 children under 1.4 metres 🚇 Lujiazui

East of the Oriental Pearl Tower is **Shanghai Ocean Aquarium**, an impressive facility with a focus on Chinese sea creatures, including the endangered Yangzi alligator. With a high percentage of exotic creatures, such as the alien-looking Japanese spider crab and dramatic displays, it has a high "ooh" factor. The marine tunnel, in which sharp-toothed sharks and giant rays swim lazily overhead at 155 metres (509ft) and never ceases to amaze the kids (and adults too).

Riverside Promenade ❺
Bīnjiāng Dàdào 滨江大道

Continuing north, you'll pass the **Shanghai International Convention Centre** (Shanghai Guoji Huiyi Zhongxin), flanked by bizarre double globes; it has been the venue for the Fortune and APEC conferences in the past. Hugging the eastern banks of the Huangpu River from Pudong Road to Yin Cheng Road is the **Riverside**

Promenade, a 2.5km (1½-mile) long walkway that offers spectacular views over the water to the Bund, especially at night. Enjoy the view from the river, or sit at one of the restaurants and cafés that line the promenade.

Strolling south along the promenade leads to **Super Brand Mall** (Zhen Da Guangchang), Pudong's largest, at 168 Lujiazui Road, which is filled with a lively mix of bars, restaurants, shops and a cinema.

Just south of Super Brand Mall is a cluster of Shanghai's newest and

ABOVE: The Super Brand Mall.
BELOW: Shanghai Ocean Aquarium.

The Shanghai World Financial Centre, China's tallest building.

BELOW: the Grand Hyatt's spiralling atrium at the Jin Mao Tower.

fanciest hotels: the **Ritz-Carlton**, the **Park Hyatt**, the **Gran Melia** along with older stalwarts, the **Shangri-La** and the **Grand Hyatt**.

Jin Mao Tower ⑥
Jīnmào Dàshà 金茂大厦

✉ 88 Century Boulevard   📞 5047 5101   ⏰ observation deck daily 8.30am–9.30pm   💲 RMB 70   🚇 Lujiazui

The **Jin Mao Tower** stands out against the Pudong skyline, and not just because it is the world's fifth-tallest building at 420 metres (1,378ft). "I wanted to evoke the subtle memory of a pagoda, the ancient Chinese high-rise and marker for the landscape," explained the building's American architect, Adrian Smith. Designed around the factor of eight, like the pagoda, the 88-storey building was built in 1999 and was China's tallest for almost a decade (the Shanghai World Financial Centre next door eclipsed it in 2008). The Jin Mao's stunning art deco design elements makes it an architectural summation of the city. Inter-

estingly, the 88th-floor observatory offers city views from an almost identical perspective to the Oriental Pearl Tower. The world's highest hotel, **Grand Hyatt Shanghai** (Jinmao Kaiyue Dajiudian) occupies the 54th–87th floors; the 56th-floor atrium affords a breathtaking view of the building's core, rising in a dizzying concentric spin to the 88th floor.

Shanghai World Financial Centre ⑦ Shànghǎi Huánqiú Jīnróng Zhōngxīn
上海环球金融中心

The **Shanghai World Financial Centre**, across from Jin Mao Tower, is the world's third-tallest building at 492 metres (1,614ft). Designed by the American architectural firm Kohn Pedersen Fox, its distinctive design feature is a trapezoidal opening at the building's apex, which locals call "the bottle-opener". The sleek and soaring wide-shouldered building contains offices, China's largest Apple store, gourmet grocery stores, boutiques and a luxury **Park Hyatt** hotel.

Recommended Restaurants & Cafés on page 235

with run-down 1970s government-built housing poking up from between shiny skyscrapers, reminders that despite the movie-set look of Pudong, a local population still lives here.

At the top end of Century Boulevard, keep an eye out for the distinctive shape of the **Shanghai Stock Exchange Building** (Shanghai Zhengjuan Jiaoyisuo), built to resemble an ancient Chinese coin with a square space in its centre. Visitors are not allowed on the trading floor. At 3,600 sq metres (38,750 sq ft), the Shanghai exchange is the largest in Asia and operates an advanced electronic trading system.

A 10-minute taxi ride from riverside Lujiazui via Century Boulevard will take you to Pudong's shopping nexus, where you'll find Asia's largest department store, the 10-storey **Next Age Department Store** (Ba Bai Ban) and, across the street, **Times Square** with its large collection of designer boutiques.

Chen Guichen's House is one of Pudong's few historic structures. The building dates back to 1917.

Chen Guichen's House
Lù Jiāzuǐ Kāifā Chénlièguǎn
(Chén Guìchūn Jiùzhái)
陆家嘴开发陈列馆 (陈桂春旧宅)

Across Century Boulevard is the only building here that looks as if it might be more than a decade old, a 1917 wood and brick courtyard house that was once the home of wealthy shipping merchant Chen Guichen. The spacious house was once part of a sprawling estate that housed several families and served as the headquarters of the Japanese army and the Kuomintang government. A museum until 2007 (rather uninspiringly known as the Lujiazui Development Showroom), the house is now closed to the public.

AROUND CENTURY BOULEVARD

Century Boulevard (Shi Ji Da Dao) Shanghai's Champs-Elysées, cuts dramatically through Pudong. The magnificent 5km (3-mile) long street, which runs from the World Financial Centre to Century Park, has a generous 100-metre (320ft) wide avenue with 10 hectares (25 acres) of greenery on either side. Designed by French architect Jean-Marie Charpentier (who also designed the Shanghai Grand Theatre), it makes for one of the city's most pleasant drives. Pudong's landmarks are well spread out on either side of the boulevard,

Qinci Yangdian Temple ❽
Qīncì Yǎngdiàn Dàoguàn
钦赐仰殿道观

LEFT: Shanghai Stock Exchange Building.
BELOW: Jin Mao Tower as seen from one of the courtyards at Chen Guichen's House.

TIP

You could take a boring taxi ride into the city from Pudong International Airport, or you could experience a heart-stopping ride on the Maglev train – which uses electromagnetic technology to glide above the guard rails at a top speed of over 430km (267 miles) an hour! The downside? The train only goes to as far as Longyang Road metro station in Pudong, where you have to lug your bags one floor down the escalator and get a taxi to town. See Transport *(page 270)* for details on the Maglev.

RIGHT AND BELOW: Shanghai Science and Technology Museum.

✉ 476 Yuanshen Road ⊙ daily 8am–4pm ⊚ RMB 5 🚇 Dongchang Road + taxi

Pudong's most important temple, with its curved, tiled roof and ochre-coloured walls, looks out of place in the forest of concrete and glass that make up Pudong. The temple was first built during the Three Kingdoms period (AD 220–280), and has been rebuilt several times over the years. The latest rebuilding, in 2007, saw the Taoist temple's Qing-era buildings demolished and replaced with brand-new buildings and gods – taking away its authencity. The temple's most powerful deity, Yan Wang, is also known as the god of hell; Qinci Yangdian also has a collection of city gods and a "treaty" god.

Shanghai Science and Technology Museum ❾
Shànghǎi Kējìguǎn 上海科技馆

✉ 2000 Century Boulevard; www.sstm.org.cn 📞 6862 2000 ⊙ Tue–Sun 9am–5pm ⊚ RMB 60 adults, RMB 20 children 🚇 Science and Technology Museum

Back on Century Boulevard, veer right at the "Oriental Light" sculpture, a contemporary sundial, to the **Science and Technology Museum**. The theme of the US$183-million museum, taking up 68,000 sq metres (731,950 sq ft) of space, is "man, nature, science and technology". The popular IMAX theatre screens daily shows (separate fee), and the five interactive science halls hold everything from an exploding volcano to a recreated rainforest with over 300 types of plants. In addition there is a simulated laboratory where experiments can be conducted, and an interactive children's area.

Shanghai Oriental Arts Centre ❿ Shànghǎi Dōngfāng Yìshù Zhōngxīn
上海东方艺术中心

✉ 425 Dingxiang Road; www.shoac.com.cn 📞 3842 4800 🚇 Science and Technology Museum

On the opposite side of Century Boulevard is the stunning **Shanghai Oriental Arts Centre**, home of the Shanghai Symphony Orchestra. Designed by Pudong Airport designer Paul Andreu in the shape of a magnolia (the city flower) when viewed from the top, the SOAC is Pudong's answer to the Shanghai Grand Theatre.

The 23,000-sq-metre (247,572-sq-ft) centre for performing arts is encircled by a lush garden and has three performance theatres and an exhibition hall. Andreu carried his theme of nature inside as well: the black granite floor symbolises the forest floor, steel girders are the

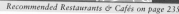
trees, and the clear, round lights, suspended at different levels, are dewdrops.

Century Park ⓫ Shìjì Gōngyuán 世纪公园

✉ 1001 Jinxiu Road 📞 3876 0588 🕐 daily 6am–6pm ⓔ free 🚇 Shiji Park

Continue down Century Boulevard to **Century Park**. French architect Jean-Marie Charpentier also designed this beautifully landscaped 140-hectare (346-acre) ecopark, its forest and park area anchored by a huge lake. The park is the site of sporting events such as the annual Terry Fox run and other large celebrations.

NANHUI AND OUTSKIRTS

Rural Nanhui District, south of the Pudong New Area, is a dramatic change in character from Pudong's business-like sterility. Nanhui is most famous for its peach orchards, which transform into a sea of pink blossoms towards the end of March and the start of April. Apart from this, Nanhui hosts an animal park for children and Shanghai's only authentic water village.

Shanghai Wild Animal Park ⓬ Shànghǎi Yěshēng Dòngwùyuán 上海野生动物园

✉ Nanfang Road, Nanhui 📞 5803 6000 🕐 daily 8am–5pm ⓔ RMB 100 adults, RMB 50 children

A 45-minute drive from Pudong takes you to this 205-hectare (506-acre) safari park. It is divided into bus and walking zones by animal type: wilder animals such as hunting leopards and South China tigers are safely viewed from buses, while the walking zones allow gentler species such as kangaroos, deer and lemurs to roam freely. There are also animal shows throughout the day. Unfortunately, keepers ignore the fact that visitors feed the animals, some of which are unnecessarily tethered, sometimes harshly, during the photo sessions and performances.

China Pavilion ⓭ Zhongguo Guan 中国馆 东方之冠

The striking interior of the Shanghai Oriental Arts Centre takes its design cue from nature.

BELOW: the Shanghai Oriental Arts Centre resembles a magnolia bloom – Shanghai's official flower – when viewed from above.

✉ corner of Pudong South Road and Shang South Road ☎ 2020 2010 ⏰ 9am–5pm 💲 RMB 20 adults, RMB 15 children

All the pavilions on the Shanghai Expo site, which covered 5.28km (3¼ miles), will be dismantled, save the iconic China Pavilion. "Crown of the East" features a traditional Chinese roof and an interlocking wooden bracket system called *dougong*; the exhibition within is themed "Chinese Wisdom in Urban Development" with sections on urban development and planning in ancient and modern China, and on a low-carbon future.

Xinchang Ancient Town
Xīnchǎng Gǔzhèn 新场古镇

This atmospheric canal town in Nan-hui District – about an hour's drive from the centre of Pudong – and dating back to the Song Dynasty (AD 960–1279) is perhaps Shanghai's best and most authentic water village, sensitively restored by one of the city's leading preservationists and as yet undiscovered by the tourist hordes.

ABOVE: sea lions at the Shanghai Wild Animal Park.
BELOW: idyllic Xinchang canal town.

Xinchang has been largely over-shadowed by better-known tourist traps like **Zhujiajiao** and **Zhou-zhuang** *(see page 243)*, offered as standard fare on most bus tours to Shanghai's outskirts. But this is a good thing and long may it remain so. Unlike the city's other water villages, Xinchang's residents still live in the houses that their ancestors built.

Xichang's Ming-era main street has been preserved along with over 20 of the town's original mansions as well as courtyard houses. Highlights include the beautiful **Zhang Mansion** (Zhang Ting) at 176 Xinchang Street, with its Dutch floor tiles and European touches. Another must-see sight is the century-old **No. 1 Teahouse** (Lou Cha Guan), an atmospheric three-storey building. ❏

BEST RESTAURANTS AND CAFÉS

Chinese

100 Century Avenue
世纪大道100
✉ 91/F, 93/F, Shanghai World Financial Center, 100 Century Avenue; www.shanghai park.hyatt.com
📞 6888 1234 🕒 daily L & D.
$$$$ [p323, D2]
The highest restaurant in China, within the Shanghai Financial Center, boasts a dramatic space – high ceilings, spectacular city views – and Chinese, Japanese and western cuisne served from seven show kitchens. There are 4,000 wines on the wine list.

Shanghai Uncle
上海阿叔
✉ 8/9F, 500 Zhangyang Road, Times Square
📞 5836 7977 🕒 daily L & D. $$ [p323, E2, off map]
A spacious, dramatic crimson-and-black space that serves the same delicious food as its branches across the river. Serves authentic Shanghainese cuisine, but with twists that make it contemporary, as well as innovative new dishes.

Continental

HoF
巧陆家嘴店

✉ Floor B1, DBS Building, 1318 Lujiazaui Ring Road; www.houseofflour.com
📞 5010 0800 🕒 Mon–Sat 3pm–midnight. $$ [p323, E2]
This bar and brasserie offer spectacular views of the Oriental Pearl Tower, and delicious bistro-style fare created by a French-trained chef. Owner Brian Tan, pastry chef and chocolatier, legendary desserts – Manjari chocolate mousse, fruit tartss and anything chocolate.

Fusion

Jade on 36
翡翠36
✉ 36/F, Tower Two, Pudong Shangri-La, 33 Fucheng Road; www.jadeon36.com
📞 6882 8888 🕒 daily D.
$$$$ [p323, D2]
Perhaps Shanghai's most avant-garde restaurant, and certainly one of its finest. Restaurant-designer-to-the-stars Adam Tihany did the décor, incorporating futuristic interpretations of ancient Chinese icons (such as the giant snuff bottles), while chef Paul Pairet creates cuisine just as inventive. His signature playful dishes include foie gras lollipop, citrus shrimp in a jar and a whole candied lemon, filled with sorbet.

Italian

Danieli
✉ 39/F, St Regis Hotel, 889 Dongfang Road 📞 5050 4567 🕒 daily D, Mon–Fri L.
$$$$ [p323, E2, off map]
Its out-of-the-way location has made this a hidden gem, but one worth seeking out. The plush setting – luxury carpets, fresh flowers and silken fabrics – is a worthy backdrop for the sophisticated Italian cuisine: beautifully cooked fish, meats and especially pasta. The service is flawless and there are a stunning views from the window tables.

Cafés

Element Fresh
新元素
✉ G/F, Super Brand Mall, 168 Lujiazui Road; www.elementfresh.com
📞 6887 7888 🕒 daily B, L & D. $$ [p323, D2]
A bright, sunny California-style casual eatery. Fresh and healthy offerings are the mainstays here, with plenty of choice among the sandwiches, salads, and pastas. There's a good Asian menu as well.

Yi Café
香格里拉咖啡
✉ 2/F, Tower Two, Pudong Shangri-La, 33 Fucheng Road 📞 6882 8888 🕒 daily B, L & D. $$ [p323, D2]
Yi Café is the city's most luxe café, with international cuisines at a series of stations prepared before your eyes. Shanghai dumplings, Indian curries, Lebanese salads, Malay satays, Japanese sashimi, Italian pastas, and more.

Prices for a three-course meal for two people, excluding drinks:
$ = under RMB 250
$$ = RMB 250–500
$$$ = RMB 500–800
$$$$ = over RMB 800

RIGHT: main dining room at Jade on 36.

Recommended Restaurants & Cafés on page 245

WESTERN SUBURBS AND CHONGMING ISLAND

Shanghai city slickers escape here for the slower pace and taste of country living. Jiading, Songjiang and Qingpu counties all have their own appeal, and further west is Chongming Island, China's second-largest island and a birdwatchers' haven

Amusement parks, Ming dynasty canal towns, ancient pagodas and nature spots run riot through the countryside that borders the city's western flank, a curious mixture of tradition, kitsch and industrialisation. Shanghai's western suburbs and Chongming Island are part of the greater Shanghai municipality, yet are still too rural to be really considered part of the city of Shanghai.

The western suburbs – which were carved out of neighbouring provinces and provided the burgeoning city with food and room for expansion – offer a taste of Old China, with scenes of lonely pagodas brooding on silent hillsides and crumbling Ming houses in forgotten lanes. The rural quiet belies what was a thriving area during the Song and the Tang dynasties, and, in the case of Songjiang County's Songze village, a history that goes as far back as Neolithic times – before the land mass of Shanghai even existed.

Today, Shanghai's long shadow still defines the character of the area. Elements of antiquity, so lacking in the city, are tarted up and gift-wrapped for Shanghai tourists. Acres of ripening fields are yielding to the city's relentless progress as

they are taken over by mega-sized factories and, increasingly these days, luxury housing.

JIADING DISTRICT

Jiading district typifies the western suburbs with its dual character, part Old China, part ultra-modern China. Once the seat of the imperial examinations, the district is dotted with classical gardens and temples. But it is also the home of the Formula One race in China, and is a leading auto-manufacturing centre.

Main attractions
JIADING TOWN
SHANGHAI INTERNATIONAL CIRCUIT AT ANTING
SHESHAN OBSERVATORY
SHESHAN CATHEDRAL
CHONGMING ISLAND

LEFT: Zhouzhuang, the largest (and also most crowded) of the suburban water villages. **RIGHT:** a countryside toddler.

Soup dumpling.

BELOW: pavilion at the
Garden of Ancient
Splendour at Jiading.

Nanxiang ❶ 南翔

Jiading's most famous export is *xiao
long bao*, from **Nanxiang**, some
17km (10½ miles) northwest of
Shanghai. The bite-sized pleated
dumplings, stuffed with pork and
enough boiling liquid inside to do
serious damage if popped into the
mouth whole, are available in seemingly every restaurant in this small
town. The quality of these dumplings
can vary, quite dramatically, though,
from one restaurant to the next.

Garden of Ancient Splendour Gǔyīyuán 古猗园

✉ 218 Huyi Road, Nanxiang
☎ 5912 2225 ⏰ daily 7am–6pm
🎫 RMB 12 🚇 Nanxiang

Designed by bamboo sculptor (and
native son) Zhun Shansong, this
Suzhou-style garden, which dates
back to 1566, retains its Ming contours despite a 1746 reconstruction
and 1949 expansion. A Song stone

pagoda and a Tang stele with Buddhist scriptures stand in the garden. A
pavilion built during the Japanese
Occupation has a corner left incomplete, held up by a defiant fist, to sig-
nify a broken China under the
Occupation.

At the Chinese pavilion on the edge
of the garden is **Guyi Garden Nanxiang Xiao Long Bao** restaurant *(see
page 245)*, where you can partake of
this delicate Nanxiang speciality.

Jiading Town ❷ Jiādìngzhèn 嘉定镇

Some 10km (6 miles) northwest of
Nanxiang is **Jiading Town**, a quiet
canal-fringed little town that is the
largest in the Jiading district.

Dragon Meeting Pond Park Huìlóngtán Gōngyuán 汇龙潭公园

✉ 299 Tacheng Road ⏰ daily 8am–
5pm 🎫 RMB 5 🚇 Jiading Xincheng

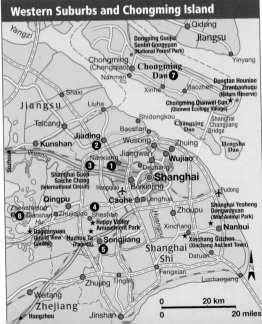

Recommended Restaurants & Cafés on page 245

The town's Ming-era park, named after the five streams that converge here, may be contemplated in relative solitude. (And yes, there is a dragon sculpture in one of the ponds.) The lovely garden is dotted with bamboo trees, pagodas and pavilions – including one with a ceiling featuring a dizzying series of concentric whorls and a mirror at its interior apex.

Confucius Temple
Kǒngmiào 孔庙

✉ 183 Nan Da Street, Jiading Town
🄲 daily 8am–4.30pm 🄾 RMB 20
🄳 Jiading Xincheng

At one time, Jiading Town was important enough to be the seat of the imperial examinations, held at the Southern Song-style **Confucius Temple**, first built in 1281. Located west of Dragon Meeting Pond Park, a massive statue of Confucius, the patron saint of scholars, dominates the main hall of the temple, with statues of his favourite students lining one wall.

Examination candidates would offer prayers to Confucius, and in return, the Yuan dynasty sculpture of a fish and dragon over the temple's main gate would bless the scholars with good luck. The sculpture is a visual representation of the saying "a carp leaping over the dragon gate", a metaphor for achieving success. There is more symbolism along the stone fence that fronts the temple, with its 72 stone lions representing the 72 disciples of Confucius.

The temple grounds are also home to the beautifully designed **Imperial Examination Museum** (Zhongguo Keju Bowuguan; daily 8am–4.30pm), which documents the rigorous examination system that dominated China's civil service from the Han dynasty until its abolishment in 1904. Among the exhibits are books, original lists of successful scholars, dioramas featuring the examination

A prayer tied to a tree next to the main prayer hall at the Confucius Temple.

LEFT: the main entrance to the Confucius Temple.
BELOW: the main prayer hall.

The Formula One race track at the Shanghai International Circuit in Anting, designed by the German-born Hermann Tilke, is reputedly one of the most challenging on the circuit.

cells, and profiles of successful candidates who later became famous.

Fahua Pagoda Fǎhuátǎ 法华塔

Exit the temple at Nan Da Street and head north towards the graceful Southern Song-era **Fahua Pagoda**, rebuilt in 1919. Legend has it that Jiading's examination candidates uniformly failed the imperial examinations until the pagoda was built; today, visitors can climb the seven-storey pagoda to the top via a wooden staircase for views over the city.

Garden of Autumn Clouds
Qiūxiápǔ 秋霞圃

✉ 314 Dong Da Street ⊙ daily 8am–4.30pm ⊚ RMB 10

A stroll up north along Lianqiu River leads to Shanghai's oldest garden and certainly one of its loveliest, with scenic spots aplenty. Laid out in 1502 as the private garden of a Ming official called Gonghong, the garden has been renovated several times.

Shanghai International Circuit ❸ Shànghǎi Guójì Sàichē Chǎng 上海国际赛车场

RIGHT: the Garden of Autumn Clouds in Jiading is Shanghai's oldest public garden.
BELOW: Formula One fans in Anting.

These days, Jiading is best known as the home of the **Formula One** race which takes place in the **Shanghai International Circuit** in Anting every September until 2010. The site includes a world-class Hermann Tilke-designed track *(see box left)* and is also the home of VW China.

Nearby is a kitschy German-themed residential town, designed by Albert Speer, son of Hitler's favourite architect, called "Anting New Town", one of a series of themed residential developments that are being built throughout suburban Shanghai.

SONGJIANG COUNTY

Songjiang County, 30km (19 miles) southwest of Shanghai and the site of Neolithic remains at Songze village, is known as the cradle of Shanghai civilisation. Today, its most famous site is the French Jesuit-built cathedral in **Sheshan ❹**. The county is also taking advantage of its lush, natural setting to reinvent itself as a weekend getaway, complete with outlet shopping.

Sheshan Observatory
Shéshān Tiānwéntái 余山天文台

✉ Sheshan Hill 🕿 5765 3423
⊙ daily 7.30am–5pm ⊚ RMB 30 for both observatory and cathedral; cable car costs an additional RMB 10
🚇 Sheshan

Anting

Every spring, Shanghai goes car crazy: that's when the city hosts the Chinese Grand Prix, the Formula One race in Anting, Jiading district. Drivers say that the Hermann Tilke-designed track may well be the best on the circuit – fast, technical and consisting of seven left and seven right turns, including a series of double-snail bends and hairpin turns cleverly designed in the shape of the character *shang*, which means "above" (from "Shanghai", meaning "above the sea"). In addition, the 1.2km (¾-mile) straightaway allows drivers to get up to speeds of 326kmh (203mph). Thanks to F1, Anting has gone from being a backwater to Shanghai's "automobile city". Volkswagen has a manufacturing base here, and there is also an automobile college, exhibition centre and hotels. Anting "New Town", bizarrely styled after a German town, is part of an urbanisation programme that will see 11 new towns taking root throughout Shanghai's suburbs by 2010.

Recommended Restaurants & Cafés on page 245

Once regarded as one of the most important in Asia, the 1898 observatory stands on the highest point in Shanghai municipality. Visitors can either walk up the 100-metre (328ft) high hill, or take the cable car up for a bird's-eye view of the surroundings. The century-old telescope is still intact, and the observatory is now a small museum dedicated to the history of Chinese stargazing. A new telescope was installed just below the crest of the hill, but as recently as 1986, the old machine was used to track and take photos of Halley's Comet for scientific use – just as the Jesuits who built the observatory did when the comet visited in 1910.

Sheshan Cathedral Shéshān Tiānzhǔjiàotáng 佘山天主教堂

✉ Sheshan Hill ☏ 5765 1521 ⏱ daily 8am–4pm; mass Mon–Sat 7am (6.30am in summer), Sun 8am (7.30am in summer)

The Jesuits also built the sturdy church next door, first named the Holy Mother Cathedral in 1866

and, subsequently, in 1935, the Basilica of Notre Dame. A subtle "M" (for Mary) and "SJ" (Society of Jesus, ie the Jesuits) are inscribed in the old iron gate in the southwestern corner of the churchyard. The lovely bronze *Madonna and Child* on the steeple is a recent replacement for the one that was pulled down during the Cultural Revolution years. Pilgrims usually walk up the south gate, lined with grottoes and shrines, stopping to say prayers or the rosary along the way. Local Catholics make a pilgrimage here each May.

Happy Valley Amusement Park Huān lè gǔ 欢乐谷

✉ Linyin Lu, Sheshan, Songjiang ☏ 3355 2222 ⏱ daily 9am–6pm; July–Aug 9am–10pm ⓒ RMB 200, children under 1.2 metres RMB 100, includes all rides ☐ Sheshan + shuttle bus

Billed as China's largest theme park, Happy Valley has rides in six different themed areas, along with China's only

The Sheshan Observatory in Songjiang county.

BELOW:
Sheshan Cathedral was built by Jesuit Catholic missionaries.

wooden roller coaster and some truly scary rides. Try Space Shot, Turbo Drop and the Diving Coaster (two nearly vertical drops!) if you dare, but there are also plenty of tamer rides, making it ideal for a family outing.

Square Pagoda
Fāngtǎyuán 方塔园

✉ 235 Zhongshan Rd (E) 📞 5782 2157 🕐 daily 8.30am–4.30pm
💰 RMB 12

Continue on to **Songjiang Town** ❺ and its pride, the **Square Pagoda**. Built in 1077, the 50-metre (160ft) structure will reward climbers with views of the countryside. The 14th-century brick screen wall that fronts the pagoda depicts the legendary monster *tan*, with deer antlers, a lion's tail and ox's hooves, which tried to devour the sun but ended up drowning instead – the moral being that greed is not good.

Other sights

The Garden of Drunken Poet Bai (Zuibai Chi; daily 9am–4.30pm), a 5-minute walk west of Square Pagoda, dates back to the 17th century. It was commissioned by a Qing official who was a fan of the Tang poet Bai, who fell into a pond while drunkenly trying to capture the moon's reflection in the water.

Songjiang county's 300-strong Muslims, descended from the soldiers who were part of the Yuan-era Mongol army, flock to the lovely **Songjiang Mosque** (Songjiang Qingzhen Si; daily 8am–7pm) every Friday for prayers. The 1367 Chinese-style mosque is one of the oldest in China.

QINGPU COUNTY

Rural Qingpu county's proximity to Shanghai means that it is a favourite playground for city dwellers, who are regular visitors to its parks, water villages and other sights.

The romance of Ming and Qing water villages such as **Zhujiajiao** and **Zhouzhuang** (*see page 243*) are rapidly eroding with the onset of tourism. The original residents have moved out and are replaced by souvenir shops; shopping plazas now ring the historical areas and the narrow lanes are cheek-to-jowl with tourists. The situation in Zhujiajiao is so bad that it does not warrant a mention in this guidebook; Zhouzhuang is only passably better.

Grand View Garden
Dàguānyuán 大观园

✉ 701 Qingshang Highway, Qingpu
📞 5926 2831 🕐 daily 8am–5pm
💰 RMB 50 adults, RMB 30 children

Just off Qingshang Highway is a glimpse of ancient China at the **Grand View Garden** on the edge of **Dianshan Lake** (Dianshan Hu). A theme park based on the classic Chinese novel *Dream of the Red Mansion*, the garden's re-creations of the novel's buildings, set in a Suzhou-style garden, are enhanced by Chinese musicians and re-enactments of scenes from the book by actors in period garb.

Tour guide at Grand View Garden.

BELOW: Grand View Garden in Dianshan Lake.

Recommended Restaurants & Cafés on page 245

Zhouzhuang ❻ 周庄

🕒 daily 8am–5pm 💰 RMB 60, includes admission to 11 sights

Shanghai's most famous water village, 900-year-old **Zhouzhuang**, located about 80km (50 miles) southwest of Shanghai, has become a kitschy Chinese Disneyland of sorts. Listed as a World Heritage site "under preparation", Zhouzhuang was made famous by renowned Shanghai artist Chen Yifei, whose paintings of a pre-tourist Zhouzhuang were snapped up by the late Armand Hammer, the noted art collector. Now fronted by a shopping plaza and an endless supply of tour buses that ensures crowds at all times, Zhouzhuang's narrow, winding streets are lined with souvenir shops, restaurants, freshwater pearl shops and art galleries. Chen Yifei wannabes can be seen earnestly painting the sights, and tourists strike poses on the bridges, the most famous of which is the Ming dynasty **Double Bridge** (Shuangqiao).

A more worthwhile option is to visit the lesser-known water villages, such as **Xinchang** *(page 234)*, **Tongli** *(page 255)* or **Xitang** *(page 256)*.

CHONGMING ISLAND ❼

Chongming Island (Chongming Dao) lies in silt-muddied waters at the mouth of the Yangzi River. China's second-largest island (after Hainan) at 1,200 sq km (463 sq miles), the island is home to some 750,000 residents. Chongming's main business is agriculture, and it provides the fish, crabs and vegetables that feed Shanghai.

Chongming has doubled its size over the last half-century through land reclamation and the constant silting of the Yangzi River. And it continues to grow: 140 metres (460ft) eastwards and 80 metres

ABOVE: *tipang*, or stewed pork rump, is a delicacy often seen at restaurants in Zhouzhuang.
BELOW: Zhouzhuang is a commonly visited sight on day trips from Shanghai.

A great egret at Dongtan Nature Reserve. The species is under threat due to pollution, poaching and encroaching urbanisation.

(262ft) north each year. With 30,000 hectares (74,130 acres) of beaches and a migratory bird conservation zone, the island has more wild creatures than people at certain times of the year. Plans are now under way to turn it into the world's first sustainable "green" island. Already the **Dongtan Eco-City** is under construction on the eastern tip of the island, and should be completed by the time the World Expo takes place in 2010.

For most of its 1,300-year history, Chongming has battled the sea. The town has been relocated five times – and rebuilt six times – due to the flooding that destroys the sea walls.

Getting to Chongming

The Yangzi River Tunnel and Bridge Project connects Chongming with Pudong via Changxiang Island. Metro Line 9 will also connect the island eventually, or you can get there the old-fashioned way, by boarding a ferry from one of Shanghai's three northeastern ports of Wusong, Baoyang and Shidongkou. Depending on which of Chong-

BELOW: Chongming Island's Dongtan Nature Reserve is a haven for rare bird species.

ming's three gritty port towns you arrive at – Nanmen, Xinhe or Baozhen – head westwards for the island's main attraction – Dongping National Forest Park.

Dongping National Forest Park Dōngpíng Guójiā Sēnlín Gōngyuán 东平国家森林公园

☎ 5964 1841 ⏰ daily 8am–5pm
💰 RMB 40

Dongping National Forest Park covers 360 hectares (890 acres) of Chongming's western half. A boulevard of soaring cone-shaped deep-green metasequoias fringe a canal leading to the entrance of eastern China's largest man-made forest.

The park began life as a tree farm in 1959 and has a fishing pond and lake. The myriad paths that criss-cross the interior, coupled with clean air and birdsong, are reasons enough to visit. However, Chongming's park administration is taking no chances: the lake is stocked with paddle boats, there is a Go-Kart track, a slightly grungy swimming pool (and a man-made beach), and downhill grass skiing. On

the forest's edge is a modern hotel, the **Bao Dao Resort** (tel: 5933 9479).

Qianwei Ecology Village
Chóngmíng Qiánwèi Cūn
崇明前卫村

☎ 5964 9261 ◷ daily 8.30am–10pm; accommodation and dining options also available ◉ RMB 40

Most of Chongming's population is concentrated in the port towns, with the remainder in scattered villages. **Qianwei Ecology Village**, on the island's eastern edge, is a traditional village with restored Qing-era thatched roof farmhouses and farmers who practise ecologically sound cultivation. The farmers here grow organic vegetables, and some have turned their houses into bed and breakfast places. Qianwei encourages visitors to try out farm living and working in the fields. It also houses the **Yingzhou Ancient Village Museum** (Yingzhou Lao Shi Bowuguan; daily 9am–5pm), which occupies a number of thatched-roof earthen houses; each one is given over to a designated task, like weaving, cooking or milling grain.

Dongtan Nature Reserve
Dōngtān Hòuniǎo Zìránbǎohùqū 东滩候鸟自然保护区

Trekking into the remote marshes and mudflats at **Dongtan Nature Reserve** (daily 6am–6pm; free) on the island's eastern edge, is a highlight. Thousands of birds, sandpipers, terns, plovers, egrets and herons – 116 species and which represent one-tenth of the total species in China – flit among the shore grasses, shrieking and cooing, including migratory birds en route from Australia to Siberia. The birds, like everywhere else in China, are under threat due to pollution, poaching and urbanisation. ❏

ABOVE: giant metasequoia trees at Dongping National Forest Park on Chongming Island.

RESTAURANTS AND CAFÉS

Note: With the exception of what's listed below, local restaurants in the areas covered in this chapter are likely to be run-of-the-mill. It's safer to stick to eateries within hotels where you can find one.

Nanxiang's most famous dish is served in a gorgeous Chinese pavilion at the entrance of Guyi Gardens, making for an idyllic setting. The dumplings here are hearty and thick-skinned – not as elegant as their delicate, thin-skinned Shanghai cousins.

Nanxiang

Guyi Garden Nanxiang Xiao Long Bao
南翔小笼
✉ 218 Huyi Road, Nanxiang Town ☎ 5917 4635
◷ daily B, L & D. **$**

Sheshan

Lake View Restaurant
月湖轩
✉ Le Meridien, 1288 Linyin Xin Road, Sheshan ☎ 5779 9999 ◷ daily L & D. **$$$**
A contemporary Chinese restaurant, Lake View features bright colours, clean lines, smiling service, and stunning views across Yuehu Lake and Sheshan Forest Park. The dishes are similarly well prepared and contemporary in flavour; updated versions of Shanghainese and Cantonese classics.

Le Café

月湖西餐厅
✉ Le Meridien, 1288 Linyin Xin Road, Sheshan ☎ 5779 9999 ◷ daily B, L & D. **$$**
Inspired by an European food market, Le Café offers a seemingly endless international buffet of dishes for breakfast, lunch and dinner. Almost every international cuisine – French, Italian Indian, Chinese and even Latin – seems to be represented here.

Prices for a three-course meal for two people, excluding drinks:
$ = under RMB 250
$$ = RMB 250–500
$$$ = RMB 500–800
$$$$ = over RMB 800

Recommended Restaurants & Cafés on pages 264–5

EXCURSIONS FROM SHANGHAI

Suzhou and Hangzhou are perfect side trips for visitors wanting to escape the frenzy of Shanghai. There are also the water villages of Tongli and Xitang, and for the more adventurous, the mist-shrouded mountain resort of Moganshan, near Hangzhou

For almost a century, people from other parts of China have come to Shanghai to see what the West looks like. Even today, one is often reminded that urban Shanghai is not the real China. Fortunately, some of the country's most famous classically Chinese sights are within a couple of hours of Shanghai. But even in these places, you can't really leave Shanghai behind. There are historical links and contemporary connections to the big city, as the spill-over from the Shanghai economic boom ignites growth and modernisation in these neighbouring outposts.

The combination of an efficient train system and high-speed highway makes getting out of the city easy. Only on China's three one-week-long holidays (Chinese New Year, 1 May and 1 October), when all transport routes are hopelessly jammed, does travelling become a major challenge.

SUZHOU ❶ 苏州

The ancient city of **Suzhou**, just 80km (50 miles) northwest of Shanghai, has an intricate mosaic of canals and classical gardens that led Marco Polo to describe it as the "Venice of the East".

PRECEDING PAGES: sunrise over West Lake, Hangzhou. **LEFT:** the Humble Adminstrator's Garden, Suzhouu. **RIGHT:** Five Gate Bridge in Suzhou.

Founded in 600 BC by He Lu, the emperor of the Wu Kingdom, Suzhou only began to flourish after the completion of the Grand Canal, a millennium later. Its prosperity soared further when neighbouring Hangzhou (and later, Nanjing) became the imperial capital of China. Silk production thrived, and imperial officials began laying out the famous classical gardens – almost 200 at its peak.

The city walls are now gone, but the moat that followed the wall's

Chinese gardens are more than what meets the eye: in the pavilions, rockeries, fish pools, gnarled trees and shrubs, and delicate blossoms are expressions of Chinese poetry, philosophy and art – a microcosm of the world. The pine trees, for instance, symbolise long life, the fat goldfish money, the peony blooms nobility. Rocks and ponds always feature prominently because the Chinese word for landscape is shanshui, literally "mountain-water".

RIGHT:
Temple of Mystery.

contours remains, as do almost 200 ancient humpback bridges. Today, the historic city is ringed by tomorrow: the Suzhou–Singapore industrial park surrounds Old Suzhou, drawing into a 21st-century world of fast food, modern industries and five-star hotels.

Suzhou's protected historical district, with its cobblestone streets and ancient stone dwellings, still retains its medieval character. But it is the tranquil gardens, now a Unesco World Heritage site, that are the soul of the city. Just 70 gardens remain; each with its own distinct personality, yet all a microcosm of the world, perfectly balanced in terms of harmony, proportion and variety.

Temple of Mystery Ⓐ
Xuánmiào Guàn 玄妙观

✉ 94 Guanqian Road Ⓒ daily 7.30am–5pm Ⓒ RMB 10

This 3rd-century Taoist temple, once the heart of an ancient-style Suzhou

bazaar is still a shopping magnet, today surrounded by a thriving street market. The temple has an Old China aura and an impressive scale: a great courtyard leads to the massive **San Qing Hall** (San Qing Tang), with its 60 magnificent red-lacquered columns, classic two-tiered roof with upturned eaves and vibrantly painted Taoist gods. The temple was badly damaged during the 19th century – probably during the Taiping Rebellion – but escaped further Cultural Revolution damage when the Red Guards commandeered it for their own use.

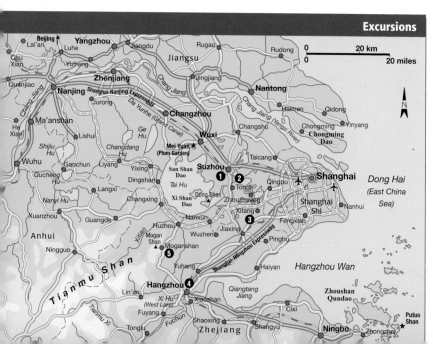

Recommended Restaurants & Cafés on pages 264–5

Kunqu Opera Museum ⓑ
Kūnqǔ Bówùguǎn 昆曲博物馆

✉ 14 Zhongzhang Jia Xiang ⓒ daily 8.30am–4.30pm ⓖ free

A 10-minute walk east, following the side of the canal, leads to the **Kunqu Opera Museum**, where Suzhou's own 5,000-year-old Kunqu opera tradition is chronicled. Predating Beijing opera by 2,000 years, Kunqu, or Kunju, opera *(see page 53)* is still performed in this Ming dynasty building under a stunning wooden dome embellished with an intricate seashell-like whorl pattern. Across the courtyard, another building houses a display of costumes, opera masks, musical instruments – even a model orchestra – as well as documents on the opera's history.

Just next door, Suzhou's ancient storytelling song tradition called Pingtan *(see page 53)* comes alive each afternoon with performances (at 1.30pm daily) at the **Pingtan Museum** (Pingtan Bowuguan). The performances, which are accompanied by Chines string instruments, are in the local Suzhou dialect.

Lion Grove ⓒ Shīzi Lín 狮子林

✉ 23 Yuanlin Road ⓒ 512 6727 2428 ⓒ daily 7.30am–5.30pm ⓖ RMB 30

It's a short taxi ride northwest to **Lion Grove**. A Buddhist temple garden laid out in 1342 by the monk Tian Ru in honour of his master, Lion Grove is a poem to the mountain. Encircled by a covered corridor, the garden has intricate piles of rocks taken from nearby Lake Tai – many lion-shaped – weathered by the elements and set among lakes and pavilions. Last owned by a branch of the well known Chinese architect I.M. Pei's family, Lion Grove is said to be Emperor Qianlong's inspiration for Yuanmingyuan, the old Summer Palace on the outskirts of Beijing.

Suzhou Museum ⓓ Sūzhōu Bówùguǎn 苏州博物馆

✉ 204 Dongbei Road; www.sz museum.com ⓒ 512 6754 1534 ⓒ daily 9am–5pm ⓖ RMB 20

I.M. Pei, drawing on his family connection to Suzhou *(see above)* for

One of the pavilions at the Lion Grove Garden.

BELOW LEFT: the stage at Kunqu Opera Museum.
BELOW: Lion Grove garden.

inspiration, designed the landmark **Suzhou Museum** in 2006, a short walk north of Lion Grove. The US$40-million white and grey building reinvents traditional Suzhou architecture in a spectacular Modernist form. There is plenty of glass and light, and Chinese touches like a Chinese garden and footbridge. The massive museum features a collection of artefacts from early Suzhou, and includes a rare pearl stupa, porcelain, funeral relics unearthed from the mud of Dongshan Island, antique maps of Suzhou and the Grand Canal, and Song dynasty art and calligraphy.

The Humble Administrator's Garden, the largest of the Suzhou gardens.

Humble Administrator's Garden ⓔ Zhuōzhèng Yuán 拙政园

✉ 178 Dongbei Road ☎ 512 6751 0286 ⏰ 7.30am–5pm 💰 RMB 70

Just to the northeast is the **Humble Administrator's Garden**, whose name refers to a line of Jin dynasty poetry that says cultivating a garden is the work of a humble man. But this 4-hectare (10-acre) garden, the largest of the Suzhou gardens, is far from a humble undertaking.

Laid out by retired Ming imperial official Wang Xianchen in 1513, the three main areas are thematically linked by water, used in pools and ponds of varying sizes. Twisting and turning rock-lined paths burst open onto a classical landscape: an expansive lotus pond crossed by zigzag bridges and pavilions perched on hillsides and in hollows.

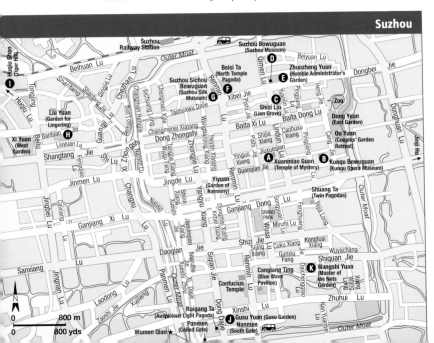

Recommended Restaurants & Cafés on pages 264–5

North Temple Pagoda **F**
Běisì Tǎ 北寺塔

✉ 652 Renmin Road 🕒 daily
8am–6pm 💰 RMB 25

To the west, this 76-metre (250ft)
high mustard and vermilion pagoda
on the site of the Wu Kingdom ruler
Sun Quan's childhood home, dominates the city. First built during the
3rd century and completely rebuilt in
the 16th century, a climb to its summit offers spectacular views of the
surrounding area, including the 17th-
century **Nanmu Hall** on the grounds,
with a teahouse just behind.

Suzhou Silk Museum **G**
Sūzhōu Sīchóu Bówùguǎn
苏州丝绸博物馆

✉ 661 Renmin Road (opposite North
Temple Pagoda) 📞 512 6753 1977
🕒 daily 9am–5pm 💰 RMB 7

Across the street, the **Suzhou Silk
Museum** recounts the history of silk
in China. Especially interesting are the
rare antique silk pieces, and the section on sericulture: one room has
large woven pans holding wriggling
silkworms (when in season) feasting
on mulberry leaves, while on another
shelf, silk cocoons sit neatly in rows.
Weavers at the museum demonstrate
how young girls ruined their hands in
the old days by plunging them into
boiling water to separate the cocoon
threads into single strands. The big
looms, strung with jewel-tone silk
threads, bob up and down in the
skilled hands of the weavers.

Garden for Lingering **H**
Liú Yuán 留园

✉ 338 Liuyuan Road 📞 512 6533
7940 🕒 7.30am–5.30pm 💰 RMB 40

To the west, outside the city gates, is
the Ming-era **Garden for Lingering**.
Here, a 700-metre (2,300ft) walkway
links the garden's four scenic areas.
Laid out by Ming dynasty minister
Xu Taishi, the corridor has inscribed
tablets bearing flowery descriptions of
the garden by poets and noted visitors. Its most famous pavilion, the
Mandarin Duck Hall (Yuanyuang),
has separate viewing rooms for men
and women, both of which overlook
the garden's pride: the 6.5-metre
(21ft) 5,000kg (11,000lb) **Cloud
Crowned Peak** (Junyun Feng), the
largest rock from Lake Tai in any of
the Suzhou gardens.

Tiger Hill **I** Hǔqiū
Shān 虎丘山

✉ 8 Huqiu Road 📞 512 6723 2305
🕒 daily 7am–6pm 💰 RMB 60

A visit to Suzhou without seeing
Tiger Hill, located far in the north-

*A silk brocade
Mao-style jacket on
display at the Suzhou
Silk Museum.*

TOP MIDDLE:
the contemporary
Suzhou Silk Museum.
BELOW:
Garden for Lingering.

RIGHT: Tiger Hill with Cloud Rock Pagoda in the background.
BELOW: Master of the Nets Garden.
BOTTOM: picturesque Gusu Garden.

west of the city, would be incomplete, wrote Song poet Su Shi. Less formal and manicured than the others, Tiger Hill contains the tomb of Suzhou's founder, the 6th-century Wu king He Lu. The garden gets its name from the mythical white tiger that appeared on the third day after his death to guard the grave. Archaeologists suspect it may be that grave, which lies beneath the seven-storey octagonal brick **Cloud Rock Pagoda** (Yunyan Ta) on the hilltop, that is causing the pagoda's severe tilt. Tiger Hill's **Thousand Men Rock** (Qian Ren Shi), at the foot of the hill, is reputedly the gruesome spot where the tomb builders were executed to keep secret the location of the tomb and its treasures, while **Sword Pond** (Jianchi) is said to be where the king's 3,000 swords were buried.

Gusu Garden ❶
Gūsū Yuán 姑苏园

✉ 1 Dong Dajie ⏰ daily 7.30am–5pm
💲 RMB 25

Head southeast to **Gusu Garden**, just south of the Sheraton Suzhou.

Here you can climb the well-worn steps of **Five Gate Bridge** (Wumen Qiao), Suzhou's tallest bridge, for a vista of boats and barges sliding past the canal. **Pan Gate** (Pan Men), the only remaining stretch of Suzhou's 3rd-century city wall, is a short walk away. The climb up the 300 metres (980ft) of original city wall is rewarded with a view of fishing boats, arched bridges, graceful willows over canals and the 1,000-year-old **Ruigang Pagoda** (Ruigang Ta).

Master of the Nets Garden
❿ Wǎngshī Yuán 网师园

✉ 11 Kuojiatou Xiang ☎ 512 6529 3190 ⏰ 7.30am–5.30pm 💲 RMB 30

The loveliest Suzhou garden is also one of the smallest: the exquisite **Master of the Nets Garden**. Dating from 1770, its name refers to the ambition of its retired court official owner, who longed to be a fisherman. The intimate garden's charm comes from its delicate, scaled-down courtyards, pavilions and rockeries. Contained in its pavilions are some of Suzhou's most exquisite antique furniture, especially in the **Peony Study** (Dianchun Yi), which has been replicated at New York's Metropolitan Museum of Art. On summer nights, the beautifully lit

Recommended Restaurants & Cafés on pages 264–5

pavilions are the setting for traditional performances – opera, music and dance – that transport the viewer to the days of the imperial court (daily 10-minute shows from 7.30–10pm; RMB 80). On moonlit nights, visitors may be given access to the **Moon Watching Pavilion** (Yue Dao Feng Lai Ting), where they can see the moon thrice over: in the sky, in the pond reflection, and in a mirror.

TONGLI ❷ 同里

📞 512 6349 3027 for English-speaking guides from the Tongli Tourist Information Centre ⏰ daily 7.45am–5.30pm ⓞ Entrance to Old Town free; RMB 80 for entrance to major sights

The Song dynasty water village of **Tongli**, 20km (12 miles) southeast of Suzhou (and 80km/50 miles from Shanghai), is so pretty that it's often used as a backdrop for Chinese films and television shows. Be warned: it is touristy – residents no longer live here in the old houses – and it can get crowded during weekends and holidays.

Surrounded by five streams, Tongli is made up of seven islets, connected by ancient stone bridges. A boat trip on the canals is a pleasant way to get a perspective on the town. **Mingqing Street** (Mingqing Jie) is lined with wooden Ming and Qing dynasty houses, now occupied by tourist shops and restaurants. At the end of the street is the classical Chinese garden, the **Retreat and Reflection Garden** (Tuisi Yuan), built in 1886 and now a World Heritage site.

East of the garden is the famous **Museum of Ancient Chinese Sex Culture** (Zhongguo Gudai Xing Wenhua Bowuguan; tel: 512 6332 3388; daily 8am–5pm; RMB 40) with over 1,200 artefacts on the history of Chinese sexuality. Created by noted Shanghai University professor Liu Danyi, the artefacts – everything from statues of copulating couples to wooden penises – are graphic (parents with young children should take note).

Also worth a visit are Tongli's old residences – **Gengle Hall** (Gengle Tang), **Jiayin Hall** (Jiayin Tang) and **Chongben Hall** (Chongben Tang) – all of which are open to visitors.

Statue at Tongli's Museum of Ancient Chinese Sex Culture.

BELOW: canal activity at Tongli.

Life in the quaint water village of Xitang moves at a gentle pace.

XITANG ❸ 西塘

✉ Jiashan county, Zhejiang province; www.xitang.com.cn ◎ RMB 60 allows access to all sights in Xitang

Nine rivers converge in the charming water village of **Xitang**, located some 90km (56 miles) from Shanghai. Xitang is still relatively quiet and authentic – especially when compared to more overexposed water towns like **Zhouzhuang** *(see page 243)*. Xitang's popularity received a boost in 2006 when it was featured in the film *Mission Impossible III*.

Xitang's riverside walkways are all covered and stretch for more than 1,300 metres (4,265ft); at night, the roofs are all strung up with pretty lanterns. Adding to the town's charm are some 122 lanes paved with slate meandering through the town, and more than 100 ancient bridges that connect the waterways.

Xi Yuan, the town's exquisite classical Chinese garden, was once the home of the Zhu family. Xitang's attractions include **Xue's House** (Xue Jia), the home of a wealthy merchant, the rear of the house facing the river,

BELOW: Xitang and its covered riverside walkways.

as well as **Zhongfu House** (Zhongfu Jia), dating from the Ming and Qing era, with its seven courtyards. Also worth visiting is the **Shang Tang Temple** (Shang Tang Miao), dedicated the military hero of the same name.

HANGZHOU ❹ 杭州

Located 185km (115 miles) southwest of Shanghai is **Hangzhou** – a classical Chinese beauty and the capital of Zhejiang province. Hangzhou was built on wealth, earned by its fortuitous position as the southern terminus of the Grand Canal (which connected all the way to the capital, Beijing), and by royal privilege as China's imperial capital during the Song dynasty. It quickly became an important centre for the silk industry and, as a favourite retreat for China's emperors, a place where the noble arts and leisure were cherished.

The Taiping Rebellion razed the city in 1861; this was followed by a period of prosperity as a Treaty Port in 1895, and then another period of destruction during the Cultural Revolution. Today, Hangzhou is on an upswing again, as it grows as a

Recommended Restaurants & Cafés on pages 264–5

centre for industry, pharmaceuticals and telecommunications. All this has given rise to a frenzy of construction in Hangzhou, mainly of hotels, office buildings and shopping malls.

West Lake Ⓐ Xīhú 西湖

Boat tours *(see margin tip page 258)* are an ideal way to see the famous 5.5-sq-km (2¼-sq-mile) freshwater **West Lake** and its attractions. Past **Mid-Lake Pavilion** (Huxinting) and **Ruan Yuan's Mound** (Ruangong Dun), most visitors disembark at **Xiao Ying Island** (Xiao Ying Dao) for views of the three 17th-century stone pagodas floating on the lake. Called the **Three Pools Mirroring the Moon** (San Tan Yin Yue), this is one of the 10 legendary views of West Lake.

Gu Shan Island Ⓑ
Gūshān Dǎo 孤山岛

The 1.5km (1-mile) **Bai Causeway** (Bai Di), named after the Hangzhou poet-governor Bai Juyi, cuts a path around the northern section of the lake, connecting Hangzhou's mainland to **Gu Shan**, the island on the lake's northwest shore. At the entrance

of Bai Causeway is **Broken Bridge** (Duan Qiao), so called because when winter snow on the bridge melts, it appears as if the bridge has been spilt into two. The bridge is famous as the setting for the Hangzhou folk tale *Lady White Snake (see margin note)*.

Further down the Bai Causeway is **Autumn Moon on a Calm Lake** (Pinghu Qiuyue), one of the traditional spots from which to view the lake, and, on a small road to the right, **Crane Pavilion** (Fanghe Ting), built in 1915 in memory of the Song poet Lin Hejing, who is said to have lived here alone with only a crane for company.

"Lady White Snake" recounts the tale of a white snake who changes herself into a beautiful woman, and falls in love with a young man. They meet for the first time near Broken Bridge.

ABOVE: a "dragon boat" moored at West Lake.
BELOW: different vistas of West Lake.

TIP

At West Lake, boats can be hired along the shore, near Gu Shan Island and along the eastern side of the lake near Hubin Road. Look out for the booths which sell tickets for everything from small boats that you row yourself to larger junks and ferries.

RIGHT: Zhejiang Provincial Museum.

Zhejiang Provincial Museum Zhèjiāng Shěng Bówùguǎn 浙江省博物馆

✉ 25 Gushan Road ☎ 571 8797 1177 ⏰ Tue–Sun 9am–5pm ⓔ free; audio guide RMB 10

On Gu Shan Island itself is **Zhejiang Provincial Museum**, built in 1929 on the grounds of the Emperor Qianlong's imperial palace. There are 100,000 cultural relics in its seven halls, including the famous Celadon Hall (Zhejiang was once the main producer of Chinese celadon).

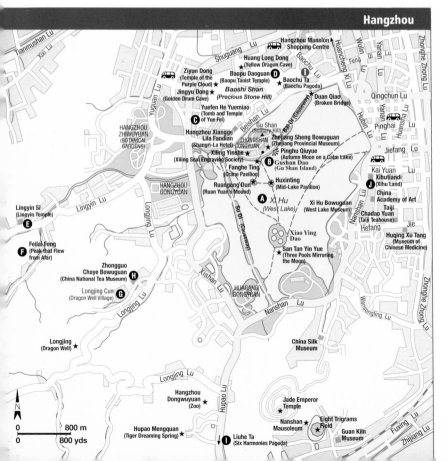

Recommended Restaurants & Cafés on pages 264–5

Other sights on Gu Shan

The **Xiling Seal Engraving Society** (Xiling Yinshe; 8.30am–4.30pm; free), a short walk west, displays seal engravings on the walls of several pavilions strewn on the hillside.

A path to the rear leads gradually uphill, on whose summit is found the 11-storey unrestored **Pagoda of Avatamsaka Sutra** (Huayanjing Ta), built in 1924.

The **Sigillography Museum** (Zhongguo Yingxue Bowuguan; daily 8.30am–4.30pm; free), just before the bridge, recounts the history of the Chinese seal and has some lovely exhibits. Displays range from rough clay shards to tiny carved seals with calligraphy to match.

Tomb and Temple of Yue Fei  Yuèfén Hè Yuèmiào 岳坟和岳庙

✉ West of Beishan Road ☎ 521 8798 6663 ☉ daily 7am–6pm ◉ RMB 25

On the northwestern shore of the mainland is the **Tomb and Temple of Yue Fei**, a popular memorial to the 12th-century Song patriot commander who, despite his success against invaders from the north, was framed, arrested and killed with his son Yueyang on trumped-up charges. He was exonerated and given a proper burial 21 years later in 1163. Yue Fei's temple was destroyed during the Cultural Revolution in 1966 and rebuilt in 1979. No longer a functioning temple, its main hall is dominated by a Yue Fei statue with a plaque that reads, "Recover our lost territories" (modern-day implications with regard to Taiwan do not go unnoticed). Eight murals in the back tell the story of Yue Fei's life. Laid out as a Song dynasty garden, the temple is connected to the tomb grounds.

The back of the temple leads to the **Temple of the Purple Cloud** (Ziyun Dong), the oldest natural cave on the ridge. From here, it's a pleasant walk away from the tourists and into the peaceful surrounds of **Precious Stone Hill** (Baoshi Shan). From here are views of the 10th-century **Baochu Pagoda** (Baochu Ta) to the east.

Baopu Taoist Temple  Bàopǔ Dàoyuàn 抱朴道院

☉ daily 6am–5pm ◉ RMB 5

Grounds of the Seal Engraving Society.

This lovely yellow-coloured temple, teetering over the rock face in nearby **Ge Hill**, is newly renovated but still retains an old-world charm. Black-clad nuns with tightly pulled buns can often be seen meditating in the temple. Originally built during the Jin dynasty (AD 317–420), the temple has been extended and restored several times. It is named after the Taoist master and alchemist Ge Hong, also known as Baopu, who was famous for producing the elixir of life.

Lingyin Temple  Língyǐn Sì 灵隐寺

☉ daily 5am–6pm ✉ RMB 65

Found in the hills west of West Lake is **Lingyin Temple**, which translates as

BELOW: statue of Yue Fei at the temple named after him.

Burning joss sticks as offerings at Lingyin Temple.

the Temple of the Soul's Retreat. This is Hangzhou's second-biggest attraction, as affirmed by the heaving crowds. **Liugong Pagoda** (Liugong Ta), the ancient hexagonal seven-storey pagoda at the entrance, contains the remains of the Indian monk Huili who built the temple in AD 326.

One of the five famous Chan (Zen) sect Buddhist temples of China, Lingyin Temple has been rebuilt several times since – at least 16 times according to one source. The temple was spared during the Cultural Revolution, and thus has retained treasured relics such as the 10th-century stone pagodas in front of the **Hall of the Four Heavenly Kings**. Inside is an image of the Maitreya (Future) Buddha, protected by an 800-year-old statue of Skanda, the Guardian of Buddhist Law and Order. Behind this building is the **Grand Hall** – accessed via a courtyard – where a 20-metre (65ft) tall statue of Sakyamuni Buddha stands. Carved from 24 blocks of camphor wood in 1956, it is China's largest sitting Buddha and a replica of an original Tang dynasty statue.

RIGHT: rock carving of the Laughing Buddha, near Lingyin Temple.
BELOW: statuary at Lingyin Temple.

Peak That Flew from Afar
F Fēilái Fēng 飞来峰

South of Lingyin Temple is the **Peak That Flew from Afar**, so named because the monk Huili exclaimed that it looked so much like the one in his native India that it must have flown here. Indeed, the peak – actually a cliff – is smaller than the surrounding peaks, and is the only one made of limestone, not sandstone.

The 470 **stone carvings** on the rockface, mostly intact, date from the 10th to the 14th century, with the oldest ones being the 10th-century

Recommended Restaurants & Cafés on pages 264–5

Guanyin (Goddess of Mercy) in the **Deep Dragon Cave** (Longhong Dong) and the carvings in the **Shot of Gleam Cave** (Shexu Dong). Everyone's favourite carving is that of the famous jolly Laughing Buddha, as the crowds in front of it attest.

Dragon Well Village
Lóngjǐng Cūn 龙井村

Southwest of West Lake is **Dragon Well Village**, where Hangzhou's famous tea of the same name is grown in nearby terraced plantations. Further southwest is **Dragon Well** (Longjing), the legendary spring after which the tea is named. What is unusual is that the two levels of springs that feed the pond create a line when the water is disturbed, instead of the usual concentric circles. Young girls often splash their faces with the cool water, believing that it will improve their complexion.

China National Tea Museum
Zhōngguó Cháyè Bówùguǎn 中国茶叶博物馆

✉ Longjing Road 📞 571 8796 4221
🕐 Tue–Sun 8.30am–4.30pm 💲 free

North of the village is the **Tea Museum of China**, which does an excellent job of documenting the history and culture of tea production in five linked buildings. One of its highlights is the re-creation of the tea rooms of different ethnic minorities.

Six Harmonies Pagoda
Liùhé Tǎ 六和塔

🕐 daily 6am–6.30pm 💲 RMB 30

About 3km (2 miles) southwest of West Lake is **Six Harmonies Pagoda**. Standing near the northern bank of the Qiantang River, it overlooks a large bridge. Built in 970 in the hope that it might control the river's mighty tidal waves, the seven-storey pagoda was last rebuilt in 1900, although its interior dates to 1123.

The pagoda, its Song dynasty structure still intact, is the traditional spot to watch the river's famous tidal bore on the autumn equinox in mid-September *(see margin)*.

Xihutiandì 西湖天地

Towards the east of West Lake is **Hangzhou City**, where a frenzy of construction is creating plazas and shopping malls, all concentrated around **Yanan Road** and **Hubin Road**. There is plenty of brand-name shopping at the "Hubin International Boutique Compound", which has stores selling everything from Tag Heuer to Valentino.

South of Hubin Road, against a beautiful backdrop of historic buildings and the shores of West Lake, is **Xihutiandi**. Like its Shanghai sister, Xintiandi *(see page 154)*, this is an upscale dining and nightlife complex.

Further south is **Hefang Street** (Hefang Jie), a shopping street dedicated to Chinese knick-knacks and local snacks in a Qing dynasty setting. **Taiji Teahouse** (Taiji Chadao Yuan), at No. 184, is one of the best places in town to enjoy a cup of the local brew.

Six Harmonies Pagoda along the northern bank of the Qiantang River. In mid-September, hundreds gather at the nearby bridge to watch the wall of water surging to as high as 6 metres (20ft), caused by the river's famous tidal bore.

BELOW: tea plantations near Dragon Well Village.

"In the heart of the Bamboo, 1,800 feet above sea. Beautiful scenery! Swimming Pool! Private Park! Healthy climate! Cool nights!" – from a 1930s Hotel Mokanshan (sic) brochure.

Just off Hefang Street is the **Museum of Chinese Medicine** (Huqing Xu Tang; daily 8.30am– 5pm; RMB 10), a stunning Qing-era building that is a working pharmacy and clinic, reputedly the oldest in China. Continuing east is the **Drum Tower Antique Market** (Gulou Guwan Shichang), which has stalls selling reproductions and the occasional genuine article.

MOGANSHAN ❺

Hangzhou makes a good base for exploring **Moganshan**, located some 65km (40 miles) north of Hangzhou and 195km (120 miles) west of Shanghai. An early start from Hangzhou allows a full day of exploration; if coming direct from Shanghai, an overnight stay is recommended. Nestled in the mountains of north Zhejiang province, the highland resort of Moganshan – with its cool evenings and summer temperatures no higher than 27°C (80°F) – made it the ideal hill station for Concession-era foreigners longing for a more comfortable climate.

Before the first missionaries ven-

RIGHT: waterfall at Moganshan.
BELOW: lush bamboo forests at Moganshan.

tured here in the 1890s, there were only Chinese farmers living here, cultivating the bamboo that still grows thickly on Moganshan. Barely scraping a living, they were quite happy to rent their houses to the first foreigners who summered here. The frugal missionaries could only afford to rent houses, but later they were joined by wealthier citizens, some of whom even brought their architects from Shanghai to construct holiday

Recommended Restaurants & Cafés on pages 264–5

villas using the grey stone quarried from the nearby hills. By the 1930s, there was a full-fledged summer community in Moganshan with post offices, two churches and nearly 160 houses. In the 1960s, when the Sino-Soviet split raised fears of a nuclear war, the resort was turned into a military garrison; it was only reopened to the public in the mid-1980s.

Things to see

Today, Moganshan is experiencing a renaissance of sorts with many of the old villas restored as retreats, and it has become something of an escape for Shanghai urbanites, thanks to its quiet relaxing pace. Moganshan is best explored by wandering along its hilly paths, still paved with the stone laid a century ago, breathing the fresh mountain air and discovering the once-grand mansions tucked away in the hills.

Start at Moganshan village, where along Yingshan Street is the **Bamboo Museum** (Zhuzi Bowuguan; daily 10am–5pm). It is amazing to see the many creative uses of bamboo for which Moganshan is famous.

Southwest of the village, on a grooved mountain road, is **No. 126**, a grey stone house with curved turrets and Gothic doors and windows, and framed against the pine and bamboo forest. Mao Zedong stayed in this house while he was working on China's Constitution in 1954.

Back on Yingshan Street, heading east up a steep hill above the post office and past the power station, is the former **Protestant church**. The parsonage next to it once served as a primary school, but is now abandoned in preparation for a new use. East of the church, thick bamboo pipes lead to the lonely stream-fed **swimming pool**, almost eerie in the swirling mists. The **tennis courts**, which once had Chinese pavilions for spectators, are just north of here on the hill, but in rough shape today.

Head back south on the main road, past the Moganshan Management Office, to the **Yellow Temple** (Huang Si), a simple Buddhist temple where locals say gunpowder was stored in the aftermath of the Sino-Soviet split.

The atmospheric home of 1930s Shanghai mafia boss Du Yuesheng, in the northeast, has been turned into a Radisson-managed guesthouse, the **Du Yuesheng Villa** (Du Yuesheng Binguan; tel: 572 803 3601), while further north is the one-time villa of another luminary, Kuomintang leader Chiang Kai-shek, now the **Wuling Hotel** (Wuling Binguan; tel: 572 803 3218).

Also part of the local scene is **Naked Retreats** (Shanghai office tel: 6431 8901; www.nakedretreats.cn), a boutique eco-hotel featuring restored farmhouses on the bamboo hillside. The idea is to get back to nature, so the farmhouses are rustic (but with the amenities city dwellers need), meals are cooked by a local woman, and guests can avail themselves of activities that incude hiking the many Moganshan trails, biking, tea-picking, yoga and massage. ❑

TIP

All the excursions covered in this chapter can be done as day trips out of Shanghai, although in the case of Hangzhou and Moganshan, you would be really stretching it. An overnight at most of these places is recommended; even the water villages of Tongli and Xitang take on a very different atmosphere at night.

BELOW: Wuling Hotel, where Chiang Kai-shek once lived.

BEST RESTAURANTS AND CAFÉS

Suzhou

CHINESE

De Yue Lou

得月楼

✉ 27 Taijian Lane ☎ 512 6522 6969 ⏱ daily L & D. **$$**

This charming eatery is done up like an old Suzhou mansion – Chinese lanterns, Ming-style wooden furniture, classical paintings. The restaurant, which has Ming-era origins, serves Suzhou specialities almost identical to Songhelou (just across the street) – like squirrel mandarin (sweet and sour) fish, crystal prawns, and more.

Shang Palace

香宫

✉ Shangri-La Suzhou, 168 Ta Yuan Road, Levels 2 and 3 ☎ 512 6808 0168 ext 23 ⏱ daily L & D. **$$$**

Beautifully decorated in a nouveau-Chinoise style,

Shang Palace serves beautifully executed Cantonese, Hai Yang and regional specialities in an elegant environment.

Songhelou

松鹤楼

✉ 72 Tai Jian Lane, near Guan Qian Jie ☎ 512 6523 3270 ⏱ daily L & D. **$$**

This is Suzhou's most famous restaurant – Emperor Qianlong is said to have dined here – but be warned that Songhelou is now modernised, and packed with Chinese tourists trying the Suzhou specialities for which it is famous – squirrel mandarin fish, crystal shrimp, and more.

Wangsi

王四酒家

✉ 35 Taijian Lane ☎ 512 6522 7277 ⏱ daily L & D. **$$**

Smaller and less famous than its neighbours De

Yue Lou and Songhelou, Wangsi nevertheless serves good meals in a simple setting. Its Beggar's Chicken, a tender, whole chicken baked in mud, is a speciality.

INTERNATIONAL

Garden Brasserie

萃英

✉ Sheraton Suzhou Hotel and Towers, 259 Xin Shi Road ☎ 512 6510 3388 ⏱ daily 6am–11pm. **$$$**

A bright, sun-filled restaurant overlooking landscaped gardens, the Garden Brasserie is open all day (unlike most Suzhou restaurants), making it a good place to stop between tours. The menu spans the globe, from European classics to Southeast Asian favourites and, of course, Chinese dishes.

Hangzhou

CHINESE

A Simple Diet

粗菜馆

✉ R'Tin Hotel, 12 Macheng Road ☎ 571 8775 5977 ⏱ daily L & D. **$**

Located next to R'Tin Hotel, this modern restaurant serves up excellent Hangzhou dishes at a steal. The portions are big and the service attentive (and

there is an English menu). Particularly good are the lotus root with sweet sticky rice, the red-roasted pork and steamed bread, and the chopped green peppers with minced pork.

Crystal Jade Garden

翡翠花园酒家

✉ House 10, Xihutiandi, 147 Nanshan Road ☎ 571 8702 6618/7887 ⏱ daily 10am–10.30pm. **$$**

Set among trees in Xihutiandi, Crystal Jade has both an airy conservatory and discreet, dark panelled private rooms. The food – a range of Chinese dishes – is consistently good, making this a favourite with both local business types as well as expats.

Green Club

绿野乡村俱乐部

✉ 68 Waidaqiao Road, South Meiling Road ☎ 571 8533 2482 ⏱ daily L & D. **$**

Rustic little gem set in an old farmhouse serving Hangzhou country specials, including shrimps fried with green tea – well worth the 30-minute taxi ride from the city centre. The area surrounding Green Club is lush with bamboos and tea plantations offering walks – if you're so inclined.

LEFT: Shang Palace at the Shangri-La Suzhou hotel.
RIGHT: Beggar's Chicken – a Hangzhou speciality.

Hubin 28
湖滨28

✉ 1/F, Hyatt Regency Hangzhou, 28 Hubin Road ☎ 571 8779 1234 © daily L & D. **$$**

Sleek and chic, the dimly lit Hubin 28 blends strong modern lines with touches of Old China. Its Chinese fare features dishes from all over the country, including Hangzhou favourites such as *dongpo* pork with chestnut pancakes, and pan-fried bean curd stuffed with mushroom.

Jinjiang Seafood Street
近江海鲜美食街

© daily D. **$**

It's loud and lively, and you'll either love it or hate it. The street is always packed with hungry hoards feasting on anything from fleshy prawns to tender squids, all cooked to perfection by one of the many restaurants lining the road. The process is simple – pick your desired catch, then ask the *laoban* (the owner of the restaurant) to cook it for you – unless you want your fish cooked a particular way, let him set his creative juices loose.

Louwailou
楼外楼

✉ 30 Gushan Road; www.louwailou.com.cn ☎ 571 8796 9023 © daily L & D. **$$**

Somewhat of a Hangzhou institution, this large restaurant with an equally large terrace overlooking Xihu Lake serves all the best Hangzhou specialities, including West Lake vinegar fish, *dongpo* pork, Beggar's Chicken and dried bell tofu – a must for anyone wanting to sample the local cuisine. Weather permitting, the terrace is an ideal place from which to watch the sun set across the lake while having dinner.

Yee Chino
玉玲珑

✉ 171 Zhongshan Road (N) ☎ 571 8707 0777 © daily L & D. **$$**

Deliciously decadent restaurant set in an Alice in Wonderland world of pink and purple hues, complete with hanging chandeliers, green leaf-shaped oversized chairs and cheeky little parrots. Food orders are penned with long, pink feathers and served equally theatrically on oversized plates. *Bobo* chicken and cod cooked with peanuts are especially good.

CONTINENTAL

Jamaica Café
牙买加咖啡

✉ House 12, Xihutiandi, 147 Nanshan Road ☎ 571 8702 6598 © daily 9am–midnight. **$**

Spanish chain serving good hits of coffee and home-made sandwiches as well as tapas. Overlooking West Lake, the pleasant outdoor tables, nestled among the trees, are a good place to chill.

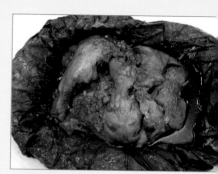

Provence
普罗旺斯法国餐厅

✉ 1 Baishaquan, Shuguang Road; www.provence-hz.com ☎ 571 8797 6115 © daily 11am–10.30pm. **$**

Authentic fuss-free French food at reasonable prices. The owner, Eric, who helped establish the very successful Epicure in Shanghai, has set up his own eatery in a renovated two-storey house with an outdoor terrace. There is a modestly priced café menu, as well as the pricier "chef's recommendation", which is still great value. Wide selection of wines too.

TEAHOUSE

Taiji Teahouse
太极茶道苑

✉ 184 Hefang Street ☎ 571 8780 1791 © daily 7.30am–midnight. **$**

Old-world teahouse with lovely original features in the heart of Hefang Street. Everything, from the tea menu handwritten in Chinese characters on a bamboo scroll to the traditional method of pouring tea with a long-spouted brass teapot, brings you back to times long gone.

Moganshan

The Moganshan Lodge
莫干山 咖啡厅

✉ Songliang Shanzhuang, Yin Shang Street; www.moganshanlodge.com ☎ 572 803 3011 © daily 8am–midnight. **$$**

Perched on the hills of Moganshan, this little café-cum-restaurant-cum-bar has a lovely homey feel (the outside terrace is the perfect place to enjoy a freshly brewed cup of coffee). The lodge serves Western food with a distinct home-made taste throughout the day – dinners are cooked to order, so be sure to phone and arrange in advance, particularly during busy summer weekends.

Prices for a three-course meal for two people, excluding drinks:

$ = under RMB 250
$$ = RMB 250–500
$$$ = RMB 500–800
$$$$ = over RMB 800

✵ INSIGHT GUIDES

SHANGHAI
Travel Tips

TRANSPORT

GETTING THERE AND GETTING AROUND

The boom in car ownership in Shanghai has meant that traffic congestion is a way of life, and getting around the city by car can be slow during peak hours. Still, this is a fairly compact city, and many of its neighbourhoods are easily (and best) seen on foot. Although taxis are inexpensive – flagfall begins at RMB 11 – they can be scarce during rush hour and when it rains, so some advance planning is required. As a backup, the metro is a fast, efficient option, but during peak times the carriages can get crowded.

GETTING THERE

By Air

Pudong International Airport

Most international flights arrive at the modern, designer-built **Pudong International Airport** (Pudong Jichang; tel: 9608 1388; www.shairport.com), located about 30km (18½ miles) from the city centre. See Getting Around *(page 270)* for details on getting to the city.

The airport's two terminals handle about 35 million passengers with a capacity of 80 million passengers annually in four connected halls – arrival halls are on the lower level, while departure halls are on the upper level.

Arriving passengers are quickly whisked through the terminal on a combination of travellators and escalators to immigration; after clearing immi-

gration, take the escalator one level down to baggage claim (carts are free) and customs.

The arrival hall is lined with hotel information desks, currency exchange facilities and ATMs, as well as the Tourist Information Centre and China International Travel Service (CITS) counters.

Hongqiao Airport

Most domestic flights arrive at **Hongqiao Airport** (Hongqiao Jichang; tel: 5260 4620; www.shairport.com), located 13km (8 miles) from the city centre. See Getting Around *(page 270)* for details on getting to the city.

Hongqiao's second terminal opened in 2010, giving the 35 million travellers who come through more breathing room. Domestic arrivals at Hongqiao don't need to go through immigration and can proceed directly to baggage claim. After clearing customs, hotel reservation booths are located on the left in the arrival hall. There is a Bank

of China office, ATMs and a Tourist Information Centre.

Key Airline Offices

Air China: Room 101B, Changfeng Centre, 1088 Yanan Road (W); tel: 5239 7227; www.airchina.com.cn.
British Airways: Room 703, Central Plaza, 227 Huangpi Road; tel: 6835 5633; www.britishairways.com.
China Eastern Airlines: 1720 Huaihai Road (W); tel: 6247 5953; www.ce-air.com.
China North West Airlines: 258 Weihai Road; tel: 6267 4233; www.cnwa.com.

TRAINS TO HK & BEIJING

Beijing – The Z21/Z22 is a de luxe overnight service from Shanghai to Beijing (a journey of 12 hours). It has been described as a "super-luxury star-rated moving hotel" with en suite bathrooms, TV and Internet access. Trains in both directions depart at 7pm and arrive at 7am the following morning.

Hong Kong – A comfortable train service runs on alternate days from Kowloon's Hung Hom Station to Shanghai – if you don't mind the journey time of 25 hours (see www.kcrc.com for details). The K100 departs from Kowloon at 3pm and arrives in Shanghai at 4.30pm the next day. The K99 departs from Shanghai at 10.24am and arrives at Kowloon at 1.10pm the next day.

Book tickets directly at the Shanghai Railway Station, or contact a travel agent.

Dragonair: Suite 2103–4, Shanghai Plaza, 138 Central Huaihai Road; tel: 6375 6000/6375 6375; www.dragonair.com.
Northwest Airlines: Suite 207, East Podium, 1376 Nanjing Road (W); tel: 6279 8100; www.nwa.com.
Qantas: Room 3202, K. Wah Centre, 1010 Central Huaihai Road; tel: 6145 0188; www.qantas.com.au.
Shanghai Airlines: 212 Jiangning Road; tel: 6255 0550; www.shanghai-air.com.
Singapore Airlines: Room 1106, Tower 1, Plaza 66, 1266 Nanjing Road (W); tel: 6288 7999; www.singaporeair.com.
United Airlines: Room 3301, Central Plaza, 381 Central Huaihai Road; tel: 3311 4567; www.ual.com.
Virgin Atlantic: Room 221, 12 Zhongshan No. 1 Road (E) (the Bund); tel: 5353 4600/5353 4605; www.virginatlantic.com.

By Rail

Most trains arrive and depart from the main **Shanghai Railway Station** (Xin Ke Zhan; 100 Molin Road (tel: 6317 9090, 6354 5358/ 3193), but be sure to check, as some trains arrive and depart from the **Shanghai South Train Station** at 289 Laohumin Road (tel: 6404 1317, 6317 9090).

Same-day and next-day train tickets may be purchased at the Shanghai Railway Station. Hotel concierges and travel agencies will also book tickets for you.

Train Classes

"Hard" and "soft" describe the different classes on the trains ("first" and "second" class are politically incorrect terms).

Ying Zuo (Hard Seat) is the classic China train experience, with too many tickets issued for too few spaces (you may end up standing for the duration of the journey), cigarette smoke and a constant din.

Ruan Zuo (Soft Seat) is a less crowded, more comfortable experience. Comfortable soft-seat tourist trains run between Shanghai and the popular tourist destinations nearby – Hangzhou, Suzhou and Nanjing.

Ying Wo (Hard Sleeper) has two narrow three-tier bunks (six beds in total) to a compartment, no doors and no air conditioning or heating. The lowest bunk is the most expensive – which converts into the communal train seat during the day. The top berth is the cheapest.

Ruan Wo (Soft Sleeper) has two bunks (four beds in total) in a closed-door compartment, with air conditioning.

By Bus

High-speed highways linking Shanghai with its neighbours (Suzhou, Hangzhou, Nanjing etc.) make buses an efficient budget option for linking up to nearby as well as long-distance destinations. For general bus inquiries, call: 9621 6800.

By Sea

Luxury cruise liners stop in Shanghai, and there are also luxury ferries to Korea and Japan. There are two piers; ships from Hong Kong, Korea and Japan dock at the **International Passenger Terminal** (Guoji Keyun Matou) at 100 Yangshupu Road, tel: 6595 9259, just north of the Bund area. Domestic ships and ferries dock at the **Wusong Passenger Terminal** (Shanghai Gang Wusong Keyun Zhongxin) at 251 Songbao Road, tel: 5657 5500.

Tickets can be booked by travel agencies as well as directly from the ferry booking offices. General ticket information, tel: 6326 1261.

BELOW: the main hall of the Southern Railway Station.

GETTING AROUND

From Pudong International Airport

Taxis

There is a well-organised taxi line outside the arrival hall (expect a long queue at peak hours, but it moves quickly). At the end of the queue, tell the taxi handler your destination, or, better yet, hand him a piece of paper with your destination written out in Chinese characters (taxi drivers in Shanghai generally don't speak English). Taxis to the city centre in Puxi cost roughly RMB 150–200 (before 11pm; night rates are higher), and will take about an hour, depending on traffic conditions. Trips to downtown Pudong will cost a little less. Make sure the taxi meter is turned on at the start of your journey. Avoid touts who may approach you at the arrival hall – their rates are at least three times higher.

Airport Buses

There are six routes from the airport to different points in the city, and the pick-up point is between Doors 7 and 15 in the arrival hall. Tickets (which range from RMB 15–20) may be purchased at the airport bus ticket counter (tel: 6834 6912) in the arrival hall or on the bus itself. The buses run from 6am until the last flight at night, and take about 75–90 minutes to reach the city centre.

Hotel Shuttles

A private car transfer (expect to pay RMB 500 and above per trip) can be arranged when you book more upscale hotel accommodation. If so, either your name or the name of your hotel will be prominently displayed by someone holding up a signboard. If you haven't arranged for a car transfer, most of the major hotels have counters at the airport that can arrange such transfers.

Maglev Train

The high-speed Maglev (short for magnetic levitation) train runs from the airport to Pudong's Longyang metro (subway) station, a 30km (19-mile) journey that takes only eight minutes to cover, at up to a dizzying 430km (267 miles) an hour. Tickets are priced at RMB 50 for a single trip (RMB 40 if you have a boarding pass to show that you arrived by plane that same day). The trains run from 9am–5pm and tickets are available at the entrance gate. Take it for the novelty factor, as the metro is more convenient.

Metro

Metro Line 2 (located between Terminal 1 and Terminal 2) links Pudong International Airport with the heart of town and the metro network. The same line serves Hongqiao Airport *(see below)* as well, which is around a two-hour journey. Fares start at RMB 3.

Approximate journey time is 20 minutes to downtown Pudong from the airport (current text gives distance from Longyang), 35 minutes to Puxi.

Inter-Airport

The 40km (25-mile) distance between Pudong and Hongqiao airports is one of the longest taxi rides you can take in Shanghai, so take note if you have to make a connection from an international flight to a domestic one (or vice versa). There are regular airport shuttle buses between the two, costing RMB 30, while a taxi (60–90 minutes) will set you back by at least RMB 240. Meanwhile, airport authorities are working on connecting the two airports more efficiently by metro, but nothing has materialised yet.

From Hongqiao Airport

Taxi

The taxi line at Hongqiao Airport is notoriously long, but it moves quickly. Taxis to the city centre in Puxi cost approximately RMB 60 for the 30–45-minute ride. Avoid the taxi touts who hang around the arrival hall and invariably charge much more.

Airport Bus

Hongqiao Airport's shuttle bus runs several routes from the airport to the city. The cost is RMB 5–7 and journey time is about 45 minutes.

Metro

Metro lines 2 and 10 extend to Hongqiao; the station is located near Terminal 2 and the

BELOW: Shanghai's Maglev train is the fastest in the world.

Hongqiao Railway Station. with the heart of town and the metro network. Metro Line 2 also serves Pudong International Airport (see above) as well, which is around a 2-hour journey. Fares start at RMB 3.

Inter-Airport
See Pudong Airport (opposite).

Orientation

The Huangpu River separates Pudong district, literally "east of the Huangpu", from the rest of Shanghai, or Puxi, "west of the Huangpu". The Suzhou Creek divides the thriving mid-section of Puxi (just after the Bund) from its quieter northern suburbs.

There are places to stay and things to do all over the city, but travellers will find the highest concentration of sights, restaurants, entertainment spots and hotels in the Nanjing Road (E) corridor in Puxi, anchored by the Shanghai Centre and continuing east to People's Square, after which it

ABOVE: the metro is a fast and convenient way of getting around.

becomes Nanjing Road (W), just a few blocks away from the Bund. This is where the majority of shopping, museums and attractions lie.

Pudong's Lujiazui area is largely made up of concrete and glass skyscrapers, and has much less soul. This is, after all, a designated economic zone. There are a few places of interest, mainly along or close to the banks of the Huangpu River. Travellers with business in Pudong have a wide range of hotels to choose from.

Overall, the streets in Puxi run north to south and east to west in a grid-like fashion, except for oval-shaped Nanshi and the old racetrack contours that ring People's Square. The major streets run the length of the city and have directional tags: for example, Huaihai Road (W) or West, Central Huaihai Road or Huaihai Road (E) or East (see box below for translations).

The city is bisected from east to west by the Yan'an Road Elevated Highway and from north to south by the Chongqing Road Elevated Highway.

Crossing Huangpu River to Pudong from Puxi can be done via ferry, metro, the Nanpu, Yangpu or Lupu bridges, or several tunnels.

Note: see also Addresses (page 296).

Public Transport

Metro (Subway)

Shanghai's slick metro system (di tie) is an efficient way to get around the city and avoid traffic jams, although the metro during rush hour has human jams of its own. The metro is fairly easy to navigate: entrances are identified by the letter "M", there are metro maps, in English and Chinese, at the stations, and the ticket machines have an English language option. Announcements on the train are made in both English and Chinese.

Single-journey metro tickets

USEFUL STREET TRANSLATIONS

Road signage in Shanghai is generally bilingual, in English first, with the Chinese characters written below. All this is part of Shanghai's efforts to sell itself as an international city. The reality is somewhat different. Few people on the street speak English, and you are better off saying the street name in Chinese when asking for directions. Keep the following basic translations in mind when deciphering road signs:

English	Chinese	English	Chinese
Central	Zhong	Road	Lu
East	Dong	Street	Jie
West	Xi	Avenue	Da Dao/Jie
South	Nan	One	Yi
North	Bei	Two	Er

Here are a few sample translations to give you a better idea.

English	Chinese
Central Huaihai Road	Huaihai Zhong Lu
Nanjing Road (E)	Nanjing Dong Lu
Nanjing Road (W)	Nanjing Xi Lu
Henan Road (S)	Henan Nan Lu
Henan Road (N)	Henan Bei Lu
Zhongshan No. 1 Road (E)	Zhongshan Dong Yi Lu
Ruijin No. 2 Road	Ruijin Er Lu

TRANSPORT

ACCOMMODATION

SHOPPING

ACTIVITIES

A – Z

LANGUAGE

TRANSPORT CARD

If you're taking public transport, it is worth getting the **Shanghai Public Transport Card** (Jiaotong Ka), a stored-value contactless card that can be used for metro, bus and taxi rides. The card itself costs RMB 20 (which is refundable), and any denominations can be added. The card can be purchased at all metro stations and selected convenience stores. When the card is swiped on the sensor located at metro turnstiles or at scanners found in the bus and dashboards of taxis, the correct fee is automatically deducted.

may be purchased at ticket machines or counters at all metro stations. Trains operate daily from 5.30am to 11pm.

Metro Hotline: 6318 9000/ 6437 0000 (no English spoken).

There are **12 lines** currently in operation and there will eventually be 18, including one to Pudong Airport. For a map of the metro system, see page 337 or check: www.travelchinaguide.com/ images/map/shanghai/subway-line.

• **Metro Line 1** runs a north–south path from Gongfu Cun (or Village), via the Shanghai Railway Station, to Xinzhuang in the southern suburbs.

• **Metro Line 2** runs an east–west axis from Zhangjiang (in Pudong) past Longyang (where a transfer can be made to the Maglev), via People's Square (where it intersects with Metro Line 1) to Songhong Road in the west. There are plans to extend Metro Line 2 to Hongqiao Airport in the east and Pudong Airport in the west, but so far no work has started on this.

• **Metro Line 3** is a mostly elevated 36km (22-mile) line that runs from north to south from Jiangwan to Shanghai South Railway Station. The line is not of much use for tourists except for visiting some of the sights in Hongkou (see page 211). The

line also connects with Metro Line 1 at Zhongshan Park.

• **Metro Line 4** forms almost a complete circle around the city. Along the way it intersects with Metro Lines 1 and 2 and 3 at certain points.

• **Metro Line 5** runs from Xinzhuang, the terminal station of Metro Line 1 in the south, to the Minhang Development Zone in the southwest.

• **Metro Line 6** runs north–south between Gangcheng and South Lingyan roads. Also called the Pudong Light Railway, it is located entirely within Pudong district.

• **Metro Line 7** links downtown Shanghai and Pudong with Baoshan district, running from Shanghai University (Baoshan to Meilanhu).

• **Metro Line 8**, the Yangpu Line, runs north–south from Shiguang Road (Yangpu District) to the Aerospace Museum (Minhang); it is one of Shanghai's busiest lines.

• **Metro Line 9** runs east–west from Songjiang New City (Songjiang District) to Yanggao Central Road (Pudong).

• **Metro Line 10's** main line runs from New Jiangwan Town to Longxi Road, with a branch from Longxi Road to Hangzhong Road. An extension to Hongqiao Airport will be completed by the end of 2010, connecting the airport with downtown Shanghai and the Yangpu and Hongkou districts.

• **Metro Line 11** has two lines: A, the main line, and B, the branch line. Line A starts at Jianding North and Line B starts from Anting and connects with the Formula One racetrack, Shanghai International Circuit; the lines have the same route and stations after Jiading New City.

• **Metro Line 13** runs north-south from Madang Road to Shibo Avenue.

Buses

Many of the downtown buses now have announcements and signage in English, but drivers and conductors only speak Chinese. During rush hour, buses can get very crowded, but otherwise are quite a pleasant way to get around – if you are not in a tearing hurry. Most buses run from 6am to midnight, while some special services operate 24 hours. Fares cost from RMB 1–5; tickets can be bought on board or use your stored-value Shanghai Public Transport Card (see box).

Taxis

Taxis are one of Shanghai's great deals – they can be hailed anywhere off the street, cost only RMB 11 at flagfall, and average RMB 15–30 for a journey in central Shanghai. The city's taxi drivers are also generally a reliable and honest lot – to the point of telling you if they don't know your destination. But as incomes rise, more and more people are taking taxis these days, making them scarce during peak times and in bad weather.

Taxi drivers generally speak only Chinese, so it is crucial that you have the name and address of your destination written out in Chinese, and, failing that, the name of the street and the cross-street in Chinese.

Taxis are metered and drivers turn it on as a matter of course. Fares cost RMB 11 for the first 3km (1¾ miles), and RMB 2.10 per additional km after that. Trips after 11pm start at RMB 14 for the first 3km, and revert to RMB 2.10 per additional km after that. Tips are not expected.

BELOW: taxis are plentiful.

TRANSPORT ◆ **273**

TRANSPORT

ACCOMMODATION

SHOPPING

ACTIVITIES

A – Z

LANGUAGE

Payment is either by cash or by the stored-value Shanghai Public Transport Card (see box opposite).

Rear seats rarely have safety belts, or else the belts seem stuck to the seat and are unusable. If this is a problem for you, sit in front. For some reason the back door on the driver's side is always locked, so always board and alight on the other side.

Always ask for a printed receipt (fa piao in Chinese) which records the taxi number and the taxi company's telephone number; this will help in the event you leave something behind in a taxi. With the exception of mobile phones, things are usually returned promptly. For complaints on taxi service, contact tel: 6323 2150.

Taxis can be booked in advance for a surcharge. They can also be hired for the whole day. The following taxi companies operate in Shanghai.
Da Zhong Taxi: tel: 800 6200 1688/6258 1688
Jin Jiang Taxi: tel: 6275 8800
Qiang Sheng Taxi: tel: 6258 0000
Shanghai Taxi: tel: 5481 1630, www.shanghai-taxi.com. This company only accepts pre-bookings.

Private Car Rental

Tourists are no longer expressly prohibited from driving in Shanghai, but neither are they encouraged – car rental agencies generally recommend hiring a car with driver. Expect to pay RMB 600–800 a day. Petrol cost is usually included in the rates.
Shanghai Anji Car Rental (a joint venture with Avis), tel: 6229 1119, www.avischina.com.
Dazhong, tel: 6318 5666.

Trips out of Shanghai

The trips to the places covered in the Western Suburbs (page 237) and Excursions (page 249) chapters can be organised either on your own or with the aid of a good travel agency (see page 294).

The cheap option is to use the special sightseeing buses that depart from several venues around town, but these are mainly used by domestic tourists and don't cater to foreigners (ie people who don't speak Chinese).

Trains are one good option for independent travel to Suzhou and Hangzhou; tickets can be booked through your hotel or directly at the **Shanghai Railway Station** at 100 Molin Road, tel: 6317 9090, 6354 3193.

You could also arrange to hire a private car with a driver. This option would give you the most flexibility. Some travel agencies also have English-speaking guides who will accompany you – this is useful for translation purposes, but be aware that the "guide" may not know much about the destination itself. Places of interest in the Western Suburbs chapter like Jiading District, Songjiang County and Qingpu County are easily covered in a day, depending on how many sights you wish to see. Expect to pay RMB 500 for a half-day car hire with driver and RMB 600 or more for a full-day's hire to these areas.

Some places (like Zhouzhang and Suzhou) are standard day tours offered by travel agents. Some companies also sell a Hangzhou day trip, but this is a bit of a stretch. Ask about 2-day package tours to Hangzhou that include a night's accommodation and sightseeing.

Chongming Island

By Ferry: Take a taxi to Baoyang port in northeastern Shanghai, where you can board the ferry to Nanmen port on Chongming; the boat ride takes 30–40 minutes. At Nanmen, take a taxi to your hotel or final destination.
Baoyang to Nanmen ferries run 13 times a day, with an additional trip at the weekends. Ferries run from 7.10am–5pm daily, tel: 5667 1205.
Nanmen to Baoyang ferries run from 6.30am–4.30pm daily, tel: 6961 2710/2711.
By Car: The Yangzi River Bridge and Tunnel Project connects Chongming Island with Pudong via Changxiang Island (a journey of about 40 minutes).

Suzhou

By Train: Trains run regularly between Shanghai Railway Station and Suzhou Train Station. The journey is under an hour.
By Car: The expressway is the fastest way to travel to Suzhou, getting you there in just over an hour. A one-way car trip with driver will cost about RMB 420. A same-day return trip (with waiting time included) will cost around RMB 900.

Hangzhou

By Train: Trains leave regularly for the Hangzhou Train Station from both the Shanghai Railway Station and the Shanghai South Train station. The trip takes about 2½ hours.
By Car: The drive to Hangzhou via the expressway will take about the same time as the train, depending on road conditions. A one-way car trip with driver will cost about RMB 900.
Note: Suzhou and Hangzhou are connected by overnight passenger boats sailing on the Grand Canal. Tickets (RMB 128–788) can be purchased at hotel tour desks in either Suzhou (tel: 512-6520 5720) or Hangzhou (tel: 571-8515 3185).

Moganshan

By Car: Moganshan is best done as a side trip from Hangzhou. From there, get a hired car or taxi. The ride from Hangzhou to Moganshan takes about an hour.

Tongli and Xitang

By Car: Both these water villages are more easily accessed from Suzhou. Enquire with the hotel desk in Suzhou about car rental cost. If going direct from Shanghai, a rented car with driver will cost about RMB 900 for a day trip to either of the villages. A combined trip to both villages will not cost much more.

A CCOMMODATION

SOME THINGS TO CONSIDER BEFORE YOU BOOK THE ROOM

S hanghai is an expensive place to bed down. Demand for accommodation still outstrips supply, even though there are plenty of options available in all the different price categories – so book early, or risk there being no room at the inn. Rates, and occupancies, peak during the autumn and spring high season, and during major events and conferences.

Choosing a Hotel

Shanghai is mainly dominated by international four- and five-star hotels, but there is, increasingly, much more choice. Chinese hotel brands Hengshan and Jinjiang own and manage several key upmarket properties, and the number of mid-range hotels, particularly the international brands, is growing, although they are often not as centrally located as the five-star ones.

China's first budget motel chains, like Motel 168, have opened throughout the city, but these can be difficult for non-Chinese-speakers to navigate. Boutique hotels are a recent, and welcome, addition to the scene.

Discounts are usually available during the summer (July–Aug) and winter (Dec–Feb) months.

Hotel Areas

Although there are hotels throughout the city, most are concentrated in areas with the highest concentration of tourists and business travellers – like Jingan, Fuxing Park area (the former French Concession), the Bund, Hongqiao and Pudong. All these areas have a mix of both luxury and moderate options.

Jing An is the traditional hotel district; the hotels in this area are mainly international five-stars, targeted at business and high-end leisure travellers. **Fuxing Park** and surroundings have hotels that bear the character of the former French Concession – this is where

you will find the city's historic hotels, some of them located in the mansions of old Shanghai tycoons.

The **Bund**, which until this century had no luxury lodgings except for the Peace Hotel, is now home to several brand-new and upmarket hotels as well as a few moderately priced ones.

Hongqiao, in the suburbs, was the first area in the city to open international hotels; the offerings here include state guesthouses, convention hotels as well as international five-star ones.

Pudong is the site of the some of the snazziest hotels in the city, whose profiles dominate its futuristic skyline.

Prices and Bookings

The following listings – in RMB, as this is how prices will appear on your bill – are organised according to price brackets. The categories are based on one

CHINESE STARS

Luxury hotels in Shanghai usually exceed their Western counterparts in terms of space, comfort and service, but star rankings in China can vary widely. Five-star and the new platinum five-star accreditation is determined by a central body, but below this, local bodies decide on the rankings.

night's accommodation in a double room, not including breakfast. A service charge of 15 percent is usually added on in all the categories except the budget hotels.

Always ask if there are any special offers, packages or discounts available: hotels may not mention these if you don't ask. Reservations are usually best made by e-mail or via telephone; make sure you get a reservation number from the hotel, or a printout of the confirmation.

Serviced Apartments

Short-stay serviced apartments with kitchen facilities, maid services and security are ideal for those who are staying for a month or more. But they are also great for a few nights for families with children or people who just want more elbow room.

Ascott Pudong
浦东雅诗阁酒店公寓
3 Pudong Avenue, Pudong
Tel: 6886 0088; www.the-ascott.com
[p323, E1]

The Shanghai Centre
上海商城
Suite 742, 1376 Nanjing Road (W)
Tel: 6279 8600; www.shanghaicentre.com
[p321, C3]
Somerset Grand Shanghai
上海盛捷高级服务公寓
8 Jinan Road, Luwan District
Tel: 6385 6888; www.the-ascott.com
[p326, B1]
Somerset Xuhui Shanghai
上海徐汇盛捷服务公寓
888 Shanxi Road (S), Xu Hui District
Tel: 6466 0088; www.the-ascott.com
[p325, D3]

A C C O M M O D A T I O N   L I S T I N G S

THE BUND AREA

Luxury

Fairmont Peace Hotel
和平饭店
20 Nanjing Road (E)
Tel: 6321 6888
www.fairmont.com/peacehotel
[p322, C1]
This heritage hotel has been brought into the 21st century with no expense spared. From the opulent lobby to six on-site restaurants and 270 luxury bedrooms and suites bristling with amenities – and many

with stupendous river or city views – this hotel is clearly aiming to impress.
The Peninsula Shanghai
上海半岛酒店
B1-1/F, 32 Zhongshan Road (E) No. 1
Tel: 2327 2888
www.peninsula.com
[p322, C1]
Featuring a stunning decor of Art Deco and chinoiserie, the Peninsula is possibly Shanghai's favourite luxury

hotel. Amazing high-tech rooms feature the finest linens; amazing bathrooms; free VOIP calls; vast plasma televisions, even nail driers are provided. The only drawback? You might never want to leave.
Waldorf Astoria Shanghai on the Bund
上海外滩华尔道夫酒店
88 Central Sichuan Road
Tel: 6322 9988
www.waldorfastoriashanghai.com
[p322, C2]
The Waldorf Astoria is

a sophisticated hotel in two parts; the older – formerly the 1911 landmark Shanghai Club contains elegant suites and a faithful recreation of the famous original Long Bar – is joined to a modern tower where de luxe rooms offer swish bathrooms with in-mirror TVs and a host of amenities that well-heeled globetrotters would expect.

BELOW: a luxury suite at The Peninsula.

PRICE CATEGORIES

Price categories are for a double room without taxes:
Luxury: over RMB 1,500
Moderate: RMB 1,000–1,500
Inexpensive: RMB 500–1,000
Budget: under RMB 500

Inexpensive

Broadway Mansions
上海大厦
20 Suzhou Road (N)
Tel: 6324 6260
www.broadwaymansions.com
[p322, C1]
This 22-storey, four-star hotel dates back to 1934, when it started out as the former site of the Foreign Correspondents' Club. It was fully renovated in 2006, offers comfortable rooms and an ideal location – just across Suzhou Creek from the Bund – for forays to both the Bund and the Jewish quarter. Rates for rooms with views of Suzhou Creek, the Bund and Pudong are a little higher, but are well worth the extra. The rooftop terrace has fabulous views.

Budget

Astor House Hotel
浦江饭店
15 Huangpu Road
Tel: 6324 6388
www.pujianghotel.com
[p323, C1]
Located just a few minutes from the Bund across Suzhou Creek, this 1910 gem was once Shanghai's top hotel, hosting celebrities from Albert Einstein to Charlie Chaplin. The rooms retain their high ceilings and original trim, and most of the old architecture is still intact.

PEOPLE'S SQUARE AREA

Luxury

JW Marriott Hotel
JW万豪酒店
399 Nanjing Road (W)
Tel: 6360 0503
www.marriotthotels.com
[p322, A3]
Marriott's first premium "JW" branded hotel in China is part of the striking Tomorrow Square complex, occupying levels 38 to 60 – the highest floor – of the building. From its tastefully designed rooms to its restaurants, pool and fitness centre, and the Mandara Spa, the JW spells pure luxury and indulgence. The sweeping views of the city from its rooms and public areas are breathtaking, and the hotel occupies prime position near People's Square, with major museums and the Grand Theatre at its doorstep.

Le Royal Meridien
世茂皇家艾美酒店
789 Nanjing Road (E)
Tel: 3318 9999
www.starwood.com
[p322, A2]
The 66-storey hotel has an ultra-modern design that stands out in the skyline and one of the best locations in the city – on the main shopping section of Nanjing Road (E), near People's Square, only a short walk away from the Bund. Rooms are comfy, the bathrooms are spacious and the hotel has an impressive array of in-house restaurants, including the award-winning French eatery Allure.

Moderate

Howard Johnson Plaza
古象大酒店
595 Jiujiang Road
Tel: 3313 4888
www.hojoshanghai.com
[p322, A2]
An 8-minute walk to the Bund and right next to the Nanjing Road shopping section. Don't mistake this for the cookie-cutter Howard Johnson motels found in the US – this is a de luxe property. Excellent facilities and spacious rooms have quickly made it a favourite of business travellers; gourmands rave about its Riviera restaurant.

Park Hotel
国际饭店
170 Nanjing Road (W)
Tel: 6327 5225
www.parkhotel.com.cn
[p322, A2]

Once Shanghai's tallest hotel and the building that inspired a young I.M. Pei to study architecture, renovations in 1999 removed the historic interior in favour of a more contemporary feel. Still, the historic Ladislau Hudec-designed Art Deco exterior remains a Nanjing Road landmark. The rooms are international-standard and comfortable. Located across from People's Square, the hotel is ideally situated for the museums and the Grand Theatre.

Sofitel Hyland Hotel
索菲特海仑酒店
505 Nanjing Road (E)
Tel: 6351 5888
www.accorhotels-asia.com
[p322, B2]
A four-star with an excellent location along the Nanjing Road pedestrian street, close

BELOW: bathroom with a view at JW Marriott.

to both shopping and sightseeing at the Bund. The Sofitel has a very standard-issue feel to it, but the higher floors have excellent views over Nanjing Road and the Huangpu River.

Inexpensive

Pacific Hotel
金门大酒店
108 Nanjing Road (W)
Tel: 6327 6226

[p322, A2]
A three-star historic hotel managed by the local Jinjiang Group, the Pacific is a no-frills hotel located in the historic Union Insurance Building. There is not much in the way of facilities, but its central location across People's Square makes it ideal for visits to the area's major museums and the Shanghai Grand Theatre.

Budget

East Asia Hotel
东亚饭店
680 Nanjing Road (E)
Tel: 6322 3223
[p322, B2]
An excellent location in the heart of everything, on Nanjing Road (E), the two-star East Asia hotel was recently renovated. Not many frills, and little English is spoken by the staff, but they are helpful.

YMCA Hotel
青年会宾馆
123 Xizang Road (S)
Tel: 6326 1040
www.ymcahotel.com
[p322, B3]
Located in the beautiful former Chinese YMCA, built in 1929, it's a little worn, but the rooms are clean, and the location, just a block from People's Square, the museums and the metro station, is hard to beat.

FUXING PARK AREA

Luxury

88 Xintiandi
88新天地会所
380 Huangpi Road (S)
Tel: 5383 8833
www.88xintiandi.com
[p326, A1]
An unbeatable location in Xintiandi, with rooms and suites overlooking the shops and the lake. The contemporary and stylishly furnished rooms are kitted out with all the mod-cons including plasma screen TVs, Internet access, printers/scanners as well as kitchenettes. A café/lounge is on the third floor and guests have access to a fitness centre.

Langham Xintiandi
99 Madang Road, Xintiandi
Tel: 2330 2288
http://xintiandi.langhamhotels.com
Opened in 2010, the ultra-luxury Langham occupies an iconic building directly across the street from Xintiandi and just steps from the shopping on Huaihai Road. 375 rooms and suites, an indulgent spa

ABOVE: opulent Okura Garden Hotel.

and top-notch international and Chinese restaurants.

Mansion Hotel
自席公馆酒店
82 Xinle Road
Tel: 5403 9888
www.chinamansionhotel.com
[p325, D1]
The renovated French Concession villa of a former mob boss, the Mansion is a luxury period jewel. The feel is European, and the rooms have been refurbished to retain a vintage, very luxurious

feel. The rooftop restaurant overlooks the former St Nicholas Russian church.

Okura Garden Hotel
花园饭店
58 Maoming Road (S)
Tel: 6415 1111
www.gardenhotelshanghai.com
[p325, D1]
An opulent five-star managed by Japan's Okura Group, the public areas of the hotel occupy the renovated Cercle Sportif Français (French Club), with many of the historic details and sprawling gardens still intact. Guest rooms, located in the modern hotel tower to the rear, offer modern amenities, including an indoor swimming pool, health club and business centre. Centrally located, just around the corner from the stores on Central Huaihai Road.

Pullman Shanghai Skyway
上海仕维格丽致酒店
15 Dapu Road
Tel: 3318 9988
www.pullmanhotels.com

[p325, E3]
Set in a 52-storey skyscraper, the Pullman Shanghai Skyway offers 645 luxuriously appointed rooms and 78 suites. The hotel opened in 2007 as the Skyway Landis, and features top-notch Chinese, French and international restaurants, plus a well-equipped fitness centre. It's situated close to the metro station, and is convenient for the business and shopping districts.

PRICE CATEGORIES

Price categories are for a double room without taxes:
Luxury: over RMB 1,500
Moderate: RMB 1,000–1,500
Inexpensive: RMB 500–1,000
Budget: under RMB 500

ABOVE: old-world charm at Ruijin Guesthouse.

Moderate

Jinjiang Hotel
锦江饭店
59 Maoming Road (S)
Tel: 6258 2582
http://jj.jinjianghotels.com
[p325, D1]
This pair of five-star hotels, now managed by the local Jinjiang group, was built by old Shanghai tycoon Victor Sassoon as the Cathay Mansions and Grosvenor House. Centrally located off Central Huaihai Road. Renovations have created anonymous standard hotel interiors, although details like fireplaces and some old trimmings remain. More reminiscent of old-world grandeur are the 26 suites, furnished with vintage Shanghai pieces. Health club, with swimming pool, bowling alley and restaurants on site.

Jinjiang Tower
新锦江大酒店
161 Changle Road
Tel: 6415 1188
www.jinjianghotels.com
[p325, E1]
The five-star flagship of the Jinjiang group dominates the neighbourhood with its 43-storey circular hotel tower. Rooms are small but well appointed, and most have great views of the city. Facilities include an outdoor pool, a business centre and shopping arcade. Popular with package tour groups.

Pudi Boutique Hotel Fuxing Park
璞邸精品酒店
99 Yandang Road
Tel: 5158 5888
www.accorhotels-asia.com
[p325, E1]
A lovely 52-room boutique hotel located on the Yandang Road pedestrian street, close to Fuxing Park and the shopping on Central Huaihai Road. Pudi is part of the Accor Group, and the French pedigree shows in the chic, European-style decor and the presence of a cigar bar. There is a fitness centre but no eateries on the premises.

Ruijin Guesthouse
瑞金宾馆
118 Ruijin No. 2 Road
Tel: 6472 5222
www.ruijinhotelsh.com
[p325, E2]
Five renovated historic villas set in the expansive former Morriss Estate, its gardens dotted with fountains and pavilions. Located right in the heart of the French Concession. Face Bar, Hazara Indian restaurant and

La Na Thai restaurant are in Building No. 4 on the grounds, and the shops of Central Huaihai Road are close by.

Taiyuan Villa
太原别墅
160 Taiyuan Road
Tel: 6471 6688
[p325, E2]
One of the loveliest mansions in the French Concession and dating back to the 1920s, Taiyuan Villa has been the home of General George Marshall as well as Mao's wife in the past. Refurbished using 1930s-style Shanghai furniture, the rooms overlook the villa's sprawling lawns.

Budget

Anting Villa Hotel
安亭别墅花园酒店
46 Anting Road
Tel: 6433 1188
[p324, C3]
Occupying an old mansion, this hotel is located on a quiet street, yet within walking distance of many of the major sights in the French Concession.

HENGSHAN ROAD

Moderate

Hengshan Picardie Hotel
衡山宾馆
534 Hengshan Road
Tel: 6437 2929
www.hengshanhotels.com
[p324, B4]
Built in 1936 as the Picardie Apartments, it lost much of its historic charm after a 2002 refurbishment that modernised and updated rooms and added a decidedly gilded touch to public areas. Conveniently located in the diplomatic district on the edge of Xujiahui, and close to the Xujiahui business and shopping districts, and the Hengshan Road bar street.

Regal International East Asia Hotel
富豪环球东亚酒店
516 Hengshan Road
Tel: 6415 5588
www.regal-eastasia.com
[p324, B3/4]
This slick modern five-star is located in the diplomatic district, just outside Xujiahui and a 10-minute drive from Central Huaihai Road. Excellent tennis centre, gym and pool. Hengshan Park and Xujiahui Park are across the street, the Xujiahui shopping and business

district is a 5-minute walk, and the Hengshan Road strip of bars and restaurants is just a block away.

JING AN

Luxury

Four Seasons Shanghai
四季大酒店
500 Weihai Road
Tel: 6256 8888
www.fourseasons.com/shanghai
[p321, D3]
The luxury and service associated with the Four Seasons chain have made this a favourite of businesspeople and wealthy tourists, despite the small rooms, decidedly unglamorous building and slightly out-of-the way location.

Hilton Hotel
希尔顿饭店
250 Huashan Road
Tel: 6248 0000
www.hilton.com
[p324, B1]
A Shanghai institution, the five-star Hilton runs smoothly and periodic refurbishments keep it looking young. Broadband, indoor pool, gym, business centre and swish spa. Centrally located between Central Huaihai Road and Nanjing Road (W), and a 5-minute walk from the Julu Road bar strip.

JC Mandarin
锦沧文华大酒店
1225 Nanjing Road (W)
Tel: 6279 1888
www.jcmandarin.com
[p321, D3]

Well run and a great location – across the street from the Shanghai Centre and right next to the Shanghai Exhibition Centre. The Mandarin Club Executive Floor often wins kudos from business travellers. Facilities include a business centre, indoor pool, squash and tennis courts.

Jia Shanghai
Jia上海
931 Nanjing Road (W)
Tel: 6217 9000
www.jiashanghai.com
[p321, D3]
A 1926 apartment building was gutted to create this 55-room slick, ultra-modern hotel in the heart of Nanjing Road (W). Each room features a kitchenette, and there is an executive floor as well as a pair of penthouse suites. The rooftop terrace serves complimentary breakfast and afternoon tea. Convenient for the Nanjing Road shops and metro station.

Portman Ritz-Carlton
波特曼丽嘉酒店
1376 Nanjing Road (W)
Tel: 6279 8888
www.ritz-carlton.com
[p321, C3]
Anchoring the Shanghai Centre, this hotel is a

favourite of business travellers and state visitors, including recent US presidents. The service is excellent, the dining options are varied, and there is a full complement of facilities including fitness centre, tennis courts, indoor-outdoor pool and the gourmet Italian restaurant Palladio.

Moderate

Hengshan Moller Villa
衡山马勒别墅
30 Shanxi Road (S)
Tel: 6247 8881
www.mollervilla.com
[p321, D4]
A landmark Gothic fantasy dominated by steeples and spires, and built in 1936, refurbished and converted into a charming small hotel in 2002. The historic older building is often booked by government dignitaries and rooms may not be open to the public, but it doesn't hurt to ask.

Inexpensive

Jing An Hotel
静安宾馆
370 Huashan Road
Tel: 6248 1888
[p324, B1]
Right next door to the Hilton, the main building of this locally managed hotel was built in the Spanish style in 1935 (an adjacent, less attractive, annexe was added in 1985). Guestrooms have been renovated, but several of the function rooms retain their vintage glamour. Facilities are

basic, but the sprawling garden compensates.

The Old House Inn
老时光酒店
No. 16, Lane 351,
Huashan Road
Tel: 6249 6118
www.oldhouse.cn
[p324, B/C1]
A charming lane house with original details, romantic four-poster beds and vintage Chinese furnishings. Chic bistro café is on the premises, and it's just steps from the Hilton and within walking distance of the Julu-Fumin bar and restaurant street. Book early.

Budget

Motel 168
莫泰168
678 Anyuan Road
Tel: 6316 8168
www.motel168.com
[p320, A2]
On the border of Jing An and Putuo districts, it's close to Jade Buddha Temple, as well as the lures of Nanjing Road. Clean and well run.

PRICE CATEGORIES

Price categories are for a double room without taxes:
Luxury: over RMB 1,500
Moderate: RMB 1,000–1,500
Inexpensive: RMB 500–1,000
Budget: under RMB 500

BELOW: suite style at Jia Shanghai.

(side tab labels) TRANSPORT · ACCOMMODATION · SHOPPING · ACTIVITIES · A – Z · LANGUAGE

HONGQIAO AND CHANGNING

Luxury

Marriott Hongqiao
万豪虹桥大酒店
2270 Hongqiao Road
Tel: 6237 6000
www.marriott.com
An efficiently run business hotel with a resort-like atmosphere – from the low-rise building to the palms in the lobby and the outdoor pool. The Marriott is 8 minutes from Hongqiao Airport, close to exhibition centres if you're here for business, and right in the heart of expat suburbia.

Sheraton Grand Taipingyang
喜来登豪达太平洋大饭店
5 Zunyi Road (S)
Tel: 6275 8888
www.sheratongrand-shanghai.com
The former Westin Taipingyang has been re-branded as the more luxurious Sheraton Grand, but the European-style flair and service remain. A business traveller's favourite, the Sheraton has a great location for work – next to the INTEX Convention Centre and close to the Shanghai Everbright Convention and Exhibition Centre. The hotel has one of the city's best Italian restaurants, Giovanni's.

Xijiao State Guesthouse
西郊宾馆
1921 Hongqiao Road
Tel: 6219 8800
www.hotelxijiao.com
Queen Elizabeth II once stayed here – in the Presidential Suite in Building No. 7 – but what really sets this place apart is its

ABOVE: Holiday Inn Vista Shanghai.

picturesque setting in an 80-hectare (200-acre) woodland park. Extensively refurbished in 2005, there are stylishly appointed rooms as well as villas. The latter are for long-term guests and are scattered throughout the beautiful grounds among flowers and trees, with walkways by the river. Convenient for business in the Hongqiao area, but it's a good 20-minute drive from the city centre.

Moderate

Cypress Hotel
龙柏饭店
2419 Hongqiao Road
Tel: 6268 8868
www.jinjianghotels.com
The hotel block itself is modern but it is set in a historic location – in the rambling grounds of Old Shanghai Jewish tycoon Victor Sassoon's former estate (his villa itself is not open to guests), allowing for strolls through rambling woods. Facilities are adequate at best and service is a bit patchy. Shanghai Zoo is a 5-minute walk away.

Hongqiao State Guesthouse
虹桥迎宾馆
1591 Hongqiao Road
Tel: 6219 8855
www.hqstateguesthotel.com
The renovated rooms rooms in the main building are small but comfortably appointed. More interesting are the vintage villas in a range of Western architectural styles and set in land-scaped rolling grounds. These are only open for long-term rentals, however, and for use by state visitors. Facilities include a café and several restaurants, Clark Hatch fitness centre and an outdoor pool.

Radisson Plaza Xingguo Hotel
兴国宾馆
78 Xingguo Road
Tel: 6212 9998
www.radisson.com
[p324, A2/3]
This contemporary high-rise sits at the edge of the former Butterfield & Swire compound and is closer to the French Concession area than it is to Changning. The hotel is just minutes from Central Huaihai Road by taxi. On its vast lawns are several old villas (only open to state visitors and long-term guests), including the historic Building Number One, where Mao Zedong stayed whenever he was in town. Excellent facilities with tastefully furnished and generous-sized rooms.

Renaissance Yangtze
扬子江万丽大酒店
2099 Yan'an Road (W)
Tel: 6275 0000
www.marriott.com

This hotel's great asset (if you are in Shanghai for business) is its location in the midst of all the convention centres – SITC, INTEX and Shanghai Mart. Facilities include an indoor pool, health club and spa.

Inexpensive

Holiday Inn Vista Shanghai
上海古井假日酒店
700 Chang Shou Road
Tel: 6276 8888
www.shanghai-vista.holiday-inn.com
[p320, A2]
Some 20 minutes from Hongqiao Airport and close to Hongqiao's convention centres, the Holiday Inn is designed for business travellers. Contemporary and comfortable, the hotel offers dining, a fitness centre, and Internet access on the executive floor and in public areas.

Budget

Jinjiang Inn
锦江之星
No. 5, Lane 1600,
Changning Road
Tel: 5373 1568
www.jj-inn.com
Close to Zhongshan Park and the metro station, this hotel is good for those who plan to spend time in Shanghai's western neighbourhoods.

HONGKOU

The hotels closest to the Bund area (near Suzhou Creek) have already been covered on pages 275–6. The hotels listed here are located further northwest of town.

Moderate

Crowne Plaza Fudan
复旦皇冠假日酒店
199 Handan Road
Tel: 5552 9999
www.ichotelsgroup.com
A little out of the way for the average visitor, but for those who need to be close to the area's universities, it offers one of the few hotel options in the neighbourhood. Located opposite Fudan University and close to the Wanda commercial centre and shopping mall.

Inexpensive

Four Points by Sheraton Shanghai, Daning
上海福朋喜来登大酒店
1928 Gonghe Xin Road
Tel: 2602 2222
www.starwoodhotels.com
Convenient for the university district and close to the Shanghai Railway Station but far from Shanghai's major tourist attractions and most businesses. The hotel has all the amenities you'd expect from this second-tier brand of the Sheraton – indoor pool, spa, restaurants – and is located within the Life Hub @ Daning, which is filled with numerous shops and restaurants.

Budget

Motel 168
莫泰168
300 Huoshan Road
Tel: 6585 0888

www.motel168.com
Very convenient for touring the old Jewish neighbourhoods, Motel 168 is part of a chain of clean, comfortable and well-run budget hotels. The Huoshan Road branch in particular offers good value for money.

PUDONG

Luxury

Park Hyatt Shanghai
金茂凯悦大酒店
88 Century Avenue
Pudong New Area
Tel: 6888 1234
www.shanghai.park.hyatt.com
[p323, E2]
The highest hotel in the world is a high-design beauty located between the 54th and 88th floors of China's second-tallest building, the Jin Mao Tower. Situated in the heart of Pudong's Lujiazui financial district, this is where high-tech meets Shanghai style, with plenty of "world's highest" experiences, from bars to bubble baths and swimming pools. Rooms are spacious, and those that face the Huangpu River command premium rates. Good range of bars and restaurants, plus PU-J's nightclub in the basement.

Pudong Shangri-La
浦东香格里拉大酒店
33 Fucheng Road
Tel: 6882 6888
www.shangri-la.com
[p323, D2]
An extensive refurbishment and the addition of a second, 36-storey tower has moved this elegant riverside hotel into the ultra-luxury category. A business travellers' favourite, expect spacious, luxury accommodation, first-class service, stunning views, and some of the best dining in the city, with Yi Café and the avant-garde French fusion restaurant called Jade on 36.

Ritz-Carlton Pudong
瑞吉红塔大酒店
8 Century Avenue, Lujiazui
Tel: 2020 1888
www.ritz-carlton.com

BELOW: classical chic at Park Hyatt Shanghai.

PRICE CATEGORIES

Price categories are for a double room without taxes:
Luxury: over RMB 1,500
Moderate: RMB 1,000–1,500
Inexpensive: RMB 500–1,000
Budget: under RMB 500

[p323, D2]
Reaching for the sky, this hotel occupies the top 18 floors of the Shanghai IFC Building. Rooms are spacious, beautifully designed and feature curved, floor-to-ceiling windows that offer some of the city's best views. Service is friendly and attentive and the rooftop bar is not to be missed.

Moderate

Oriental Riverside Hotel Shanghai
上海东方滨江大酒店
2727 Riverside Avenue
Tel: 5037 0000
www.shicc.net
[p323, D1]
Pudong's only "five-star convention hotel" lacks the gloss of its brand-name five-star competitors, but makes up for it

with an unbeatable location for conference goers: directly next to the International Conference Centre in the heart of the Lujiazui financial district. Pay a little extra and ask for a room with a river view.

Inexpensive

Courtyard by Marriott
齐鲁万怡大酒店
838 Dongfang Road
Tel: 6886 7886
www.marriott.com
[p323, E2, off map]
Comfortable hotel geared for the business traveller with an eye on the balance sheet. Rooms have generously sized work desks, two phones with dataports and the full range of business amenities, including meeting facili-

ties. Located close to Lujiazui, across the street from the St Regis.

Holiday Inn Shanghai Pudong
上海浦东假日酒店
899 Dongfang Road
Tel: 5830 6666
www.ichotelsgroup.com
[p323, E2, off map]
Close to the financial institutions and department stores of Pudong, the Holiday Inn is a comfortable, but not fancy, hotel. It offers amenities like a business centre, pool and gym plus a Mediterranean and a Cantonese/Shanghainese restaurant.

Novotel Atlantis Shanghai
海神诺富特大酒店
728 Pudong Avenue
Tel: 5036 6666
www.accorhotels-asia.com

[p323, E2, off map]
The city's most elegant four-star hotel is good value for money. The rooms are smallish, but the hotel has a European sense of style. Restaurants include the revolving ART50 restaurant with interesting art exhibits, a cigar bar and pub.

Ramada Pudong Airport
浦东机场华美达大酒店
1100 Qi Hang Road
Tel: 3849 4949
www.ramadainternational
[p323, E2, off map]
Located close to Pudong Airport, this hotel is a boon for travellers with tight flight connections. Rooms include high-speed Internet access. There is a full range of restaurants and a health club.

OUTSIDE SHANGHAI

CHONGMING ISLAND

Inexpensive

Bao Dao Resort
宝岛度假村
Chongming Island
Tel: 521 5933 9479
www.bao-dao.com
Startlingly modern hotel located on the edge of Dongping National Forest Park. The architecture doesn't really complement the lush green surroundings, but that doesn't seem to faze the mainly Chinese guests. Facilities include bowling alley, gym, tennis courts and a swimming pool.

SUZHOU

Expensive

Gloria Plaza Hotel Suzhou
苏州凯莱大酒店
535 Gan Jiang East Road
Tel: 512 6521 8855
www.gloriahotels.com
Extensively refurbished in 2007, this well-appointed business-class hotel is located close to the Singapore Industrial Park but is equally convenient for visits to Suzhou's many gardens. Facilities include a café, seafood restaurant, bar, business centre and fitness club.

Shangri-La Hotel Suzhou
苏州香格里拉
168 Ta Yuan Road
Suzhou National New and Hi Tech Development Zone
Tel: 512 6808 0168
www.shangri-la.com
The Shangri-La's location in the heart of Suzhou's business zone makes this a natural choice for business travellers. Suzhou's gardens are a 20-minute drive away. Located on the 28th to the 51st floors in one of Suzhou's tallest buildings, this luxury five-star offers beautiful views over the city. Spacious, tastefully appointed rooms feature the latest technology. Facilities include restaurants, indoor pool, gym and a putting green.

Sheraton Suzhou Hotel and Towers
吴宫喜来登大酒店
388 Xin Shi Road
Tel: 512 6510 3388
www.starwoodhotels.com
This low-rise resort hotel is designed in traditional Chinese style around a beautifully laid-out classical garden. The stunning design, spacious rooms and excellent service compensate for its

location, which is not especially near any of the major gardens. Facilities include restaurants, an indoor pool, gym, business centre.

Inexpensive

Nanlin Hotel
南林饭店
20 Gun Xiu Fang Road, Shi Quan Jie
Tel: 512 6801 7888
Popular with tour groups and renovated in 2005, the Nanlin is laid out over 3.5 hectares (8½ acres) of expansive gardens in southeast Suzhou. Rooms have Chinese-style decor and amenities include a swimming pool, fitness centre, business centre and shopping arcade.

Budget

Scholar's Inn
书香门第商务酒店
277 Jingde Road
Tel: 512 6521 7388
A charming budget hotel with decor, albeit simple, that is a nod to its Chinese heritage. Good value for money.

BELOW: Sheraton Suzhou Hotel.

HANGZHOU

Luxury

Hyatt Regency Hangzhou
杭州凯悦酒店
28 Hubin Road
Tel: 571 8779 1234
www.hangzhou.regency.hyatt.com
The Hyatt is part of a lakefront development that includes residential apartments and a department store. This luxury hotel caters to business guests as well as holidaymakers, with Internet access in the rooms, spa and fitness centre, and Camp Hyatt for children under 12. The chic Hubin 28 restaurant serves excellent Chinese food.

Shangri-La Hangzhou
杭州香格里拉饭店
78 Beishan Road
Tel: 571 8797 7951
www.shangri-la.com
Ideally situated overlooking West Lake, the Shangri-La has two wings. Most of the standard rooms are in the east wing, while the

west-wing rooms are larger and have nicer views of West Lake. Both wings are set among sprawling wooded grounds intersected by tree-lined pathways. Good restaurants, health club and indoor swimming pool on site.

Moderate

Ramada Hangzhou Haihua
华美达广场杭州海华大酒店
298 Qingchun Road
Tel: 571 8721 5888
www.ramadahangzhou.com
A stylish four-star modern high-rise on the northeastern shore of West Lake in the heart of the business district. Business centre, indoor pool, and 10 minutes from the train station.

Sofitel Westlake Hangzhou
杭州索菲特西湖大酒店
333 West Lake Avenue
Tel: 571 8707 5858
www.sofitel.com
This French-managed hotel has an excellent location on the eastern banks of West Lake and close to the attractions of Hubin Road. Rooms are contemporary in style and spacious, most with views of the lake area. Facilities include an indoor swimming pool, two restaurants, bar and fitness centre. Note: don't confuse this with the nearby **Sofitel Xanadu Resort**, located about 15km (9 miles) from central Hangzhou.

Budget

Jiexin Century Hotel
杰欣世纪酒店
220 Nanshan Road
Tel: 571 8707 0100

An excellent location for its price, on the eastern fringes of West Lake. The hotel was recently renovated.

MOGANSHAN

Moderate

Du Yuesheng Villa
杜月笙别墅
547 Moganshan Mountain
Tel: 572 803 3601 ext 801
The mountain villa of Shanghai gangster Du Yuesheng has been modernised to international standards, and is managed by the Radisson hotel group.

Naked Retreats
Shanghai Office: 1st Floor, No. 62 Gao An Road, Xuhui
Tel: 6431 8901
www.nakedretreats.cn
Get back to nature in this peaceful complex of converted old village houses. Bring your own food or enjoy the rustic cooking offered; walk in the bamboo forest; go fishing or just curl up with a book or in front of one of their complimentary DVDs.

Priest Villa
牧师别墅
329 Moganshan Mountain
Tel: 572 803 3601 ext 801
The former home of a Moganshan missionary, Priest Villa (managed by the Radisson hotel group) has been refurbished to international standards.

PRICE CATEGORIES

Price categories are for a double room without taxes:
Luxury: over RMB 1,500
Moderate: RMB 1,000–1,500
Inexpensive: RMB 500–1,000
Budget: under RMB 500

TRANSPORT

ACCOMMODATION

SHOPPING

ACTIVITIES

A – Z

LANGUAGE

SHOPPING

BEST BUYS

Shanghai's shopping runs the gamut from brand-name designers on the Bund to streetside tailors and sprawling markets where virtually everything imaginable is on sale. Some of Shanghai's best buys are unique to the city: boutiques selling contemporary products that feature local design; antiques from the Concession era; propaganda posters from the 1960s; and custom-designed clothes, jewellery and furniture. The Shanghainese love to shop, so you'll have plenty of company, especially at weekends and during the run-up to Chinese New Year.

WHERE TO BUY

Nanjing Road (W), Central Huaihai Road and Xujiahui are the city's major shopping areas, filled with large shopping centres, department stores and brand-name designer shops. One-of-a-kind-boutiques are mainly found along Maoming Road, Taikang Road and in Xintiandi. See also the **Shopping** feature on page 74 of this guide.

Most large malls and department stores are generally open daily from 9–10am to 9–10pm. Smaller shops may operate shorter hours, so call first.

Shopping Malls

Malls are a relatively new concept in China – most have been built from the late 1990s onwards. In the Nanjing Road (W) area, they tend to be lavish affairs, filled with designer brands and imports, along with high-end food outlets.

Some of the malls are a little less lavish on Central Huaihai Road (but they are much more crowded), while Xujiahui and Pudong's offerings are targeted at everyman.

Nanjing Road (W) Area

CITIC Square
中信广场
1168 Nanjing Road (W)
Home to Asia's largest Montblanc store, and other trendy boutiques.

D-Mall/Hong Kong Shopping Centre
迪美香港购物中心
221 People's Avenue (at Nanjing Road, under People's Square)
Funky streetwear in the old bomb shelter underneath People's Square. Popular with teens.

Jiu Gang City Plaza
久光城市广场
1618 Nanjing Road (W)
Located above Jing An metro, this mall has a supermarket and a food court in the basement, plus a department store and upscale shops like Tiffany's and Burberry.

Plaza 66
恒隆广场

1266 Nanjing Road (W)
Marbled and glass mall, very chic and stocked with all the major designer brands. Wide range of restaurants and cafés.

Raffles City
莱福士广场
268 Central Xizang Road
Hugely popular mall (just across People's Square) with young, trendy labels such as Levi's and Nike, a cineplex, eateries and a large food court called Megabite.

Westgate Mall
梅陇镇广场
1038 Nanjing Road (W)
Anchored by Isetan department store, Westgate offers a plethora of shops, eateries and a cineplex.

Central Huaihai Road

Isetan
伊势丹
523 Central Huaihai Road
Popular Japanese department store, with a good selection of household items.

Parksons
百盛
918 Central Huaihai Road
Parksons department store
anchors this mall, which also has
a supermarket and restaurants.

Times Square
时代广场
99 Central Huaihai Road
Slick and stylish mall, with brand-
name boutiques as well as
restaurants and a bookstore
(Charterhouse Book Traders).

Xujiahui

Grand Gateway
港汇广场
1 Hongqiao Road
The city's biggest mall, with
crowds to match. A good range of
both mid-range and high-end
shops, restaurants and cafés,
plus a cineplex on the 5th floor.

Oriental Shopping Centre
东方商厦
8 Caoxi Road (N)
Recently refurbished to compete
with Grand Gateway, this has
a good department store in
addition to the usual retail mix.

Taipingyang
太平洋
932 Hengshan Road
An excellent selection of clothing,
cosmetics, shoes and housewares, all affordably priced.

Pudong

Next Age Department Store
第一八佰伴
501 Zhangyang Road
Asia's largest department store
has an immense array of off-the-
rack clothing, as well as toys,
shoes, houseware and more.

Super Brand Mall
正大广场
168 Lujiazui Road
Gigantic 10-storey mall known for
its mega supermarket and cafés
and restaurants, in addition to
the usual apparel boutiques.

Markets and Bazaars

Dongtai Road Antiques Market
东台路古玩市场
Dongtai Road (at Liuhekou Road)
This is Shanghai's largest

antiques market. Its stalls and
shops carry an array of antiques –
some fake, some real – from the
Qing dynasty to the Cultural Revolution, with plenty of treasures
from the Concession era too.

**Longhua Fashion and
Gifts Market**
龙华服饰礼品市场
2465 Longhua Road
Many of the vendors from
Shanghai's famous fake goods
market, Xiangyang, relocated
here in 2006. You'll find the
same selection of counterfeit
goods – clothing, shoes, decor,
toys, electronic games – in over
600 stalls on three floors.

**Shanghai South Bund
Fabric Market**
面料市场
399 Lujiabang Road
All types of fabric, including traditional Chinese silk, Thai silk, cotton, linen etc. Bargaining hard is
de rigueur. Most stalls have tailors
who offer their services at reasonable prices. Make sure there is
time for fittings (a second one may
be necessary). Good idea to bring
along a piece of clothing you wish
to be copied or a page ripped out
of a fashion magazine.

**Yatai Xinyang Fashion and
Gift Market**
亚太盛汇广场
Shanghai Science and Technology Museum metro station
An underground warren of counterfeit clothes, bags, shoes, soft-
ware, toys and more. Shop here if
your conscience doesn't prick you.

Yu Garden Bazaar
豫园商城
(bordered by Anren Street,
Fuyou Road, Jiujiaotang Road
and Fangbang Road)
A must-visit, for its shops
specialising in chopsticks,
walking sticks, all manner of
Chinese souvenirs and jewellery.
Check out also the **Fumin Street
Smallware Market** and **Fuyou
Road Merchandise Mart** in the
vicinity (see page 142).

Antiques

Honest antiques dealers in
Shanghai will tell you that genuine
Chinese antiques are dwindling
rapidly. There are still late Qing-
era pieces to be found, but there
are far more copies masquerad-
ing as the real thing. Shanghai Art
Deco pieces are more plentiful at
the time of writing, but even
copies of these are being found.

Art Deco in Shanghai
上海装饰艺术
Building 7, 50 Moganshan Road
Tel: 6277 8927
Artist Ding Yi's Art Deco furniture
shop has a collection of some of
the finest original pieces you'll
see anywhere in Shanghai, with
equally high prices to match.

Cang Bao Building
藏宝楼
459 Fangbang Road
This replica Ming-era building in
Nanshi houses mostly junk and
souvenir stalls, but if you dig deep
enough there is some original Art

BELOW: Dongtai Road Antiques Market.

Deco furniture, late Qing-era items and Tibetan artefacts.

Chine Antiques
艺林
Dongtai Road Antiques market, near Liuhekou Road
Tel: 6387 4100
This reputable shop stocks some late Qing pieces and fine reproduction pieces (especially furniture).

Hu and Hu Antiques
胡胡
No. 8, Lane 35, 1885 Caobao Road
Tel: 3431 1212
www.hu-hu.com
Late Qing-era pieces, old-style countryside furniture and custom-made pieces. Marybelle Hu, the proprietor, is probably Shanghai's most honest dealer: she will tell you straight off if a piece is a copy.

Shanxi Antique Furniture
山西古董家具
731 Hongxu Road
Tel: 6401 0056
Well-respected shop with a good selection of antique furniture.

Books

Bookazine Shanghai
中图书店
Citic Square, Unit 522, 1168 Nanjing Road (W)
Tel: 5292 5214, and
C4, Green Sports & Leisure Center, No.600, Lan Tian Road
Tel: 5030 6879
www.cnpiecsb.com
Part of a reputable chain of bookshops owned by China National

BELOW: Asian Era ceramics.

Publications Import and Export Corp. Stocks newspapers, magazines as well as foreign books.

Chaterhouse Book Traders
Shop B-1E, Times Square, 93 Central Huaihai Road
Tel: 6391 8237, and
Shop 68, 6F SuperBrand Mall, 168 West Lujiazui Road
Tel: 5049 0668
www.chaterhouse.com.cn
Stocks the city's best and most current selection of English-language books.

Foreign Languages Bookstore
外文书店
390 Fuzhou Road
Tel: 6322 3200
Good collection of English books, including classics and bestsellers.

Garden Books
花园书店
325 Changle Road
Tel: 5404 8729
www.gardenbooks.cn
A good selection of English language books, and a café.

Shanghai Book City
上海书城
465 Fuzhou Road
Tel: 6352 2222/6391 4848
Its small English-language section, focusing mainly on design books, is on the 6th floor.

Home Accessories

Angel & Tony's Antique Shop
劢发家具
398 Jianguo Road (W), Puxi
Tel: 6433 0050
A good selection of antiques, restored and unrestored, as well as home and garden decor, in two locations: Puxi and Pudong – the factory is in the Pudong location.

Annabel Lee
安梨家居
No. 1, Lane 8, Zhongzhan No. 1 Road (E), The Bund
Tel: 6445 8218
www.annabel-lee.com
Its stylish Bund store sells a lovely range of silk home items like placemats, cushion covers and table runners, as well as women's accessories like hand-bags, shawls and slippers.

Kava Kava
吉木坊
167 Anfu Road
Tel: 5404 3873
www.kavakavahome.com
Kava Kava specialises in traditional Chinese-style furniture for modern homes – turning wooden Ming-style chests into television cabinets and finding contemporary uses for altar tables. Most pieces are new.

Little Dragon
龙子
No. 15, 339 Changle Road
Tel: 5403 9867
www.hu-husofa.com
Custom-made and ready-made sofas, chairs and soft furnishings in the best range of furniture styles and upholstery fabric available in Shanghai.

Le Platane
梧桐
127 Yongfu Road
Tel: 6433 6387
Owned by a French lawyer and a former *Vogue* editor, it offers an eclectic collection of beautiful things for the home and self.

Lehman & Qian
雷门九歌
119 Madang Road, Xintiandi
Tel: 6385 1805
www.lehmanqian.com
Best known for its hand-painted silk wallpaper with classical chinoiserie designs, this shop also carries lamps, screens and furniture that fuse Chinese and 18th-century Western design.

Madame Mao's Dowry
毛太设计
207 Fumin Road
Tel: 5403 3551
Collection of rare original Cultural Revolution artefacts – posters, statues, records – as well as furniture, paintings, books and more.

Simply Life
逸居生活
1–2 & 5 Xintiandi, 123 Xingye Road
Tel: 6387 5100, and
9 Dongping Road
Tel: 3406 0509
www.simplylife-sh.com
High-end home accessories that reflect both a Chinese and South-

ABOVE: Shanghai Tang boutique.

east Asian aesthetic. The range includes tableware, ceramics, linen and glassware.

Spin Ceramics
Building 3, 758 Julu Road
Mobile tel: 139 1631 4424
This showroom features a collection of glazed pale green, China blue and underglazed porcelain, made according to the traditional techniques used at the imperial porcelain factory at Jingdezhen.

Shanghai Trio
上海组合
181 Taicang Road
Tel: 6466 6884
www.shanghaitrio.com.cn
Innovative Chinese-inspired designs for linens, shawls, trendy gifts and souvenirs.

Torana Carpets
图兰纳家苑
164 Anfu Road
Tel: 5404 4886
www.toranahouse.com
Tibetan rugs are the core offering at Torana, but the small, well-stocked store also has a good supply of Chinese, Persian, Xinjiang and antique rugs.

Fabrics

Chinese Printed Blue Nankeen Exhibition Hall
中国蓝印花布馆
No. 24, Lane 637, Changle Road
Te: 5403 7947
Chinese blue *nankeen* fabric with intricate patterns can either be purchased by the metre, or in the form of ready-made clothing, slippers and accessories.

Fabric Depot
剪刀石头布
1269 Wuzhong Road
Tel: 6405 6890
Four floors of top-of-the-line upholstery and curtain fabric at wholesale prices. On-site tailors can make up curtains, cushion covers, sofa covers, etc.

Silk King
真丝商厦
139 Tianping Road, tel: 6282 1533; 66 Nanjing Road (E), tel: 6321 2193; 819 Nanjing Road (W), tel: 6215 3114; 550 Central Huaihai Road, tel: 6327 5566; and 1371 Sichuan Road (N), tel: 6324 0790; www.silkking.com.cn
This state-owned chain of silk stores has a wide selection of silk fabrics and provides on-site tailoring services as well.

Pearl Jewellery

Pearl farms dot Shanghai's suburbs, and supply high-end stores like Tiffany's and Neiman Marcus. Quality varies enormously, as do designs, but prices are still considerably lower than you would pay elsewhere.

Amylin's Pearls
艾敏林氏
www.amy-pearl.com
1445 Gubei Road
Tel: 6275 3954, and
No. 30, 3rd floor, FenShine

UNIQUELY SHANGHAI

Suzhou Cobbler
苏州绣鞋
17 Fuzhou Road, Room 101
Mobile tel: 139 1818 7760
www.suzhou-cobblers.com
Hand-embroidered silk Chinese slippers, with traditional as well as whimsical motifs.

Blue Shanghai White
海上青花
No. 17-103 Fuzhou Road
Tel: 6323 0853
www.blueshanghaiwhite.com
Unique ceramics inspired by Shanghai blue and white porcelain – all handcrafted by owner and ceramics artist Haichen.

Fashion & Accessories Plaza, 580 Nanjing Road (W)
Tel: 5228 2372
Beautifully designed pearl jewellery – Amy's is a favourite of celebrities visiting Shanghai. The helpful staff speak English.

China Pearl City
上海珍珠城
2nd and 3rd Floors, 558 Nanjing Road (E)
A vast pearl market with wholesale pearls; some ready-made items on sale, or you can create your own designs.

Hong Qiao New World Pearl Market
虹桥国际珍珠城
Hong Mei Road, on the corner of Hong Qiao Road
Hundreds of stalls selling pearl jewellery as well as loose pearls.

Fashion

inSH
200 Taikang Road
Tel: 6466 5249
www.insh.com.cn
Owned by a young Shanghainese fashion designer, inSH – the name stands for "in Shanghai" – features slinky dresses, T-shirts, *qipaos* and children's clothing.

Shanghai Tang
上海滩
59 Maoming Road (S), Shop E, Jinjiang Hotel Promenade
Tel: 5466 3006, and
181 Taicang Road, 15 North Block, Xintiandi
Tel: 6384 1601
www.shanghaitang.com
Traditional Chinese fashion with a contemporary flavour: Neonbright, beautifully cut *qipaos*, Mao jackets for men, children's clothes, and tableware too.

Younik
2/F, Bund 18,
No. 1 Zhongshan Road (E)
Tel: 6323 8688
This boutique, in the stylish Bund 18 building, carries clothes by some of Shanghai's hottest young designers. Rising designers Lu Kun and Jenny Ji's latest collections are featured here, as is jewellery by designer Jiang Qiong Er.

ACTIVITIES

THE ARTS, NIGHTLIFE, EVENTS & FESTIVALS, SIGHT-SEEING, SPORTS, SPAS AND CHILDREN'S ACTIVITIES

An old Shanghai song calls it "new paradise… the city that never sleeps", and true to its reputation, Shanghai has plenty going on at all hours of the day – as well as night. Cultural events and festivals are mainly concentrated during the peak spring and autumn seasons (so time your visit to coincide with these if you wish), but the museums, galleries and nightlife spots thrive all year round. Plus there are spas, golfing and plenty to do for children, as well.

THE ARTS

For a more complete coverage on Shanghai's arts scene, read the chapters on **Performing Arts** *(page 51)* and **Visual Arts** *(page 59).*

Museums

Part of Shanghai's drive to become a world-class city has been to establish world-class museums. For the most part, it has succeeded, with the Shanghai Museum easily the best, not just in Shanghai but in China. All the museums charge an entrance fee, but most offer discounts to children, students and senior citizens. All the major arts-related museums have been covered in the Places section. Check the index for the specific names.

Art Galleries

The largest concentration of art galleries is at **M50** (a snazzy name for No. 50 Moganshan Road). Clustered here in old warehouses by Suzhou Creek are some of the city's most interesting galleries *(see photo feature on pages 222–3 and box opposite).*

The city's big artfest, the **Shanghai Biennale**, takes place in even-numbered years. This is when some of the biggest names in the international and domestic contemporary art worlds exhibit their works in Shanghai. In between, a number of art fairs are organised, some government-sponsored (such as the Shanghai Art Fair) and some privately run (like ShContemporary).

Only a few of the better-known art galleries are listed here. Entrance to galleries is usually free, and most are closed on Sundays (it's best to call ahead to confirm).

DDM warehouse
东大名创库
3/F, 713 Dong Da Ming Road
Tel: 3501 3212
www.ddmwarehouse.org
All types of contemporary art –

paintings, photography, video, sculpture, even performance art – are exhibited in this shabby-chic warehouse space.

Elisabeth de Brabant Chinese Contemporary Art
博雅珊艺术中心
299 Fuxing Road (W)
Tel: 6466 7428
www.elisabethdebrabant.com
A small, well-curated gallery in an atmospheric French Concession lane house, Elisabeth de Brabant focuses on Chinese contemporary artists, including well-known names such as Xiao Hui Wang and Shan Sa. The gallery also represents a small collection of international names.

James Cohan Gallery
科恩画廊
1/F, Building 1, No.1 Lane
Tel: 5466 0825
www.jamescohan.com/gallery
A branch of the New York gallery of the same name, James Cohan's Shanghai branch fea-

THE BEST M50 GALLERIES

The clutch of cutting-edge art galleries at 50 Moganshan Road, collectively known as **M50** *(see also pages 219 and 222–3)*, should not be missed if you're a serious art aficionado. Choice art galleries at M50 include:

Art Scene Warehouse
艺术景仓库
2/F, Bldg 4
Tel: 6277 4940
www.artscenechina.com
Together with its second location in Fuxing Road, this gallery hosts regular exhibitions by the 25 or so big-name Chinese contemporary artists it represents.

Eastlink
东廊艺术
5/F, Bldg 6
Tel: 6276 9932
www.eastlinkgallery.cn
Founded by Shanghai art pio-

neer Li Liang, the gallery holds its own avant-garde version of the "Shanghai Biennale" as well as regular exhibitions.

ShanghART Gallery and **H-Space**
香格纳画廊
Bldg 16 and 18
Tel: 6359 3923
www.shangartgallery.com
Opened in 1995, the sprawling warehouse gallery features paintings, sculpture and installations by some of China's leading contemporary artists.

Studio Rouge
红寨当代艺术画廊
Bldg 7
Tel: 5252 7856
www.studiorouge.cn
Regular exhibitions by good but not yet famous contemporary Chinese artists. Second location at 17 Fuzhou Road, near the Bund.

Theatre, Opera & Concerts

Shanghai's stylish new theatres (and a few charming old ones) regularly stage musicals, concerts, dance performances, Chinese opera, drama and even rock concerts throughout the year. There is plenty of foreign star-power on offer, from Yo-Yo Ma to Beyoncé and *Les Misérables*, but there are also plenty of high-quality local troupes who perform in Chinese.

Local talent includes three orchestras, the **Shanghai Symphony Orchestra**, the **Shanghai Philharmonic Orchestra** and the **Shanghai Broadcast Symphony Orchestra**. There is also the excellent **Shanghai Ballet**, and for contemporary dance fans, the **Jin Xing Modern Dance Company**.

The Shanghai Grand Theatre hosts both Western and Chinese opera but the centre for **Beijing Opera** is Yifu Theatre. Occasionally, the Shanghainese form of Chinese opera (called Kunju) is performed here too.

Another must-see is the **Shanghai Acrobatic Troupe**, justly renowned for their breathtaking contortions, who perform at Circus World and the Shanghai Centre Theatre.

OV Gallery
OV画廊
19 Shaoxing Road
Tel: 5465 7768
www.oriental-vista.com
The gallery represents about 15 Chinese contemporary artists, and shows regular, well-curated exhibitions of their paintings, photography and installations.

Shanghai Deke Erh Centre
上海尔冬强艺术中心
Bldg 3, Lane 210, Taikang Road
Tel: 6415 0675
Renowned Shanghai photographer Deke Erh's gallery space is used for exhibitions, concerts and even book readings.

For a detailed list of performances in Shanghai, check the website: www.culture.sh.cn.

Theatres

Lyceum Theatre
兰心大戏院
57 Maoming Road (S)
Tel: 6256 5544
Dating to 1930, this Art Deco theatre was restored in 2003. It mainly hosts traditional Chinese performing arts (like Pingtan) and children's dramas and recitals.

Majestic Theatre
美琪大戏院
66 Jiang Ning Road
Tel: 6217 4409
This Art Deco theatre started life as a movie theatre, but today hosts primarily ballets and plays.

Shanghai Centre Theatre
上海商城剧院
1376 Nanjing Road (W)
Tel: 6279 8663/7132
The Shanghai Acrobatic Troupe (www.shanghaiacrobats.com) holds regular performances here (7.30pm daily). The 90-minute show is worth every cent so get the best seats.

Shanghai Circus World
上海马戏城
2266 Gong He Xin Road
(at Da Ning Road)
Tel: 5665 3646/6652 7750
The Shanghai Acrobatic Troupe performs a more elaborate high-tech show with special effects called ERA Intersection of Time (www.era-shanghai.com) at this out-of-the-way location.

BUYING TICKETS

Tickets for most arts performances can be purchased either direct from the venue or from the **Shanghai Cultural Information and Booking Centre** (272 Fengxian Road; tel: 6217 2426; www.culture.sh.cn). The website has comprehensive listings for theatres and performance spaces in town. In the pipeline are plans to provide online booking.

Shanghai Concert Hall
上海音乐厅
523 Yan'an Road (E)
Tel: 6386 2836
The classic 1930s Shanghai Concert Hall – where the Shanghai Philharmonic Orchestra is based – hosts local and visiting symphonies and classical musicians.

Shanghai Dramatic Arts Centre
上海话剧艺术中心
288 Anfu Road
Tel: 6433 5133
This is where cutting-edge Chinese contemporary plays, some with English subtitles, are performed.

Shanghai Grand Stage
上海大舞台
1111 Caoxi Road (N) (inside the Shanghai Stadium)
Tel: 6438 5200/4952
This stadium is the venue for many of Shanghai's rock concerts, from Linkin Park to the Rolling Stones and Beyoncé.

Shanghai Grand Theatre
上海大剧院
300 People's Avenue
Tel: 6372 8701/8702
www.shgtheatre.com
Designed by French architect Jean-Marie Charpentier, this is the city's premier venue for highbrow culture – theatre, dance, music and opera. The Shanghai Broadcast Symphony Orchestra is based here.

Shanghai Oriental Arts Centre
上海东方艺术中心
425 Dingxiang Road, Pudong
Tel: 3842 4800
www.shoac.com.cn
Pudong's answer to the Shanghai

Grand Theatre. Comprising a 2,000-seat concert hall, a 1,000-seat lyric theatre and 330-seat hall for chamber music, this is the home of the Shanghai Symphony Orchestra. A mixed bag of arts events take place here, including ballet, opera and classical music.

Yifu Theatre
逸夫舞台
701 Fuzhou Road
Tel: 6351 4668
The home of Beijing opera in Shanghai, Yifu also features performances of Kunju opera. Performances on Sat and Sun at 1.30pm and 7.15pm.

Film

Despite the preponderance of cheap counterfeit DVDs, cineplexes continue to be popular. Most Chinese films are shown without subtitles. Hollywood blockbusters (albeit heavily censored) are screened in English (with Chinese subtitles) only at selected cinemas; otherwise they are dubbed in Chinese. The following cinemas cater to English-speakers:

Kodak Cinema World
柯达电影世界
5/F, Metro City, 1111 Zhaojiabang Road (at Tianyaoqiao Road)
Tel: 6426 8181
http://cinemaworld.kodak.com/english.htm

Paradise Warner Cinema City
永华电影城
6/F, Grand Gateway,
1 Hongqiao Road

Tel: 6407 6622
Studio City
环贸电影院
10/F, Westgate Mall,
1038 Nanjing Road (W)
Tel: 6218 2173
UME International Cineplex
UME新天地国际影城
Xintiandi, 4/F, No. 6, Lane 123 Xingye Road
Tel: 6373 3333

NIGHTLIFE

Shanghai's bar and nightclub scene is hot, and increasingly sophisticated, with its fair share of drugs and prostitution. The more upscale bars are along the **Bund**, **Xintiandi** and in the five-star hotels. Popular bar strips are also found at **Julu Road** and **Hengshan Road**.

The club scene attracts international DJ icons from overseas, and while Shanghai's live music scene is not as vibrant as Beijing's, the city does manage to hold its own. Drink prices are generally similar to big-city prices anywhere in the world; look out for happy hours, two-for-one drink deals and ladies' nights, when women get a free drink.

See also the **Shanghai Nights** chapter *(page 81)* for more on the city's nightlife scene.

Shanghai's free listings magazines provide pages and pages of every bar and nightclub as well as upcoming events. The most reliable are: *That's Shanghai*, www.thatsshanghai.com; and *City Weekend*, www.cityweekend.com.cn.

Bars and Pubs

The Bund
Bar Rouge
7/F, Bund 18,
Zhongshan No. 1 Road (E)
Tel: 6339 1199
Located on the top floor of a beautifully restored building, expect gorgeous red-tinged interiors and a terrace with views of the Bund.

BELOW: Beijing opera performance at Yifu Theatre.

Very popular with the Euro set.

Bund Brewery
11 Hankou Road
Tel: 6321 8447
Located just off the Bund in a historic building, it serves micro-brewed fresh beer (both dark and light), brewed in the copper stills that dominate the bar.

D&G Martini Bar
G/F, Bund 6,
Zhongshan No. 1 Road (E)
Tel: 6323 2277
Located on the same floor as the Dolce & Gabbana boutique, this low-key bar (unlike the loud D&G clothes) is owned by the store and modelled on the Martini bar in the flagship Milan store.

The Glamour Bar
(at M on the Bund)
魅力酒吧 (米氏西餐厅)
6/F, Bund 5,
Zhongshan No. 1 Road (E)
Tel: 6350 9988
www.m-theglamourbar.com
Pink neon, a silver bar shaped like a high-heeled shoe and floor-to-ceiling views of the river and the Bund. Funky DJs, great cocktails and long lines at the door – it's Shanghai's most happening bar at the moment.

Hengshan Road Area

The Blarney Stone
岩烧
5A Dongping Road
Tel: 6415 7496
Shanghai's most authentic Irish pub, down to the brogue of the bartenders. Good live music.

O'Malley's Irish Pub
欧玛莉爱尔兰酒吧
42 Taojiang Road
Tel: 6474 4533
www.omalleys-shanghai.com
Located in a French Concession villa with a lovely garden, the Guinness and home-brewed O'Malley's ale is popular with the city's expatriates.

Paulaner Brauhaus
宝莱纳
150 Fenyang Road, tel: 6474 5700; House 19–20, North Block Xintiandi, tel: 6320 3935; and Riverside Promenade, Binjiang Avenue, tel: 6888 3935

Paulaner has three locations – in a vintage French Concesssion villa, in a Xintiandi *shikumen* house, and on the river overlooking the Bund in Pudong. Brews its beer right on the premises of each venue.

Sasha's
萨莎
House 11, 9 Dongping Road
(at Hengshan Road)
Tel: 6474 6166
www.sashas-shanghai.com
The stylish bar in this old Soong family mansion gets smoky and crowded after 8pm. The garden is a nice retreat when the press of people gets to you. A favourite stop on the Hengshan pub crawl.

Julu Road

Manifesto
梅萨
748 Julu Road
Tel: 6289 9108
Located on the second floor of a renovated French Concession electronics factory, Manifesto offers an excellent wine list – and an inviting terrace.

Xintiandi

Cube
181 Taicang Road, Building 2,
North Block, Xintiandi
Tel: 5351 0007
Located in a *shikumen* house and next to dessert bar Sugar – it specialises in dessert cocktails in a frothy, pink-hued setting. Perfect for a girls' night out.

DR Bar
15 Lane 181, Taicang Road
North Block, Xintiandi
Tel: 6311 0358
Owned by Xintiandi architect Ben Wood, this tiny, sultry bar serves some of the best martinis in town. Artsy and celebrity types are drawn here.

Paulaner Brauhaus
宝莱纳
No.19–20, North Block Xintiandi,
Lane 181 Taicang Road
Tel: 6320 3935
www.bln.com.cn
The Xintiandi branch of this Shanghai institution features hearty German meat-and-

ABOVE: international nightlife scene.

potatoes dishes, live music and an even livielier atmosphere, all fuelled by the house speciality: micro-brewed Paulaner beer.

Tou Ming Si Kao (TMSK)
透明思考
Unit 2, House 11, Lane 181,
Taicang Road, North Block
Xintiandi
Tel: 6326 2227
Beautiful coloured-glass sculpture is the theme here – from the bar counter to the bar stools and designer wine glasses.

Elsewhere

Barbarossa
芭芭露莎
231 Nanjing Road (W)
Tel: 6318 0220
A Moroccan-themed bar with a decidedly *Arabian Nights* feeling. A great place to chill out with a drink. Fabulous views from the rooftop.

Jade on 36 Bar
翡翠36酒吧
Level 36, Pudong Shangri-La Hotel
Tel: 6882 3636
Designed by über-restaurant designer Adam Tihany, this pink and green bar boasts spectacular views of the Bund and Pudong as well as a creative drinks list.

Clubs and Live Music

Brown Sugar
红糖爵士音乐餐厅
Bldg 15, Xintiandi North Block,
Lane 181, Taicang Road
Tel: 5382 8998
www.brownsugarjazzclub.com
As befits its Xintiandi location, this is an upscale jazz club fea-

turing international and local jazz most nights of the week, well-crafted cocktails and a more mature – and touristy – crowd.

Cotton Club
棉花俱乐部
8 Fuxing Road (W)
Tel: 6437 7110
A Shanghai legend, the Cotton Club features its own band, open-mic nights and guest artistes – Wynton Marsalis jammed here when he was in town. This is where some of the city's best blues and jazz are played.

House of Blues & Jazz
布鲁斯与爵士之星
60 Fuzhou Road
Tel: 6323 2779
Live blues and jazz as well as jazz selections from the CD player in one of the most authentic retro settings in Shanghai.

The Jazz Bar
Fairmont Peace Hotel
20 Nanjing Road (E)
Tel: 6138 6883
www.fairmont.com/peacehotel
Reopened following several years of renovation work, this venerable old venue is a great place to see live jazz.

JZ Club
爵士酒吧
46 Fuxing Road (W)
Tel: 6431 0269
www.jzclub.cn
Owned by a Beijing jazz musician, JZ's is where local jazz musicians come to jam after-hours. Excellent acoustics, a good crowd, and perhaps the best jazz in Shanghai.

Mao Live House
570 Huaihai Road (W)
Tel: 5258 9999
www.maolive-sh.com
A good-sized space with an excellent sound system and a good selection of rock music acts (local, national and international) makes Mao one of the best concert venues in the city. Frequented by young locals as well as expats, there's live music almost every night of the week.

Muse
The New Factories
68 Yuyao Road
Tel: 6218 8166
www.museshanghai.com
Located in the edgy setting of a warehouse in the New Factories hub, Muse features house and R 'n' B. The downside: there's not much else in the surrounding area.

Shelter
庇护所
5 Yongfu Road
Tel: 6437 0400
A former bomb shelter that is a favourite underground dance music venue. Local musicians, DJs, alternative dance acts and a cheek-to-jowl crowd in this over-heated, loud – but enjoyable – venue.

Yin Yang
轮回
125 Nanchang Road
Tel: 6466 4098
One of Shanghai's oldest bars, YY (the downstairs dance floor is "warm" and the upstairs chill-out lounge "cool" – go to both spaces and your yin and yang will be balanced) has an Old Shanghai-style feel with its wooden interior and the portrait of Mao, good cocktails and hip young Chinese.

Yuyintang
育音堂 **Yuyingtang**
851 Kaixuan Road
Tel: 5237 8662
www.yuyintang.org
One of Shanghai's oldest, and best, live music venues, Yuyintang has underground rock bands every weekend, both local and international.

Zhijiang Dream Factory
上海芷江梦工厂
4/F, Building B, 28 Yuyao Road

BELOW: live performance.

Tel: 5213 5223
A live music warehouse for larger shows, featuring mostly better-known Chinese and international bands, theatre groups and parties. Upstairs is a more upscale space for drinks, with a contemporary Asian design.

Gay and Lesbian Venues

Note: Gay venues are still fairly underground because of occasional brushes with the authorities; they sometimes close down and pop up elsewhere. The ones listed here have been around for several years, but it is still a good idea to call beforehand.

The Box
B1/F, 10 Hengshan Road
Tel: 139 1894 9817
www.shthebox.com
The largest LGBT bar in Shanghai, this centrally located venue is packed out at weekends, with movie screenings, drag shows, theme parties and lots and lots of dancing – most of the action takes place late.

Eddy's
1877 Central Huaihai Road
Tel: 6282 0521
www.eddys-bar.com
A longstanding favourite, with a loyal following who manage to find it every time it moves.

Red Bar
2/F E4B, Life Hub @ Daning
1978 Gonghe Xin Road
Mobile tel: 133 9115 9298
Lesbian bar with house music and pole-dancing for whoever wants to try. Open bar every Wednesday.

Red Station
4/F, 200 Taikang Road
Tel: 6415 8695
It's a young, local crowd of la-las (Chinese slang for lesbians) who come here, especially on weekends. There's plenty of dancing (to hip-hop, mostly).

Shanghai Studio
1950 Central Huaihai Road, No. 4
Tel: 6283 1043
www.shanghai-studio.com
Private rooms and meandering tunnels add interest to this small bar, as does the art on the walls.

EVENTS & FESTIVALS

January–February

Spring Festival (Chun Jie, or Chinese New Year). A three-day public holiday plus the weekend. Takes place in either January or February, depending on the lunar calendar. For an entire week, all transport and hotels in Shanghai will be fully booked. The city gets dressed up for the holiday, and shops are filled with goodies. The Lantern Festival (Deng Jie) is held on the 15th day of the new year, and celebrated with a lantern display at Yu Garden.

March

Shanghai International Literary Festival. China's biggest international literary event, the festival has attracted big names (like Gore Vidal, Amy Tan) as well as emerging local writers on China.

April

Formula One. The Shanghai International Circuit in Anting (in the outskirts of Shanghai) hosts this exciting race in April.

Qing Ming. A public holiday. The first week of April brings the "Clear and Bright Festival", known in English as the "Tomb-Sweeping Day". Chinese visit the graves of their ancestors bearing gifts of food and fake paper money to be burnt for use in the afterlife.

May

Labour Day. A public holiday in honour of China's workers.

June

Dragon Boat Festival. A public holiday in honour of Qu Yuan, a 3rd-century poet and patriot who drowned himself when he learnt that his home state had fallen to the enemy. People went out in boats, beating drums and tossing rice dumplings into the water so that fish would stay away from

ABOVE: dragon boat racing.

his body. *Zongzi*, the leaf-wrapped rice dumplings are eaten, and dragon boat races take place.
Shanghai International Film Festival. Attracts local celebrities as well as top Hollywood names.

September–October

Mid-Autumn Festival. A public holiday. The 15th night of the eighth lunar month, when the moon appears the roundest, is an occasion for people to celebrate by nibbling on mooncakes filled with sweet red bean or lotus nut paste, with an egg yolk embedded in the centre.

October

National Day. A three-day holiday plus the weekend in celebration of the founding of the People's Republic of China on 1 Oct 1949 – expect plenty of fireworks, and another mass exodus of people and congested roads.

November

International Fashion Week. A showcase for the brightest domestic fashion designers, the festival also attracts international fashion names.
Shanghai Biennale. This event brings together some notable cutting-edge contemporary artists from both the Chinese and Western worlds.
Shanghai International Arts Festival. A month-long festival that features a programme of international as well as Chinese performing arts.

Shanghai ATP Masters. ATP's season ending finale brings some of tennis's biggest names to Shanghai.

HSBC Champions Golf Tournament. Golf's top players compete in this tournament, held in Sheshan, just outside Shanghai.

December

Christmas and New Year. Decorations light up the shopping hubs along Nanjing Road and Central Huaihai Road. On New Year's Eve, the Longhua Temple fair has fireworks and lion dancing. New Year's Day is a public holiday.

SIGHTSEEING

If time is limited, there are day tours that will show you the city's highlights, as well as day trips and overnight tours to nearby scenic spots such as Suzhou, Hangzhou and the water villages. The main agencies, CITS and Jinjiang, are government-owned, however, and their tour guides will give you the official version of history – so bear this in mind. Many Shanghai hotel desks can arrange day tours with the aforementioned agencies or with private companies.

China International Travel Service (CITS): 1277 Beijing Road (W); tel: 6289 4510; www.scits.com

Jinjiang Optional Tours Centre: 191 Changle Road; tel: 6445 9525/6466 2828; www.jjtravel.com

Synwalk Travel: 16G, Tower B, Yue Da International Plaza, 1118 Chang Shou Road; tel: 5169 5100; www.synwalk.com

River Cruises

Shanghai Huangpu River Cruise Company
153 Zhongshan No. 2 Road (E)
Tel: 6374 4461/6329 9992
Seeing Shanghai from the river that has powered so much of the city's history and trade can be exhilarating. Several companies operate boat tours near the south-

ern end of the Bund at Jinling Pier (near the Meteorological Signal Tower), but this one seems to be the most popular. It offers 1-hour round-trip cruises to the Yangpu Bridge and 3½-hour cruises all the way to the Yangzi River and back. There are day and night cruises, depending on the season. Tickets can also be booked through hotel tour desks.

Specialist Tours

Art Tours
e-mail: info@shanghaiculture.com
www.shanghaiculture.com
Local expert Xhingyu Chen leads tours of art galleries and artist studios, offering a unique insight into the Chinese art scene.

Historic Shanghai Walks & Talks
e-mail: info@historic-shanghai.com
Half- and full-day tours of historic Shanghai by experts on Shanghai's history and architecture. Tours can be customised and are limited to 10 people. Bookings should be made in advance by contacting the e-mail address given.

Shopping Tours
Tel: 6366 4361
Mobile tel: 137 6193 6595
www.eastofthesun-asia.com
Shanghai-based expat Francine Martin offers shopping adventures that will unearth unique Shanghai treasures. Tours are customised to the shoppers' wish list. Ideal for individual or small groups.

Tours of Jewish Shanghai
Mobile tel: 130 0214 6702
www.shanghai-jews.com
Half- and full-day tours that focus on the history of the Jews in Shanghai with knowledgeable Israeli journalist Dvir-Bar Gal.

SPORTS

Urban Shanghai has its share of city sports – mostly of the indoor variety – and a number of international tournaments that draw big-name sports figures to the city. The **Shanghai Sharks** basketball team (which Yao Ming, now of the

Houston Rockets, previously played for and now owns) is based at the Luwan Stadium while the popular football team **Shanghai Shenhua** plays at the Hongkou Stadium. International tournaments include the **Shanghai ATP Masters**, which brings the top names in tennis to town and the **HSBC Champions Golf Tournament**, which does the same for golf. Both events take place annually in November.

Basketball and Football

Shanghai Shenhua (football)
Hongkou Stadium
715 Dong Ti Yu Hui Road
Tel: 6553 2388 (ticket info)
Shanghai Sharks (basketball)
Luwan Stadium
128 Zhao Jia Bang Road
Tel: 6467 5358 (ticket info)

Golf

Shanghai's golf courses are mostly located on its outskirts, about 30 minutes to an hour from the city. They range from nine-hole courses to the 54-hole one at the Shanghai Binhai Golf Club. Greens fees cost between RMB 400 to RMB 1,600 (at weekends). Most golf courses are private but five-star hotels in Shanghai can arrange for guests to play.

Hongqiao Golf Club
虹桥高尔夫俱乐部
555 Hongxu Road
Tel: 6421 5522
www.happygolf.com.cn
Shanghai Binhai Golf Club
上海滨海高尔夫俱乐部
Binhai Resort, Nanhui, Pudong
Tel: 5805 8888
www.binhaigolf.com
Sheshan International Golf Club
佘山国际高尔夫俱乐部
Lane 288, Linyin Xin Road
Tel: 5765 5765
www.sheshangolf.com
Shanghai Tianma Country Club
上海天马乡村俱乐部
1 Tianmashan Zhen
Tel: 6268 5500
Shanghai Tomson Golf Club
汤臣高尔夫俱乐部

1 Longdong Road
Tel: 5833 8888
www.tomson-golf.com

SPAS

Indulgent (and pricey) five-star hotel spas may be new to Shanghai, but the neighbourhood clinics and massage centres that have been dispensing no-frills versions of age-old Chinese remedies for years are not. Popular therapies include *tuina*, the Chinese-style massage which focuses on restoring the balance of the body's energy, or *chi*, as well as foot reflexology, acupressure massage and acupuncture.

Body & Soul – The TCM Clinic
身心佳中医门诊部
14/F, Suite 5, Anji Plaza
760 Xizang Road (S)
Tel: 5101 9262
www.bodyandsoul.com.cn
A Traditional Chinese Medicine (TCM) clinic owned by a Chinese-trained Western TCM specialist, it offers all the traditional therapies.

Banyan Tree
悦榕水疗
3/F, Westin Hotel
88 Central Henan Road
Tel: 6335 1888
www.banyantreespa.com.shanghai
Expect an indulgent Asian resort experience with Balinese, Thai, Swedish and Hawaiian massage and other body treatments.

Dragonfly
悠庭保健会所
206 Xinle Road

Tel: 5403 9982
www.dragonfly.net.cn
Located in a French Concession lane house, Dragonfly offers foot and body massages. Candle lights and Buddhist stone statues add to the atmosphere. More than 10 branches throughout the city; check website for details.

Evian Spa
依云水疗
2/F, Three on the Bund
2 Zhongshan No. 1 Road (E)
Tel: 6321 6622
www.threeonthebund.com
A contemporary setting for hydrotherapies and French beauty treatments. "Express" treatments include blow dries, manicures and facials in under an hour.

Green Massage
春
58 Taicang Road
Tel: 5386 0222
www.greenmassage.com.cn
Simple yet stylish setting for massage, aromatherapy, foot massage and "ear candling". Massage beds are divided by bamboo screens. Close to Xintiandi.

Magpie
风雅堂
685 Julu Road
Tel: 5403 3867
Dim lighting and antique Chinese furniture give this place a bit of an opium den feel. Oil massage is its speciality.

Mandara
蔓达梦水疗中心
6/F, J W Marriott, Tomorrow Square, 399 Nanjing Road (W)
Tel: 5359 4969
www.mandaraspa.com

The Marriott's exquisite Asian spa takes on a Shanghai look: *shikumen* grey brick walls, Shanghai Deco furniture and pampering Eastern therapies from all over Asia.

Shile Boutique Lifestyle Centre
十乐
No. 1, Lane 599, Fangdian Road
www.jjtshile.com
Contemporary lines and natural materials give this "boutique lifestyle centre" the feel of an Asian resort. Massage therapies, as well as a restaurant and bar.

CHILDREN'S ACTIVITIES

China's one-child policy has created a generation of parents eager to offer their "Little Emperors" plenty of diversions. So in addition to being a child-friendly city, Shanghai offers an array of entertainment options for children. Many of these have already been covered in the Places chapters, including **Changfeng Ocean World** *(page 209)*, **Dino Beach** *(page 199)*, **Jinjiang Amusement Park** *(page 199)*, **Shanghai Museum of Natural History** *(page 121)*, **Shanghai Natural Wild Insect Kingdom** *(page 228)*, **Shanghai Ocean Aquarium** *(page 228)*, **Shanghai Science and Technology Museum** *(page 232)*, **Shanghai Wild Animal Park** *(page 233)* and **Shanghai Zoo** *(page 203)*. Also universally loved by children is taking the high-speed lift up the **Oriental Pearl Tower** *(page 227)* and watching gravity-defying stunts performed by the **Shanghai Acrobatic Troupe** at the **Shanghai Centre Theatre** *(page 289)*.

Most parks have playgrounds and sometimes paddle boats and rides. Recommended for kids are **Fuxing Park** *(page 156)*, **Gongqing Forest Park** *(page 216)*, **Jing An Park** *(page 188)*, **Lu Xun Park** *(page 218)* and **Zhongshan Park** *(page 207)*. The **Shanghai Botanical Gardens** *(page 198)* in south Shanghai are another place for a great day out with the children.

BELOW: soaking off the stress.

AN ALPHABETICAL SUMMARY OF PRACTICAL INFORMATION

A ddresses

Buildings are usually sequentially numbered, odd numbers on one side of the street and even numbers on the other. Because the major streets often run the entire length of the city, it helps to know what the nearest cross-street is when trying to locate an address, such as Central Huaihai Road near *(kaojing)* Gao'an Road. It's easier with newer buildings as the street address now indicates building numbers within an area, for example, Central Huaihai Road 1000–2000. *See also Orientation and Useful Street Translations, page 271.*

B udgeting Your Trip

Shanghai is as cheap or as expensive as you want it to be. Accommodation can cost from as little as RMB 50 for a dorm bed to upwards of RMB 2,500 for one of the city's de luxe five-star hotels.

Similarly, a meal in a simple Chinese restaurant costs about RMB 25 per person, while you can easily pay RMB 500 at the one of the city's swankier Chinese or Western eateries. Local beer costs as little as RMB 25; imported beer is three times more. A glass of wine at an expensive restaurant costs RMB 80 and upwards.

The city's efficient public transport system is cheap – a bus or metro ride within the downtown area won't cost more than RMB 5. Taxi rides are also inexpensive, running about RMB 20 for trips within the city centre.

Entry fees to most attractions are under RMB 20, except for premier attractions like the Oriental Pearl Tower, where the most expensive ticket costs RMB 100.

Business Hours

Shops generally open at 10am and close around 7pm, though some stay open until 10pm. Government offices are open from 9am to 5pm during weekdays with a 1–2-hour lunch break. Banks may stay open until 6pm or 7pm; some currency exchange desks are open around the clock; and ATMs are everywhere.

Most large malls and department stores are generally open daily from 9–10am to 9–10pm. Smaller shops may have shorter hours, so call first. Keep in mind that most businesses are closed during Chinese New Year and other national holidays (see page 302).

Business Travellers

Business is the driving force in Shanghai, the Manhattan of China, and most things are set up for the needs of the business traveller. Most hotels – and not just the top end – are well equipped with business centres, in-room Internet, interpreter and support services. The city is also establishing itself as a key convention and exhibition centre, and is home to several international-standard venues.

The local Shanghai government is very pro-business. For more information on business and investing in Shanghai, see the website: www.investment.gov.cn. See also the chapter on **Business and Economy** (page 44).

C hildren

Shanghai loves children. There is not a museum, a restaurant or a theatre where your child will feel unwelcome. The downside is a loss of privacy: your kids will be touched, stared at, talked to and photographed – just take a positive attitude about the whole thing and you'll meet new friends and gain fresh insights.

Hotels often allow children to stay with parents in a double room at no extra charge. Extra beds are available for a small surcharge. Reliable babysitters, called ayi (aunty), are easily available. If planning to be in Shanghai for any length of time, consider a serviced apartment with kitchen (see page 275).

Climate

Shanghai has a northern subtropical monsoon climate with four distinct seasons. Rainfall is plentiful throughout the year, though most of it falls during the rainy season from June to September. Expect hot and muggy summers with temperatures hovering in the mid-30s°C (95°F) in July and August, and chilled-to-the-bone damp winters in December and January. January is the coldest month, although temperatures rarely dip below zero. Snow is rare in Shanghai, although there are the occasional late December/January flurries. Shanghai's mildest weather (and best times to visit) is in spring (mid-March to May) and autumn (September to early November).

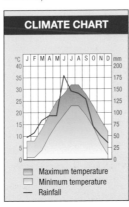

CLIMATE CHART

Maximum temperature
Minimum temperature
— Rainfall

Clothing

Shanghai errs on the side of casual, but it is a city of unrelenting style: you'll be forgiven for not wearing a tie, but never for looking like a bumpkin. Light, breathable clothes work best in the hot, humid summertime, with a light wrap for the over-air-conditioned restaurants and offices. In winter, several layers of clothing is the key to staying warm. Savvy travellers always carry a foldable umbrella with them to protect against sudden showers.

Crime & Safety

Shanghai is a relatively safe city, but petty crimes like pickpocketing do happen in crowded areas like train stations, markets and on busy streets. There is very little violent crime against foreigners, but tourists should be aware of scams. One of the better-known ones involves locals asking foreign tourists to dinner in order to "practise their English". After the end of a meal, an extortionate bill arrives, with the local having disappeared, or simply professing that they're "too poor" to pay.

It's a safe city for women, too, who are able to walk alone, even at night, safely and without being harassed – but again, you should be on your guard.

Every neighbourhood has its own police station or post, often labelled in English. This is the place to report any crime,

TRANSPORT

ACCOMMODATION

SHOPPING

ACTIVITIES

A – Z

LANGUAGE

although you might have to wait for the Public Security Bureau officer in charge of foreigners to handle your case. Otherwise, contact the **Public Security Bureau** directly. See below for a list of Emergency Numbers.

Customs Regulations

Duty-free allowance per adult is as follows: two bottles of liquor (75cl each), 400 cigarettes, 50g of gold or silver, and perfume for personal use. On arrival, tourists have to fill out a baggage declaration form and hand it in to customs; be sure to retain the duplicate copy to show upon exit. There is no limit to the amount of foreign currency and Chinese Renminbi traveller's cheques that can be brought in; the unspent portion may be taken out. There is a long list of prohibited items, including animals, firearms, plant material and media deemed "detrimental" to China's social and political security. For up-to-date details see www.china.org.cn. Note: antiques require a government stamp in order to be exported; most reputable dealers can take care of the necessary paperwork.

D isabled Access

Most of Shanghai's modern hotels, buildings and museums are all wheelchair-accessible, but older buildings and the myriad overpasses and underpasses are not. Newer metro stations all have wheelchair ramps, and the older ones are adding them.

Shanghai's wheelchair-bound use motorised wheelchairs to get around. **Bashi Taxi** (tel: 6431 2788) has several minivans that cater for the wheelchair-bound.

E lectricity

Local electricity is 220 volts; 50 cycles AC. Chinese-to-foreign conversion accessories – whether conversion plugs or voltage converters – are easily available at department stores and hotels.

Embassies & Consulates

Australian Consulate: 22/F, CITIC Square, 1168 Nanjing Road (W); tel: 5292 5500; www.china.embassy.gov.au.
British Consulate: Suite 301, Shanghai Centre, 1376 Nanjing Road (W); tel: 6279 7650; www.uk.cn.
New Zealand Consulate: 1605–1607A, 989 Changle Road; tel: 5407 5858; www.nzembassy.com.
Singapore Consulate: 89 Wanshan Road; tel: 6278 5566; www.mfa.gov.sg/shanghai.
United States Consulate: 1469 Central Huaihai Road; tel: 6433 6880; also **American Citizen Services**: 8/F, Westgate Mall, 1038 Nanjing Road (W); tel: 3217 4650, after-hours emergencies tel: 6433 3936; http://shanghai.usconsulate.gov.

Emergency Numbers

Public Security Bureau: 710 Hankou Road; tel: 6321 5380
Ambulance: 120
Fire: 119
Police: 110

Entry Requirements

Passports should be valid for at least six months before you step out of your home country.

Most visitors to China require a visa. There are several ways of procuring one. The easy way is to use the services of a travel agent. There will be a commission charge on top of the visa-processing fee paid to the visa office of the Chinese embassy or consulate. If you are part of a group tour, the travel agent will issue a group visa for all the members of the tour party.

Individual travellers may also apply for a visa directly with the Chinese embassy or consulate in their home country. For more details and to download a visa form, check the **Chinese Ministry of Foreign Affairs** website at www.fmprc.gov.cn/eng. To locate the relevant section, click on "About

ABOVE: t'ai chi on the Bund.

China"– "Travel to China" – "Visa Information".

Two passport-size pictures, the completed application form and the fee are required. There are additional requirements for first-time visa applicants who are foreign-born but of Chinese descent, or who were born in China but have migrated overseas.

It takes about 7–10 working days to process your China visa, so make sure you apply for one well before your intended departure. Visa fees vary by country, so check with the respective Chinese embassy or consulate. The fee also depends on the length of stay. The standard tourist visa is a single-entry 30-day visa. Multiple-entry and 60-day visas are also available at higher cost.

Business and student visas usually allow multiple-entry and come with three- to six-month validity. However, these require supporting documentation confirming your status.

Visas in Hong Kong

As many people combine a trip to China with Hong Kong, another option is to get your China visa issued in Hong Kong. Many nationalities only require a valid passport for entry into Hong Kong. Once there, you can either apply for a visa directly with the local Chinese visa office *(see opposite)*, or use the services of a travel agent or the China Travel Service office (CTS). Obtaining visas in Hong Kong is both

TRANSPORT

ACCOMMODATION

SHOPPING

ACTIVITIES

A – Z

LANGUAGE

inexpensive and speedy – most are issued within 2–3 working days and same-day service is available at premium rate.

Consular Dept of China's Foreign Ministry in Hong Kong: 7/F, Lower Block, China Resources Building, 26 Harbour Road, Wan Chai, Hong Kong; tel: 852 3413 2300; fax: 852 3413 23127; www.fmcoprc.gov.hk. Mon–Fri 9am–noon, 2–5pm.

China Travel Service: CTS House, 78–83 Connaught Road, Central, Hong Kong; tel: 852 2853 3533; fax: 852 2543 2671; www.china travelone.com. Check the website for branch locations.

Visa Extensions

In Shanghai, tourist visas can be extended for a maximum of 30 days. To extend a business visa, a letter of sponsorship from a Chinese *danwei* (work unit) is required; student visa extensions must be accompanied by a letter from the school. The process usually takes three business days. All visa extensions require two passport-size photos and are processed at the **Public Security Bureau** in Pudong, No. 1500 Minsheng Road, tel: 2895 1900; nearest metro station: Science and Technology Museum; Mon–Sat 9am–5pm.

Etiquette

Bear in mind the following rules:
• Shoes should be removed when entering homes; sometimes slippers will be provided.
• Use both hands to present business cards at meetings.
• Tea should be offered when you visit someone, whether at home or in a business setting.
• If you invite someone for dinner, you are expected to pay for the entire meal – Shanghainese do not go Dutch. Nevertheless, the Shanghainese are very forgiving of foreigners when it comes to local rules of etiquette, so you will be excused of most gaffes.

The most serious breaches of etiquette tend to involve politics rather than manners: although the atmosphere is far more open now, it is still wise to stay away from political discussions, especially involving sensitive topics like Taiwan and Tibet.

G ay & Lesbian Travellers

Homosexuality is frowned upon in China – it was downgraded from a mental illness only in 2001 – but in liberal Shanghai, the gay scene is increasingly open, albeit a predominantly male one. Nevertheless, discretion prevails; China is still basically a conservative society, so flagrant displays of affection are best avoided. See also page 293 for a list of gay and lesbian nightlife venues. For more information on this subject check www.utopia-asia.com/chinshan.htm.

H ealth & Medical Care

Healthcare is good in Shanghai, and improving all the time. There are Western-staffed clinics and designated foreigners' clinics in local hospitals with English-speaking personnel. Other hospitals will treat foreigners, but only in emergencies. For more serious and complicated issues, patients often return to their home countries or seek treatment in Hong Kong. Visitors to Shanghai should therefore have health insurance that includes repatriation expenses.

Similarly, all the medication you might need – over-the-counter and prescription – should be brought with you, as not all medication can be found in Shanghai.

Vaccines

Other than requiring a yellow fever vaccination certificate from travellers coming from tropical South America or sub-Saharan Africa, Shanghai does not require any immunisations.

The Centre for Disease Control (CDC) in Atlanta, US, recommends the following vaccines for travellers to Shanghai. For more information, check its website: www.cdc.gov.

Be sure to consult your doctor at least 4 to 6 weeks before your trip so that there is sufficient time for the shots to take effect.

Hepatitis A – A food and water-borne viral infection of the liver.

Hepatitis B – An estimated 10 to 15 percent of the Chinese population carry hepatitis B, which is transmitted through bodily fluids and can lead to liver disease. The vaccine is recommended if you might be exposed to blood, have sexual contact with the local population, stay longer than six months, or risk exposure through medical treatment.

Japanese encephalitis – This is only recommended if you plan on visiting rural areas for four weeks or more, except under special circumstances, like an outbreak of the disease.

Rabies – Recommended if there is risk of exposure to wild animals.

BELOW: traditional Chinese medicine.

Hospitals

Shanghai Huashan Hospital
Foreigner's Ward: 19th Floor,
12 Central Wulumuqi Road
Tel: 6248 9999, ext 1900
A mid-sized general hospital
which offers most specialities
except obstetrics and gynaecology, and paediatrics.
Pudong Children's Medical Centre
1678 Dongfang Road, Pudong
Tel: 5873 2020
A large, modern teaching hospital
built as a Sino-US joint venture.
Ruijin Hospital
197 Ruijin No. 2 Road
Tel: 6437 0045, ext 8101
(outpatients and emergencies
only); 6324 0090, ext 2101
(24-hour house calls)
Large teaching hospital with
most specialities. The foreigners'
clinic is located in Guang Ci
Hospital, on the grounds.

Clinics

**Parkway Health – Shanghai
Centre Clinic**
Suite 203, West Retail Plaza,
Shanghai Centre,
1376 Nanjing Road (W)
Tel: 6445 5999
www.parkwayhealth.cn
Reputable clinic with overseas-trained and English-speaking doctors and staff. Offers a wide
range of speciality clinics, including dentistry. Operates clinics
throughout the city. For 24-hour
assistance, call 6445 5999.
**Shanghai East International
Medical Centre**
551 Pudong Road (S), Pudong
Tel: 5879 9999
www.seimc.com.cn
Opened in 2003, this international-class facility is operated by
Shanghai East Hospital and a
California-based healthcare company. Provides both outpatient
and in-patient medical services.

Pharmacies

Parkway Health centres will fill
prescriptions *(see above)*.
Shanghai No. 1 Dispensary: 616
Nanjing Road (E), tel: 6322
4567; daily 9am–10pm.
Watsons: 789 Central Huaihai

Road; tel: 6474 4775; daily
9am–10pm. Branches all over
the city.

Chinese Medicine

At the core of Traditional Chinese
Medicine (TCM) is the philosophy
that disease is due to an imbalance of *yin* and *yang* in the body.
Illness is cause by an interruption
of the flow of energy *(qi)* through
the channels, or acupuncture
points, of the body. Restoring the
body to health requires the
correction of this imbalance or
disruption through acupuncture
and herbal medicines.

English-speaking TCM doctors
run clinics at Parkway Health
centres *(see above)*. Other
places exist, but little or no
English is spoken.

I nternet & E-mail

Most business-class hotels either
have in-room WiFi, rooms that are
equipped with computer ports
that allow for high-speed Internet
connections or a business centre
where this facilty is available for a
fee. There are wireless cafés all
over the city as well.

L eft Luggage

Luggage can be left at the airport
and the train station.
Pudong International Airport:
Arrival Hall, tel: 6834 6078;
Departure Hall, tel: 6834 5035.
Hongqiao Airport: Arrival Hall,
tel: 5114 4520. Rates depend
on size of luggage.
Shanghai Railway Station: tel:
6354 3193 (RMB 80 per day).

Lost Property

If you lose your passport, it's
best to contact your consulate
immediately. Some consulates
have emergency 24-hour
numbers for this. For items left in
taxis, refer to the taxi receipt for
the telephone number to call (the
receipt also has the taxi number
on it, which will help the company
locate the vehicle).

M aps

Free tourist maps of Shanghai in
English and Chinese are available at the concierge desks of
most hotels. The maps sold at
the bookshops are usually in
Chinese. Recommended is the
Insight Fleximap Shanghai,
laminated for durability.

Media

Newspapers

Shanghai has two major daily
English-language newspapers:
the **Shanghai Daily** (www.shanghai
daily.com or http://english.eastday.
com) published locally with a
local perspective on information
is the choice for most people;
the second paper, **China Daily**
(www.chinadaily.com.cn) is published out of Beijing. *China
Daily*'s Shanghai edition has
two weekly supplements, one
on business and the other on
entertainment. The English edition of the Chinese-language
People's Daily is available on
the Internet at http://english.people
daily.com.cn.

Foreign newspapers and publications are available from the
city's four- and five-star hotels.
One of the best sources is The
Portman Ritz-Carlton Shanghai,
which carries the *South China
Morning Post*, *International
Herald Tribune*, *Asian Wall Street*

Journal and magazines like *Economist*, *Time* and *Newsweek*.

Magazines

Shanghai is awash with free English-language publications of varying quality, most with useful listings of restaurants, bars and entertainment spots. Among the best are **City Weekend** (www.city weekend.com.cn), **That's Shanghai** (www.thatssh.com) and **Time Out**, which provide insightful, timely articles as well as listings. Most of the magazines are available at bars and restaurants around town.

Television

Shanghai Broadcast Network (SBN) has the news in English at 10pm from Monday to Saturday; *Citybeat*, a cultural programme in English fills in the same time slot on Sundays. The news in English is also broadcast on **China Central Television** (CCTV) at 4, 7 and 11pm on weekdays and at noon on weekends.

Most four- and five-star hotels have cable channels with **Star World**, **CNN**, **HBO** and **ESPN**.

Radio

BBC World Service is accessible on radio. English-language programming is on FM 101.7 and FM 103.7.

Money

Chinese Currency

The Chinese yuan (CNY) is also known as renminbi (RMB). One yuan or renminbi (colloquially called *kuai*) is divided into 10 jiao (or *mao*); one jiao is divided into 10 fen. RMB bills are issued by the Bank of China in the following denominations: one, two five, 10, 50 and 100. China's fifth set of new currency was rolled out over several years beginning in the 1990s, with the most recent (and final) addition to the set being the new purple 5 RMB note and 5 jiao coin in 2002. Old notes, particularly the fives and 100s (issued in

ABOVE: Chinese renminbi notes.

1999), are still in circulation, so don't be surprised if you receive currency of the same denomination that looks different.

Jiao and fen are issued in bills and coins, although the paper jiao and fen are being phased out in favour of coins. Coins come in denominations of 1 RMB, 1, 2 and 5 jiao and 1, 2 and 5 fen. These days, fen isn't used much.

Exchanging Money

At the time of press, US$1 was roughly equivalent to RMB 6.6 while £1 bought about RMB 10.5.

All rates are uniform regardless of whether you exchange money at a bank or hotel. Major currencies can be changed at hotels – but you must be a registered guest – as well as at banks and some department stores. The same applies for traveller's cheques. Slightly better exchange rates are offered for traveller's cheques as opposed to cash.

Convertibility

When you change money, you'll receive a foreign exchange receipt, showing the amount exchanged. Any unused RMB can be changed back into foreign currency at the end of your visit, but you must show the foreign exchange receipt.

In theory, because the Chinese RMB isn't convertible, you won't be able to exchange it back into foreign currency (or vice versa) outside of China. However, in practice, many countries that

share borders with China or have business contacts with China are likely to have RMB. Check with banks and money exchange outlets in your country.

Emergency Money

Western Union, a reliable international money transfer agency, will wire money through the China Courier Service Corp. Identification is required for collection, tel: 6356 6666; or visit the website www.westernunion.com.

Cash Machines

If you find yourself short of cash, international credit cards and bank cards (Cirrus, Plus, Visa, MasterCard, American Express) can be used to withdraw local currency from ATMs, which are found throughout the city.

Bank of China will issue credit card cash advances with a 3 percent commission in US$ or RMB. The following are helpfully located ATMs:

Bank of China, Hongqiao Airport Arrival Hall; Pudong International Airport Arrival Hall; 139 Ruijin No. 1 Road; and 1377 Nanjing Road. **Citibank**, Pudong International Airport Arrival Hall; and Zhongshan Road (next to Peace Hotel).

Hongkong and Shanghai Bank, Ground Floor, West Retail Plaza, Shanghai Centre, 1376 Nanjing Road (W); Hong Kong Plaza, 282 Central Huaihai Road; at the Bund, 15A Zhongshan No. 1 Road (E).

Credit Cards

International credit cards are now accepted at major hotels and most restaurants – although many Chinese restaurants and small hotels only take cash or domestic credit cards. Cash is also king in the markets and most smaller local shops, although department stores do take credit cards.

American Express Hotline: 6279 7183. Daily 9am–5.30pm.

MasterCard Hotline: 10-800 110 7309.

Visa Hotline: 10-800 110 2911.

Foreign Banks

For a comprehensive list of banks in Shanghai, check the **Shanghai Banking Association** website: www.sbacn.org.

P ost Offices

The main **Shanghai Post Office** is at 395 Suzhou Road (N), tel: 6393 6666 – just across Suzhou Creek from the Bund. The international mail section is open daily from 8am to 10pm.

Every neighbourhood in Shanghai city has a post office, open 8 to 12 hours a day depending on the area. Post offices in the busiest areas, ie Sichuan Road, Central Huaihai Road, Nanjing Road and Xujiahui, are open 14 hours, while the Luwan district post office is open 24 hours.

In addition to mailing and selling stamps, post offices also deliver local courier packages. Most large hotels will post letters to international destinations for you.

Overseas Courier Services

DHL-Sinotrans: Shanghai International Trade Centre, 2200 Yan'an Road (W), tel: 6275 3543; and 303 Jinian Road, tel: 6536 2900, www.dhl.com.

FedEx: 10/F, Aetna Building, 107 Zunyi Road, tel: 6275 0808, www.fedex.com.

UPS: Room 1318, Central Plaza, 318 Central Huaihai Road, tel: 6391 5555, www.ups.com.

ABOVE: credit cards are widely used in Shanghai.

Local Courier Services

Express Mail Service (EMS): Offices at the following locations: 1337 Central Huaihai Road, tel: 6437 4272; 431 Fuxing Road, tel: 6328 3322; 2 Century Boulevard, Pudong, tel: 5047 2288; 146 Gao Qiao Shi Jia Road, Pudong, tel: 5867 5114.

Public Holidays

Since January 2008, four new public holidays have been added to the calendar. The list of holidays is as follows (*denotes holidays determined by the lunar calendar):

New Year's Day: 1 Jan
Spring Festival: Jan/Feb*
Qing Ming: Apr*
Labour Day: 1 May
Dragon Boat Festival: June*
Mid-Autumn Festival: Sept/Oct*
National Day: 1 Oct

Note that **Spring Festival** (or Chinese New Year) and **National Day** are week-long holidays. Schools and government offices are open the weekend before or after the one-week holiday.

The seven-day holiday is meant to encourage domestic travel, and as a result, not only is Shanghai jam-packed during the holidays, so are all forms of transport in and out of the city. This is especially true during Spring Festival, when Shanghai's migrants return to their villages for the festivities. Try to avoid visiting Shanghai, and China as a whole, during these periods.

Public Toilets

Public toilets are plentiful, but toilet paper always seems to be in short supply (so always carry a pack of tissues with you). Payment – usually a few jiao – is often required, but toilets aren't always clean. If you are squeamish, head for a nice hotel or shopping mall, where the public facilities are almost always user-friendly.

R eligious Services

China has five official religions: Buddhist, Taoist, Catholic, Protestant and Islam. Religion may no longer be the opium of the masses but, predictably, there are controls. For instance, Shanghai's 140,000 Chinese Catholics look to the local Catholic Patriotic Association as their head, not the Pope.

To discourage proselytising, Chinese nationals are not allowed by law to attend church services conducted for Shanghai's foreign community. At such services, foreigners may be required to carry their passports – just in case spot checks are done by the authorities.

Catholic

Dongjiadu Cathedral
175 Dongjiadu Road
Tel: 6377 5665
Chinese-language Sunday mass only at 7.30am.

St Ignatius Cathedral
158 Puxi Road
Tel: 6469 0930
Sunday mass (in Shanghainese) at 7am and 10.30am, and 6pm.

Foreigners may attend.
St Peter's Catholic Church
270 Chongqing Road (S)
Tel: 6467 8282
English-language Sunday mass at
Shanghai's expatriate's church is
at 10.30am; Saturday evening
mass is 5pm.

Protestant

Shanghai Community Church
53 Hengshan Road
Tel: 6437 6576
English-language service for
foreigners is at 4pm on Sunday.

Jewish

The Shanghai Jewish Centre
Shang-Mira Garden Villa No. 2,
1720 Hongqiao Road
Tel: 6278 0225
For times of Shabbat services
and to make reservations for
Shabbat meals, check its
website at www.chinajewish.org.
Chabad Jewish Centre of Pudong
Yanlord Garden, Apt 2B, Building
11, Alley 99, Puming Road, Pudong
Tel: 5878 2008
www.jewishpudong.com

Muslim

Xiaotaoyuan Mosque
52 Xiaotaoyuan Street (off Fuxing
Road (E) at Henan Road)
Tel: 6377 5443
Daily 8am–7pm.

Buddhist/Taoist

Jing An Temple
1686 Nanjing Road (W)

BELOW: offering prayers.

Daily 7.30am–4pm.
Jade Buddha Temple
170 Anyuan Road
(at Jiangning Road)
Daily 8am–noon, 1–5pm.

🅣 axes

Four- and five-star hotels add a
10 or 15 percent tax – really a
service charge in disguise – to
their bills. No service charge is
levied on restaurant bills, and tip-
ping is not encouraged.

Telephones

The **country code** for China is **86**;
the **city code** for Shanghai is
021. When calling Shanghai from
overseas, drop the prefix zero.
When making a **domestic** call
from one province to another in
China, dial the city code first
(including the prefix zero). **Local**
calls within Shanghai do not
require the city code.

To make an **international
direct dial** call from Shanghai,
dial the international access
code: 00, followed by the country
code, the area code and the local
telephone number.
Local directory assistance: 114
International operator: 116

The following are city codes of
places covered in the Excursions
section of this guidebook:
Hangzhou 0571
Moganshan 0572
Suzhou 0512

Mobile Phones

Most mobile phone users with a
roaming facility will be able to
hook up with the GSM 900
network that China uses. The
exceptions are users from Japan
(unless they have a tri-band
phone). Check with your service
provider before leaving home.

To save on expensive mobile
phone charges, consider using a
local prepaid phone card. These
are available in denominations of
RMB 100 and up at magazine
stands and convenience stores
throughout the city. You will be
given a SIM card and a local num-

ber to use. Incoming and outgoing
calls are charged by the minute.
The main service providers are
Shanghai Telecom, **Shanghai
Mobile** and **China Unicom**.
Note: local mobile numbers
begin with 13 or 15.

Public Telephones

Most public telephones in China
use prepaid phone cards, which
can be used for local, long
distance and international (IDD)
calls. Prepaid phone cards are
available in amounts of RMB 20,
RMB 30, RMB 50 and RMB 100.

Call charges are RMB 0.20 for
three minutes, while a call exceeding three minutes is charged RMB
0.10 for every six seconds (or RMB
0.60 for the fourth minute). For
some strange reason, it becomes
more expensive after the third
minute, presumably because the
authorities don't want users
hogging public phones.

International long-distance call
rates vary, but are usually fairly
expensive, over RMB 10 a minute.
Discounted rates often apply on
public holidays.

Time Zones

Shanghai (and all of China) is on
Beijing time, which is 8 hours
ahead of Greenwich Mean Time
(GMT). There is no daylight savings.

Tipping

Locals do not tip, but many
tourists do, probably because
they are used to doing so back
home. For taxis and many restaurants, you needn't tip, but in
international restaurants it is
becoming accepted. RMB 10 per
day is reasonable for a tour guide.

Tourist Information

Local Tourism Offices

A **Tourist Hotline** (tel: 6252
0000) operates daily from 10am
to 9pm. Information can be
patchy depending on who you get
on the line. Be sure to ask for an

TRANSPORT ACCOMMODATION SHOPPING ACTIVITIES A – Z LANGUAGE operator who speaks English.

The **Shanghai Tourist Information and Service Centre** (http://lyw.sh.gov.cn/en) operates branches in each of Shanghai's districts, including one at the ground level of the arrival hall of Pudong International Airport. They are geared towards Chinese-speaking travellers and are seldom of much use to foreign travellers – the level of English spoken at the counter staff varies from one service centre to another. The service centres can book hotel rooms and tours, but of more use are the free brochures and maps they give out. Also very helpful are hotel concierges in five-star hotels and local tourist magazines *(see page 301)* and websites *(see right)*.

Following are some of the more centrally located info centres:

Jingan District Tourist Information & Service Centre: 699 Nanjing Road (W); tel: 3214 0042.
Luwan District Tourist Information & Service Centre: 127 Chengdu Road (S); tel: 5386 1882.
North Huangpu Tourist Information & Service Centre: 518 Jiujiang Road; tel: 6350 3718.
South Huangpu Tourist Information & Service Centre: 159 Jiujiaochang Road; tel: 6355 5032/5033.
Pudong New Area Tourist Information & Service Centre: Super Brand Mall, 168 Lujiazui Road (W); tel: 3878 0202.

If you're in **Xintiandi**, stop by the **Shanghai Information Centre for International Visitors** at No. 2, Lane 123, Xinye Road (tel: 6384 9366), just round the corner from the Shikumen Open House Museum. It has a good range of free brochures and maps, and if you're lucky, English-speaking counter staff.

Overseas Tourism Offices

The **China National Tourism Offices** abroad are useful sources for maps, brochures and travel information. Check its website at www.cnto.org. It's likely that the

CNTO branches will recommend that you book your holiday packages with its affliated CITS – **China International Travel Service** (www.cits.net) or the CTS – **China Travel Service** (www.ctsho.com), both of which are government-run travel agencies. They handle tours, hotels, flights (international and domestic) and train tickets. You can opt to use CITS or CTS agencies even before you set foot in Shanghai. Or you can fly to Shanghai and then book your trips locally, either with the CITS or CTS office in Shanghai or a privately run travel agency *(see page 294)*.

Because language makes independent travel in China a bit of a challenge, package tours are a good option for the less adventurous. Just be warned that the government agencies might give you the official perspective on Shanghai – so you'll miss the chamber pots, filthy but charming lanes and much of Shanghai's European history in favour of modern buildings and the much-vaunted successes of the Chinese Communist Party.

Below are addresses of key CNTO offices abroad:

CNTO Australia: 19th floor, 44 Market Street, Sydney, NSW 2000, Australia; tel: 61-2 9299 4057; fax: 61-2 9290 1958.
CNTO Canada: 480 University Avenue, Suite 806, Toronto, Ontario, M5G1V2, Canada; tel: 1-416 599 6636.
CNTO Singapore: 7 Temasek Boulevard, 12–02, Suntec Tower One, Singapore 038987; tel: 65-63372 220; fax: 65-6338 0777.
CNTO UK: 4 Glentworth Street, London, NW1 5PG, UK; tel: 44-20 7935 9787; fax: 44-20 7487 5842.
CNTO USA: New York, 350 Fifth Avenue, Suite 6413, Empire State Building, New York, NY 10118, US; tel: (toll free) 1-888 760 8218; fax: 1-212 760 8809; **Los Angeles**, 550 North Brand Boulevard, Suite 910, Glendale, CA 91203, US; tel: (toll free) 1-800 670 2228, tel: 1-818 545 7507; fax: 1-818 545 7506.

ABOVE: a street vendor.

Websites

The following websites provide a variety of information on travel-related subjects on Shanghai.
General Information
www.china.org.cn
China Foreign Ministry
www.fmprc.gov.cn/eng
Shanghai Government
www.shanghai.gov.cn
www.investment.gov.cn
Health Matters
www.worldlink-shanghai.com
Banks in Shanghai
www.sbacn.org
Airport Information
www.shanghaiairport.com
Government Travel Services
www.cits.net; www.ctsho.com;
www.cnto.org; www.cnta.gov.cn
Local Media
http://english.eastday.com
www.chinadaily.com.cn
http://english.peopledaily.com
Entertainment and Events
www.cityweekend.com.cn
www.thatsshanghai.com
www.smartshanghai.com
Hotel Bookings
www.book-a-hotel-in-shanghai.com
www.shanghaihotels.com

Weights & Measures

China uses the metric system of weights and measures. Traditional Chinese measurements like *jin* (½ kg) and *chi* (1 metre) are commonly used, particularly in the local markets and more traditional shops.

L ANGUAGE

UNDERSTANDING THE LANGUAGE

General

Mandarin is the official national language of China. In addition to Mandarin, known as *putonghua*, most Chinese speak local dialects. In Shanghai, the dialect is Shanghainese, or *Shanghai-hua (see text box right)*.

Written Chinese uses characters based on pictograms, which are pictorial representations of ideas. The standard Romanisation system for Chinese characters is known as *hanyu pinyin*. It has been in use since 1958, and is used throughout this book.

Some 6,000 to 8,000 characters are in regular use; 3,000 characters are sufficient for reading a newspaper. In mainland China, simplified characters *(jian tizi)* are used, while in Hong Kong and Taiwan, complex characters *(fan tizi)* are used.

Basic Rules

Tones make it difficult for foreigners to speak Mandarin correctly, as different tones give the same syllable completely different meanings. Take the four tones of the syllable *ma*, for instance: the first tone *mā* means "mother"; the second tone *má* means "hemp"; the third tone *mǎ*

means "horse"; and the fourth tone *mà* means "to scold". There is also a fifth "neutral" tone.

There is a standard set of diacritical marks to indicate which of the four tones is used:
mā = high and even tone
má = rising tone
mǎ = falling then rising tone
mà = falling tone

Pronunciation

The pronunciation of the consonants in *hanyu pinyin* is similar to those in English: b, p, d, t, g, k are all voiceless; p, t, k are aspirated; b, d, g are not aspirated. The i after the consonants ch, c, r, sh, s, z, zh is not pronounced; it indicates that the preceding sound is lengthened.

Pinyin/Phonetic/Sound

a/a/f**a**r
an /un/r**u**n
ang/ung /l**u**ng
ao/ou/l**ou**d
b/b/**b**ath
c/ts/ra**ts**
ch/ch/**ch**ange
d/d/**d**ay
e/er/d**ir**t
e (after i,u,y)/a/tr**a**m
ei/ay/m**ay**
en/en/wh**en**
eng/eong/**ng** has a nasal sound

SHANGHAI DIALECT

Most Shanghainese prefer to speak their own dialect, *Shanghaihua*. A lilting language that sounds almost Japanese, *Shanghaihua* is unintelligible to speakers of Mandarin and other dialects. It is derived from the Wu region, south of the Yangzi River.

er/or/honour
f/f/**f**ast
g/g/**g**o
h/ch/lo**ch**
i/ee/k**ee**n
j/j/**j**eep
k/k/ca**k**e
l/l/**l**ittle
m/m/**m**onth
n/n/**n**ame
o/o/b**o**nd
p/p/tra**pp**ed
q/ch/**ch**eer
r/r/**r**ight
s/s/me**ss**
sh/sh/**sh**ade
t/t/**t**on
u/oo/sh**oo**t
u (after j,q,x,y)/as in German ü
u+/mu+d**e**
w/w/**w**ater
x/sh/as in **sh**eep
y/y/**y**ogi
z/ds/re**ds**
zh/dj/**j**ungle

Greetings

Hello	Nǐ hǎo	你好
How are you?	Nǐ hǎo ma?	你好吗?
Thank you	Xièxie	谢谢
Goodbye	Zài jiàn	再见
My name is…	Wǒ jiào…	我叫…
My last name is	Wǒ xìng	我姓…
What is your name?	Nín jiào shénme míngzì?	您叫什么名字?
What is your last name?	Nín guìxìng?	您贵姓?
I am very happy…	Wǒ hěn gāoxìng…	我很高兴…
All right	Hǎo	好
Not all right	Bù hǎo	不好
Can you speak English?	Nín huì shuō Yīngyǔ ma?	您会说英语吗?
Can you speak Chinese?	Nín huì shuō Hànyǔ ma?	您会说汉语吗?
I cannot speak Chinese	Wǒ bù huì hànyǔ	我不会汉语
I do not understand	Wǒ bù dǒng	我不懂
Do you understand?	Nín dǒng ma?	您懂吗?
Please speak a little slower	Qǐng nín shuō màn yìdiǎn	请您说慢一点
What is this called?	Zhège jiào shénme?	这个叫什么?
How do you say… ?	…Zěnme shuō?	…怎么说?
Please	Qǐng/Xièxie	请/谢谢
Never mind	Méi guānxi	没关系
Sorry	Duìbuqǐ	对不起

Pronouns

Who/who is it?	Shuí?	谁?
My/mine	Wǒ/wǒde	我/我的
You/yours (singular)	Nǐ/nǐde	你/你的
You/yours (respectful)	Nín/nínde	您/您的
He/his/she/hers	Tā/tāde/tā/tāde	他/他的/她/她的
We/ours	Wǒmen/wǒmende	我们/我们的
You/yours (plural)	Nǐmen/nǐmende	你们/你们的
They/theirs	Tāmen/tāmende	他们/他们的

Travel

Where is it?	Zài nǎr?	…在哪儿?
Do you have it here?	Zhèr… yǒu ma?	这儿有… 吗?
No/it's not here/there aren't any	Méi yǒu	没有
Hotel	Fàndiàn/bīnguǎn	饭店/宾馆
Restaurant	Fànguǎn	饭馆
Bank	Yínháng	银行
Post office	Yóujú	邮局
Toilet	Cèsuǒ	厕所
Railway station	Huǒchē zhàn	火车站
Bus station	Qìchē zhàn	汽车站
Embassy	Dàshǐguǎn	大使馆
Consulate	Lǐngshìguǎn	领事馆
Passport	Hùzhào	护照
Visa	Qiānzhèng	签证
Pharmacy	Yàodiàn	药店
Hospital	Yīyuàn	医院
Doctor	Dàifu/yīshēng	大夫/医生
Translate	Fānyì	翻译
Bar	Jiǔbā	酒吧
Do you have…?	Nín yǒu… ma?	您有…吗?
I want to go to…	Wǒ yào qù…	我要去…
I want/I would like	Wǒ yào/wǒ xiǎng yào	我要/我想要
I want to buy	Wǒ xiǎng mǎi…	我想买…
Where can I buy it?	Nǎr néng mǎi ma?	哪儿能买吗?

This/that	Zhège/nàge	这个/那个
Ticket	Piào	票
Postcard	Míngxìnpiàn	明信片
Letter	Yì fēng xìn	一封信
Airmail	Hángkōng xìn	航空信
Postage stamp	Yóupiào	邮票

Shopping

How much?	Duōshǎo?	多少?
How much does it cost?	Zhège duōshǎo qián?	这个多少钱?
Too expensive, thank you	Tài guì le, xièxie	太贵了, 谢谢
Very expensive	Hěn guì	很贵
A lot	Duō	多
Few	Shǎo	少

Money Matters, Hotels, Transport, Communications

Money	Qián	钱
Chinese currency	Rénmínbì	人民币
One yuan/one kuai (10 jiao)	Yì yuán/yí kuài	一元/一块
One jiao/one mao (10 fen)	Yì jiǎo/yì máo	一角/一毛
One fen	Yì fēn	一分
Traveller's cheque	Lǚxíng zhīpiào	旅行支票
Credit card	Xìnyòngkǎ	信用卡
Foreign currency	Wàihuìquàn	外汇券

Where can I change money?	Zài nǎr kěyǐ huàn qián?	在哪儿可以换钱?
I want to change money	Wǒ xiǎng huàn qián	我想换钱
What is the exchange rate?	Bǐjià shì duōshǎo?	比价是多少?
We want to stay for one (two/three) nights	Wǒmen xiǎng zhù yì (liǎng/sān) tiān	我们想住一(两, 三)天
How much is the room per day?	Fángjiān duōshǎo qián yì tiān?	房间多少钱一天?
Room number	Fángjiān hàomǎ	房间号码
Single room	Dānrén fángjiān	单人房间
Double room	Shuāngrén fángjiān	双人房间
Reception	Qiántái/fúwùtái	前台/服务台
Key	Yàoshi	钥匙
Clothes	Yīfu	衣服
Luggage	Xíngli	行李

Airport	Fēijīchǎng	飞机场
Bus	Gōnggòng qìchē	公共汽车
Taxi	Chūzū qìchē	出租汽车
Bicycle	Zìxíngchē	自行车
Telephone	Diànhuà	电话
Long-distance call	Chángtú diànhuà	长途电话
International call	Guójì diànhuà	国际电话
Telephone number	Diànhuà hàomǎ	电话号码

Computer	Diàn nǎo	电脑
Check e-mail	Chá diànxìn	查电信
Use the Internet	Shàngwǎng	上网

Time

When?	Shénme shíhou?	什么时候?
What time is it now?	Xiànzàijǐ diǎn zhōng?	现在几点钟?
How long?	Duōcháng shíjiān?	多长时间?
One/two/three o'clock	Yìdiǎn/liǎng diǎn/sān diǎn zhōng	一点/两点/三点钟
Early morning/morning	Zǎoshàng/shàngwǔ	早上/上午
Midday/afternoon/evening	Zhōngwǔ/xiàwǔ/wǎnshang	中午/下午/晚上
Monday/Tuesday	Xīngqīyī/Xīngqī'èr	星期一/星期二
Wednesday/Thursday	Xīngqīsān/Xīngqīsì	星期三/星期四
Friday/Saturday	Xīngqīwǔ/Xīngqīliù	星期五/星期六

Sunday	Xīngqītiān/Xīngqīrì	星期天/星期日
Weekend	Zhōumò	周末
Yesterday/today/tomorrow	Zuótiān/jīntiān/míngtiān	昨天/今天/明天
This week/last week/next week	Zhège xīngqī/shàng xīngqī/ xià xīngqī	这个星期/上星期/下星期
Hour/day/week/month	Xiǎoshí/tiān/xīngqī/yuè	小时/天/星期/月
January/February/March	Yíyuè/èryuè/sānyuè	一月/二月/三月
April/May/June	Sìyuè/wǔyuè/liùyuè	四月/五月/六月
July/August/September	Qīyuè/bāyuè/jiǔyuè	七月/八月/九月
October/November/December	Shíyuè/shíyīyuè/shí'èryuè	十月/十一月/十二月

Eating Out

Attendant/waiter/waitress	Fúwùyuán/xiǎojiě	服务员/小姐
Eat	Chīfàn	吃饭
Breakfast	Zǎofàn	早饭
Lunch	Wǔfàn	午饭
Dinner	Wǎnfàn	晚饭
Menu	Càidān	菜单
Chopsticks	Kuàizi	筷子
Knife	Dāozi	刀子
Fork	Chāzi	叉子
Spoon	Sháozi	勺子
Cup/glass	Bēizi/bōlibēi	杯子/玻璃杯
Bowl	Wǎn	碗
Plate	Pán	盘
I want…	Wǒ yào…	我要…
I do not want…	Wǒ bú yào…	我不要…
I did not order this	Zhège wǒ méi diǎn	这个我没点
I am a vegetarian	Wǒ shì chī sù de rén	我是吃素的人
I do not eat any meat or fish	Wǒ suóyǒude ròu hé yú dōu bù chī	我所有的肉和鱼都不吃
Please fry it in vegetable oil	Qǐng yòng zhíwù yóu lái chǎo	请用植物油来炒
Beer	Píjiǔ	啤酒
Liquor	Bái jiǔ	白酒
Red/white wine	Hóng/bái pú táo jiǔ	红/白葡萄酒
Mineral water	Kuàngquánshuǐ	矿泉水
Soft drinks	Yǐnliào	饮料
Green tea/black tea	Lǜchá/hóngchá	绿茶/红茶
Coffee	Kāfēi	咖啡
Tea	Cháshuǐ	茶水
Fruit	Shuǐguǒ	水果
Rice	Mǐfàn	米饭
Soup	Tāng	汤
Stir-fried dishes	Chǎo cài	炒菜
Beef/pork/lamb/chicken	Niúròu/zhūròu/yángròu/jīròu	牛肉/猪肉/羊肉/鸡肉
Vegetables	Shūcài	蔬菜
Spicy/sweet/sour/salty	Là/tián/suān/xián	辣/甜/酸/咸
Hot/cold	Rè/liáng	热/凉
Can we have the bill, please	Qǐng jié zhàng/mǎidān	请结帐/买单

Numbers

One/two/three/four/five	Yī/èr/sān/sì/wǔ	一/二/三/四/五
Six/seven/eight/nine/ten	Liù/qī/bā/jiǔ/shí	六/七/八/九/十
Eleven/twelve/twenty/thirty/forty	Shíyī/shíèr/èrshí/sānshí/sìshí	十一/十二/二十/三十/四十
Fifty/sixty/seventy/eighty/ninety	Wǔshí/liùshí/qīshí/bāshí/jiǔshí	五十/六十/七十/八十/九十
One hundred	Yìbǎi	一百
One hundred and one	Yìbǎi língyī	一百零一
Two hundred/three hundred	Liǎng bǎi/sān bǎi	两百/三百
Four hundred/five hundred	Sì bǎi/wǔ bǎi	四百/五百
One thousand	Yìqiān	一千

FURTHER READING

History

Life and Death in Shanghai by Nien Ching, HarperCollins, 1995. A beautifully written account of a privileged woman's ordeal during the Cultural Revolution in Shanghai.

Red Azalea by Anchee Min, Berkeley Publishing Group, 1995. An honest memoir of growing up during the Cultural Revolution in Shanghai, chronicling the injustices and torments through the eyes of a teenage girl.

In Search of Old Shanghai by Lynn Pan, Joint Publishing Co., 1982. Meticulously researched and the best historical account of Old Shanghai.

The Soong Dynasty by Sterling Seagrave, Vintage, 1992. Well-researched book that reads like a novel on the Soongs, Old Shanghai's "first family", whose rise parallels China's story in the first half of the 20th century.

Strangers Always: A Jewish Family in Wartime Shanghai by Rena Krasno, Pacific View Press, 1992. Krasno, born and raised in Shanghai, used her diaries and letters as the basis for this account of wartime Shanghai.

Architecture

Building Shanghai: The Story of China's Gateway by Edward Denison and Ren Guangyu, Wiley, 2006. A captivating account of the evolution of the city's architecture – beautifully illustrated with archival maps and photographs.

A Last Look: Western Architecture in Old Shanghai by Tess Johnston and Deke Erh, Old China Hand Press, 2003. Shanghai's legacy of Western architecture – some of it already gone – cap-

tured over 25 years by historian Johnston and photographer Erh.

Phantom Shanghai by Greg Girard, Magenta Foundation, 2007. A photographic documentation of the architectural destruction and reinvention of Shanghai.

Shanghai Art Deco by Tess Johnston and Deke Erh, Old China Hand Press, 2006. Johnston and Erh document Shanghai's signature Art Deco style in architecture, interior design and objects. Archival photographs and maps are also included.

Contemporary China

Chinese Lessons: Five Classmates and the Story of New China by John Pomfret, Henry Holt & Co., 2006. Former *Washington Post* Beijing bureau chief Pomfret insightfully relates the experiences of his five classmates from Nanjing University, and through them, examines the dramatic changes in recent Chinese history.

Country Driving: A Journey Through China from Farm to Factory by Peter Hessler, HarperCollins, 2009. The former *New Yorker China* correspondent's final chapter in his trilogy of a changing China: Hessler drives through China, chronicling the human side of the China boom.

Factory Girls: From Village to City in a Changing China by Leslie Chang, Spiegel & Grau, 2008. *Wall Street Journal* correspondent Chang tells the story of the exodus of China's rural population through the lives of two teenage girls. A remarkable portrait of a side of China that is often hidden.

One Billion Customers: Lessons from the Front Lines of Doing Business in China by Jim McGre-

gor, Free Press, 2005. Journalist-turned-businessman McGregor's clear-eyed account of two decades of doing business in China.

Operation Yao Ming: The Chinese Sports Empire, American Big Business and the Making of an NBA Superstar by Brook Larmer, Gotham Books, 2005. Former *Newsweek* journalist Larmer chronicles the rise of Shanghai boy Yao Ming. Vividly illustrating the strictures of the sports system and modern Chinese society.

The Party: The Secret World of China's Communist Rulers by Richard McGregor, Harper, 2010. An investigation into the inner workings of the Communist Party is banned in China and key to understanding the country.

FEEDBACK

We do our best to ensure the information in this book is as accurate and up to date as possible. The books are updated on a regular basis, using local contacts. However, some mistakes and omissions are inevitable and we are ultimately reliant on our readers to put us in the picture.

We welcome your feedback on your experiences of using the book "on the road". We'll acknowledge all contributions and offer an Insight Guide to the best letters received.

Please write to us at:
Insight Guides
PO Box 7910
London SE1 1WE
United Kingdom
Or send an e-mail to:
insight@apaguide.co.uk

ART & PHOTO CREDITS

PHOTO FEATURES

SHANGHAI STREET ATLAS

The key map shows the area of Shanghai covered by the atlas
section. An index of street names and places of interest
shown on the maps can be found on the following pages. For
each entry there is a page number and grid reference

Map Legend

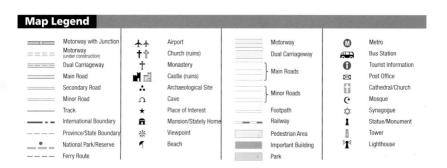

	Motorway with Junction	✈ ✈	Airport		Motorway	Ⓜ	Metro
	Motorway (under construction)	† ✝	Church (ruins)		Dual Carriageway	🚌	Bus Station
	Dual Carriageway	†	Monastery	}	Main Roads	❶	Tourist Information
	Main Road	🏰 🏚	Castle (ruins)			✉	Post Office
	Secondary Road	∴	Archaeological Site	}	Minor Roads	✝	Cathedral/Church
	Minor Road	∩	Cave			☾	Mosque
	Track	★	Place of Interest		Footpath	✡	Synagogue
	International Boundary	🏛	Mansion/Stately Home		Railway	🗼	Statue/Monument
	Province/State Boundary	✳	Viewpoint		Pedestrian Area	⬭	Tower
	National Park/Reserve	🏌	Beach		Important Building	🎇	Lighthouse
	Ferry Route				Park		

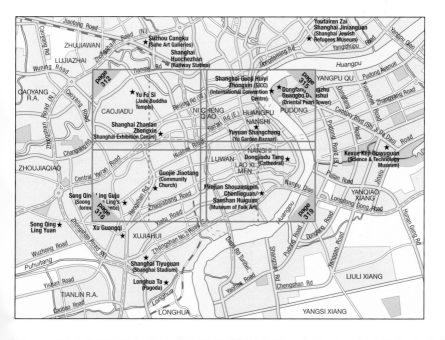

HONGHOU
虹口區

Tiantong Rd

Suzhouhe Road

Guoqing Road

Beisuzhou Road

Zhejiang Road North

Fujian Road North

Shanxi Road North

Tiantong Road

(Wusong)

Henan Rd N.

Suzhouhe Rd

Waitan
(former
Consu

Peni
Sha

Suzhou Creek

(Beisuzhou Lu)

(Suzhouhe Lu)

Zhou Creek

Central Henan Road

Shanghai Waitan Meishuguan
(Rockbund
Art Museum)

Yuanmingyuan Rd

Zhongguo Yin!
(Bank of C

Dianchi R

HUANGPU
黄浦區

Huangpu
Theatre

Zhongguo
Theatre

Xinzha Road

Xiamen

Beijing Road East

Guling Road

Huanghe

Wenzhou Rd

Road (Tibet (Xizang) Beilu)

Zhejiang Rd N.)

(Beijing Donglu)

Central Fujian Road

Lihe Road

Central Yunnan Rd

Guizhou Road

Guangxi Road

Niuzhuang Rd

Ningbo Road

Tianjin Road

Tianjin Road

Nanjing Road Pedestrian Mall

(Tianjin Lu)

Henan Rd

NANJING
ROAD EAST
南京東路 Ⓜ

Heping Fanc
(Fairmont Peace He

Heping Huiz
Fa
(Swate
Peace

Hong Miao
(Holy Trinity,
Red Temple)

Hankou Ro

Laohaig
(Customs Ho

Jiujiang

Shanghai №1
Department
Store

Nanjing Road East

Raffles City

(Jiujiang Lu)

(Hankou Lu)

Pudong Fazhan Yi
(Pudong Development

Foreign Languages
Bookstore

Central Shandong

Henan Zhong Lu)

Huaxia
M on the

PEOPLE'S
SQUARE
人民廣場站

Fengyang

Daguangming
Dian Ying
(Grand Cinema)

PEOPLE'S PARK
(RENMIN GONGYUAN)

Xincheng Road

Nanjing Rd West

Mu'en Tang
(Moore Church)

Renmin Grand
Stage Theatre

Hankou Road

Jiujiang

Rd

(Fujian Zhonglu)

(Fuzhou Lu)

Fuzhou
Road

Guangdong Road

(Guangdong Lu)

Ruose
(St Jose

Shanghai
Dangdai
Yishu Guan
(MoCA)

Chengshi Guihua Guan
(Urban Planning Centre)

PEOPLE'S SQUARE
人民廣場站 Ⓜ

Yifu Wutai
(Theatre)

Fuzhou Road

Guangxi Road

Zhejiang Road

Beihai North

Yan'an Freeway (elevated)

Shanghai Ziran Bowuguan
(Museum of Natural History)

Shenze Road

Shandong Rd S.

(Yan'an Do

Jiangy

Shanghai
Meishu Guan
Laoguan
(Art Museum)

Shanghai Renmin
Zhengfu
(City Hall)

Jiangyin Rd

Shanghai Dajuyuan
(Grand Theatre)

Renmin Guangchang
(People's Square)

Renmin Da Dao)

People's Avenue

Central (Xizang) Tibet Road

Da Shijie
(Great World)

Yongshou Road

Ninghai Hubei
Rd S. L.

Jinling Road

Zhejiang Rd S.

Henan Road South

Central

Ruose
(St Jose

Central
Plaza

Weihai Rd

Wusheng Road

Huangpi Road North

Wusheng Road

Shanghai Bowuguan
(Shanghai Museum)

Yan'an Road East

Shanghai
Yinyueting
(Concert Hall)

Guangxi Road South

Yunnan Road South

Shanghai
Cybermart

Fuyou Road

Fuyou Lu Qingzhensi
(Fuyou Rd Mosque)

Chenxi
(Nu

Chongqing Rd North

Dagu Road

PEOPLE'S PARK
(RENMIN GONGYUAN)

HUANGPI ROAD SOUTH
黄陂南路站 Ⓜ

Central Jinling Road

Pu'an

Road

(Huaihai Zhonglu)

Tibet (Xizang) Road (Tibet Lu)

Times
Square

Taoyuan
Road

Shouning Rd

(Renmin Nanlu)

Qinglian St

Dongtaidian St

Luxiangyuan Rd

Jiangyin St

Baiyun Guan
(Taoist Temple)

Dajingge
(Dajing Tower)

Wanzhu St

Dajing

(Fangbang Zhonglu)

Qinglian Rd

Shidong

Cang Bao Lou
(Can Bao Bldg)

Cent

(Henan Nanlu)

Jinling Road West

Hong Kong
Plaza

Renmin Bellu)

Central Huaihai Road

Songshan Road

HUAIHAI
GONGYUAN

Dongtai Lu
Shichang
(Antiques Market)

Kuaiji

Central Fangbang Rd E.

Jinjia Fang

Xiaotaoy
Qingzhe
(Peach Ore
Mosqu

Chongqing Rd South (Chongqing Bellu)

Shui On
Plaza

Central
Plaza

Xing'an Road

Taicang Road

Danshui Road

Xing'an Road (Xing'an Lu)

(Taicang Lu)

Chongde Road

Ji'an

Zizhong Road

Dongtai Road

Fuxing Road East

Kongjia Long

Shigi Long

LAOXIMEN
老西门站 Ⓜ

Xintiandi

TAIPINGQIAO
GONGYUAN

Liuhekou Road (Liuhekou Lu)

Madang Road

Shanghai Wanshang
Huaniaoi Shichang
(Wanshang Bird & Flower Market)

Jingxiu St

312

A   B

N

JINGAN
GONGYUAN

JIANGSU ROAD
江苏路站
Ⓜ

(Yuyuan Lu)

Zhenning Road (Zhenning Lu)

Zhu'anbang Road East

Nanjing Road West

Shi Shaonian Gong
(Municipal Children's
Palace)

Yan'an Freeway (eleva

Husham Road

Cai Yuanpei G
(Cai Yuanpei
former residence

Julu

1

Yuyuan Road

Central Yan'an Road (Yan'an Zhonglu)

Huadong
Hospital

Central Wulumuqi Road

Hilton
Hotel

(Huashan Lu)

Changshu Road (Changshu

Ch

Anhua Road (Anhua Lu)

Jiangsu Road (Jiangsu Lu)

Zhenning Road

Huashan Road

Huashan
Hospital

(Huashan Lu)

(Changle Lu)

Lixi Road (Lixi Lu)

Changle Road

(Anfu Lu)

Wuyi Road

(Changle Lu)

Anfu Road

Wulumuqi Zhonglu

(Wuyuan Lu)

CHANGSHU ROA
常熟路站

2

Jiangsu Road

Caojiayna Lu

Changle Road

Jiangsu Road

DINGXIANG
HUAYUAN
(GARDEN)

(Huashan Lu)

Wukang Lu

Wuyuan Road

Cotton
Club

CHANGSHU ROA

Panyu Road

Huashan Road

Xinguo Road (Xinguo Lu)

Gaoyou Road

Fuxing Road West (Fuxing Xilu)

JZ

Nie Er

Faguo Lingsh
(French Consul
General's Res

Le Passage
Fuxing

Meiguo Lingshiguan
(US Consulate-General)

Dongp

Wulumuqi Rd S.

(Hunan Lu)

Hunan Road

Riben Lingshiguan
(Japanese Consul-
General's Residence)

Taojiang

Panyu Road (Panyu Lu)

Hunan Road

SHANGHAI LIBRARY
上海图书馆 Ⓜ

Shanghai Tushuguan
(Shanghai Library)

Sha
Yingyue Xu
(Conserva
Music Middle S

Niuqiaobang

Xingguo Road (Xingguo Lu)

Ferguson
Lane

Wukang Road

Lao Meiguo Xuesheng
(former Shanghai
American School)

Guojie
(Shang
Interna
Commu
Church

3

Huashan Lu

Tai'an Road (Tai'an Lu)

(Huaihai Zhonglu)

Wuxing Road

Gao'an Road

HENGSHAN ROAD
衡山路站 Ⓜ

Hengshan Rd

Wukang Road

Wukang Dalou
(Normandie Apartments)

Gao'an Rd

Yongjia Road

Anting Road

Fahuazhen Road (Fahuazhen Lu)

Central Huaihai Road

Wanping Rd

Kangping Road

Song Qingling
(Soong Ching Ling's
former residence)

Shanghai Ying Cheng
(Shanghai Film Art Centre)

Regal International
East Asia

Gao'an Lu

Jianguo Rd W.

Xinhua Road
(Xinhua Lu)

Tianping Road

Yuting Road

Zhongguo Gongchandang
Shanghai Shi Wei Yuanhui
(Communist Party HQ)

Wanping Lu

(Hengshan Lu)

Hengshan
Picardie
Hotel

DONGAN

Panyu Rd

Hualhai Road West (Huaihai Xilu)

Jiaotong Daxue
(Shanghai Jiaotong
University)

HENGSHAN
GONGYUAN

Zhongguo Tielu
Gongren Jinian Ta
(Chinese Railroad
Workers)

Wuxing Lu

4

Huashan Road

Guangyuan Road

Hengshan Road

Xiao Hong Lou
(La Villa Rouge)

Wanping Lu

Zhaojiabang Road

东

(Tianping Lu)

(Huashan Lu)

Kangping Lu

Hengshan Road

XUJIAHUI
GONGYUAN

Zhaojiabang Road

Shangha
Univ

0   500 m

0   500 yds

A   B

313

(Julu Lu)

(Julu Lu)

Jinxian Road (Jinxian Lu)

(Changle Lu)

Changle Road

Lanxin Daxiyuan
(Lyceum Theatre)

Central Huaihai Road

Xing'an Rd

Chongqing Road South (Chongqing Rd)

Chongqing Road South (Chongqing Beilu)

Isetan

Yandang Entertainment Street

Road

1

Xiangyang Road North (Xiangyang Beilu)

Shaanxi Road South

Maoming Road South

New Hualian
Commercial Building

Nanchang

(Changle Lu)

Xinle Road

Xinle Road

Baisheng Gouwu
Zhongxin
(Parkson Department
Store)

Guotai Dianyingyuan
(Cathay Cinema)

Jinchan
Hotel

Sheng Nigulasi Jiaotang
(former St Nicholas
Church)

Gaolan Road

FUXING
GONGYUAN

Mansion
Complex

XIANGYANG
GONGYUAN

Zhonglu

(Huaihai)

SHAANXI
ROAD SOUTH
陕西南路站

Sun Zhongshan Guju
(former Residence of
Sun Yat-sen)

Donghu Road

Xiangshan
Road

Central Fuxing Road

ongguo Lanyin
abu Guan
inese Printed Blue
nkeen Exhibition Hall)

SHAANXI
ROAD SOUTH
陕西南路站

Nanchang Road

(Fuxing Zhonglu)

(Shaanxi Nanlu)

Zhou Enlai Guju
(former residence of
Zhou En-lai)

North-South Freeway (elevated)

Central Huaihai Road

Yinyue Xueyuan
(Conservatory
of Music)

Ruijin No.2 Road

Hefei Rd

2

(Fenyang)

Ruijin
Guesthouse

Damuqiao Road

ntral Fuxing Road

Fenyang Rd

Wenhua
Guangchang
(Cultural Square)

Shanghai Gongyi
Meishuguan
(Arts & Crafts Museum)

Yongjia Road

Yongkang Road

(Sinan Lu)

Ruijin Yi Yuan
(Ruijin Hospital)

shkin
angle

(Yongjia Lu)

Jiande Road

Sinan Rd

Puxijin
(Pushkin)

Shaoxing Road (Shaoxing Lu)

Central Jianguo Road

(Xiangyang Nanlu)

Tianzi Fang
(Art Centre)

Taikang Road

3

Taiyuan Road

(Jianguo Xilu)

(Shaanxi Nanlu)

Jianguo Road West

Ruijin 2-Lu

Xujiahui Road

(Xujiahui Lu)

Yueyang Road

(Damuqiao Lu)

Zhaojiabang Road

Dapu Road

DAMUQIAO ROAD
大木桥路站

Zhaojiabang Road

Yueyang Lu

Shanghai Gongan Bowuguan
(Museum of Public Security)

Xietu Road

(Zhaojiabang Lu)

(Zhaojiabang Lu)

Damuqiao Road (Damuqiao Lu)

(Dapu Lu)

4

Pingjiang Road

(Pingjiang Lu)

(Yixueyuan Lu)

Xiaomuqiao Road

Xietu Lu

Ruijin Branch

Rihui Branch

ueyuan Road

Fenglin Road (Fenglin Lu)

Qingzhen Road

(Qingzhen Lu)

(Xiaomuqiao Lu)

Xietu Road

(Quxi Lu)

Quxi Rd

Zhongshan
Hospital

Pediatric
Hospital

Chaling Road

318

314

A B

Yangdang

Entertainment Street

Nanchang
Road

FUXING
GONGYUAN

317

Xing'an Rd

Xing'an Lu

Taicang Lu

(Taicang Lu)

Chonde Road

Liuhekou Road (Liuhekou Lu)

Chongqing Road South (Chongqing Belu)

Chongqing Road South (Chongqing Belu)

Xintiandi

Zhonggong
Yidahuizhi
(Site of the First
National Congress
of the CPC)

Xintiandi

TAIPINGQIAO
GONGYUAN

Danshui Road

Zizhong
Road

Huangpi Road South

Jian Rd

(Fuxing Zhonglu)

Shunchang
Road

(Hefei Lu)

Central Fuxing Road

LUWAN
卢湾区

Hefei Road

North-South Freeway (elevated)

Central
Jianguo Rd

Tianzi Fang
(Art Centre)

Taikang Road

Xujiahui Road (Xujiahui Lu)

Dapu Road

Xiexu Road

Nantangbang Rd

Xietu Road

(Dapu Lu)

(Danshui Lu)

Madang Lu

Madang Road

Jianguo Road East

Yongnian Road

Mengzi Road

Xiexu Road

Luban Road (Luban Lu)

Luban Road (Luban Lu)

LUBAN ROAD
鲁班路站 Ⓜ

0   500 m
0   500 yds

(Xiexu Lu)

(Huangpi Namlu)

Shunchang Lu

Road

Lujiabang Road

Jumen Road

Mengzi Rd W.

Xiexu   Road

(Xietu Lu)

(Nantangbang Lu)

Mengzi Lu

(Jumen Lu)

Wuliqiao Road (Wuliqiao Lu)

Mengzi
Road

Quxi Road (Quxi Lu)

Jumen
Road

Runan Road

Quxi Road

Dongtai Lu Shichang
(Antiques Market)

Dongtai Road

Renmin

Road

Shanghai Wanshang
Huaniaoi Shichang
(Wanshang Bird
& Flower Market)

Jinjia Fang

Kongjia
Long

Fuxing Road East

Xicangon

Jingxiu St

Menghua St.

(Zizhong Lu)

Ji'an Road

Dongjia Lu

Zhaozhou Road

Tanglawan Rd

LAOXIMEN
老西门站

Wen Miao
(Confucius Temple)

Wen Miao Rd.

Tibet (Xizang) Road South

Zhonghua Road

Penglai Road

Xuegian Street

Anian Road

(Dajj Lu)

Daxing

Road

(Jianguo Donglu)

Zhizaoju Road

Fangxie Road

Dajj Road

Hunan
Stadium

Dalin Road

(Zhizaoju Lu)

Jiangyin Lu

(Lujiabang Lu)

(Liyuan Lu)

(Huining Lu)

Liyuan Road

Huining Road

Xietu Road

Xilingjiazhai Road

XIZANG ROAD SOUTH
西藏南路站 Ⓜ

Tibet (Xizang) Nanlu

Tibet (Xizang) Road South

(Quxi

Lu)

Zhizaoju Road

Zhongshan No.1 Road South (Zhongshan Nan 1-Lu)

World EXPO 2010

Gaoxiong Ro

1

2

3

4

D E

N

NANSHI
南市

Wangyun Road

Guangqi Road South (Guangqi Nanlu)

(Penglai Lu)

Lingji St

Fuxing Rd East

Laoxin St

Doushi Street

Waima Road

Penglai Rd

Maojia Road

Meijia St

Ningle Road

Qiaojia Road

(Miezhu Lu)

Wailangjiaqiao Street

Xinmatou Street

(Waima Lu)

Yujia Long

Xundao Street (Xundao Jie)

Zhonghua Road (Zhonghua Lu)

Zixia Road

Huayi Rd

Beishija

Long

Zhuhangmatou St

Zhongshan Road South Zhongshan Nanlu

(Wangjiamatou Lu)

ngwen Road

Huangjia Road

Wangjiamatou Road

Miezhu Road

Wangliazuijiao Street

Waicang-qiao St

Wanyumatou St

Gongyimatou St

(Zhonghua Lu)

Dongjiadu Road (Dongjiadu Lu)

Wanyu St

Dongjiadu
Tianzhutang
(Dongjiadu
Cathedral)

(Henan Nanlu)

(Jiangyin Jie)

Xigouyu Road

Sanguyuan Street

Dongjiangyin Street

Nangu St

Nancang Street

Laiyimatou Rd

Luxi Street

Waima Road

HUANGPU
黄浦區

Lujiabang Road

Liushi Road

(Dongjiangyin Jie)

Duojia Road

Xuejiabang Rd

DONGJIADU
董家渡

(Huining Lu)

nzhushan Rd

Hainan Long W.

**South Bund
Fabric Market**

(Duojia Lu)

Puyu Road West

Haichao Road

Caoxieyan Road

Youchematou St

(Waima Road)

Huangpu

Xietu Road East (Xietu Donglu)

East

Nanjiang St

NANPU BRIDGE
南浦大橋站

Chezhan Road East

Puyu

(Quxi Lu)

PUDONG
浦东

Chezhan Rd
West

nzhu Lu)

njian Shoucangpin
Chenlieguan/
Sanshan Huiguan
Museum of Folk Art)

Miaojiang Rd

Nanpu Qiao (Nanpu Bridge)

AI
UAN

ongshan Road South (Zhongshan Nanlu)

World E X P O 2010

Tannan Road

Miaojiang Rd

Nanmatou Road

Jiaohan Road

rld E X P O 2010

Sanliqiao Road East

Barsongyuan Rd

Huayuangang Rd

World E X P O 2010

Yinan Road

(Yinan Lu)

(Nanmatou Lu)

Pusan Rd

Pudong Road South

orld Expo Museum

A B

Legend
- Hotel
- Restaurant

1

Guangfu Road W. (Guangfu Xilu)
Suzhou Creek (Wusong)
Guilin Road
Changde Road
Jiaozhou Road

Macao Rd
Xikang Road
Shaanxi Rd North
CHANGSHOU PARK
(Shaanxi Beilu)
Changshou (Changshou Lu)
Xikang Lu
Jiangning Road
Changhua Road
Xinhui Lu
Xisu

Anyuan Road
(Jiangning Lu)

CHANGSHOU ROAD
常熟路站

Xinhui Road
(Aiyuan Lu)
Renne Road
Shaanxi Road North
(Haifan

2

Changshou Road
Holiday Inn Vista Shanghai

Motel 168
Anyuan Road

Changde Lu
Xikang Road
Haifang Road

JING'AN
静安区

Shaanxi
(Jiaozhou Lu)
CHANGPING ROAD
昌平路站
(Changping Lu)
Kangding Lu
Xikang

Yuyao Lu
Yanping Road
Jiaozhou Road

3

Wuning Road South (Wuning Jielu)
Changping Road
(Kangding Lu)
Kangding Road
Changde Road

Yuyao Road
Wuding Road
(Wuding Lu)
Xinzha Road

Kangding Road
(Yanping Lu)
Kangding Road
Wanhangdu Road
(Wuding Xilu)
Xinzha Road

Beijing Road West
Ma

4

(Wanhangdu Lu)
Wanhangdu Road (Wanhangdu Lu)

Le Bouchon

Wuding Road West
Zhenning Road
Wulumuqi
Yuyuan Road
(Yuyuan Lu)

Yuyuan Road
Jiu Gong City Plaza

Jingan Si
(Jing An Temple)
JINGAN TEMPLE
静安寺站
Hueshan

Bali Laguna

JING AN GONGYUAN

CHANGNING
长宁区

Jiangsu Road

N
0 — 500 m
0 — 500 yds

Yuyuan Road (Yuyuan Lu)
Zhenning Road
Road North

Nanjing Road West
Shi Shaonian Gong
(Municipal Children's Palace)

Hilton Hotel

Yan'an Freew

Cai Yuanpe
(Cai Yuanpei
former resid

A B

Legend:
- Hotel
- Restaurant

HONGKOU
虹口区

HUANGPU
黄浦区

LAOXIMEN
老西门站

Map labels (A column):
Zhejiang Road North
Tiantong Rd
Guoqing Road
Tibet (Xizang) Rd N
Suzhouhe Road
Beisuzhou Road
Zhejiang Rd N
Xiamen
Xinzha Road
Huangho
Wenzhou Rd
Beijing Road East
Guling Road
Central Yunnan Rd
Luhe Road
Guizhou Road
Jinmen Dajiudian (Pacific Hotel)
Guoji Fandian (Park Hotel)
Fengyang
PEOPLE'S SQUARE
人民广场站
Barbarossa Lounge
Nanjing Rd West
Xinchang Road
Xizang
Shanghai Meishu Guan Laoguan (Art Museum)
Art Lab
Shanghai Dangdai Yishu Guan
PEOPLE'S SQUARE
人民广场站
Kathleen's 5
JW Marriott Hotel
Shanghai Renmin Zhengfu (City Hall)
Shanghai Dajuyuan (Grand Theatre)
Wagas
Central Plaza
Weihai Road
People's Avenue (Renmin Da Dao)
Renmin Guangchang (People's Square)
Huangpi Road North
Shanghai Bowuguan (Shanghai Museum)
Wusheng Road
Wusheng Road
Chongqing Rd South (Chongqing Beilu)
Dagu Road
Yan'an Road East
PEOPLE'S PARK (RENMIN GONGYUAN)
HUANGPI ROAD SOUTH
黄陂南路站
Central Jinling Road
Jinling Road West
Hong Kong Plaza
Central Huaihai Road
Shui On Plaza
Central Plaza
Xing an Road (Xing an Lu)
Danshui Road
Taicang Road
Madang Road
T8
Xintiandi
Crystal Jade, Din Tai Fung
TAIPINGQIAO GONGYUAN
Xing an Road
Liuhekou Road (Liuhekou Lu)
Chengde Road
Jinan Rd
Zizhong Road
HUNHAI GONGYUAN

Map labels (B column):
Henan Rd N.
Tiantong Road
Fujian Road North
Shanxi Road North
(Wusong)
Central Jiangxi Road
Suzhou Creek
(Suzhouhe Lu)
(Beisuzhou Lu)
Central Henan Road
Beijing Donglu
Niuzhuang Road
(Tianjin Lu)
NANJING ROAD EAST
南京东路站
Central Fujian Rd
Ningbo Road
Tianjin Rd
East Asia Hotel
Nanjing Road Pedestrian Mall
(Jiujiang Lu)
Yang's Fry Dumplings
Allure East
Nanjing Rd
Le Royal Meridien
Sofitel Hyland
(Hankou Lu)
Central Shandong Rd
Fuzhou Rd
Howard Johnson Plaza
Jiujiang
Central Zhejiang Road
Fujian
Hubei
(Fuzhou Lu)
Hamilton House
Mao Zhu Shi Jia Xiang Cai
Hankou Road
Fuzhou Road
Zhejiang
Henan Zhong Rd
Guangdong Road
(Guangdong Lu)
iiijit!
Guangdong Rd
Lost Heaven
Beihai Road
Central (Xizang) Tibet Road
Zhongr
Yan'an Freeway (elevated)
Fujian Rd S.
Shenxiang Rd S
Shandong Rd S
Henan Road South
Ruose (St Jo
Ninghai Road
Hubei Rd S.
Jinling Road E.
Da Shijie (Great World)
Guizhou Road South
Yongshou Road
Zhejiang Rd S.
Jinling Road E.
YMCA Hotel
Shanghai Yinyue Ting (Concert Hall)
Tibet (Xizang)
Rd South
(Huaihai Zhonglu)
Luxiangyuan
Fuyou Road (Fu
Chenxiang (Nunne
Sh
Rest
Shanghai
Cybermart
Times Square
Taoyuan Road
Shouning Road
Yunnan (Nanlu)
Renmin Lu
Qinlian St
Donggangnian St
Baiyun Guan (Taoist Temple)
Dajingge (Dajing Tower)
Daijing
Wanzhu St
Kuaiji
Renmin
Qinglian St
Fangbang Rd (Fangbang Zhonglu)
Zifu St
Road
Shidi St
(Henan Nanlu)
Songxue St
Shipi Long
Jinilia Fang
Kongjia Long
Fuxing Road East
Jingxiu St
Central Fangbang Rd

u Music Café
Xindalu Chinese Kitchen
use Hotel

Huangpu

0   500 m
0   500 yds

Renmin Yingxiong Jinianbei
(Monument to the People's Heroes)

Li
al Cuisine

NGPU
NGYUAN

altan Canguang Sui Dao
und Sightseeing Tunnel)

Shanghai
Guoji Huiyi
Zhongxin (SICC)
(International Convention
Centre)

MINGZHU
GONGYUAN

Shanghai Haiyang
Shuizuguan
(Ocean Aquarium)

Dongfang Mingzhu
Guangbo Dianshui
(Oriental Pearl Tower)

Yijian Rd Tunnel

Yincheng Road North

Bank of India
Shanghai HQ

Pudong Road South (Pudou Nanlu)

Novotel Atlantis Shanghai

N

1

Fenghe Road

Oriental Riverside
Hotel

Dongguang Rd

Yincheng
Road

Dongchen Rd (Pudon Nanlu)

LUJIAZUI
陆家嘴

Ye Shanghai

RIVERSIDE
PARK

LUJIAZUI
陆家嘴站

Ritz-Carlton
Pudong

100 Century
Avenue

Zhen Da Guangchang
(Super Brand Mall)

International
Financial
Centre

Century

LUJIAZUI
GONGYUAN

Boulevard

HoF

Chen Guichun Jiuzhai
(Chen Guichen's
House)

Lujiazui Road East

Shanghai Zhengjuan
Jiaoyisuo
(Stock Exchange
Building)

Daniel 1

the

s
v Heights,
ampoa Club,
n Georges

Yan'an Road East Tunnel

Element
Fresh

Yi Café

Fucheng Road

Jade on
36

Pudong
Shangri-La

Yincheng Road West

Park Hyatt
Shanghai

Jinmao Dasha
(Jin Mao Tower)

Huayuanshiqiao Road

Yincheng Rd

Shanghai
World Financial
Centre

Shanghai Tower
(under construction)

Yincheng Road South

(Shi Ji Da Dao)

2

Shanghai Uncle,
Courtyard by Marriott,
Holiday Inn Shanghai Pudong,
Ramada Pudong Airport

Jinling Dong Lu Ma Tou
(Jinling Pier)

onglu

nyong'an Rd

nmin
Road

Anren St
iang St

GUCHENG
GONGYUAN

iang
tou
n Green Wave
Pavilion

uxinting
eahouse

Xianmingju
(City Temple of Shanghai)

gbang Rd
(Fangbang Zhonglu)

Zhongshan No 2 Road East

Dajieng Road

Gangu St
Wutong
Road

Tucheng Lu

Dongchang Road

P U D O N G
浦 东

Purmin Road (Purmin Lu)

Sangcheng Road

Qixin Road

3

Zhoujin Rd

hai
use

Rd Pudou

ailou
Road

Xueyuan Road (Xueyuan Lu)

Shiliu Puhong Qixlang
(Cloth Market)

Dong Street

Waxiangua

Laotaiping St

Zhonghua Road

Xinmatou St

Zhongshan Road South (Zhongshan Nanlu)

Fuxing Road East Tunnel

Caolontang Rd

4

Sipailou Road

Xiyajie Long

(Fuxing Donglu)

N A N S H I
南 市

Lingji St

Guangqi Road South

Meijia St
Penglai Rd

Xundao Street

Zhonghua Road

Miezhu Road

Fuxing Road E.

Laoxin St

Joushi Street

Joushi
Road

Waima Road (Waima Lu)

Stiller's

Table #1

Huangpu

Wangyun Road

Maojia

Road

The Waterhouse at South Bund

320

A **B**

Hotel
Restaurant

JIANGSU ROAD
江苏路站

(Yuyuan Lu)

Zhenning Road (Zhenning Lu)

Zhu'anbang Road East

Nanjing Road West

Shi Shaonian Gong
(Municipal Children's Palace)

JING AN
GONGYUAN

Yan'an Freeway (elevated)

Guyi Huna
Restaurar

Cai Yuanpei Guju
(Cai Yuanpei
former residence)

Julu Lu

Hushan Road

Central Wulumuqi Road

1

Yuyuan Road

Da Marco

Central Yan'an Road (Yan'an Zhonglu)

Huashan Road

Zhenning Road

Hilton
Hotel

Jing An
Hotel

The Old
House Inn

(Huashan Road)

Changle Road

(Changle Lu)

Changshu Road (Changshu Lu)

Changle

Anhua Road (Anhua Lu)

Lixi Road (Lixi Lu)

Wuyi Road

Jiangsu Road (Jiangsu Lu)

Caoujayna Road

Changle Road

(Changle Lu)

Jiangsu Road

Changle Road

Anfu Road

(Anfu Lu)

(Wulumuqi Zhonglu)

Wuyuan Road

CHANGSHU ROAD
常熟路站

2

1221

Yan'an Road West (Yan'an Xilu)

Johnny Moo's

Simply Thai

Xian Yue
Hien

Huashan Road

DINGXIANG
HUAYUAN
(GARDEN)

Wukang Road

Boxing Cat
Brewery

South
Beauty

Taojiang

Fuxing Road West (Fuxing Xilu)

Ginger
Café

Caoou Road

Boonna 2

Arugula

O'Malley's
Irish Pub

Dongping

Wulumuqi Rd S.

Madison

Azul

Sim
Th

Radisson Plaza
Xingguo Hotel

Huashan Road

Xingguo Road (Xingguo Lu)

(Hunan Lu)

Hunan Road

Coffee Tree,
Franck

Shanghai
Tushuguan
(Shanghai
Library)

Pasta Fresca
di Salvatore

Sasha'
Yang's
Kitchen

3

Niuqiaobang

Hunan Road

Ferguson
Lane

Wukang Road

SHANGHAI LIBRARY
上海图书馆

Gao'an Road

HENGSHAN ROAD
衡山路站

Hengshan Rd

Lin Yutong Road (Linyutong Lu)

Huashan Road

Tai'an Road (Tai'an Lu)

(Huaihai Zhonglu)

Wuxing Road

Wukang Dalou
(Normandie Apartments)

Song Qingling
(Soong Ching Ling's
former residence)

Kangping Road

Regal International
East Asia Hotel

Yongjia Road

Anting
Villa
Hotel

Anting Road

Panyu Road

Fahuazhen Road (Fahuazhen Lu)

Central Huaihai Road

Yuqing Road

Jianguo Rd West

4

Xinhua Road
(Xinhua Lu)

Panyu Rd

Huaihai Road West (Huaihai Xilu)

Huashan Road

Guangyuan Road

Jiaotong Daxue
(Shanghai Jiaotong
University)

Kangping Road

Tianping Road

Hengshan Road

Wanping Rd

Hengshan
Picardie Hotel

HENGSHAN
GONGYUAN

Keven
Café

Wuping Lu

XUJIAHUI
GONGYUAN

DONGAN RO
东安路

Zhaojiabang Road

Zhaojiabang Road

Shanghai
Univ

0 ————— 500 m

0 ————— 500 yds

Old Station Restaurant,
Fwuh Luh Pavilion,
Bistrow by Wagas

Xiao Hong Lou
(La Villa Rouge)

A **B**

321

D

E

326

Mesa

Shintori

Baoluo

The Mansion

Mansion Complex

ushi Oyama

The 7

The Grape

El Willy

Citizen Café

Chun

Osteria Rest.

Yakitori Fukuchan

Okura Garden Hotel

Jinjiang Hotel

The Tandoor

Jinjiang Tower

Isetan

Nanchang

Pudi Boutique Hotel Fuxing Park

FUXING GONGYUAN

Sun Zhongshan Guju (former Residence of Sun Yat-sen)

Central Huaihai Road

Xing'an Rd

Yandang Entertainment Street

Xiangyang Road North, Xiangyang Beilu

Julu Lu

Julu Lu

Jinxian Road

Jinxian Lu

Jinxian Lu

Changle Road

Changle Lu

Maoming Road South

Xinle Road

Xinle Road

Donghu Road

Zhonglu

SHAANXI ROAD SOUTH
陕西南路站

XIANGYANG GONGYUAN

(Huaihai)

Shaanxi Nanlu

Nanchang Rd

Maoming Nanlu

Nanchang Lu

Rujin No.2 Road

Gaolan Road

Shanxi Lu

Chongqing Rd S (Chongqing Nalu)

Changle Lu

Changle Lu

SHAANXI ROAD SOUTH
陕西南路站

Central Huaihai Road

Yinyue Xueyuan (Conservatory of Music)

Central Fuxing Road

ntral Fuxing Road

Shanghai Gongyi Meishuguan (Arts & Crafts Museum)

1931 Bar & Restaurant

Blue Frog

Wenhua Guangchang (Cultural Square)

Ruijin Guesthouse

Central Fuxing Road

CPK

Zhou Enlai Guju (former residence of Zhou En-lai)

Ruijin Yi Yuan (Ruijin Hospital)

Hefei Rd

North-South Freeway (elevated)

Xiangshan Road

Fenyang Lu

Fenyang Rd

Xiangyang Road South

Nanchang Rd

Damuqiao Road

Shaanxi Road South

Yongkang Road

Shaanxi Nanlu

Yongjia Road

Ruijin No.2 Road

Shanxi Lu

Pushkin Triangle

Taiyuan Bieshu (Taiyuan Villa)

Vienna Café

Tianzi Fang (Art Centre)

Somerset Xuhui Shanghai

Jiande Road

Central Jianguo Road

Jianguo Road West

Taikang Road

Xujiahui Road

Pullman Shanghai Skyway

Yueyang Road

Taiyuan Road

Yongjia Lu

Xiangyang Lu

Taiyuan Road

Shaanxi Nanlu

Shaoxing Lu

Jianguo Xilu

Ruijin 2-Lu

Xujiahui Lu

Dapu Road

hui g

Zhaojiabang Road

Zhaojiabang Road

DAMUQIAO ROAD
大木桥路站

Shanghai Gongan Bowuguan (Museum of Public Security)

Zhongshan Hospital

Zhaojiabang Lu

Zhaojiabang Lu

Xiangqiaozhao Road

Pingjiang Road

Pingjiang Lu

Fenglin Road Fenglin Lu

Xueyuan Road

Qingzhen Road

Qingzhen Lu

Yixueyuan Lu

Damuqiao Road

Damuqiao Lu

Xietu Road

Xietu Lu

Xietu Road

Chaling Road

Xietu Lu

Rihui Branch

Ruijin Road

Ouxi Rd

Dapu Lu

Ouxi Lu

Xietu Road

D

E

322

325

A B

A **B**

Yandang Road

Xing'an Rd

Chongqing Road South (Chongqing Nan Lu)

Xing'an Lu

Taicang Road

(Taicang Lu)

T8

Chongde Road

Dongtai Lu Shichang
(Antiques Market)

Renmin Road

Jinjia Fang

Yongjia Long

Fuxing Road East

Xintiandi

Nanchang
Road

Entertainment Street

Pudi
Boutique
Hotel
Fuxing
Park

Crystal Jade,
Din Tai Fung

88 Xintiandi

Xintiandi
Road

Liuhekou Road (Liuhekou Lu)

TAIPINGQIAO
GONGYUAN

(Zizhong Lu)

Zizhong
Road

Danshui Road

Huangpi Road South

Shunchang Road

(Fuxing Zhonglu)

Somerset
Grand Shanghai

Lian
Road

Jian
Road

Shanghai Wanshang
Huanaioi Shichang
(Wanshang Bird
& Flower Market)

Yongjia

Jingxiu St

Xicangqiao

LAOXIMEN
老西门站

Menghua St.

Wen Miao
(Confucius Temple)

Wen Miao Road

Penglai Road

Xueqian Street

**FUXING
GONGYUAN**

Central Fuxing Road

(Hefei Lu)

Tangwaxan Rd

Ji'an
Road

Dongtai Lu

Zhaozhou Road

Fouxie

Tibet (Xizang) Road South

(Daji Lu)

Anran Road

Daxing
Road

Zhonghua Road

Sinan Mansions

**LUWAN
卢湾区**

Hefei
Road

North-South Freeway (elevated)

Central
Jianguo Rd

Madang Road

(Danshui Lu)

Jianguo Road East

Madang Road

Yongnian Road

Lujiabang Road

(Jianguo Donglu)

(Shunchang Lu)

Zhizaoju Road

Fangxie Road

**Hunan
Stadium**

Dalin Road

(Zhizaoju Lu)

Liyuan Road

Tibet (Xizang Nanlu)

Hunong Road

(Lujiabang Lu)

Dalin Lu

Jiangyin Street

(Lyuan Lu)

(Huning Lu)

Taikang Road

Xujiahui Road (Xujiahui Lu)

Xiexu Road

Mengzi Road

Jumen Road

Mengzi Rd W.

Xiexu Road

(Xiexu Lu)

Hunong Road

(Xiexu Lu)

(Nantangbang Lu)

(Xietu Lu)

Xietu Road

Jumen Lu

Zhizaoju Lu

Xizang Road South
西藏南路站

Pullman
Shanghai
Skyway

Dapu Road

Nantangbang Rd

Luban Road (Luban Lu)

(Mengzi Lu)

Wuliqiao Road (Wuliqiao Lu)

Xilingjiazhai Road

Quxi

Xietu Road

(Dapu Lu)

Runan Road

Jumen Road

(Quxi
Lu)

LUBAN ROAD
鲁班路站

Quxi Road (Quxi Lu)

Quxi Road

Mengzi Road

Jumen Road

Gaoxiong Road

World EXPO 2010

Zhongshan No. 1 Road South (Zhongshan Nan 1/4 Lu)

0 _____ 500 m

0 _____ 500 yds

323

D
E

N

NANSHI
南市

Fuxing Rd East

Wangyun Road

Guangqi Road South (Guangqi Nanlu)

Lingli St

Laoxin St

Doushi Street

Maojia

Road

Stiller's

Table #1

**The Waterhouse
at South Bund**

Penglai Rd

(Penglai Lu)

Ningjie Road

Qiaojia Road

Meijia St

Xundao Street (Xundao Jie)

Zhonghua Road (Zhonghua Lu)

Miezhu Lu

Zixia Road

Wailangjiaqiao Street

Huayi Rd

Beishija St

Xinmatou Street

Zhonghua Road South (Zhongshan Nanlu)

Waima Lu

Waima Road

1

Yujia Long

Wangjiamatou Road

Wangjiamatou Street

Xincang St

Waicang

Zhuhangmatou

long

(Wangjiamatou Lu)

South

ngwen Road

Huangjia Road

Miezhu Road

Wanyumatou St

St

(Zhonghua Lu)

Dongjiadu Road (Dongjiadu Lu)

Gongyimatou

St

(Henan Nanlu)

Xigouyu Road

Nangu St

Laiyimatou Rd

Gongyimatou
St

Waima Road

HUANGPU
黄浦區

(Jiangyin Jie)

Sangyuan Street

Dongjiangyin Street

Nancang Street

Luxi Street

■ Dongjiadu
Tianzhutang
(Dongjiadu
Cathedral)

Zhongshan Road South (Zhongshan Nanlu)

2

(Huining Lu)

Lujiabang Road

Liushi Road

(Dongjiangyin Jie)

Duojia Road

DONGJIADU
董家渡

nzhushan Rd West

Hainan Long W.

East

Haichao Road

Xueqianbang Rd

South Bund
Fabric Market

(Duojia Lu)

Puyu Road East

Puyu

Caoyezhan Road

Nanjiang St

NANPU BRIDGE
南浦大桥站

Youchematou

Waima Road

Huangpu

Xietu Road East (Xietu Donglu)

Road

Youchematou Rd

3

Chezhan Road East

Puyu

(Quyu Lu)

PUDONG
浦东

Chezhan Rd
West

njian Shoucangpin
Chenlieguan/
Sanshan Huiguan
(Museum of Folk Art)

Miaojiang Rd

Nanpu Bridge (Nanpu Qiao)

GLAI
YUAN

Zhongshan Road South (Zhongshan Nanlu)

World EXPO 2010

Bansongyuan Road

Miaojiang Rd

Huayuangang Rd

Tangnan Road

Nanmadou Road

Jiaonan Road

4

rld EXPO 2010

Sanliqiao Road East

World EXPO 2010

Yinan Road

(Yinan Lu)

Nanmatou Lu

Pudong Road South

Pusan Rd

World Expo
Museum

China Pavilion

D
E

STREET INDEX

GENERAL INDEX